The Economic Cycle and the Growth of the Chinese Economy

The nature of the economic cycle has been a long-standing problem for economists, given much attention especially by Malthus, Marx and Keynes. Key questions include: What are the causes of the economic cycle? Are the causes endogenous or exogenous? And why is the economic cycle irregular? Economists' views on these matters have differed, some concluding that governments can intervene effectively to stimulate economic growth, while others argue that government intervention is ineffective and even harmful. This book explores the theory of the economic cycle in relation to economic growth in China, and especially in relation to income distribution and the demand for consumer durables. The book concludes that the cause of the economic cycle is endogenous, that the periodic fluctuation of economic growth and its dynamic equilibrium are natural aspects of the growth of the economy, and it puts forward a new model of the economic cycle which confidently predicts the future trajectory of China's economic growth.

Li Jianwei is a Senior Research Fellow at the Development Research Center of The State Council of the People's Republic of China.

Routledge Studies on the Chinese Economy

Series Editor
Peter Nolan
Director, Centre of Development Studies;
Chong Hua Professor in Chinese Development; and
Director of the Chinese Executive Leadership Programme (CELP),
University of Cambridge

Founding Series Editors
Peter Nolan, University of Cambridge and
Dong Fureng, Beijing University

The aim of this series is to publish original, high-quality, research-level work by both new and established scholars in the West and the East, on all aspects of the Chinese economy, including studies of business and economic history.

56 **China's Centralized Industrial Order**
Industrial Reform and the Rise of Centrally Controlled Big Business
Chen Li

57 **China's Exchange Rate Regime**
China Development Research Foundation

58 **China's WTO Accession Reassessed**
China Development Research Foundation

59 **US–China Relations in the Twenty-First Century**
A Question of Trust
Michael Tai

60 **Understanding China**
The Silk Road and the Communist Manifesto
Peter Nolan

61 **Being Middle Class in China**
Identity, Attitudes and Behaviour
Ying Miao

62 **Governing the Commons in China**
Yan Zhang

63 **The Economic Cycle and the Growth of the Chinese Economy**
Li Jianwe

The Economic Cycle and the Growth of the Chinese Economy

Li Jianwei

Routledge
Taylor & Francis Group
LONDON AND NEW YORK

First published 2017 by Routledge

2 Park Square, Milton Park, Abingdon, Oxfordshire OX14 4RN
52 Vanderbilt Avenue, New York, NY 10017

Routledge is an imprint of the Taylor & Francis Group, an informa business

First issued in paperback 2018

British Library Cataloguing in Publication Data
A catalogue record for this book is available from the British Library

Library of Congress Cataloging in Publication Data
A catalog record for this book has been requested

ISBN: 978-1-138-24291-3 (hbk)
ISBN: 978-0-367-17979-3 (pbk)

Typeset in Times New Roman
by Wearset Ltd, Boldon, Tyne and Wear

Contents

Figures

Tables

Preface

Since the nineteenth century, economists have been trying to explain two problems of the economic cycle: what are the causes of the economic cycle and are the causes endogenous or exogenous? Why is the economic cycle irregular? Before the nineteenth century, most of the classical theories argue that the economic cycle results from a single exogenous factor. However, this analysis does not provide a rigorous and systematic theoretical basis. The exceptions during this period are Malthus' insufficient consumption theory and Marx's theory of economic crisis. After the nineteenth century, two schools of economics, the Keynesian school and the neoclassical school, further developed research on the economic cycle. The Keynesian school argues that economic growth is disequilibrium and the economic cycle is endogenous to some extent, while the neoclassical school argues that economic growth is equilibrium and economic cycle is exogenous. The divergent views of the two schools have led to different approaches toward the role of macro-regulation policy. The Keynesian school suggests government policy intervention is effective to stimulate economic growth, while the neoclassical school suggests government policy intervention is ineffective and even harmful.

Over 16 years ago, I began to research China's economic growth and economic cycles. In 2012, my research found that the residents' income distribution demonstrated statistical normal distribution. This is a theoretical breakthrough on research of the economic cycle. Based on the normal distribution of residents' income, I find that the distribution of the consumption of goods is also statistically normal, which leads to the conclusion that the cycle of consumption and that of the whole economy must be endogenous. This finding has settled the debate on whether the economic cycle is endogenous or exogenous and provides a good explanation of economic growth as well as the relationship between income distribution and economic growth. It demonstrates that the periodic fluctuation of economic growth and its dynamic equilibrium are actually two aspects of the growth of the economy.

The research of this book was originally published in June 2015 as a book in Chinese entitled *Economic Cycle: Endogenous Mechanism and Dynamic Equilibrium*. I have since continued the research on the relationship between income distribution and economic growth, as well as the economic cycle. This English version is based on the original research, but I have incorporated new results and also made revisions. I would like to share my research insights with readers, especially with scholars and researchers on the economic cycle and the growth of the Chinese economy.

This book provides empirical evidence on the cycle of China's consumer durables that is determined by the distribution of income, and discusses the relationship between the cycle of demand for durable goods and the economic cycle. It then constructs an economic cycle model to predict the fluctuation of the cycle of the Chinese economy and its dynamic equilibrium. It is found that the growth rate of the Chinese economy will decline in the next ten years, with an average growth rate of 6.5 percent and a fluctuation in the rate between 5 and 8 percent. The book also discusses policy implications, including stabilizing the growth rate in the short-term and stabilizing exports, improving the structure of consumption, promoting enterprise innovation and upgrading the economic structure in the medium to long term.

The research in this book makes an original contribution to the theoretical and empirical study of the economic cycle. First, the research proves that the economic cycle is endogenous by the normal distribution of residents' income, which provides microeconomic grounds to support the endogenous cycle theory. Second, the research finds the state of economic growth is unbalanced due to its cyclical fluctuations. It also finds that there exists a state of dynamic equilibrium of economic growth. This solves the theoretical divergence between the Keynesian approach and the neoclassical approach. Third, the book finds that a moderate income gap is essential for rapid and steady economic growth. Fourth, technical progress and enterprise innovation are key factors to maintaining sustainable economic growth. Finally, the book provides a more convincing theoretical explanation on the successive development and cyclical fluctuations of the Chinese economy in the past 30 years. It also constructs a mathematical model and provides a forecast for the growth of the Chinese economy in the next ten years.

The book has 12 chapters. The main content of each chapter is discussed below.

Chapter 1 analyzes the main argument of the classical and modern cycle theories as well as the limitations of each theory. Classical cycle theories focus on the fluctuations of the total economy, and most of them lack a solid theoretical foundation. I have divided the modern cycle theory into two schools of economics – the Keynesian school and the neoclassical school, and analyzed their respective theoretical arguments and limitations. I point out that the key difference between the two groups is on the nature of economic operation. The Keynesian school holds that economic growth is unbalanced and the economic cycle is endogenous, while the neoclassical group holds that economic growth is balanced and the economic cycle is exogenous.

Chapter 2 analyzes the features of residents' income distributions from 1997 to 2005 in China, and finds that rural and urban residents' income distributions are bell-shaped, which is the typical shape of a normal distribution. It estimates the normal distribution functions of rural residents' income distributions and urban residents' income distributions respectively, and proves residents' income distributions are indeed normal.

Chapter 3 demonstrates the relationship between the normal distribution of residents' income and the endogenous mechanism of the economic cycle. The analytical approach is as follows: on the condition that residents' income distribution is subject to a normal distribution, the distribution of demand for durable goods is also subject to a normal distribution, and the demand for non-durable goods is distributed as the integration of a normal distribution. It is then obtained that the first derivative of the distribution of demand for durable goods is a whole process of the cycle, while the first derivative of the distribution of demand for non-durable goods is only half of the process of the cycle. This means that the growth rate of consumption is cyclical, and the replacement demand and the demand for new products make the cycle of the growth of demand continuous. And then the growth rate of investment is also cyclical, meaning the growth rate of the whole economy is cyclical.

Chapter 4 analyzes the normal features of American and Japanese residents' income distributions. With the assumption that residents' income distributions are subject to normal distributions, it is concluded that the growth rate of the world's consumption is cyclical, so one country's growth rate of exports is also cyclical, and it is deduced that the economic growth rate is still cyclical under the initial condition.

Chapter 5 discusses two types of economic cycle. One is determined by the normal features of income distribution, which we call the income distribution cycle. Its wavelength is determined by the level of residents' income and the price of consumer goods. The higher the growth rate of residents' income and the smaller the income gap, as well as the lower the consumer goods price and the larger the price decline, the shorter the wavelength of the income distribution cycle. The other is the actual cycle and its wavelength is determined by supply lag or product service life or product innovation frequency or exports, which we call the price-adjusted cycle, replacement demand cycle, innovation demand cycle and export cycle. The actual cycle could change the wavelength of the income distribution cycle by its effectiveness on the price of consumer goods and the level of residents' income.

The amplitudes of different cycles fluctuate greatly. Chapter 6 discusses the main factors causing the fluctuations. The variance of the ratio of price to income is the key factor determining the amplitudes of income distribution cycles; the bigger the variance, the smaller the amplitude. The larger the price elasticity of supply, or the smaller the price elasticity of demand, the bigger the amplitude of the price-adjusted cycle. The longer the service life of durable goods, or the lower the innovation frequency, the bigger the amplitude of the replacement demand cycle and the innovation demand cycle.

Chapter 7 demonstrates the dynamic equilibrium of the economic cycle and argues that the stable state of neoclassical growth theory is only one type of dynamic equilibrium state of the economic cycle.

To demonstrate and apply the theory of the economic cycle, Chapter 8 analyzes the cycles of China's demand for durable goods in the form of household appliances and passenger cars, and the relationship between the cycle of demand for durable goods and the cycle of the economy.

Applying the theory of the income distribution growth cycle, Chapter 9 analyzes the income distribution cycle of the urban passenger car in China. The analytical focus is to estimate the demand function of passenger cars and the relationship between the demand for passenger cars and the level of residents' income, as well as the income gap. It also analyzes the relationship between the cycle of passenger cars and the cycle of heavy industry, as well as the Chinese economy.

Chapter 10, employing filtering technology, divides China's GDP growth rate into five sectors as a short-term wave, middle term wave, middle-to-long-term wave, long-term wave and dynamic equilibrium. Regression analysis is conducted to estimate the contributions of consumption, investment and export to the economic cycle.

Chapter 11 applies the mathematic model built on the theory of the economic cycle and predicts the trend of China' economic growth from 2015 to 2025. It concludes that China's economic growth rate will cyclically decrease to a middle-to-high rate: 6.5 percent, with fluctuation at a rate of 5–8 percent in the next ten years.

Chapter 12 demonstrates the theoretical basis and the structure of the mathematical model the author has built on the economic cycle.

This book would not have been published without support from the following people. I wish to express my deep appreciation to my supervisor, Professor Liu Guoguang, for his consistent guidance, support and encouragement over the past 20 years, and his help to keep me focused on my research and this original contribution to the study of economic cycle and the growth of the Chinese economy. I wish to express my special appreciation to Professor Peter Nolan, my supervisor during my stay in Cambridge University as an academic visitor, for his warm encouragement and acknowledgment of my research contribution. I also would like to express my gratitude to the group of PhD students who helped me improve the English translation: Tao Xin, Xiao Chunwen, Hou Mutian, He yuan, Liu Yunxiang and Fu Zhenyu. I wish to express my special thanks to Dr. Zhang Jin for her great help in the translation of the whole book and for her helpful advice on the revision of the research. I would like to express my thankfulness to my colleagues at the Development Research Center of the State Council, who gave me many helpful suggestions about the research. Finally, I would like to give special thanks to Mr. Peter Sowden, editor of Routledge, for his patience and professionalism in making the publication of this book possible.

Li Jianwei
Cambridge, England
June 26, 2016

1 Traditional economic cycle theories and their limitations

The study of economic cycle originated in the nineteenth century. Economists found regular cyclical fluctuations in the process of economic development, among which the fluctuation of the absolute value of British economic aggregates is the most remarkable. In 1921, Hayek defined the economic cycle as the circular deviation from economic equilibrium (Hayek, 1929). Since then economists have been using this definition as the starting point of the study of the economic cycle. Later, the integration of economic cycle theory and economic growth theory led to the development of growth cycle theory, which is divided into two major groups – Keynesian and neoclassical theories. The neoclassical school believes the origin of the economic cycle is exogenous because a temporary deviation of economic activities from the steady-state invalidates the effectiveness of government interventions. On the other hand, the Keynesian school argues that the economic growth cycle is endogenous, and government intervention can be effective in stimulating economic growth.

The classical economic cycle theory

Following the British economic crisis of 1825, the first generation of economic cycle theories, known as the "classical economic cycle theories," emerged. The classical economic cycle theories mainly focused on the study of the circular fluctuations of economic aggregates, many of which regarded the economic cycle as fluctuations caused by exogenous factors. This approach lacks a systematic and rigorous theoretical basis.

Agricultural economic cycle and other exogenous economic cycle theories

The early studies of the economic cycle in the nineteenth century treated it as exogenous. They believed that the economic cycle is rooted in the change of factors outside the economy and not affected by economic factors. One of the most influential theories was the agricultural economic cycle theory.

William Jevons and Henry Moore were representatives of the agricultural economic cycle theorists. Using the grain farming cycle as a reference point, this school focuses their study on the influence of agricultural fluctuations on business activities. This led to the sunspot theory, which argues that the change of sunspots is the cause of the fluctuation of agricultural production and overall economic cycle. Due to the economic structure of that time, the agricultural cycle theory confined its perspective to the fluctuation of agriculture and environment, and lacked systematic observation and analysis.

Other typical exogenous economic cycle theories include the nonmonetary overinvestment theory and political economic cycle theory. The nonmonetary overinvestment theory holds that the economic cycle is caused by territory expansion, technology invention, population growth and the accompanying investment fluctuation. The political economic cycle theory argues that the economic cycle is caused by political factors, such as elections and policies on inflation and employment.

Insufficient consumption theory

In the early nineteenth century, Thomas Malthus and Jean Charles Léonard de Sismondi established causality of overcapacity and the associated economic crisis to the insufficient consumption caused by the poverty of laborers. Economic recession and crisis are caused by the fact that the growth of demand for consumer goods cannot keep up with the growth of the production of consumer goods. Furthermore, this theory argues that insufficient consumer demand will lead to insufficient demand for capital goods and trigger an economy-wide overproduction crisis. The main cause of insufficient consumption is income inequality, which is responsible for the lack of purchasing power of the poor and the excess savings of the rich.

Sismondi states in his book *New Principle of Political Economy: The Relationship between Wealth and Population* that the only purpose for societies to use labor and engage in production is to satisfy people's demand (Sismondi, 1964). Production mainly depends on the demand of non-laborers, which will lead to unlimited expansion of production, and at the same time reduce the consuming power of laborers and cause overproduction crises and economic cyclical fluctuation. The insufficient consumption theory is innovative because it makes an assumption of the endogeneity of the economic cycle.

Long cycle (long wave) theory

The representative figures of long cycle theory include Joseph Schumpeter, Alexander Parvus and Nikolai Kondratiev. Kondratiev proposed a version of long wave economic cycle theory based on empirical observations. However, the theory is mostly derived from price fluctuations and lacks a theoretical foundation. On this basis, Schumpeter put forward a long wave model based on short-term inventory cycles. Later, Arthur Burns and Wesley Mitchell further developed the long wave theory (Schumpeter, 1939). They identified the long wave as being composed of a series of cycles, with each cycle having two major phases: the industrial phase and the speculation phase.

There are two major limitations of the long cycle theory:

1 The long cycle theory fails to provide a reasonable explanation for short-term economic fluctuations. The Great Depression of 1929 posed a major empirical challenge to this theory, as it is inconsistent with the predictions of long cycle theory.
2 Scholars such as John Maynard Keynes are more concerned about short-term cycles with wavelength of no more than 100 years. The long cycle model proposed by Parvus and others was mainly driven by innovations, which is hardly affected by economic policies, and therefore left no room for government intervention.

Infrastructural investment cycle theory

In 1930, Simon Kuznets analyzed the fluctuations of the economic cycle of various countries and discovered a type of economic cycle with durations ranging from 15 to 25 years (average 20 years). Influenced by the long wave (cycle) theory, he defined this cycle as mid-cycle. He demonstrated that the cyclical fluctuation of construction investment was the main driver of this type of economic cycle. Because mid-cycle theory treats the rise and fall of the construction industry as the main driving force, it is also known as the "construction cycle."[1]

Population cycle theory

In his study of economic cycles, Kuznets also paid attention to the relationship between changes in population structure and economic cycles. Unlike the construction (mid-) cycle theory, population cycle theory argues that the structural change of population is the core driver of long-term economic fluctuation. Population growth will bring about the growth of consumption, and stimulate investment for expanded reproduction, and promote economic development. As the younger generation enters the labor market, their income will be depressed, and consumer demand will decline, the economy will enter a period of recession. Kuznets established linkages between the fluctuations in economic activities and immigration, population growth and labor force growth, laying a solid foundation for later studies of population and economic cycles. However, there are still some controversies over the mechanism through which population cycle and economic cycle interact.

Marxist theory of economic crisis

In light of the worldwide economic crisis of 1825, Marx and Engels put forward the argument that bourgeoisie greed was the root of economic crisis. This theory is laid out in *Das Kapital*. The first volume of *Das Kapital* was published in 1867. The drafts of the second and third volumes were published by Engels in

1885 and 1894 respectively. The fourth volume, *Theory of Surplus Value*, was edited and published by Karl Kautsky in 1905–1910. On the prosperity and recession brought about by the economic cycle, Marx states in his *Das Kapital* that the root of the problem lies in the irreconcilable contradictions between the capitalist productive forces and production relations, which is the fundamental contradiction of capitalism. Marxists believe that the economic cycle in capitalist societies is caused by the repetition of such crises, and the contradictory internal mechanism of capitalism is the foundation of crisis. Marxism thinks social polarization caused by the unfair distribution under private ownership and the exploitation of workers is the reason for economic crisis. To eliminate the negative impact of recession, it is necessary to first and foremost eliminate private ownership.

Psychological economic cycle theory

Arthur Pigou emphasizes the influence of psychological factors such as irrational behavior on the economic cycle. In his book *Industrial Fluctuations*, Pigou argues that the economic cycle is caused by the combined influence of real factors, psychological factors and independent economic factors. Optimism and pessimism both influence economic cycles. He also thinks that the panic-inducing effect of bankruptcy, rather than the capital loss it caused, can cause the greatest harm to the economy. Because of the fear of bankruptcy, people's willingness to invest will fall (Pigou, 1928).

Pigou doesn't think the "invisible hand" is able to restore the troubled economy to a balanced state. He thinks that changes in price and the damages to economic plans during recessions are difficult to restore. With price rigidity, the recession will cause a series of problems preventing the market from clearing.

Keynesian school

The Great Depression from 1929 to 1933 presented a major challenge to economic cycle theories. Keynesianism came into being against the background of the Great Depression. Keynesian theory is a major milestone in the development of economic cycle theories. With disequilibrium growth theory at the core of the study of economic cycle endogeneity, Keynesianism provided a theoretical basis for government intervention, and thus plays an important role in modern economics.

Classic Keynesian theory

Keynes' masterpiece, *The General Theory of Employment, Interest and Money*, discusses the relationship between employment and economic fluctuation and its effects on market equilibrium. Keynes challenged Say's Law of market clearing and the full employment hypothesis, two basic assumptions of classical economics. He has created a new theoretical framework and thinking paradigm for the study of economic cycle. Keynes argues that economic fluctuation and crisis are caused by insufficient effective demand, so state intervention is an effective measure to solve this problem.

Keynes gives an in-depth discussion on the economic cycle in the *General Theory*. He goes beyond the perspective of economic equilibrium growth and analyzes economic cycle as endogenous to economic growth. Keynes argues that the duration of economic cycle was usually 5–10 years under the circumstances of that period of time. Based on an analysis framework underpinned by investment, consumption and multiplier effects, the Keynesian school argues that there are two types of factors that contributed to the economic cycle: first, the scarcity of capital leads to increasing marginal returns of capital; second, under the influence of inventory level, when marginal return of capital rises, investment and speculative demand will expand, and the economy will enter the next cycle. Given the social and economic context of their time, the classic Keynesian school focused its study of the economic cycle on the question of how to response to economic crises, thinking that the main cause of economic recession was the negative impact of crises on the supply side's expectations (such as constrained liquidity). In response to the economic crisis, expansionary policies should be used, including deficit fiscal policy, low interest rates, and bond issuance. The Keynesian school holds that raising money for government expenditure can stimulate effective demand and reduce overcapacity of production. The economic policies of the Keynesian school put the idle funds of the market in a pool so as to serve the state and poor people, which will ease social polarization while stimulating economic development.

General Theory is of great significance to the development of economic cycle theory. The theory of economic growth in disequilibrium that Keynes put forward in his works triggered a fierce debate between followers of the Keynesian school and the neoclassical school (with monetary cycle theory and actual economic cycle theory as representatives). The focuses of the study on the economic cycle in that period include analyses of the relationship between saving, investment and economic growth, the policy transmission mechanism and effect measurement, monetary supply and demand and inflation, interest rates and the credit mechanism. But the classic Keynesian theory still has some deficiencies in the interpretation of economic cycle. First, classic Keynesian theory lacks a micro-foundation for the analysis of the economic cycle, so it's hard to reconcile the theory with traditional microeconomics. Second, the most criticized part of Keynesianism is that it struggles to deal with the problem of stagnation, or the coexistence of high inflation and sluggish growth.

New Keynesian theory

In order to address the weakness of classic Keynesian theory, the New Keynesian school introduced the micro-foundation in the 1980s, which improved the theoretical foundation and policy recommendation of classic Keynesianism. The New Keynesian theory established several frameworks to study the economic cycle, including Domar model, Cobweb model, Harrod model, Hicks dynamic model and chaos theory. It provides a more solid foundation for the Keynesian school to explain the economic cycle problem.

In the 1970s, the New Keynesian scholars such as M. Gertler, R. Clarida and J. Gali argued for effectiveness of monetary policy. They studied the relationship between monetary policies and the economic cycle by looking at the theories of non-market clearing, sticky wage and sticky prices. The core opinion of the New Keynesian theory is that monetary change will affect real economic growth, and effective monetary policy can stabilize total output and employment. Therefore governments should adjust short-term interest rates to accommodate the economic fluctuations and to reduce the impact of the expected inflation on economic fluctuation. The best monetary policy should implement inflation targeting. E. Phelps and J. Taylor (1977) found that even under the rational expectations assumption, macroeconomic policy is still effective.

The representative figures of New Keynesianism include G. Mankiw, J. Tinbergen, O. Blanchard and P. Samuelson. In comparison with traditional Keynesianism, however, New Keynesianism still holds the core viewpoint of Keynesianism that an incomplete market is the main cause of the economic cycle; it discards the classic Keynesian policies such as frequent countercyclical interventions. New Keynesianism focuses on the incompleteness of the market, replacing the traditional price rigidity with price stickiness and highlighting the importance of monetary policy for addressing the economic cycle. So in the view of New Keynesianism, countercyclical policies are very important for smoothing the economic cycle.

The New Keynesian school divides the economic cycle into two or four periods. The two periods are the contraction and expansion periods. The four periods are prosperity, recession, depression and recovery. As price is gradually adjusted, aggregate demand and aggregate supply would be affected by the fluctuation of consumption, investment and money supply, which form the core drivers of economic cycle fluctuations.

Later on, New Keynesianism developed many branches. Starting from the basic assumptions, these branches have enriched the New Keynesian economic cycle theory in different ways. The New Keynesian economic cycle model covers the theory of wages, price stickiness and economic cycle fluctuations, the theory of staggered price setting, the theory of monopolistic competition and aggregate demand fluctuation, the theory of market structure and macroeconomic fluctuation, the theory of market strategy and coordination failure, the theory of price stability and the economic cycle, and so on. These branches have explored the causes of economic cycle fluctuations and the relationship with economic growth from different angles. Among them are two theoretical models that have far-reaching effect on the subsequent studies of economic cycle theory. The first one is Samuelson's multiplier-accelerator theory, which analyzes the relationship between investment and total production and its influence on the economic cycle. The second is Tinbergen's cobweb model, which uses elasticity theory to explain the fluctuations of certain commodities with longer production cycles under the situation of disequilibrium.

Multiplier-accelerator theory

In the late 1930s, New Keynesian economists represented by Samuelson proposed the multiplier-accelerator theory. According to this theory, the economic cycle is jointly determined by the changes of investment and income, and hence jointly decided by multiplier and accelerator. The core idea of the multiplier-accelerator model is that investment, national income and consumption influence and regulate each other. With fixed government expenditure, which means no government intervention, the economic cycle will emerge on the basis of the economy regulating itself. Each period of economic cycle is the result of the interaction between multiplier and accelerator. In this kind of spontaneous adjustment, investment is the key factor because the economic cycle is mainly caused by investment. Rapid increase of production stimulates the rapid growth of investment, and large-scale investment in turn stimulates production to increase even faster. Such a process of positive stimulus will continue until the economic potential is completely exhausted, after which the economic growth rate starts to fall, and the slowing growth, in turn, leads to less investment. This process will then lead to recession.

In the multiplier-accelerator model, the multiplier principle emphasizes the effect of autonomous investment on national income, while the accelerator principle emphasizes the effect of the fluctuation of aggregated national income on investment. Samuelson combines multiplier and accelerator to explain economic fluctuations. The increase of income or consumption demand will lead to disproportional increase in investment, while disproportional decrease of income or consumption demand will lead to multiplied reduction of investment. The basic theoretical framework is:

$$Y_t = C_t + I_t + G_t \tag{1}$$

In this formula, Y_t refers to total output, C_t refers to total consumption, I_t refers to total investment and G_t refers to total government expenditure.

Consumption is defined as the product of marginal consuming propensity (b) multiplying last period income ($Y_t - 1$), namely:

$$C_t = bY_{t-1} \tag{2}$$

Investment is defined as the acceleration coefficient (v) multiplied by the change of consumption, namely:

$$I_t = v(C_t - C_{t-1}) = v(bY_t - bY_{t-1}) = vb(Y_t - Y_{t-1}) \tag{3}$$

When government expenditure (G_t) is fixed, the core formula of the multiplier-accelerator principle can be derived:

$$Y_t = b(1+v)Y_{t-1} - bvY_{t-2} + G_t \tag{4}$$

This last equation is a second-order differential equation of Y_t. The nature of the differential equation shows that when the marginal consumption propensity and accelerator meet certain conditions, the output will come into a regular pattern of periodic fluctuations. Multiplier-accelerator theory reveals the process of how different economic variables interact with each other. It shows the path of economic growth under different multiplier and accelerator factors. It reveals that the economic cycle is endogenous. The theory implies that government can influence the economic cycle by adjusting government investment, which mitigates the destruction of the economic cycle, flattens it and ensures more stable growth of national economies. Samuelson's theory provides a foundation for the subsequent studies and analysis.

Cobweb model

J. Tinbergen, H. Schultz, U. Ricel and N. Kaldor jointly put forward the cobweb model, introducing the time factor into equilibrium analysis, and using elasticity theory to explain the fluctuations of productions of certain commodities with longer production cycles under disequilibrium conditions. The cobweb model is based on three basic assumptions, namely: commodities need a certain period of time to be produced and in this period of time the scale of production cannot be changed; the output determines price in the current period; and current price determines output in the next period.

Tinbergen analyzes the relationship between different aggregate variables in the US and other countries to predict economic fluctuations. In his book, *Statistical Test of Economic Cycle Theory*, published in 1939, Tinbergen examined the American macroeconomic problems and created the "cobweb model" to study the economic cycle in a single market. This provides an important basis for subsequent studies of economic cycle theories. The cobweb model explains the fluctuations of the output and prices of many commodities with longer production cycles. It can be divided into three types: the divergent cobweb, continuous cobweb and convergent cobweb.

According to the basic assumptions of the cobweb model, the mathematical model of the linear cobweb model is shown as follows:

$$D_t = \alpha - \beta P_t$$

$$S_t = \delta + \gamma P_t$$

$$D_t = S_t$$

In this formula, α, β, δ and γ are positive coefficients; D_t is demand in period t; S_t is supply in period t; P_t is price in period t; P_{t+1} is price in period $t+1$.

When the market is in equilibrium, the equilibrium price would be $P_e = P_t = P_{t+1}$, and then equilibrium price is calculated as:

$$p_t = (\alpha + \delta) / (\beta + \alpha)$$

Assume that the actual output is lower than the equilibrium level in the initial period due to external interference; insufficient output will cause the rise of actual price. As responses to price change, the producers will choose to increase production in the next period, then the growth of output in the second period will cause a decline of price, which, in turn, leads to a decline of output in the third period, and then leads to the actual rise of price in the fourth period. In this continuous process, the range of fluctuations of actual output and actual price becomes bigger and bigger (or smaller and smaller), and the deviation from equilibrium output and equilibrium price becomes bigger and bigger (or smaller and smaller). When the price elasticity of supply is greater than the price elasticity of demand, the cobweb model will become divergent. When the price elasticity of supply is less than the price elasticity of demand, the cobweb will become convergent.

The neoclassical school

After the 1960s, the neoclassical school made significant theoretical contributions to explanation of the economic cycle. It has established a set of new theoretical frameworks for the study of the economic cycle, which go beyond the framework of Keynesian theory. Among them, the most representative schools include the monetarism school, rational expectation school and real economic cycle school.

Monetarism school

The monetarism school attributes all economic fluctuations to changes in the supply and demand of money. Its core ideas are that during economic cycles, individuals, enterprises and countries are all affected by money supply, and that the lack of liquidity is the core reason for economic recession. Under the assumption of quantity theory of money and full employment, the change of money supply is considered as the main factor that causes the economic cycle. Therefore, the key to dealing with economic fluctuation is to determine the quantity and channel of the money supply.

Some of the influential figures of the monetarism school are Fisher, Hawtrey, Hayek and Friedman. The monetary factor theory (Hawtrey), monetary overinvestment theory (Hayek) and monetary cycle theory (Friedman) have made important contributions to the explanation of economic fluctuations from the perspective of money supply and demand.

Fisher believes that the main reason for economic fluctuations and economic crisis is the lack of credit supply caused by the debt accumulation of enterprises and tightening monetary policies. On the basis of the concept of monetary non-neutrality, Hayek's theory is the first one to emphasize the important role of monetary policy in economic cycles. The adjustment of the production of consumer goods takes some time, but money supply can adjust faster as the supply of money increases. With the increase of money supply, a stable level of savings will stimulate the increase of consumption demand. When the growth of the supply of consumer goods cannot keep up with the growth of consumer demand, prices will rise; as governments and banks control the money and savings, consumption growth slowdown will lead to overcapacity and unemployment; then, the economy enters a recession. Hayek's theory of economic cycle was supported by Friedman's empirical results (1970). Friedman explained the economic cycle with the quantity theory of money. He takes money as an exogenous variable and illustrated the important role of money in the economic cycle with Fisher's equation.

Rational expectation school

With the stagflation phenomenon that Keynesian school cannot explain, the emergence of the rational expectation school has brought the study of economic fluctuation into a new era. The rational expectation school proposes new methods from the perspective of exogeneity to explain stagflation.

The representative figures of the rational expectation school, such as R. Barro and T. Sargent, claim that the basis of the economic cycle is rational expectation. In markets without complete information, changes in relative prices and absolute prices interact with each other, and the fluctuations of production and employment depend mainly on the producers' expectations of product demand under the influence of the external environment. When prices fluctuate, firms confuse the price rise at general level with the growth of consumer demand, and decide to expand production. When the general prices fall, they will move in the opposite decision. These decision processes underline the cause of the economic cycle.

Real economic cycle school

The real economic cycle theory emerged during the 1970s–1980s. The representative figures include R. Lucas, R. Goodwin, F. Kydland and E. Prescott, (Yang and Wang, 2004). The fundamental idea is that technology shock is the driving force of the economic cycle and that even smaller technological innovations may have great effect on economic fluctuations. The economic cycle can be seen as rational agents' optimal choice in coping with external shocks. The theoretical framework is based on the general equilibrium model of market clearing.

The basic hypothesis of real economic cycle theory is perfect competitive market and rational expectations. The early real economic cycle theory ignores market failure, monetary shocks and government intervention; therefore, the theoretical hypothesis of the real economic cycle school was fiercely attacked by the New Keynesian school. Real economic cycle theory uses the Solow residual to represent technology progress (shock) (Hall, 1988). Many researchers (Arias *et al.*, 2007) constructed real economic cycle models to study the relationship between total factor productivity (TFP) and the frequency of the economic cycle, and established significant positive correlations.

The real economic cycle theory originates from classical economics. Its focus on technology impact has significantly influenced the study of the economic cycle in modern macroeconomics. With the development and improvement of real economic cycle theory, its theoretical framework has incorporated views from other schools. This is the key to real economic cycle theory to retaining its vigor. Robert Lucas believes that the scientific examination and application of counter-cyclical policies has enabled the economic cycle theory to better explain the economic cycle in the US (Zhai, 2001). The dynamic stochastic general equilibrium model (DSGE model) based on real economic cycle theory has become an essential tool for modern macroeconomic analysis. Table 1.1 offers a summary.

Table 1.1 Comparison of classical school, Keynesian school and neoclassical school

Schools	*Classical school*	*Keynesian school*		*Neoclassical school*
		Classic Keynesianism	*New Keynesianism*	
1 Hypothesis	Long-term price elasticity; continuous market clearing	Price rigidity; market not clearing	Price stickiness; market not clearing	Short-term price elasticity and price expectation; continuous market clearing
2 Applicable situations	Long term	Short term	Short term and long term	Short term and long term
3 Model feature	Aggregate relation	Aggregate relation	Aggregate relation	Reasoned from microeconomics
4 Aggregate demand curve	Right downward	Right downward	Right downward	Right downward
5 Aggregate supply curve	Vertical	Horizontal	Right upward (short term); vertical (long term)	Right upward (short term); vertical (long term)
6 Philips Curve	Vertical	Horizontal	Right downward (short term); vertical (long term)	Right downward (short term); vertical (long term)
7 Interpretation of economic cycle	Full employment	Monetary and real factors	Monetary and real factors	Real factors
8 Role of money	Long-term monetary neutrality	Monetary non-neutrality	Monetary non-neutrality	Short-term monetary neutrality
9 Micro-foundation	None	None	Explaining the cause of price stickiness	Explaining the cause of price shrinkage
10 Policy proposals	Less government intervention	Government intervention	Government intervention	Less government intervention

Recent progress of studies on economic cycle theory

At the beginning of the twenty-first century, with the rapid development of mathematical modeling and econometrics, the study of the economic cycle has witnessed an unprecedented boom. The 2008 financial crisis has made the economic cycle a hot topic again.

The new feature of the current economic cycle study shows that researchers no longer take a single indicator like economic output or growth rate as the criterion for measuring economic fluctuation. They combine a basket of indicators, including GDP growth rate, inflation rate and unemployment rate, to make comprehensive evaluation on national economic fluctuations. In recent years, the empirical analysis school has made good progress in the study of the economic cycle. Focusing on theoretical analysis, the empirical analysis school has adopted an econometric method to study the causal factors of the economic cycle. Representative figures of the school include L. Klein and R. Frisch. They have proposed many modeling approaches for the analysis of the economic cycle, including the Klein model and Trend Filter model (Wang and Hu, 2009), all of which have made important contributions to the study of the economic cycle.

Klein firmly believes that crisis is periodical. He estimates economic cycle fluctuations with the Klein model, world model and other methods. Frisch establishes the basic mathematical model for describing the economic cycle and attributes the causes of economic cycle fluctuations to two aspects: the influences of the external environment and the responses of the internal system. With differential equations as its basis, his dynamic model has integrated capital as the main driver of the economic cycle.

The study of economic cycle theories has always been vigorous. Most of the disagreements among different schools have concentrated on the explanation of the origin of the economic cycle, focusing on whether it is endogenous or exogenous. My study on the characteristics of household income show that cyclical fluctuation is the normal state of economic activities, and at any stage of economic growth there always exists an endogenous cycle induced by the characteristics of normally distributed household income (see Chapter 3). There exist various kinds of endogenous cycles, such as the price adjustment cycle caused by lagging supply, and the demand cycle for upgrading and innovation caused by product upgrading. Cyclical economic fluctuations are determined by a variety of endogenous growth cycles (see Chapter 5). At the same time, any stage of the economic cycle is part of the equilibrium growth process, the equilibrium state of which evolves with economic structure. This is to say that cyclical fluctuation is a dynamic equilibrium state (see Chapter 7). After integrating the time factor into the Solow model, the stable equilibrium theory of the neoclassical school itself has become a model of the endogenous cycle. Its stable equilibrium state is the dynamic equilibrium of the cyclical fluctuations of economic growth. The Keynesian non-equilibrium growth theory and the neoclassical equilibrium growth theory each emphasizes one aspect of the cyclical fluctuations of economic growth and its dynamic equilibrium state.

Note

1 In his book entitled *The Longtime Movement of Production and Price*, Kuznets argues that population is the main determinant affecting economic activities, and economic activities can exert influence on population growth, so population factor is endogenous, while many economists see population as an exogenous variable. For example, in the investigation of output and unit cost, population would be regarded as an exogenous variable.

2 Normal estimation of income distribution of China's urban and rural households

The characteristics and evolution of household income distribution are the foundation for the study of consumer demand. Income difference is a ubiquitous phenomenon. The distribution of households along the income spectrum is normally bell-shaped – most households are concentrated at the middle level, and the proportions of households decrease toward both ends of the spectrum. A bell-shaped distribution is the basic feature of a normal distribution, and empirical observations show that household income distribution in most countries is approximately normally distributed. However, income distribution in different countries might be vastly different due to different degrees of income inequality and levels of national income. Thus, empirical approximation requires different normal distributions. Even in the same country, the features of household income distribution also vary from year to year for the same reasons. According to the household survey data from China, urban and rural household income distributions in different years all have bell-shaped features. As shown by the results of the normal estimation of the rural household income distribution in 1997–2005 and the urban household income distribution in 2005–2011, both the urban and rural household income distributions of China are normally distributed, with the expected value equal to the median income of the income category with the greatest population density. As average income level increases, the simulated income variance becomes higher, and the simulation normal distribution curve tends to flatten out. The increase in income variance is mainly due to the rise of the expected value and the change in income distribution structure. Since 1997, the ratio of standard deviation of income to average income for rural households has been declining steadily, and the same ratio for urban households has also been declining since 2005, showing that income inequality within the urban and rural household groups has been narrowing in recent years. On the other hand, the estimation of cross-year average rural household income distribution in 1997–2005 and cross-year average urban household income distribution in 2005–2011 show that the distribution of cross-year urban and rural households' average income is also normally distributed, with the expected value equal to the median income of the income category with the most population density.

Bell-shaped feature of urban and rural households' income distribution in China

According to the urban and rural survey data provided by the Statistic Bureau of the PRC, urban and rural household incomes in all households surveyed are basically distributed in a bell shape. More specifically, the proportion of households first increases with income and then gradually declines after reaching its peak.

It can be seen from the distribution of rural household income in 1985, that rural households with income under 100 yuan account for 0.96 percent of all households; the household groups with income of 200–300 yuan and 300–400 yuan, close to the average disposable income of 397.6 yuan, account for 25.61 percent and 24.1 percent of all households, respectively (Figure 2.1). The proportion of high-income households with disposable income of 1,500–2,000 yuan is just 0.26 percent and the figure for households with disposable income of over 2,000 yuan is just 0.16 percent. In 1990, the average income of rural households increased to 629.79 yuan. The group with the highest proportion in all income groups is the 600–800 yuan group, which represents 18.56 percent of all households. In 1997, the average income of rural households rose to 2,090.13 yuan. The households with average disposable income of 2,000–2,500 yuan, the highest proportion in all income groups, accounts for 14.93 percent. The households with

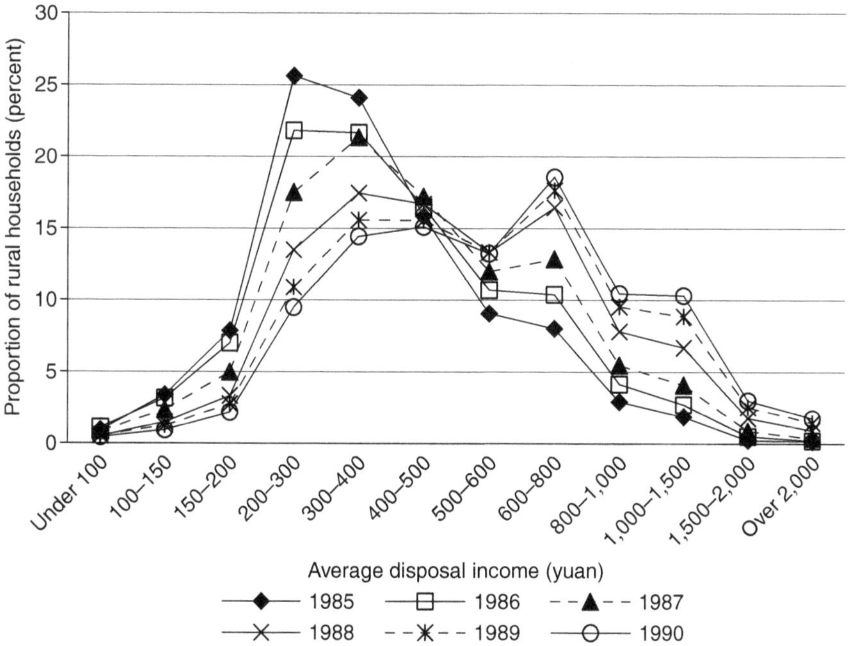

Figure 2.1 Change of proportions of rural households grouped according to average disposable income (%) (1985–1990).

Source: China Macroeconomic Database of WIND.

income below 100 yuan account for only 0.18 percent; the households with average income over 5,000 yuan account for 4.94 percent.

The distribution of rural household income in other years also has a bell shape (Figure 2.2). After 1997, the distribution of rural household income over 5,000 yuan saw an obvious tail-raising as the group of households with income over 5,000 yuan increased. However, household income over 5,000 yuan are not divided into further subgroups.

On the other hand, the urban household income distributions are in a bell shape (2005–2011) (Figure 2.3). In 2005, households with income below 10,000 yuan account for 4.85 percent. The households with income between 10,000 and 15,000 yuan account for 10.1 percent; households with income between 15,000 and 20,000 yuan account for 13.61 percent. The households with income between 20,000 and 25,000 yuan account for 14.09 percent, which is the highest proportion. After this income level, the proportion of households with higher income starts to decline. The proportion of households with income between 60,000 and 65,000 yuan fell to less than 2 percent. Besides the common feature of a bell-shaped distribution, the other important feature of the urban household annual income distribution is that the income of the households with the highest proportion steadily increases, along with the rise of the overall income level. However, the proportion of households with the highest population density has been declining over the years. For example, the households occupying the highest proportion were gradually shifting from the income group with income between 20,000 and 25,000 yuan in 2005 and 2006, to the group with income

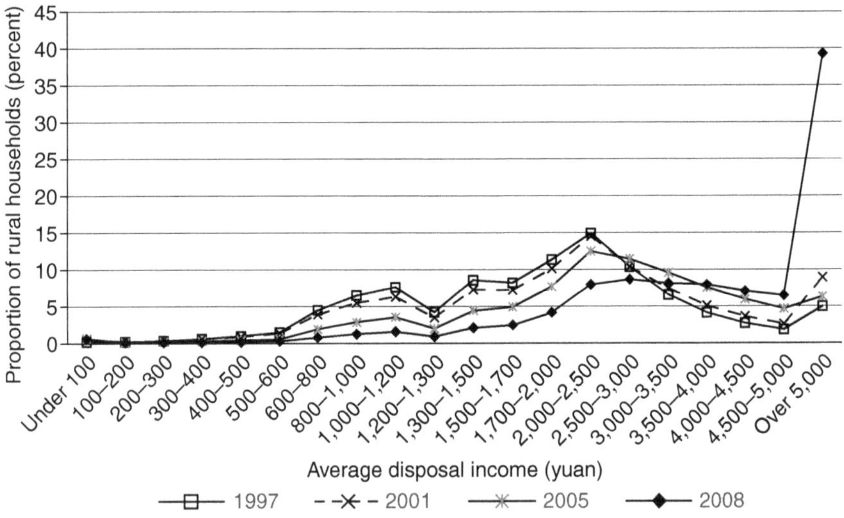

Figure 2.2 Change of proportions of rural households grouped according to average disposable income (%) (1997–2008).

Source: China Macroeconomic Database provided by WIND.

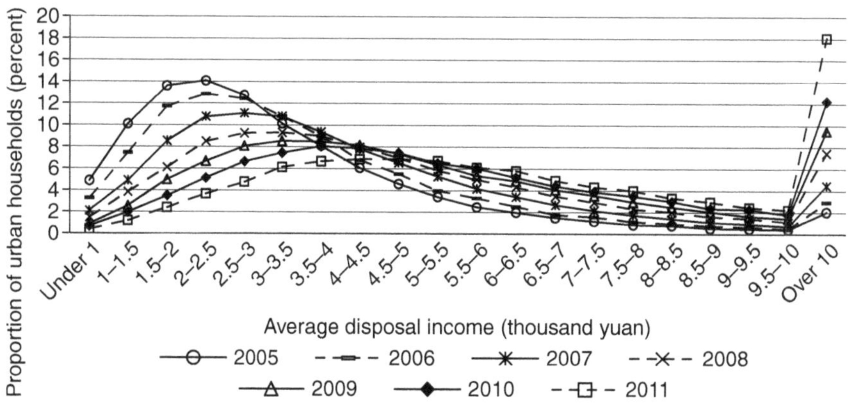

Figure 2.3 Change of proportions of urban households grouped according to average disposable income (%) (2005–2011).

Source: CEIC Macroeconomic Database.

between 25,000 and 30,000 yuan in 2007, to the group with income between 30,000 and 35,000 yuan in 2008 and 2009, then to the group with income between 35,000 and 40,000 yuan in 2010, and finally to the income group with income between 40,000 and 45,000 yuan in 2011. Furthermore, the highest proportion of households also declined from 14.09 percent in 2005 to 12.86 percent in 2006, 11.09 percent in 2007, 9.31 percent in 2008, 8.54 percent in 2009, 8.01 percent in 2010 and 6.88 percent in 2011 successively. The continuous decline of the proportion of households with the highest population density implies that the urban household income distribution curve becomes flatter, and that the income groups are expanding at both ends of the distribution curve.

Normal estimation of rural household income distribution in China

Rural household income distribution demonstrates the bell-shaped feature of normal distribution. However, the accuracy of fitting a normal distribution will be affected due to the lack of data during 1985–1990 and the maximum grouping threshold of 5,000 yuan used during 2006–2010, which will put a disproportionally large number of rural households into the group beyond 5,000 yuan. So, we use the rural household income distributions in 1997–2005 for normal simulation estimation. According to the results of the simulation estimation, the annual rural household income in China from 1997 to 2005 is normally distributed with the expected value equal to the median income of the income category with the most population density. By comparing the density functions of the annual rural income distributions, we can see that the average of the expected values of each year's distribution is 2.25; across the time dimension, variance has been gradually expanding and the distribution curve has been flattened out. But after 1997, the ratio of income standard deviation to average income has been declining and the income inequality narrowing, which has flattened the rural household income distribution. At the same time, the cross-year average income of the rural households in that period was normally distributed with the expected value of 2.25 and variance of 1.07.

Normal estimation of rural household income distribution in China (1997)

The first step of fitting a normal distribution is to estimate the expected value and variance of the samples. The expected value of a sample is the sample mean. The average disposable income of rural households in 1997 is 2,090.13 yuan. A significant number of households are located near this value: 14.93 percent of households have annual income in the range of 2,000–2,500 yuan, which has the highest density among all income groups. We choose the median of the 2,000–2,500 yuan income group as the expected value for the rural household income distribution in 1997.[1] Without the data on the distribution within each income group, we use the median of each income group as the sample value, and take the proportion of households in each income group as the weight to make an approximate variance estimation (hereinafter referred to as estimated variance). The result is that the estimated variance of rural households' income distribution is 1.5459 in 1997. This variance is less than the actual sample variance,[2] so the estimated normal distribution is steeper than the actual normal distribution curve (when the expected value is equal, the smaller the variance is, the steeper the normal distribution curve will be).

Based on the expected value and variance of rural household income distribution in 1997, we got the density function of normal distribution and its curve with location parameter 2.09 and scale parameter 1.54 through simulation with the median of income groups as a sample value (normal simulation curve). The estimated density function of the normal distribution of rural households' income in 1997 is expressed as $f(x)=\frac{1}{1.24\sqrt{2\pi}}e^{-\frac{(x-2.25)^2}{3.09}}$, abbreviated as $X\!-\!N(2.09, 1.54)$. The normal estimation curve calculated using the median of different income groups as a sample value is expressed as in Figure 2.4.

The percentage of households in an income group is the proportion of total households with income in the upper and lower limits of the income groups in all households examined. If the actual income distribution is normal, the interval integral value between upper and lower limits should be equal to the percentage of households in such an interval. Therefore, using the estimated density function, we calculate the implied percentage of household in each income group by the integration over each interval. By inspecting the actual and the estimated distributions, one can see that the estimated function lies beneath the actual function in a large interval to the left of the mean and crosses over afterwards. The

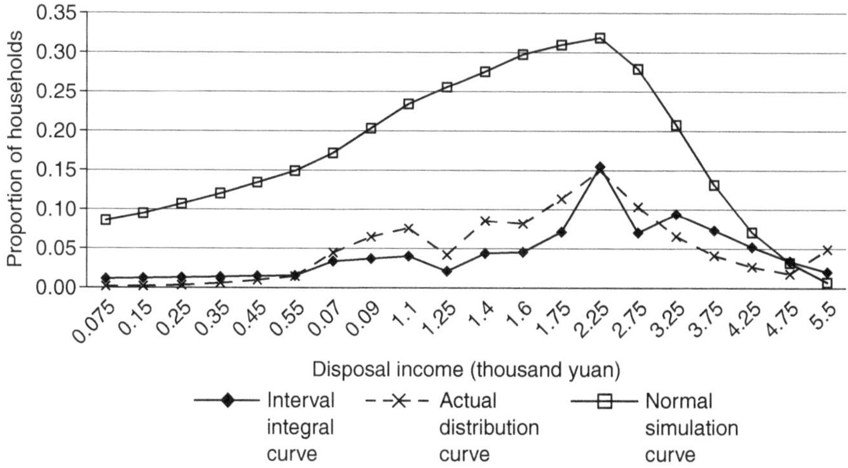

Figure 2.4 Estimation of rural household income distribution in China (1997).

Source: China Macroeconomic Database provided by WIND.

two distributions are similar in shape. The goodness-of-fit between the estimated curve and the actual distribution curve of the rural household income in 1997 is 0.9126. On this basis, it can be concluded that the distribution of China's rural household income in 1997 is normal, with the median income of the income category with the most population density as its expected value and estimated variance as the scale parameter, namely, $X\text{–}N$ (2.15,2.54) (Table 2.1; see also Table 2.2).

The regression equation of the percentage of rural household income calculated from estimated normal density function (PFNL 97) and actual value from sampling survey (PAN 97) of 1997 is:

$$\text{PAN97} = 0.93 \times \text{PFNL971} + 0.0046 + [\text{AR}(1) = 0.7272,\ \text{MA}(1) = 0.4049]$$

(5.46) (0.24) (3.08) (1.39)

R^2=0.912598; adjusted R^2=0.893869; DW=1.74. AR (1) and MA (1) are first-order autoregressive and moving average residual components. The value in parenthesis is the t-statistic.

Normal estimation of rural household income distribution in 2005

In 2005, the average disposable income of rural households in China is 3,254.93 yuan. But the income group with the highest density (12.69 percent) is the group with 2,000–2,500 yuan. The proportion of households of the group with average disposable income of 3,000–3,500 yuan is just 9.55 percent. The expected value of the estimated normal distribution should lie within the income group with the

Table 2.1 Estimation of normal simulation curve of rural household income (1997)

Income groups (yuan)	*Mid-value (yuan)*	*Household proportion (%)*	*Income variances (1.5459)*	*Normal simulation curve*
Under 100	75	0.18	0.0085	0.069
100–200	150	0.19	0.0084	0.077
200–300	250	0.34	0.0136	0.088
300–400	350	0.6	0.0217	0.100
400–500	450	0.97	0.0314	0.113
500–600	550	1.47	0.0425	0.126
600–800	700	4.49	0.1079	0.148
800–1,000	900	6.49	0.1183	0.178
1,000–1,200	1,100	7.59	0.1004	0.209
1,200–1,300	1,250	4.2	0.0420	0.232
1,300–1,500	1,400	8.56	0.0618	0.254
1,500–1,700	1,600	8.19	0.0346	0.280
1,700–2,000	1,750	11.35	0.0248	0.296
2,000–2,500	2,250	14.93	0.0000	0.321
2,500–3,000	2,750	10.35	0.0259	0.296
3,000–3,500	3,250	6.56	0.0656	0.232
3,500–4,000	3,750	4.13	0.0929	0.155
4,000–4,500	4,250	2.68	0.1072	0.088
4,500–5,000	4,750	1.81	0.1131	0.043
Over 5,000	5,500	4.94	0.5218	0.011

Source: calculated on the basis of the sampling survey data of rural household income distributions provided by WIND. Following tables use the same source.

highest density. So, we took 2,250 yuan as the expected value for the normal estimation of rural household income distribution in 2005, the medians of each income group as sample values, and the proportion of households in each income group as the weight, and the estimated variance of 3.1448 for estimating the rural household income distribution in 2005. The result is expressed as $f(x) = \frac{1}{1.77\sqrt{2\pi}} e^{-\frac{(x-2)^2}{6.29}}$, noted as $X\!-\!N(2.25, 3.14)$. Based on this, we calculate the definite integral for different income groups as the proportion household in a group implied by the estimated density function. The result is reported in Tables 2.3 and 2.4.

Through comparison between the estimated rural household income density function and the actual distribution, we can see that the estimated distribution and the actual distribution are highly consistent in trend. The results of regression analysis show that the goodness-of-fit between the estimated curve and the actual distribution curve of the rural household income in 2005 is 0.9936. On this basis, it can be concluded that the distribution of Chinese rural household income in 2005 is subject to a normal distribution with the expected value of 2.25 and variance of 3.14, namely $X\!-\!N\,(2.25, 3.14)$ (Figure 2.5).

Table 2.2 Interval integral of normal simulation function of rural household income distribution (1997)

Mid-value of income group (1,000 yuan)	*Interval of* x		$\Phi = (x-u)/ó$		$F(\Phi)$		$F(X) = F(\Phi)$		*Interval integral value*
	Lower	*Upper*	*Lower*	*Upper*	*Lower*	*Upper*	*Lower*	*Upper*	
0.075	0	0.1	–1.810	–1.729	0.0352	0.0418	0.0352	0.0418	0.0067
0.15	0.1	0.2	–1.729	–1.649	0.0418	0.0495	0.0418	0.0495	0.0077
0.25	0.2	0.3	–1.649	–1.568	0.0495	0.0582	0.0495	0.0582	0.0087
0.35	0.3	0.4	–1.568	–1.488	0.0582	0.0681	0.0582	0.0681	0.0099
0.45	0.4	0.5	–1.488	–1.407	0.0681	0.0793	0.0681	0.0793	0.0112
0.55	0.5	0.6	–1.407	–1.327	0.0793	0.0918	0.0793	0.0918	0.0125
0.7	0.6	0.8	–1.327	–1.166	0.0918	0.1220	0.0918	0.1220	0.0302
0.9	0.8	1	–1.166	–1.005	0.1220	0.1575	0.1220	0.1575	0.0355
1.1	1	1.2	–1.005	–0.844	0.1575	0.1991	0.1575	0.1991	0.0417
1.25	1.2	1.3	–0.844	–0.764	0.1991	0.2221	0.1991	0.2221	0.0230
1.4	1.3	1.5	–0.764	–0.603	0.2221	0.2743	0.2221	0.2743	0.0522
1.6	1.5	1.7	–0.603	–0.442	0.2743	0.3300	0.2743	0.3300	0.0557
1.75	1.7	2	–0.442	–0.201	0.3300	0.4207	0.3300	0.4207	0.0907
2.25	2	2.5	–0.201	0.201	0.4207	0.5793	0.4207	0.5793	0.1586
2.75	2.5	3	0.201	0.603	0.5793	0.7257	0.5793	0.7257	0.1464
3.25	3	3.5	0.603	1.005	0.7257	0.8426	0.7257	0.8426	0.1169
3.75	3.5	4	1.005	1.407	0.8426	0.9207	0.8426	0.9207	0.0782
4.25	4	4.5	1.407	1.810	0.9207	0.9649	0.9207	0.9649	0.0441
4.75	4.5	5	1.810	2.212	0.9649	0.9865	0.9649	0.9865	0.0216
5.5	5	5.5	2.212	2.614	0.9865	0.9955	0.9865	0.9955	0.0090

Note

$F(\Phi)$ is the definite integral of standard normal distribution; $F(\Phi)=\int^{b}_{a} f(\Phi)d\Phi. f(\Phi)$ is the density function of standard normal distribution, a and b are lower and upper bounds of Φ. $F(x)$ is value from the definite integration of household income distribution function $f(x)$. u and $ó$ are expected value and standard deviation of normal density function respectively. Following tables use the same notation.

Table 2.3 Estimation of normal simulation curve of rural household income (2005)

Income groups	*Mid-value (yuan)*	*Household proportion (%)*	*Income variances (1.5459)*	*Normal simulation curve*
Under 100 yuan	75	0.68	0.0241	0.1091
100–200	150	0.11	0.0038	0.1141
200–300	250	0.2	0.0061	0.1207
300–400	350	0.31	0.0084	0.1274
400–500	450	0.41	0.0099	0.1340
500–600	550	0.57	0.0120	0.1406
600–800	700	1.88	0.0318	0.1504
800–1,000	900	2.84	0.0344	0.1629
1,000–1,200	1,100	3.53	0.0286	0.1746
1,200–1,300	1,250	1.97	0.0111	0.1825
1,300–1,500	1,400	4.4	0.0158	0.1896
1,500–1,700	1,600	4.89	0.0078	0.1976
1,700–2,000	1,750	7.67	0.0048	0.2024
2,000–2,500	2,250	12.49	0.0078	0.2095
2,500–3,000	2,750	11.42	0.0642	0.2024
3,000–3,500	3,250	9.55	0.1492	0.1825
3,500–4,000	3,750	7.57	0.2318	0.1536
4,000–4,500	4,250	5.93	0.3002	0.1207
4,500–5,000	4,750	4.64	0.3509	0.0885
Over 5,000	5,500	18.97	2.3238	0.0488

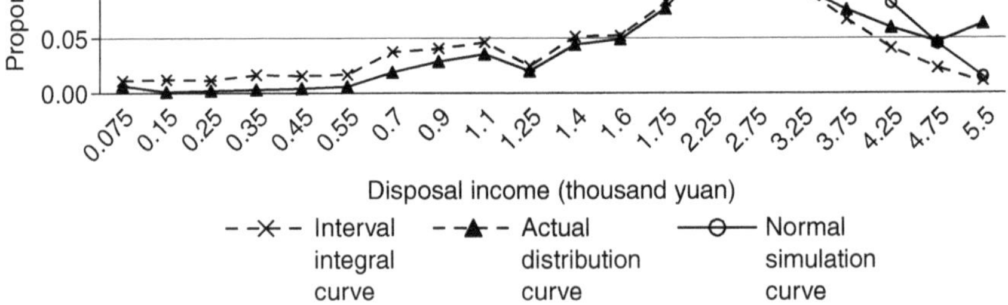

Figure 2.5 Normal simulation curve of rural household income distribution (2005).

Source: estimated using data from the China Macroeconomic Database provided by WIND.

Table 2.4 Interval integral of normal simulation function of rural household income distribution (2005)

Mid-value of income group ('000 yuan)	*Interval of x*		$\Phi = (x - u)/ó$		$F(\Phi)$		$F(X) = F(\Phi)$		*Interval integral value*
	Lower	*Upper*	*Lower*	*Upper*	*Lower*	*Upper*	*Lower*	*Upper*	
0.075	0.0	0.1	–1.269	–1.212	0.102	0.113	0.102	0.113	0.011
0.15	0.1	0.2	–1.212	–1.156	0.113	0.124	0.113	0.124	0.011
0.25	0.2	0.3	–1.156	–1.100	0.124	0.136	0.124	0.136	0.012
0.35	0.3	0.4	–1.100	–1.043	0.136	0.149	0.136	0.149	0.014
0.45	0.4	0.5	–1.043	–0.987	0.149	0.161	0.149	0.161	0.012
0.55	0.5	0.6	–0.987	–0.930	0.161	0.176	0.161	0.176	0.015
0.7	0.6	0.8	–0.930	–0.818	0.176	0.206	0.176	0.206	0.030
0.9	0.8	1.0	–0.818	–0.705	0.206	0.240	0.206	0.240	0.034
1.1	1.0	1.2	–0.705	–0.592	0.240	0.278	0.240	0.278	0.037
1.25	1.2	1.3	–0.592	–0.536	0.278	0.296	0.278	0.296	0.019
1.4	1.3	1.5	–0.536	–0.423	0.296	0.337	0.296	0.337	0.041
1.6	1.5	1.7	–0.423	–0.310	0.337	0.378	0.337	0.378	0.041
1.75	1.7	2.0	–0.310	–0.141	0.378	0.444	0.378	0.444	0.066
2.25	2.0	2.5	–0.141	0.141	0.444	0.556	0.444	0.556	0.111
2.75	2.5	3.0	0.141	0.423	0.556	0.663	0.556	0.663	0.107
3.25	3.0	3.5	0.423	0.705	0.663	0.760	0.663	0.760	0.097
3.75	3.5	4.0	0.705	0.987	0.760	0.839	0.760	0.839	0.079
4.25	4.0	4.5	0.987	1.269	0.839	0.898	0.839	0.898	0.059
4.75	4.5	5.0	1.269	1.551	0.898	0.939	0.898	0.939	0.041
5.5	5.0	5.5	1.551	1.833	0.939	0.966	0.939	0.966	0.027

The regression of the estimated density function of rural household income distribution (PFNL 05) on actual value of sampling survey (PAN 05) in 2005 gives:

$$\text{PAN05} = 0.996 \times \text{PFNL05} + 0.0012 + [\text{AR}(1) = 0.7533,\ \text{MA}(1) = 0.7531]$$
$$(18.28) \qquad\qquad (0.17) \qquad\qquad (3.75) \qquad (4.46)$$

R^2=0.993555; adjusted R^2=0.992174; DW=2.04. AR(1) and MA(1) are first-order autoregressive and moving average residual components respectively. Value in parenthesis is the *t*-statistic.

Comparison of normal estimation of rural household income (1995–2005)

China's rural household income distribution is bell-shaped from 1995 to 2010. According to the results of the normal estimation of rural household income distribution in 1997 and 2005, the rural household income distributions in other years are also subject to the normal distribution, with the median of the income group occupying the highest household proportion as the expected value. However, during the period from 2006 to 2010, the household proportion of the group with income over 5,000 yuan increased to 23.62 percent, 30.94 percent, 39.29 percent, 43.8 percent and 52.4 percent for each year. A large number of households were included in the group with income over 5,000 yuan without further division, which would directly affect the accuracy of the income variance estimation. For example, the income variance should gradually increase with the increase of average income, but the income variance from 2006 to 2010 demonstrates a lot of fluctuations. If the estimated income variance deviates from actual income variance, then this would result in a serious deviation of the simulation normal curve from the actual distribution curve. Therefore, we can only analyze the evolution of the normal distribution of rural household income from 1995 to 2005. Based on the rural household income distribution from 1995 to 2005, the income of the group with the highest population density is the group of 2,000–2,500 yuan from 1997 to 2005, while the annual income of the group with the highest population density in 1995 is the group of 1,000 to 1,200 yuan. We thus took 2,250 yuan as the expected value of the rural household income distribution, the median of each income group as the sample value, and household proportion as weight, to calculate the estimated variance of rural household income distribution of these years.

Table 2.5 shows the density function of the simulation normal distribution of rural household income distribution in each year, which is calculated according to the expected value and estimated variance.

By comparing the density functions of the estimated normal distribution of rural household income from 1995 to 2005, we can see that although the expected value is the same from 1997 to 2005, income variance has gradually risen from 1.54 in 1997 to 3.14 in 2005, causing the normal curve to flatten out. Meanwhile, the income variance is determined by the expected value of the income distribution, income difference, and income distribution structure. We consider the ratio of income standard deviation to average income as the indicator of income difference.

Table 2.5 Normal estimation of rural household income distribution (1995–2010)

Year	*Average net income ('000 yuan)*	*Expectation ('000 yuan)*	*Weighted variance*	*Ratio of standard deviation to average income*	*Density function of normal distribution*
1995	1.5777	1.1000	1.4097	0.7525	$f(x)=\frac{1}{1.19\sqrt{2\pi}}e^{-\frac{(x-1.1)^2}{2.82}}$
1997	2.0901	2.2500	1.5459	0.5949	$f(x)=\frac{1}{1.24\sqrt{2\pi}}e^{-\frac{(x-2.09)^2}{3.09}}$
1998	2.1620	2.2500	1.5986	0.5848	$f(x)=\frac{1}{1.24\sqrt{2\pi}}e^{-\frac{(x-2.16)^2}{3.2}}$
1999	2.2103	2.2500	1.6925	0.5886	$f(x)=\frac{1}{1.3\sqrt{2\pi}}e^{-\frac{(x-2.21)^2}{3.4}}$
2000	2.2534	2.2500	1.8654	0.6061	$f(x)=\frac{1}{1.37\sqrt{2\pi}}e^{-\frac{(x-2.25)^2}{3.73}}$
2001	2.3664	2.2500	2.0124	0.5995	$f(x)=\frac{1}{1.42\sqrt{2\pi}}e^{-\frac{(x-2.37)^2}{4.02}}$
2002	2.4756	2.2500	2.1403	0.5909	$f(x)=\frac{1}{1.46\sqrt{2\pi}}e^{-\frac{(x-2.25)^2}{4.28}}$
2003	2.6222	2.2500	2.3442	0.5839	$f(x)=\frac{1}{1.53\sqrt{2\pi}}e^{-\frac{(x-2.25)^2}{4.69}}$
2004	2.9364	2.2500	2.6905	0.5586	$f(x)=\frac{1}{1.64\sqrt{2\pi}}e^{-\frac{(x-2.25)^2}{5.38}}$
2005	3.2549	2.2500	3.1448	0.5448	$f(x)=\frac{1}{1.77\sqrt{2\pi}}e^{-\frac{(x-2)^2}{6.29}}$
2006	3.5870	2.2500	3.6493	0.5326	$f(x)=\frac{1}{1.91\sqrt{2\pi}}e^{-\frac{(x-2.25)^2}{7.3}}$
2007	4.1404	2.7500	3.2911	0.4382	$f(x)=\frac{1}{1.81\sqrt{2\pi}}e^{-\frac{(x-2.75)^2}{6.58}}$
2008	4.7602	2.7500	3.8448	0.4119	$f(x)=\frac{1}{1.96\sqrt{2\pi}}e^{-\frac{(x-2.75)^2}{7.68}}$
2009	5.1532	3.2500	3.0801	0.3406	$f(x)=\frac{1}{1.76\sqrt{2\pi}}e^{-\frac{(x-3.25)^2}{6.16}}$
2010	5.9190	3.7500	2.4886	0.2665	$f(x)=\frac{1}{1.58\sqrt{2\pi}}e^{-\frac{(x-3.75)^2}{4.98}}$

The greater the ratio is, the larger the income distribution deviation from the average income will be. This indicator shows that income inequality among rural households has been declining since 1997, with a decrease of its value from 0.59 in 1997 to 0.54 in 2005. The increase of the income variance from 1997 to 2005 was driven by the income distribution structure, and the narrowing income gap mediated the flattening out of rural household income distribution.

Normal estimation of cross-year average rural household income distribution (1997–2005)

Since the rural household income for each year from 1997 to 2005 is normally distributed, the cross-year rural household income distribution should also be normal. In order to verify the normality of the cross-year rural household income distribution, we average the proportion of households in each income group across years to construct the cross-year average distribution. Features of this distribution still resemble those of a normal distribution. The income of the group with the highest household density is 2,000–2500 yuan. Accordingly, we choose the median of this income group as the mean of the normal estimation, the median of each income group as the sample value and the proportion of households in each income group as its weight. After excluding the group with income over 5,000 yuan (too great a proportion may lead to overestimation), the variance of cross-year average income distribution is 1.0688. Then, the cross-year average rural household income distribution can be represented by a standard normal distribution with the mean and variance equal to 2.25 and 1.07 respectively (its density function is expressed as: $f(x)=\frac{1}{3.24\sqrt{2\pi}}e^{-\frac{(x-2.25)^2}{2.14}}$, shortened as $X{-}N[2.25, 1.07]$). The definite integrals of cross-year average income distribution for each income group represent the proportion of households in that income group as implied by the estimated distribution. These results are reported in Tables 2.6 and 2.7.

By comparing the actual and the estimated distribution of cross-year average rural household income, we can see that they are similar in shape, and only parts of the estimated distribution curve slightly deviate from the actual curve. Regression analysis shows that the goodness-of-fit between the estimated and the actual distribution is 0.9468, which suggests that normal distribution is a good approximation of the cross-year average income distribution. On this basis, it can be concluded that the distribution of cross-year average rural household income in the period considered is normal, with an expected value of 2.25 and variance of 1.07, namely $X{-}N\,(2.25, 1.07)$ (Figure 2.6).

The result from regressing the estimated density of cross-year average rural household income distribution (PFNL 9705) on the actual value of sampling survey (PAN 9705) in the period from 1997 to 2005 is:

$$\text{PAN9705} = \underset{(6.73)}{0.6218} \times \text{PFN9705} + \underset{(1.81)}{0.0197} + [\text{AR}(1) = \underset{(3.36)}{0.73041},\ \text{MA}(2) = \underset{(-488.39)}{-0.1629}]$$

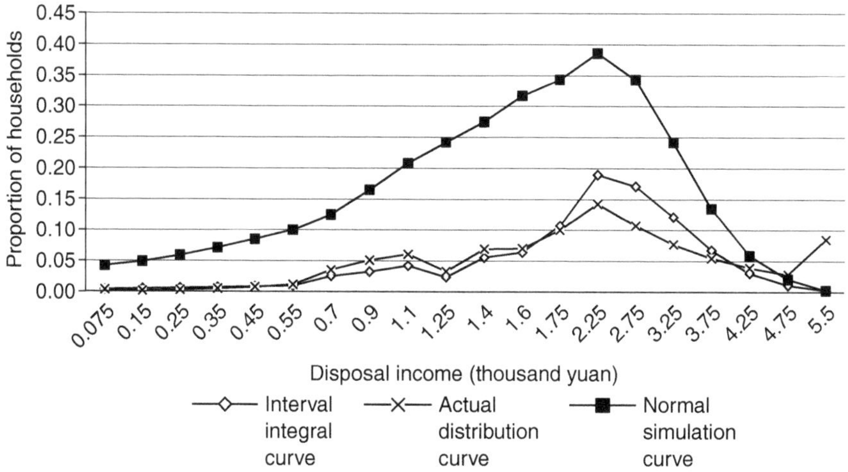

Figure 2.6 Normal simulation curve of rural household average income distribution (1997–2005).

Source: China Macroeconomic Database provided by WIND.

Table 2.6 Estimation of normal simulation curve of rural household average income distribution (1997–2005)

Income group	*Mid-value (yuan)*	*Household proportion (%)*	*Average household proportion (%)*	*Income variance*	*Normal simulation curve*
Under 100	75	3.22	0.3578	0.0169	0.042
100–200	150	1.48	0.1644	0.0073	0.049
200–300	250	2.57	0.2856	0.0114	0.059
300–400	350	4.45	0.4944	0.0178	0.071
400–500	450	6.99	0.7767	0.0252	0.085
500–600	550	10.58	1.1756	0.0340	0.100
600–800	700	31.74	3.5267	0.0847	0.125
800–1,000	900	45.82	5.0911	0.0928	0.165
1,000–1,200	1,100	54.56	6.0622	0.0802	0.208
1,200–1,300	1,250	29.85	3.3167	0.0332	0.242
1,300–1,500	1,400	62.41	6.9344	0.0501	0.275
1,500–1,700	1,600	63.04	7.0044	0.0296	0.317
1,700–2,000	1,750	90.03	10.0033	0.0250	0.343
2,000–2,500	2,250	128.42	14.2689	0.0000	0.386
2,500–3,000	2,750	96.49	10.7211	0.0268	0.343
3,000–3,500	3,250	69.42	7.7133	0.0771	0.242
3,500–4,000	3,750	49.11	5.4567	0.1228	0.135
4,000–4,500	4,250	35.2	3.9111	0.1564	0.059
4,500–5,000	4,750	25.56	2.8400	0.1775	0.021
Over 5,000	5,500	76.47	8.4967	0.8975	0.003

Table 2.7 Interval integral calculation of normal function of rural households' average income distribution (1997–2005)

Mid-value of income group ('000 yuan)	*Interval of* x		$\Phi = (x - u)/σ$		$F(\Phi)$		$F(X) = F(\Phi)$		*Interval integral value*
	Lower	*Upper*	*Lower*	*Upper*	*Lower*	*Upper*	*Lower*	*Upper*	
0.075	0.0	0.1	–2.1764	–2.0796	0.0150	0.0188	0.0150	0.0188	0.0038
0.15	0.1	0.2	–2.0796	–1.9829	0.0188	0.0239	0.0188	0.0239	0.0051
0.25	0.2	0.3	–1.9829	–1.8862	0.0239	0.0297	0.0239	0.0297	0.0059
0.35	0.3	0.4	–1.8862	–1.7895	0.0297	0.0367	0.0297	0.0367	0.0070
0.45	0.4	0.5	–1.7895	–1.6927	0.0367	0.0455	0.0367	0.0455	0.0088
0.55	0.5	0.6	–1.6927	–1.5960	0.0455	0.0554	0.0455	0.0554	0.0099
0.70	0.6	0.8	–1.5960	–1.4026	0.0554	0.0808	0.0554	0.0808	0.0254
0.90	0.8	1.0	–1.4026	–1.2091	0.0808	0.1131	0.0808	0.1131	0.0323
1.10	1.0	1.2	–1.2091	–1.0156	0.1131	0.1551	0.1131	0.1551	0.0420
1.25	1.2	1.3	–1.0156	–0.9189	0.1551	0.1788	0.1551	0.1788	0.0238
1.40	1.3	1.5	–0.9189	–0.7255	0.1788	0.2343	0.1788	0.2343	0.0555
1.60	1.5	1.7	–0.7255	–0.5320	0.2343	0.2981	0.2343	0.2981	0.0639
1.75	1.7	2.0	–0.5320	–0.2418	0.2981	0.4052	0.2981	0.4052	0.1071
2.25	2.0	2.5	–0.2418	0.2418	0.4052	0.5948	0.4052	0.5948	0.1896
2.75	2.5	3.0	0.2418	0.7255	0.5948	0.7658	0.5948	0.7658	0.1710
3.25	3.0	3.5	0.7255	1.2091	0.7658	0.8869	0.7658	0.8869	0.1212
3.75	3.5	4.0	1.2091	1.6927	0.8869	0.9545	0.8869	0.9545	0.0676
4.25	4.0	4.5	1.6927	2.1764	0.9545	0.9850	0.9545	0.9850	0.0305
4.75	4.5	5.0	2.1764	2.6600	0.9850	0.9961	0.9850	0.9961	0.0111
5.50	5.0	5.5	2.6600	3.1437	0.9961	0.9992	0.9961	0.9992	0.0031

R^2 = 0.946813; Adjusted R^2 = 0.935416; DW = 1.79; AR(1) and MA(2) are first-order autoregressive and moving average residual components respectively. The value in parenthesis is the *t*-statistic.

Normal estimation of urban household income distribution in China

The CEIC database provides data on the proportion of households of different income groups of Chinese urban households from 2005 to 2011. The data are normally distributed. We tried to fit normal distribution into each year's urban household income data. As the result shows, urban household income is normally distributed with the mean equal to the median income of the income group with the highest population density. However, because the group data of urban household income distribution were inadequate, the actual variance differs from the estimated variance, resulting in some differences between the estimated and actual distribution curves. Comparing the distributions of urban household income of different years, it can be observed that as urban households' income increases, the expected value of the estimated normal distribution moves to the right, the income variance increases, and the estimated normal distribution curve flattens. But the trend of flattening is mediated by the narrowing urban household income gap after 2005. In addition, the distribution of average urban household income for the period between 2005 and 2011 also follows the normal distribution, with the mean equal to the median of the income group occupying the highest household proportion.

Normal estimation of urban household income distribution (2005)

In 2005, the per capita income of Chinese urban residents was 11,320.77 yuan, the average household size was 2.96, and the average annual household income was 33,509.48 yuan. The income group with the greatest population density in 2005 was the group of 20,000–25,000 yuan. Given that the expected value of the normal distribution must be equal to the sample value of the income group with the highest population density, we took the median value of 22,500 yuan for the 20,000–25,000 yuan income group as the expected value of the normal estimation of urban household income distribution in 2005, the median of different income groups as the sample value and the income group's density as weight; we reached the estimated variance of 5.1817. Based on that, we can build the estimated normal distribution density function of urban household income distribution in 2005, expressed as: $f(x) = \frac{1}{2.28\sqrt{2\pi}} e^{-\frac{(x-2.25)^2}{10.36}}$, or $X \sim N(2.25, 5.18)$. Based on the normal distribution density function, we can obtain the density of different income groups of urban household by calculating definite integrals of the density function using the upper and lower bounds of different income groups. The results are shown in Tables 2.8 and 2.9.

Table 2.8 Estimation of normal simulation curve of urban household income distribution (2005)

Income groups (yuan)	*Median (yuan)*	*Household proportion*	*Income variances (5.18)*	*Normal simulation curve*
Under 10,000	7,500	0.0485	0.1095	0.1411
10,000–15,000	12,500	0.101	0.1010	0.1591
15,000–20,000	17,500	0.1361	0.0340	0.1711
20,000–25,000	22,500	0.1409	0.0000	0.1753
25,000–30,000	27,500	0.1275	0.0319	0.1711
30,000–35,000	32,500	0.1014	0.1014	0.1591
35,000–40,000	37,500	0.0811	0.1825	0.1411
40,000–45,000	42,500	0.0607	0.2428	0.1191
45,000–50,000	47,500	0.046	0.2875	0.0959
50,000–55,000	52,500	0.0341	0.3069	0.0735
55,000–60,000	57,500	0.0248	0.3038	0.0537
60,000–65,000	62,500	0.0199	0.3184	0.0374
65,000–70,000	67,500	0.015	0.3038	0.0248
70,000–75,000	72,500	0.0118	0.2950	0.0157
75,000–80,000	77,500	0.0085	0.2571	0.0095
80,000–85,000	82,500	0.0078	0.2808	0.0054
85,000–90,000	87,500	0.0053	0.2239	0.0030
90,000–95,000	92,500	0.0048	0.2352	0.0015
95,000–100,000	97,500	0.0043	0.2419	0.0008
Over 100,000	102,500	0.0207	1.3248	0.0004

Comparing the estimated and actual distribution curve of 2005, it can be observed that the integral curve and the actual curve are similar in shape, but around the expected value the integral curve is obviously below the actual distribution curve. This implies that the variance of the normal distribution function we estimated is obviously greater than the actual variance and the increase in variance has caused the distribution curve to flatten. The results of regression analysis show that the goodness-of-fit between the interval integral curve and the actual distribution curve in 2005 is 0.9714. On this basis, it can be concluded that the distribution of urban household income in 2005 is normal, with an expected value of 2.25 and variance of 5.22, namely $X–N$ (2.25, 5.22) (Figure 2.7).

The regression equation between the definite integral values of the urban household income distribution density function (PFCL05) and actual values of sampling survey (PAC05) in 2005 is

$$\begin{aligned} \text{PAC05} = 1.3599 \times &\text{PFCL05} - 0.0011 + [\text{AR}(1) = 0.7265] \\ (8.79) \qquad & (-0.11) \qquad (3.85) \end{aligned}$$

R^2=0.971399; adjusted R^2=0.967585; DW=1.34; AR(1) is first-order autoregressive item of equation residuals. The value in the bracket under variables is the t-statistic of variable significance.

Table 2.9 Definite integral of the estimated distribution density function of urban household income (2005)

Median of income group (1,000 yuan)	*Interval of* x		$\Phi = (x-u)/ó$		$F(\Phi)$		$F(X) = F(\Phi)$		*Interval integral value*
	Lower	*Upper*	*Lower*	*Upper*	*Lower*	*Upper*	*Lower*	*Upper*	
0.75	0.75	1.0	–0.6589	–0.5491	0.2546	0.2912	0.2546	0.2912	0.0366
1.25	1.0	1.5	–0.5491	–0.3295	0.2912	0.3707	0.2912	0.3707	0.0795
1.75	1.5	2.0	–0.3295	–0.1098	0.3707	0.4562	0.3707	0.4562	0.0855
2.25	2.0	2.5	–0.1098	0.1098	0.4562	0.5438	0.4562	0.5438	0.0876
2.75	2.5	3.0	0.1098	0.3295	0.5438	0.6293	0.5438	0.6293	0.0855
3.25	3.0	3.5	0.3295	0.5491	0.6293	0.7088	0.6293	0.7088	0.0795
3.75	3.5	4.0	0.5491	0.7688	0.7088	0.7794	0.7088	0.7794	0.0706
4.25	4.0	4.5	0.7688	0.9884	0.7794	0.8389	0.7794	0.8389	0.0595
4.75	4.5	5.0	0.9884	1.2081	0.8389	0.8869	0.8389	0.8869	0.0480
5.25	5.0	5.5	1.2081	1.4277	0.8869	0.9236	0.8869	0.9236	0.0367
5.75	5.5	6.0	1.4277	1.6474	0.9236	0.9505	0.9236	0.9505	0.0269
6.25	6.0	6.5	1.6474	1.8670	0.9505	0.9689	0.9505	0.9689	0.0184
6.75	6.5	7.0	1.8670	2.0867	0.9689	0.9815	0.9689	0.9815	0.0126
7.25	7.0	7.5	2.0867	2.3063	0.9815	0.9894	0.9815	0.9894	0.0080
7.75	7.5	8.0	2.3063	2.5260	0.9894	0.9942	0.9894	0.9942	0.0048
8.25	8.0	8.5	2.5260	2.7456	0.9942	0.9970	0.9942	0.9970	0.0028
8.75	8.5	9.0	2.7456	2.9653	0.9970	0.9985	0.9970	0.9985	0.0015
9.25	9.0	9.5	2.9653	3.1849	0.9985	0.9993	0.9985	0.9993	0.0008
9.75	9.5	10	3.1849	3.4046	0.9993	0.9997	0.9993	0.9997	0.0004
10.25	10.0	10.5	3.4046	3.6242	0.9997	0.9999	0.9997	0.9999	0.0002

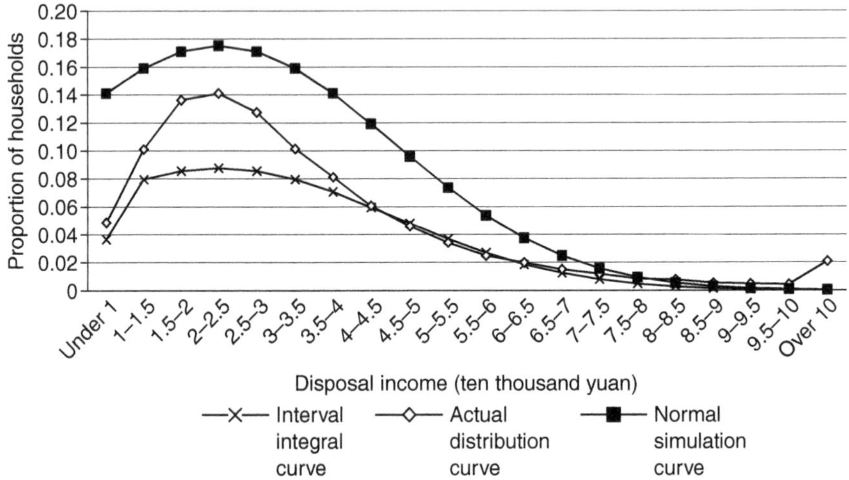

Figure 2.7 Normal estimation curve of urban household income distribution (2005).

Normal estimation of China's urban household income distribution in 2010

In 2010, the average household income of Chinese urban households was 60,576.25 yuan, while the income of the group with the highest household proportion was between 35,000–40,000 yuan. According to the principle that the expected value of normal distribution must be the sample value of the income group with the highest household density, we took 37,500 yuan, the median of the 35,000–40,000 yuan income group, as the expected value of the estimated normal urban household income distribution in 2010, the median of different income groups as the sample value and the proportion of households in each group as weights, and estimated the variance of urban household income to be 10.4764 in 2010. Then, the urban household income distribution in 2010 can be represented by a standard normal distribution with mean and variance equal to 3.75 and 10.48, respectively, with density function as $f(x) = \frac{1}{3.24\sqrt{2\pi}} e^{-\frac{(x-3.75)^2}{20.95}}$, noted as $X\text{–}N\,(3.75, 10.48)$.

Using this normal distribution density function, the proportion of urban households in each income group is calculated as the definite integral over that income range. The result is reported in Tables 2.10 and 2.11. Through comparison between the actual and the estimated rural household income density function, we can see that they are similar in shape, but the greatest part of the estimated distribution curve lies beneath the actual curve, which implies that the estimated variance is larger than actual variance. Regression analysis shows that the goodness-of-fit between the estimated curve (PFCL10) and the actual distribution curve (PAC10)

Table 2.10 Estimation of normal simulation curve of urban households' income distribution (2010)

Income groups (yuan)	*Mid-value (yuan)*	*Household proportion (%)*	*Income variances (10.48)*	*Normal simulation curve*
Under 10,000	7,500	0.0068	0.0612	0.0802
10,000–15,000	12,500	0.0198	0.1238	0.0915
15,000–20,000	17,500	0.0350	0.1400	0.1018
20,000–25,000	22,500	0.0513	0.1154	0.1107
25,000–30,000	27,500	0.0664	0.0664	0.1175
30,000–35,000	32,500	0.0745	0.0186	0.1218
35,000–40,000	37,500	0.0806	0.0000	0.1233
40,000–45,000	42,500	0.0785	0.0196	0.1218
45,000–50,000	47,500	0.0746	0.0746	0.1175
50,000–55,000	52,500	0.0650	0.1463	0.1107
55,000–60,000	57,500	0.0603	0.2412	0.1018
60,000–65,000	62,500	0.0519	0.3244	0.0915
65,000–70,000	67,500	0.0442	0.3978	0.0802
70,000–75,000	72,500	0.0388	0.4753	0.0687
75,000–80,000	77,500	0.0350	0.5600	0.0574
80,000–85,000	82,500	0.0301	0.6095	0.0469
85,000–90,000	87,500	0.0238	0.5950	0.0374
90,000–95,000	92,500	0.0229	0.6927	0.0291
95,000–100,000	97,500	0.0181	0.6516	0.0221
Over 100,000	102,500	0.1222	5.1630	0.0164

in 2010 is 0.9873. This means the estimated distribution can accurately capture the income variation across groups in 2010. The estimated variance is greater than the actual variance, thus the estimated distribution curve is flatter. This is mainly because more than 12 percent of the total households are grouped as having income over 100,000 yuan without finer division in the actual distribution.[3] In general, the urban household income distribution in 2010 is normally distributed, with the expected value of 3.75 and the variance of 10.48, namely $X–N$ (3.75, 10.48) (Figure 2.8).

The regression of the estimated proportion of urban households in each income groups (PFCL10) on the actual value (PAC10) in 2010 gives the following result:

$$\text{PAC10} = 1.0891 \times \text{PFCL10} = 0.0054 + [\text{AR}(1) = 0.9548,\ \ \text{AR}(2) = -0.3505]$$
$$(11.54) \qquad\qquad (1.37) \qquad\qquad (8.61) \qquad\qquad (-3.21)$$

R^2=0.987354; Adjusted R^2=0.984436; DW=2.48; AR(1) and AR(2) are first-order autoregressive and moving average residual components, respectively. Value in parenthesis is the t-statistic.

Table 2.11 Interval integral of normal simulation function of urban household income distribution (2010)

Mid-value of income group (1,000 yuan)	*Interval of* x		$\Phi = (x - u)/ó$		$F(\Phi)$		$F(X) = F(\Phi)$		*Interval integral value*
	Lower	*Upper*	*Lower*	*Upper*	*Lower*	*Upper*	*Lower*	*Upper*	
0.75	0.75	1.0	–0.927	–0.850	0.178	0.198	0.178	0.198	0.020
1.25	1.0	1.5	–0.850	–0.695	0.198	0.244	0.198	0.244	0.046
1.75	1.5	2.0	–0.695	–0.541	0.244	0.295	0.244	0.295	0.051
2.25	2.0	2.5	–0.541	–0.386	0.295	0.350	0.295	0.350	0.056
2.75	2.5	3.0	–0.386	–0.232	0.350	0.409	0.350	0.409	0.059
3.25	3.0	3.5	–0.232	–0.077	0.409	0.468	0.409	0.468	0.059
3.75	3.5	4.0	–0.077	0.077	0.468	0.532	0.468	0.532	0.064
4.25	4.0	4.5	0.077	0.232	0.532	0.591	0.532	0.591	0.059
4.75	4.5	5.0	0.232	0.386	0.591	0.650	0.591	0.650	0.059
5.25	5.0	5.5	0.386	0.541	0.650	0.705	0.650	0.705	0.056
5.75	5.5	6.0	0.541	0.695	0.705	0.756	0.705	0.756	0.051
6.25	6.0	6.5	0.695	0.850	0.756	0.802	0.756	0.802	0.046
6.75	6.5	7.0	0.850	1.004	0.802	0.843	0.802	0.843	0.040
7.25	7.0	7.5	1.004	1.159	0.843	0.877	0.843	0.877	0.034
7.75	7.5	8.0	1.159	1.313	0.877	0.905	0.877	0.905	0.028
8.25	8.0	8.5	1.313	1.468	0.905	0.929	0.905	0.929	0.024
8.75	8.5	9.0	1.468	1.622	0.929	0.947	0.929	0.947	0.018
9.25	9.0	9.5	1.622	1.776	0.947	0.962	0.947	0.962	0.015
9.75	9.5	10.0	1.776	1.931	0.962	0.973	0.962	0.973	0.011
10.25	10	10.5	1.931	2.085	0.973	0.981	0.973	0.981	0.008

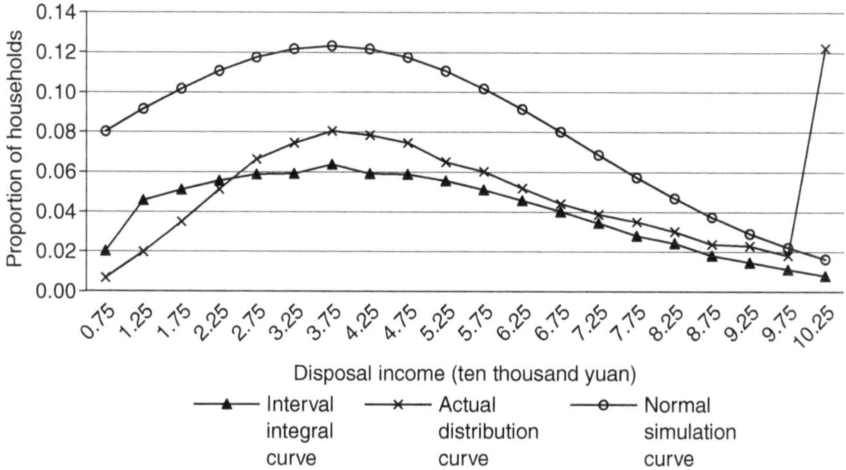

Figure 2.8 Normal simulation curve of urban household income distribution (2010).

Comparison of normal estimation of urban household income distribution (2005–2011)

The urban household income distributions in China are bell-shaped from 2005 to 2011. Based on the normal estimation results of 2005 and 2010, the urban household income in other years should also be normally distributed. In order to estimate normal urban household income distribution, we use the median of the income group that occupied the highest household proportion as the expected value, the median of each income group as the sample value and the household proportion of each income group as weight. The estimated normal distribution functions are as follows: 2005: $X=N\,(2.25, 5.18)$, 2006: $X=N\,(2.25, 6.53)$, 2007: $X=N\,(2.75, 7.38)$, 2008: $X=N\,(3.25, 8.71)$, 2009: $X=N\,(3.25, 10.42)$, 2010: $X=N\,(3.75, 10.48)$, 2010: $X=N\,(4.25, 1.22)$. The estimated normal distributions from 2005 to 2011 are shown in Table 2.12 and Figure 2.9.

Observing from the estimated normal distribution curve of urban household income in different years, we can see the expected value of the estimated normal distribution gradually shifted to the right with the increase of urban household income. However, since the income variance increased from 5.18 in 2005 to 11.22 in 2011, the estimated normal distribution curve of annual income flattened out. Meanwhile, we can see that the ratio between standard deviation of urban household income and the average household income declined from 0.68 in 2005 to 0.49 in 2011. This implies that the urban household income difference gradually decreased during this period, and that the increase of income variance was the result of the increase of average income. The narrowing of the income gap constrained the income variance and the flatness of the income distribution curve.

Table 2.12 Normal estimation of urban household income distribution (2005–2011)

Year	*Average household income (10,000 yuan)*	*Expectation (10,000 yuan)*	*Weighted variance*	*Ratio of standard deviation and average income*	*Density function of normal distribution*
2005	3.3509	2.25	5.1818	0.6793	$f(x)=\frac{1}{2.28\sqrt{2\pi}}e^{-\frac{(x-2.25)^2}{10.36}}$
2006	3.7522	2.25	6.5333	0.6812	$f(x)=\frac{1}{2.56\sqrt{2\pi}}e^{-\frac{(x-2.25)^2}{13.06}}$
2007	4.3384	2.75	7.3800	0.6262	$f(x)=\frac{1}{2.72\sqrt{2\pi}}e^{-\frac{(x-2.75)^2}{14.76}}$
2008	4.9667	3.25	8.7071	0.5941	$f(x)=\frac{1}{2.95\sqrt{2\pi}}e^{-\frac{(x-3.25)^2}{17.41}}$
2009	5.4500	3.25	10.4180	0.5922	$f(x)=\frac{1}{3.25\sqrt{2\pi}}e^{-\frac{(x-3.25)^2}{20.84}}$
2010	6.0576	3.75	10.4764	0.5343	$f(x)=\frac{1}{3.24\sqrt{2\pi}}e^{-\frac{(x-3.75)^2}{20.95}}$
2011	6.8820	4.25	11.2161	0.4866	$f(x)=\frac{1}{3.35\sqrt{2\pi}}e^{-\frac{(x-4.25)^2}{22.43}}$

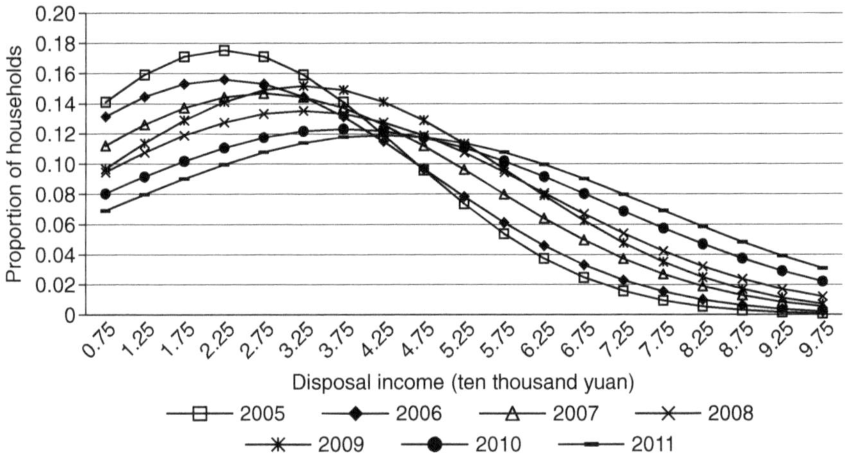

Figure 2.9 Normal simulation curve of urban household income from 2005 to 2011.

Normal estimation of urban household income distribution (2005–2011)

The distribution of urban household income in each year reflects the characteristics of normal distribution. However, whether the cross-year household income is normally distributed remains a question. We sum up the value of household population density of different income groups from 2005 to 2011 and then calculate the averages to get the cross-year average household income distribution. The distribution also conforms to a bell-shaped normal distribution. The income group with the highest population density is the group of 25,000 to 30,000 yuan. According to the feature of urban household income distribution, we took the median of the 25,000 to 35,000 yuan income group as the expected value of normal estimation, the median of different income groups as sample values and the population density of different income groups as weights. After removing the group with income over 100,000 yuan (with abnormally high density that may lead to overestimation), the variance of the urban average income distribution is 6.1 from 2005 to 2011. Assuming that the average urban resident's income distribution in this period conformed to normal distribution with expectation of 2.75 and variance of 6.1, the density function can be expressed as: $f(x) = \frac{1}{3.24\sqrt{2\pi}} e^{-\frac{(x-2.75)^2}{12.2}}$, noted as $X\text{–}N(2.75, 6.1)$. Using the density function, we calculate the population density of different income groups by calculating the definite integrals of the density function income groups in this period. The results are shown in Tables 2.13 and 2.14.

Table 2.13 Estimated distribution of urban household income (2005–2011)

Income group	*Median (yuan)*	*Total household proportion*	*Average household proportion*	*Income variance (6.1)*	*Normal simulation curve*
Under 10,000 yuan	7,500	13.63	1.9471	0.0779	0.116
10,000–15,000	12,500	32.02	4.5743	0.1029	0.134
15,000–20,000	17,500	50.88	7.2687	0.0727	0.149
20,000–25,000	22,500	61.68	8.8114	0.0220	0.158
25,000–30,000	27,500	65.02	9.2886	0.0000	0.162
30,000–35,000	32,500	63.19	9.0271	0.0226	0.158
35,000–40,000	37,500	58.67	8.3814	0.0838	0.149
40,000–45,000	42,500	51.53	7.3614	0.1656	0.134
45,000–50,000	47,500	45.36	6.4800	0.2592	0.116
50,000–55,000	52,500	38.08	5.4400	0.3400	0.097
55,000–60,000	57,500	32.44	4.6343	0.4171	0.077
60,000–65,000	62,500	28.14	4.0200	0.4925	0.059
65,000–70,000	67,500	22.86	3.2657	0.5225	0.044
70,000–75,000	72,500	19.6	2.8000	0.5670	0.031
75,000–80,000	77,500	16.51	2.3586	0.5896	0.021
80,000–85,000	82,500	14	2.0000	0.6050	0.014
85,000–90,000	87,500	11.39	1.6271	0.5858	0.008
90,000–95,000	92,500	9.94	1.4200	0.6000	0.005
95,000–100,000	97,500	8.21	1.1729	0.5747	0.003
Over 100,000	102,500	56.78	8.1114	4.5627	0.002

Table 2.14 Definitive integrals of average urban household income distribution (2005–2011)

Median of income group (1,000 yuan)	*Interval of* x		Φ = (x – u)/ó		F(Φ)		F(X) = F(Φ)		*Interval integral value*
	Lower	*Upper*	*Lower*	*Upper*	*Lower*	*Upper*	*Lower*	*Upper*	
0.75	0.75	1.0	–0.6125	–0.5359	0.2709	0.2964	0.2709	0.2964	0.0299
1.25	1.0	1.5	–0.5359	–0.3828	0.2964	0.3520	0.2964	0.3520	0.0679
1.75	1.5	2.0	–0.3828	–0.2297	0.3520	0.4090	0.3520	0.4090	0.0754
2.25	2.0	2.5	–0.2297	–0.0766	0.4090	0.4701	0.4090	0.4701	0.0781
2.75	2.5	3.0	–0.0766	0.0766	0.4701	0.5299	0.4701	0.5299	0.0796
3.25	3.0	3.5	0.0766	0.2297	0.5299	0.5910	0.5299	0.5910	0.0781
3.75	3.5	4.0	0.2297	0.3828	0.5910	0.6480	0.5910	0.6480	0.0754
4.25	4.0	4.5	0.3828	0.5359	0.6480	0.7037	0.6480	0.7037	0.0679
4.75	4.5	5.0	0.5359	0.6890	0.7037	0.7486	0.7037	0.7486	0.0575
5.25	5.0	5.5	0.6890	0.8421	0.7486	0.7995	0.7486	0.7995	0.0479
5.75	5.5	6.0	0.8421	0.9953	0.7995	0.8401	0.7995	0.8401	0.0392
6.25	6.0	6.5	0.9953	1.1484	0.8401	0.8749	0.8401	0.8749	0.0300
6.75	6.5	7.0	1.1484	1.3015	0.8749	0.9032	0.8749	0.9032	0.0215
7.25	7.0	7.5	1.3015	1.4546	0.9032	0.9272	0.9032	0.9272	0.0153
7.75	7.5	8.0	1.4546	1.6077	0.9272	0.9463	0.9272	0.9463	0.0106
8.25	8.0	8.5	1.6077	1.7608	0.9463	0.9608	0.9463	0.9608	0.0069
8.75	8.5	9.0	1.7608	1.9139	0.9608	0.9719	0.9608	0.9719	0.0042
9.25	9.0	9.5	1.9139	2.0671	0.9719	0.9808	0.9719	0.9808	0.0025
9.75	9.5	10.0	2.0671	2.2202	0.9808	0.9867	0.9808	0.9867	0.0015
10.25	10	10.5	2.2202	2.3733	0.9867	0.9911	0.9867	0.9911	0.0009

By comparing the estimated curve and the actual distribution curve of average urban household income distribution from 2005 to 2011, we can see that the estimated curve of the density function and actual distribution curve were highly consistent in shape, but the estimated curve was a little below the actual distribution curve. The regression results show that the goodness-of-fit between the estimated values of the urban household average income distribution (PFCL0511) and the actual values (PAC0511) for this period was 0.998237. This confirms that the density function of the estimated normal distribution accurately depicts the shape of the urban household average income distribution from 2005 to 2011. In general, the distribution of urban household average income from 2005 to 2011 is normally distributed with the expected mean of 2.75 and the variance of 6.1, namely $X{-}N\,(2.75, 6.1)$ (Figure 2.10).

The regression between the estimated values of urban household average income (PFCL0511) and actual value of sampling survey (PAC0511) in 2005:

$$\begin{aligned}\text{PAC0511} = {} & \underset{(53.77)}{0.9444} \times \text{PFC0511} + \underset{(14.93)}{0.0119} + [\text{AR}(1) = \underset{(9.55)}{0.5901},\ \text{AR}(2) = \underset{(-5.44)}{-0.3115}]\end{aligned}$$

$R^2 = 0.998237$; adjusted $R^2 = 0.997831$; DW = 1.6. AR(1) and AR(2) are first-order and second-order autoregressive items of equation residuals. The value in the bracket is the *t*-statistic of variable significance.

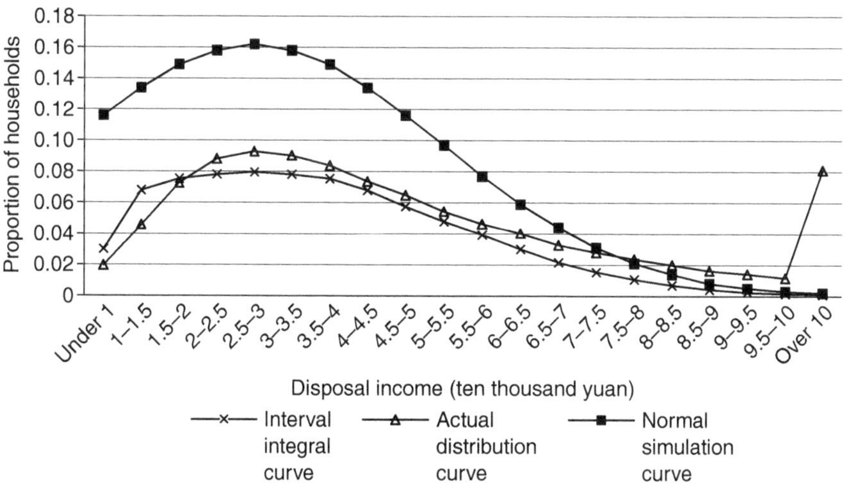

Figure 2.10 Normal simulation curve of urban household average income distribution (2005–2011).

Notes

1 Median is used instead of mean in estimating the normal distribution because the goodness-of-fit of the distribution estimated using mean is just 0.8398, much lower than the corresponding value using median.

2 The approximate variance estimated with the median of an income group or any value within the group range will be smaller than the actual sample variance. Moreover, the larger the group interval, the larger the deviation of the approximate estimation variance from the actual variance: Taking $[a, b]$ as the income group interval, assuming there are only two sample values, a and b within the group interval and the sample average is A, the actual variance in the income group is $D=[(A-a)^2+(A-b)^2]/2$, the approximate variance is $E=[A-(a+b)/2]^2$, $D-E=(a-b)^2/4>0$, namely $D>E$, and the larger the gap between a and b, the greater the deviation between the approximate estimation variance E from the actual variance D.

3 The variance of a normal distribution determines the steepness of the density function: With an underestimated variance, the density function becomes steeper because more samples are concentrated in the intervals close to the mean. Thus the value of definite integral for income groups close to the mean decreases with estimated variance.

3 The normality of household income distribution and endogenous mechanism of the economic cycle

Household income is the key determinant of household consumption. The normality of household income distribution implies that the demand for consumer goods exhibits an endogenous cycle. Given that supply is decided by demand, individual industries and the whole economy also exhibit endogenous cycles caused by the endogenous cycle of the consumer goods demand, which in turn is a consequence of the normality of household income distribution. When new products create new demand instead of replacing old products, entrepreneurial innovation could change the shape of the consumer goods demand cycle. Because the multiplier from the cycle of consumer goods demand to industrial cycle is bigger than 1, the amplitude of the latter must be greater than that of the former. The amplitude of the industrial cycle depends on the length of the production chain and its investment accelerator (the increase in investment required to produce an additional unit of consumer good). The effect of the industrial cycle on the economic cycle depends on the industrial output share of GDP and its amplitude. The rise of an emerging industry will inevitably alter the industrial structure and shape of the economic cycle at the same time. Increase in income inequality will flatten the consumer goods demand curve and enhance the demand for consumer goods in their initial development stage, but reduce the average growth rate of demand for consumer goods in their growth or maturing stage, and benefit long-term economic development through encouraging emerging industry and depressing present economic development by discouraging growing and maturing industries. On the contrary, reduction in income inequality will promote the present economic growth rate by generating demand for consumer goods in the growth and maturing stages, but depress the emerging industry and long-term economic development by weakening the demand for goods in the initial development stages. Given that both high and low income inequality can be detrimental to economic growth, moderate income inequality is necessary for maintaining sustainable and rapid economic growth.

Background

Since the discovery of various cyclic fluctuations in economic activities in the nineteenth century, economists have been trying to answer the following two questions: the first is what the causes of the economic cycle are, or whether the economic cycle is endogenous or exogenous; the second is why the shape of the economic cycle is irregular – that is, what factors have led to the huge differences in wavelength and amplitude between different cycles.

Limited by the classical theories such as the supply creating demand theory (Say's Law) and full employment theory, early studies regard economic cycles as isolated phenomena, and most of them attribute economic cycles to a single factor. For instances, William Stanley Jevons attributed the agriculture cycle to sunspot cyclic movement (Jevons, 1875), and H.L. Moore thought the grain cycle was caused by climate change (Moore, 1914). There are many other theories that attempt to pin the causes of economic cycles down to a single factor, such as attributing the short-term cycle to inventory fluctuation caused by the change of psychological or monetary factors, the mid-term cycle to cyclical fluctuation of fixed assets investment caused by equipment updating, the mid-to-long-term cycle to cyclical fluctuation caused by building construction and the long-term cycle to the fluctuation of technological progress. These early theories, such as Kitchin's inventory cycle theory, Schumpeter's technological innovation theory, Hayek's excessive investment theory, Hobson's theory of consumption shortage and others, have had profound influence on later studies of economic cycles.

The uprising of Keynesianism challenged the classical view of balanced growth, and since then economic cycles have been studied systematically as endogenous phenomena. Especially Samuelson's multiplier-accelerator model proved the endogeneity of economic cycles. Both Keynesian and New Keynesian schools hold that economic cycles are caused by many factors, some of which are endogenous and others exogenous. On the contrary, the neoclassical school that emerged after the 1960s incorporated rational expectation, and followed the classical view of balanced growth to form the rational economy cycle theory, which insists that economic cycles are only temporary deviations from equilibrium, and the economy would automatically return to equilibrium or potential growth rate. Due to the lack of satisfying theories in explaining the endogeneity and generating mechanism of economic cycles, the currents debates between the New Keynesianism and neoclassicism still focus on whether the economic cycle is endogenous or exogenous. These debates are directly relevant for the effectiveness and orientation of government policies. Therefore, it is still a critical task for current macroeconomic research to find out whether the economic cycle is endogenous and has an underlying generating mechanism. In this chapter, we present an endogenous generating mechanism for economic fluctuations that originated from the normality of household income distribution.

The normal distribution of household income and the endogenous mechanism of the cycle of demand for durables

Our research shows that household incomes in China,[1] the US and Japan[2] are all normally distributed. As a result of the normality of income distribution, the distribution of demand for consumer durables must also be normally distributed. The growth rate of durables demand will inevitably experience cyclical fluctuation. There are three inflexion points and two extrema in the function of growth rate of durables demand. According to these inflexions and extrema, we divide the service life of consumer durables into six development stages, which are the initial stage, growing stage, maturing stage, declining stage, dusk stage and terminal stage. Although all durables have limited lifespans, replacement demand will sustain the endogenous and cyclical fluctuation in the growth rate of demand for durables. If the replacement demand occurs after the maxima of original demand, the valley of the cycle of replacement demand will be postponed, and the wavelength of the cycle of replacement demand will be extended.

The relationship between household income distribution and endogenous cycle and development stages of consumer durables

Supposed that consumer durable A is a common good with the following properties: first, its output is determined by consumer demand; second, there is a saturation point for each consumer's demand for A; and finally, demand for A is a function of consumer income and the price of A – that is, a consumer with certain income level could only afford the good if the price of A is sufficiently low. Under these conditions, normally distributed household income will induce normally distributed durable good demand through the following mechanism: In the initial stage, the price of A is very high so that only high-income groups could afford it; along with the rise of household income level, the members of mid-to-high-income groups will also be able to afford A, and the increase in production of A will result in cost and hence price reduction through economies of scale, which will in turn lead to more consumers being able to afford A. Such a feedback process between demand for durable good A and reduction in both cost and price will eventually make A affordable for consumers of all income levels. Because of the normality of distribution of household incomes, the demand curve for A also exhibits features of a normal distribution, which resembles cyclical fluctuation. Maximal demand is reached when the price of A decreases to the level affordable for the income group with the highest proportion of consumers. According to the normal distribution features of demand for A, its developing process could be divided into six stages, through which the growth rate of demand for A forms a complete cycle.

The relationship between household income distribution and the endogenous cycle of consumer durables

Let's supposed that the household income distribution is normally distributed, with u as expectation and $ó$ as standard deviation; everyone's saturated demand for A is 1; and the distribution of demand for consumer good A, $Q(x)$, is also normally distributed with u as expectation and $ó$ as standard deviation, namely $Q(x) = \frac{1}{\sigma\sqrt{2\pi}} e^{-\frac{(x-u)^2}{2\sigma^2}}$, noted as $Q(x)Q(x) \sim N(u, ó)$. In this formula, x is the ratio of household income level y to the price p of A, namely y/p (hereinafter referred to as income–price ratio).

By taking derivatives of the demand function of consumer durable A, we obtain the first-order and second-order derivatives respectively, namely, $Q'(x)=\frac{1}{\sigma\sqrt{2\pi}}e^{-\frac{(x-u)^2}{2\sigma^2}}*\frac{(u-x)}{\delta^2}, Q''(x)=\frac{1}{\sigma^3\sqrt{2\pi}}e^{-\frac{(x-u)^2}{2\sigma^2}}*\left(\frac{(x-u)}{\delta^2}-1\right)$. According to the nature of derivatives, we know that the first-order derivative $Q'(x)$ of demand function $Q(x)$ is the growth rate of demand, the second-order derivative of the demand function reflects the curvature, inflexion points of demand curve and extrema of demand growth rate.

By setting $Q'(x)=0$, we get $x=u$. This means that the demand for durable good A, $Q(x)$, will reach its maximum when the income–price ratio x rises to u. While $x<u$, $Q'(x)>0$, this means that the growth rate of demand for durable A is positive while the income–price ratio is less than u. On the contrary, while $x>u$, $Q'(x)<0$, this means that the growth rate of demand for durable A is negative while the income–price ratio is greater than u.

By setting $Q''(x)=0$, we get two inflection points of $Q(x)$, which is $x=u+\delta$ and $x=u-\delta$ respectively. These two inflection points reflect the cyclic features of demand growth rate. The specific process is as follows:

1 While $x<(u-ó)$, the second-order derivative of demand function $Q'(x)$ and the first-order derivative $Q'(x)$ are both positive, these mean that the demand for A and its growth rate $Q'(x)$ are rising consistently, and the demand curve is concave downwards.
2 When $x=(u-ó)$, the second-order derivative of demand function $Q''(x)$ equals 0, and the first-order derivative $Q'(x)$ is positive, which mean that the scale of demand for A is steadily rising, but the growth rate of demand for A, $Q'(x)$ reaches its maximum at this point of $x=(u-\delta)$,which is $\frac{1}{\delta^2\sqrt{2\pi}}e^{-\frac{1}{2}}$.
3 While $(u-\delta)<x<u$, the second-order derivative of demand function $Q''(x)$ is negative and the first-order derivative $Q'(x)$ is still positive, this means that the demand for A is consistently rising, the growth rate of demand for A, $Q'(x)$, is positively and steadily declining in this interval of X. The demand curve is convex in this interval of X.
4 When $x=u$, the first-order derivative of demand function $Q'(x)$ equals 0, which means that the scale of demand for A reaches its maximum and the growth rate of demand for A reduces to 0 at the point of $x=u$.
5 While $u<x<(u+\delta)$, the second-order derivative of demand function $Q''(x)$ and the first-order derivative $Q'(x)$ are both negative, which means that the demand for A starts to decline and the growth rate of demand for A, $Q'(x)$ is consistently declining, and the demand curve is convex.
6 When $x=(u+\delta)$, the second-order derivative of demand function $Q''(x)$ equals 0, and the first-order derivative $Q'(x)$ is negative, which means that the growth rate of demand for A, $Q'(x)$, reaches its minimum at the point of $x=(u+\delta)$, which is $-\frac{1}{\delta^2\sqrt{2\pi}}e^{-\frac{1}{2}}$.

7 While $x>(u+\acute{o})$, the second-order derivative of demand function $Q''(x)$ is positive, and the first-order derivative $Q'(x)$ is negative, which means that the demand for A is consistently declining, but the growth rate of demand for A, $Q'(x)$, begins to recover from its minimum although its value is still negative in the interval of $x>(u+\acute{o})$.

In general, when the distribution of household incomes is normally distributed, the gradual rising of the income–price ratio will enable more and more households to fulfill their demand for durable good A, and the aggregate demand for A will gradually expand to reach its maximum when the income–price ratio is equal to the expected value of demand function, and as the income–price ratio continues to rise the aggregate demand for A starts to decline. Meanwhile, the growth rate of demand for durable good A will exhibit cyclical fluctuation because of the normality of household income.

The development stages of demand for consumer durables and their different features

Furthermore, we can find three inflexion points by taking third-order derivative of the demand function, $Q'''(x)=\frac{1}{\sqrt{2\pi\delta^5}}\times e^{-\frac{(x-u)^2}{2\delta^2}}\times(u-x)\times\left(\frac{(x-u)^2}{\delta^2}-3\right)$. By setting the third-order derivative to 0, we get the three inflexion points when the income–price ratio X equal to $x=u-\sqrt{3}\delta, x=u, x=u+\sqrt{3}\delta$. Based on the three inflexion points and the two extremes at $x=u-\acute{o}$ and $x=u+\delta$, we divide the developing process of consumer durables A into six stages, which are named as initial, growing, maturing, declining, dusk and terminal stages.

1 *The initial stage* takes place in the income–price ratio interval $[0,u-\sqrt{3}\delta]$. This stage begins with the emergence of durable good A and ends at the first inflexion point of demand growth rate function where the income–price ratio is equal to $(u-\sqrt{3}\delta)$. In this stage, income–price ratio is very low because the price of A is too high, and only consumers with the highest income can buy durable good A. But because the second-order and the third-order derivative of demand function are both positive, $Q'''(x)>0$ and $Q''(x)>0$, the second-order derivative $Q''(x)$, namely the acceleration of the growth rate of demand for A, is consistently rising in the initial stage, which implies the demand and demand growth rate of durable A are rising with an increasing speed in the initial stage.
2 *The growing stage* takes place in the interval $[u-\sqrt{3}\delta, u-\delta]$. This stage starts from the first inflexion point and ends when growth rate reaches its maximum. In this stage, income–price ratio has increased to a level at which the high-income and upper-middle-income groups have the ability to buy durable good A, and the demand for A expends rapidly. The second-order derivative of demand function $Q''(x)$ is still bigger than 0, which means the

scale and growth rate of demand for A are still rising consistently. But the third-order derivative of demand function becomes negative, namely $Q'''(x)<0$, which means that the acceleration of growth rate of demand for A starts to decline in the growing stage, although the growth rate of demand for A is consistently rising in the growing stage. The demand and demand growth rate of durable A are rising with a declining speed in the growing stage. And the growth rate of demand for A reaches its maximum at the end of this stage.

3 *The maturing stage* takes place in the interval $(u-\delta, u)$. In this stage, the demand for A will reach its maximum and the growth rate of demand for A will decrease to 0 by the end of the stage. As the income–price ratio rises, the middle-income class with the most population shares will be able to afford A and join the consumer team. During this stage, the demand for A increases to the maximum of its entire product lifespan. At the same time, the first-order derivative of demand function is bigger than 0, which means that the growth rate of demand for A is still positive, but the second-order and the third-order derivatives of demand function are all less than 0, namely $Q'''(x)<0$ and $Q''(x)<0$, which shows that the growth rate of demand for A is declining in this stage, and finally reduces to 0 at the end of the stage.

4 *The declining stage* takes place in the interval $(u, u+\delta)$. In this stage, demand for A begins to decrease progressively, and the growth rate of demand for A is negative. In this stage, the first-order and the second-order derivatives are all negative, but the third-order derivative of demand function is positive, which means that the growth rate of demand for A is negative and declining consistently, but the speed at which the growth rate is declining decreases as income–price ratio increases. And the growth rate will decline to its minimum when the income–price ratio rises to the level of $(u+\delta)$. In this stage, the lower mid-income group will be the new members of the consumer team of durables A.

5 *The dusk stage* takes place in the interval $[u+\delta, u+\sqrt{3}\delta]$. In this stage, the income–price ratio rises to the level at which the low-income group could afford durable A. In this interval, the first-order derivative of demand function is negative, but the second- and the third-order derivatives are all greater than 0. All of these imply that the growth rate of demand for A is recovering rapidly from its minimum, although it is still negative.

6 *The terminal stage* takes place when the income–price ratio is larger than $(u+\sqrt{3}\delta)$. In this stage, the price of durable A drops to such a low level or the income of households rises to such a high level that the lowest-income groups can afford durable A, which means that all consumers could fulfill their demands for A. In this interval, the first- and third-order derivatives of demand function are negative, but the second-order derivative is positive, which mean the growth rate of demand for A is consistently recovering, but the recovering speed is declining while the growth rate rises to zero. If there is no replacement demand or new demand for durable A, the demand for A will reduce to zero and the lifecycle of durable A will terminate at the end of this stage, because all the consumers fulfill their demand for A.

The distribution of demand for A in different stages

As we know, any kind of normal distributions can be converted to standard normal distribution. According to standard normal distribution, the intervals of the six development stages of durable A are $[0,-1.73]$ of initial stage, $[-1.73,-1]$ of growing stage, $[-1,0]$ of maturing stage, $[0,1]$ of declining stage, $[1,1.73]$ of dusk stage and $[1.73,+\infty]$ of terminal stage, respectively.

According to the definite integral of standard normal distribution, we can calculate the cumulative demand share for A in each of the six stages, which is actually the cumulative density of the ratio of demand that occurred in the current stage (hereinafter referred to as cumulative demand) to the total demand for the entire product lifespan of A (hereinafter referred to as lifetime demand). The shares in the six development stages are 0–4.18 percent in the initial stage, 4.18–15.87 percent in the growing stage, 15.87–50.00 percent in the maturing stage, 50.00–84.13 percent in the declining stage, 84.13–95.82 percent in the dusk stage and 95.82–100.00 percent in the terminal stage, respectively. Because we assumed every household's saturated demand for A is one unit, the cumulative demand for durable good A in different stages can be regarded as the proportion of households who have sufficient income to purchase A at the price in that development stage. For instance, the households who have their demands satisfied in the initial stage are only the highest-income households, which account for 4.18 percent of the total households. And in the growing stage, the households who have their demand satisfied have income levels in the top 4.18–15.87 percentile of the household income distribution. The share of satisfied households is within the 15.87–50 percentile in the maturing stage, and finally, all household demand for A will be realized by the terminal period.

The demonstration of the cycle of demand for durables

In order to illustrate more vividly the cycle of durable good demand caused by normally distributed household income, we assume that household income as well as the demand for durable A is normally distributed with a mean of 4 and variance of 1. According to the density function of normal distribution of durable good A, $Q(x)=\frac{1}{\sqrt{2\pi}}e^{-\frac{(x-4)^2}{2}}$, we plot the distribution curve of demand for A and its growth rate curve as showed in Figure 3.1.

According to the inflexion points and extrema of the demand function and its growth rate, the intervals of six development stages are: $[0,2.27]$ of the initial stage; $[2.27,3]$ of the growing stage; $[3,4]$ of the maturing stage; $[4,5]$ of the declining stage; $[5,5.73]$ of the dusk stage; and $[5.73,+\infty]$ of the terminal stage. The features of fluctuation for the cycle of demand for A in different stages are as follows.

In the initial stage, while the income–price ratio increases from 0 to 2.27, demand for A will rise from 0.01 to 8.67, and growth rate (the first-order derivative

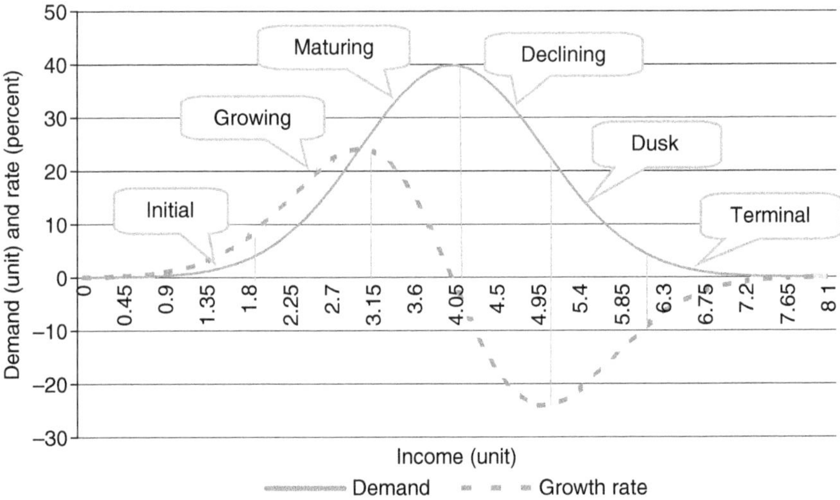

Figure 3.1 Simulation of the cycle of durable A caused by normal distribution of household income.

Note
The simulation value of demand is 1,000 times the value of normal distribution calculation.

of demand function) rises from 0.05 percent to 15.1 percent. But we should remember that the ratio of cumulative demand to lifetime demand is 4.18 percent in the initial stage, regardless of the parameters of the normal distribution.

In the growing stage, while the income–price ratio rises from 2.27 to 3, demand for A will rise from 8.67 to 24.2, and growth percent to 24.2 percent, which is the maximum in the lifespan of A. The interval rate also rises from 15.1 of cumulative demand share for A is from 4.18 percent to 15.87 percent in this stage.

In the maturing stage, while the income–price ratio rises from 3 to 4, the scale of demand will increase from 24.2 to 39.7, which is the maximum of the demand scale of A. But the growth rate begins to decrease from its extreme of 24.2 percent to 0. The interval of cumulative demand share for A is from 15.87 percent to 50 percent in this stage.

In the declining stage, while the income–price ratio rises from 4 to 5, demand will reduce from 39.7 to 24.2, and growth rate will decline from 0 to –24.2 percent, which is the minimum of the growth rate in the lifespan of A. The interval of cumulative demand share for A is from 50 percent to 84.13 percent in this stage.

In the dusk stage, while the income–price ratio rises from 5 to 5.73, demand will reduce from 24.2 to 8.67, and growth rate will recover from –24.2 percent to –15.1 percent. The interval of cumulative demand share for A is from 84.13 percent to 95.82 percent in this stage.

In the terminal stage, while the income–price ratio rises over 5.73, demand will decrease from 8.67 to 0, which means that all consumers will have fulfilled their demands for A, and the growth rate will continue to recover from –15.1 percent to 0. The interval of cumulative demand share for A is from 95.82 percent to 100 percent in this stage.

The lasting cycle of demand for durables resulted from the replacement demand for durables

Every durable has a fixed service life. The early consumer will buy a new one as a replacement when the old one reaches the end of its service life. The actual demand for durable A consists of the lower-income group's initial demands and early higher-income consumers' replacement demands. Because of the replacement demand, the cycle of demand for durable A will change from a single cycle into perpetual fluctuating cycles.

We demonstrate the influence of replacement demand on the cycle of demand for A using the same example showed in Figure 3.1. Suppose that the earliest replacement demand occurs at the time when income–price ratio rises to 5, which is at the end of the declining stage; we could find that, because of the occurrence of replacement demand, the fluctuating path of actual demand growth rate deviates from the path of initial demand growth rate. First, the declining speed of "actual demand 1" is less than that of initial demand, and the recovering speed of "actual demand growth rate 1" is bigger than that of initial demand growth rate. Second, although the scale of replacement demand is greater than the scale of initial demand, in our example actual demand will only start to rise after the income–price ratio reaches 6.5, while the initial demand scale is still declining. At the same time, "actual demand growth rate 1" will turn positive and a new cycle caused by replacement demand will begin to emerge, which we call the replacement demand cycle.

Suppose that replacement demand occurs after the maximum of initial demand, the maximum of actual demand in the replacement demand cycle comes much later than that of the initial demand. For instance, according to the earlier example, the maximum of replacement demand is reached when income–price ratio rises to 9, but the maximum of actual demand is reached when income–price ratio rises to 9.9. The peak and trough of the replacement demand cycle are postponed for the same reason, and the period of replacement demand cycle is determined by the service life or the replacement frequency of durable good A. The simulation of the replacement demand cycle is shown in Figure 3.2.

Normal distribution of household income and half-cycle of demand for non-durables

Because the service life of non-durables is very short, consumers need to repurchase non-durable goods after consumption. This creates continuous enduring demand for non-durables. Under the condition that household income is normally distributed, the distribution of demand for non-durables is the integral of

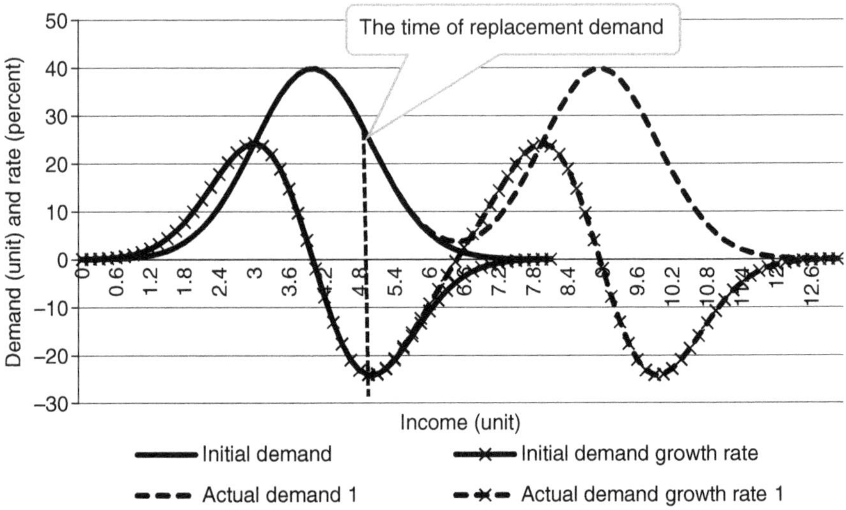

Figure 3.2 Simulation of replacement demand cycle of durable A.

normal distribution density function deduced from the normal distribution of household income, and its first-order derivative or the growth rate of demand for non-durables is a normal distribution, which is also determined by the distribution of household income. The bell shape of the growth rate of demand for non-durables looks like half of a complete cycle, so we call the cycle of demand for non-durables a half-cycle of demand for non-durables.

Let's assume the following: First, B is a non-durable good that consumers need to purchase constantly; second, there is a saturation point in demand for B; third, demand for B is a function of household income level and the price of B or the income–price ratio. Because the price of B is usually very high at the initial development stage, only high-income groups have the abilities to buy non-durable good B at the initial development stage of B. Along with the gradual decline of price of B and increase in household income, the mid-income or even low-income households will gradually be able to afford B. Because consumer good B is non-durable, the early buyers do not withdraw from the buyer pool, so the total demand for B consists of demand from the early buyers as well as from the newcomers. Suppose every consumer's saturated demand for B is one unit, then the amount of demand for B or the demand function of B, $Q(x)$, is the proportion of households with income below a threshold level of the income–price ratio particular to that stage of development. Mathematically, this is the integral of the normal distribution function of household income, namely, $Q(x) = \frac{1}{\sigma\sqrt{2\pi}}\int_0^x e^{-\frac{(x-u)^2}{2\sigma^2}} dx$, where x is the income–price ratio, u and δ are mean and variance of household income distribution.

The first-order derivative of the demand function of B is the density function of household income, $Q'(x) = f(x) = \frac{1}{\sigma\sqrt{2\pi}} e^{-\frac{(x-u)^2}{2\sigma^2}}$. As $f(x)>0$, which is normally distributed, the demand function is a continuous and monotonically increasing function. The second-order derivative of the demand function is $Q''(x) = \frac{1}{\sigma\sqrt{2\pi}} e^{-\frac{(x-u)^2}{2\sigma^2}} \times \frac{(u-x)}{\delta^2}$, and it equals 0 when x equals to u, is bigger than 0 when x is lower than u, and is lower than 0 when x is bigger than u. The features of the second-order derivative reveal the special evolution processes of demand and demand growth rate of non-durables. The demand curve for non-durables is S-shaped, which has one inflexion point when the income–price ratio x equals the expected value u of the demand function. The demand curve for B is downwards concave while income–price ratio x is less than u, and it becomes convex when income–price ratio is bigger than u. At the same time, the growth rate rises continuously when the income–price ratio x is less than u, and it reaches its maximum when the income–price ratio x is equal to u, and then the growth rate begins to decline while x is bigger than u. Compared to the complete cycle of durables demand, the cycle of non-durables demand is only half of a complete cycle, so we call it a half-cycle of demand for non-durables.

From the third-order derivative of the demand function of B, $Q'''(x) = \frac{1}{\sigma^3\sqrt{2\pi}} e^{-\frac{(x-u)^2}{2\sigma^2}} \times \left(\frac{(x-u)^2}{\delta^2} - 1\right)$, we can see that there are two inflexion points in the growth rate function, which are reached when the income–price ratio rises to $(u-\delta)$ and $(u+\delta)$, respectively. Accordingly, we can divide the whole development process of non-durables B into four stages.

The first is the initial stage. In this stage, the income–price ratio gradually rises to $u-\delta$ from 0; the growth rate of demand for B is low but accelerates rapidly throughout the stage. The cumulative demand will increase to 15.87 percent by the end of the initial stage, which means that the top 15.87 percentile of the household income distribution will be purchasing B by the end of the initial stage.

The second stage is the blooming stage. In this stage, the income–price ratio gradually rises to u from $u-\delta$, the growth rate of demand for B increases continuously until it reaches its maximum, $\frac{1}{\sigma\sqrt{2\pi}}$. But the acceleration of the growth rate is declining throughout the stage until it finally reaches 0. The cumulative demand increases to 50 percent from 15.87 percent during the blooming stage.

The third stage is the shrinking stage. In this stage, the income–price ratio gradually rises to $u+\delta$ from u. The growth rate of demand for B continues to decline from its maximum at an accelerating speed. In other words, the speed at which the growth rate is declining gets bigger and bigger during the shrinking stage. The cumulative demand increases to 84.13 percent from 50 percent in the shrinking stage.

The final stage is the saturating stage. In this stage, the income–price ratio becomes larger than $u+\delta$; the growth rate of demand for B continuously declines until it reaches 0. The speed at which the growth rate changes becomes less and less during the saturating stage. The cumulative demand increases to 100 percent from 84.13 percent, which means that all household fulfill their demands for non-durable B by the end of the saturating stage.

In order to illustrate more vividly the relationship between normally distributed household income and half-cycle of non-durables, we still assume that household income is normally distributed with a mean of 4 and variance of 1. Then the demand function of non-durable B is also normally distributed, $Q(x)=\frac{1}{\sqrt{2\pi}}\int_0^x e^{-\frac{(x-4)^2}{2}}dx$, where x is still the income–price ratio. According to this demand function, we simulate the demand curve and demand growth rate curve of non-durable B, as shown in Figure 3.3. While the income–price ratio is less than the expected value of 4, both the quantity and growth rate of demand for non-durable B are rising steadily along with the income–price ratio. When the income–price ratio rises to 4, the quantity demanded reaches its inflexion point of 39.89 units, and the growth rate reaches its maximum of 39.89 percent. When the income–price ratio becomes more than 4, the quantity demanded continues to increase until it reaches its extreme of 100 units, but the growth rate of

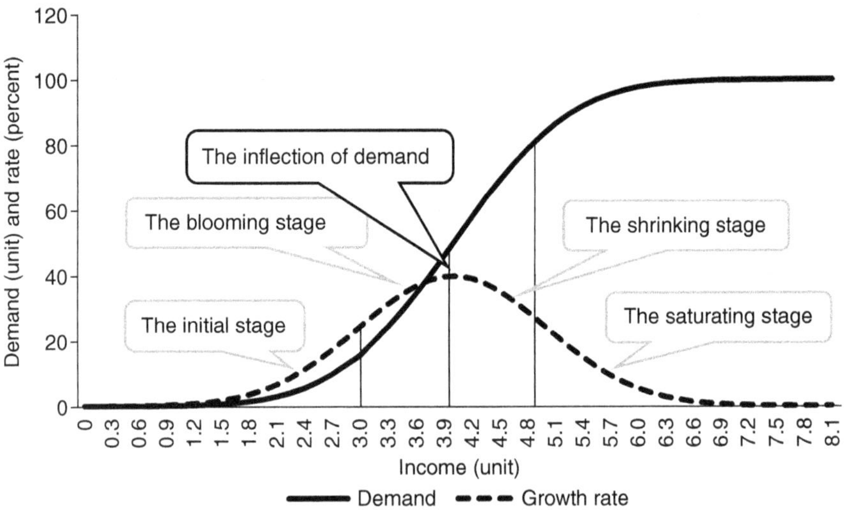

Figure 3.3 The simulation of a half-cycle of demand for non-durables caused by the normal distribution of household income.

Note

The output and simulation value of growth rate are both 100 times the calculated value of normal distribution.

demand begins to decline consistently until reaches 0. Overall, the growth rate of demand for non-durables exhibits a half endogenous cycle resulting from the normal distribution of household income.

The influence of entrepreneurial innovations on the cycle of demand for consumer goods

We didn't consider the influence of entrepreneurial innovations on the amount and growth rate of demand for consumer goods in the above analysis. At every stage of development, various innovations can affect the cycles of demand for consumer goods. We only consider two kinds of innovation here. One is a new product that can completely substitute for the original product, the other is a new product that has no substitution effect on the original product and creates new demand. When the new product is a perfect substitute of the original product, the replacement demand for the original durable will be substituted by the demand for the new product (hereinafter we call the demand for the new product innovation demand). Then the replacement demand cycle of the original durable good will be replaced by the cycle of innovation demand, and the half-cycle of demand for the original non-durable good will be replaced by the half-cycle of innovation demand for new non-durables. The shapes of both durable cycle and non-durable cycle are both unaltered. But when innovation demand is completely new demand, all is changed. When there is no substitution effect, the actual demand for durables consists of the replacement demand for original durables and innovation demand for new durables. The cycle of actual demand for durables is composed of the replacement demand cycle of original durables and the innovation demand cycle of new durables. The half-cycle of original non-durables will transform into a complete and consistent cycle owing to the emergence of innovation demand for new non-durables.

The influence of entrepreneurial innovation on the cycle of demand for durables

It is the nature of entrepreneurs to pursue and maximize profit. When the demand for durables begins to decline, the profit of entrepreneurs will shrink even if price reduction is not taken into consideration. And moreover, when the demand as well as the price of durables drops to a certain low level, the emerging surplus production capacity and financial loss must result in many bankruptcies, or many entrepreneurs are forced to exit the market. Even the surviving entrepreneurs must innovate to stimulate consumption and maintain expansion of the enterprise.

We still assume that the distribution of demand for new products generated by entrepreneurial innovation (we simply note it as innovation demand as below) is normally distributed with a mean of 4 and variance of 1, and the time that innovation demand occurs is the same as that of the replacement demand. If the innovation demand doesn't substitute the initial demand for the original product, but substitutes the replacement demand completely, then after the innovation demand occurs, the actual demand will be the innovation demand instead of replacement demand, and the actual demand cycle will be the innovation demand cycle instead of the replacement demand cycle, although the shape of the innovation demand cycle is the same as that of the replacement demand cycle, just as the curves for actual demand 1 and actual demand growth rate 1 in Figure 3.4.

If innovation demand is completely new demand, the actual demand cycle will be greatly altered. Before the demand for the original product is satisfied completely, the actual demand for durable A (actual demand 2) will be the sum of the initial demand for the original product, the replacement demand for original demand and the innovation demand for the new product. And after the demand for the original product is completely satisfied, the actual demand 2 is the sum of the replacement demand for the original demand and the innovation demand for the new product. After the innovation demand emerged, the scale as well as the growth rate of actual demand 2 will be double that of the replacement demand in the new cycle. For instance, in the new cycle, when the growth rates of replacement demand and innovation demand reach their extreme values, the growth rate of actual demand 2 will also reach its extreme values of 48.33 percent (–48.33 percent), which is double that of the initial demand growth rate, as shown in Figure 3.4.

But, we should remember that the amplification of growth rate of actual demand 2 could only last as long as the lifespan of the new product that resulted from entrepreneurial innovation. Meanwhile, because we assumed that the innovation demand and the replacement demand emerge at the same time, the

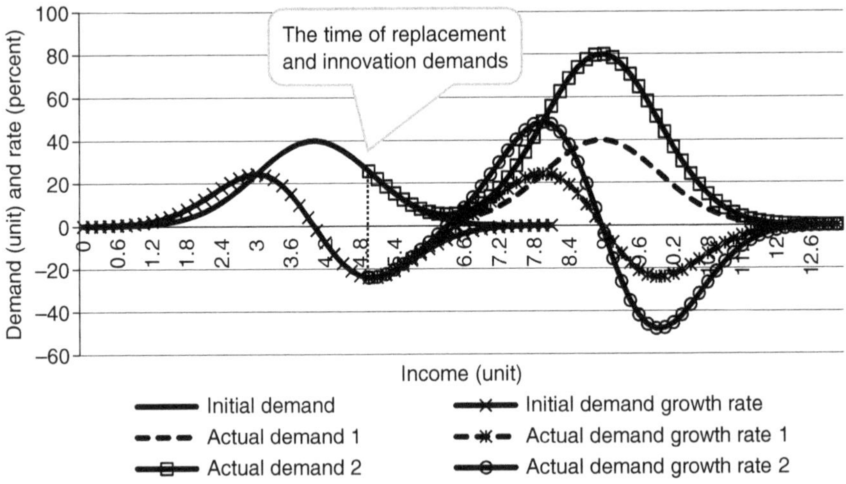

Figure 3.4 The influence of entrepreneurial innovation on the cycle of demand for durables.

Note
Actual demand 1 contains the replacement demand, and actual demand 2 contains both replacement and innovation demand.

emergence of innovation demand will only change the amplitude of the actual demand cycle, and will have no effect on the period of the actual demand cycle. If the innovation demand and the replacement demand emerge at different times, the period of the actual demand cycle will depend on the frequencies of innovations, which we will discuss in detail in Chapter 5.

The influence of entrepreneurial innovation on the cycle of demand for non-durables

The influence of entrepreneurial innovation on the cycle of demand for non-durables is similar to that of demand for durables. This implies that innovation demand could impact the shape of the cycle only when the demand for new non-durables is completely new demand instead of perfect substitution of original non-durables.

Assuming that the new non-durables emerged after the growth rate of demand for original non-durables began to decline, innovation demand for the new non-durables has two possible impacts on the cycle of actual demand for non-durable B. The first is that there is no influence on the shape of the cycle if the new non-durable is a perfect substitute for original non-durables, and the cycle of actual demand for non-durables is still a half-cycle. The second is that the half-cycle of demand for non-durables becomes a complete cycle when the innovation demand for new non-durables is completely new demand. Figure 3.5 is the simulation of the second scenario. We still use the same example shown in Figure 3.3, and assume innovation demand occurs when income–price ratio rises to 5. Because we assumed the innovation demand to be

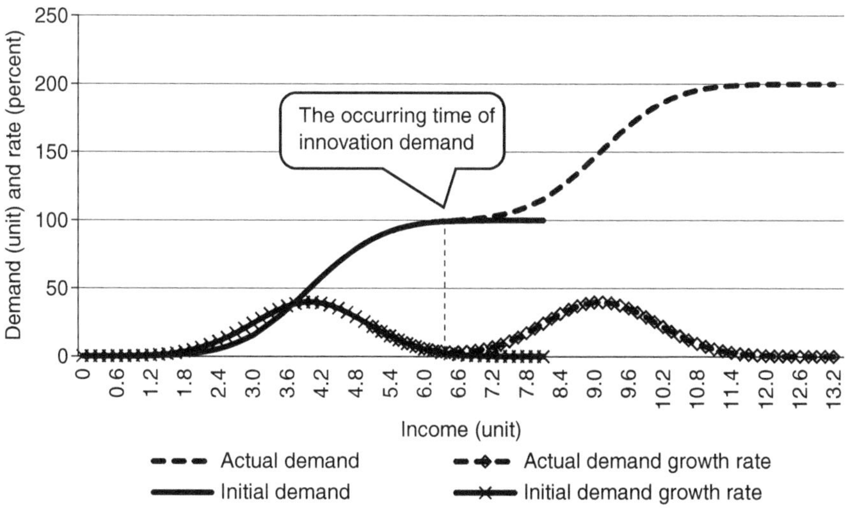

Figure 3.5 The influence of entrepreneurial innovation on the cycle of demand for non-durables.

completely new demand, the actual demand consists of the initial demand for the original product and the innovation demand for new product. And when all consumers have fulfilled their demand for the original non-durables, additional demand comes only from the innovation demand for the new non-durables, and the cycle of actual demand will be determined by the growth rate of innovation. Just like in Figure 3.5, the maximum of demand for non-durables will rise to 200 units after the innovation demand emerges, and the cycle becomes continuous.

The influence of income inequality on the endogenous mechanism of the cycle of consumer goods: the importance of moderate income inequality

Even if the mean of household income distribution is the same, different degrees of income inequality, measured by variance of household income distribution, will result in huge changes in the steepness of the income distribution curve. The shape as well as the cycle of demand for consumer goods will also be significantly different for different degrees of income inequality.

For consumer durables, the smaller the variance of income distribution is, the steeper the demand curve for durables will be, the higher the maxima of quantity demanded and demand growth rate are, and the higher the average growth rate of demand for durables in growing and maturing stages will be. In the initial stage, the smaller the variance of income distribution is, the smaller the quantity demand in this early stage is, and the lower the growth rate of demand will be. Namely, reduction in income inequality can facilitate the development of entrepreneurs whose durables are in the growing and maturing stages, but has an adverse effect on entrepreneurs whose durables are in the initial stage.

For consumer non-durables, the smaller the income variance is, the steeper the curve of demand for non-durables will be and the lower the growth rate of demand for non-durables will be in the initial stage. But the higher the extreme value of growth rate is, the higher the average growth rate will be in the blooming and shrinking stages. And similar to durables, reduction in income inequality can facilitate the development of entrepreneurs whose non-durables are in the blooming and shrinking stages, but has an adverse effect on entrepreneurs whose non-durables are in the initial stage.

In general, a more equal income distribution, i.e., smaller variance, will result in insufficient demand for entrepreneurs' products in the initial period, but will provide much more demand in growing and maturing stages or blooming and shrinking stages. On the contrary, a less equal income distribution would create more demand entrepreneurs' products in the initial stage in the short term, but has an adverse effect on the development of entrepreneurs whose products are in the growing and maturing stages or blooming and shrinking stages, owing to insufficient demand in the later development stages. After taking into consideration the double-edged effect of income inequality, moderate income inequality is essential for keeping consistent rapid growth of consumer goods demand.

The influence of income inequality on the scale and growth rate of demand for durables

When the mean is unchanged, the shape of the normal distribution is solely determined by its variance. The larger the variance is, the flatter the demand curve for consumer goods is, and vice versa. Although variation in income inequality will not change cumulative demand share (i.e., the ratio of demand arises at each stage of the development of a product to lifetime demand), it will result in changes in the lengths of different product development stages and thus affect quantity demanded per unit of time as well as growth rate.

The mechanism of the influence of income inequality on the scale and growth rate of demand for durables

According to the inflexion points and extrema of the growth rate of durable good demand, we divide the lifespan of durables into six stages, which are the initial stage in the income–price ratio interval of $[0, u-\sqrt{3}\delta]$, the growing stage in the income–price ratio interval of $[u-\sqrt{3}\delta, u-\delta]$, the maturing stage in the income–price ratio interval of $[u-\delta, u]$, decaying stage in the income–price ratio interval of $[u, u+\delta]$, the dusk stage in the income–price ratio interval of $[u+\delta, u+\sqrt{3}\delta]$ and the terminal stage in the income–price ratio interval of $[u+\sqrt{3}\delta, +\infty]$, respectively. According to the definite integral of standard normal distribution, the integral over the six intervals does not change with the variance of the distribution. That is, the cumulative demand share in the six stages are invariant to changes in variance, and remain as 4.18 percent in the initial stage over the interval of [0, 4.18 percent]; 11.69 percent in the growing stage over the interval of [4.18 percent, 15.87 percent]; 34.13 percent in the maturing stage over the interval of [15.87 percent, 50 percent]; 34.13 percent in the declining stage over the interval of [50 percent, 84.13 percent]; 11.69 percent in the dusk stage over the interval of [84.13 percent, 95.82 percent]; finally 4.18 percent in the terminal stage over the interval of [95.82 percent, 100 percent], respectively.

The time that each stage lasts will change with the variance of income distribution. Using the evolution of income–price ratio in the process of economic development as a measure of time, the lengths of the six development stages are $(u-\sqrt{3}\delta)$ in the initial stage, $(\sqrt{3}-1)\delta$ in the growing stage, δ in the maturing stage and declining stage, $(\sqrt{3}-1)\delta$ in the dusk stage, and $(u-\sqrt{3}\delta)$ in the terminal stage, respectively. When the mean u is fixed, the length of each stage is solely determined by the variance δ. When income inequality rises, as variance δ becomes bigger, the length of the initial stage decreases but the lengths of growing and maturing stages increases. This, combined with the fact that cumulative demand in each stage remains unchanged, implies that the average quantity demanded in the initial stage becomes higher, and the average quantity demanded in the growing and maturing stages becomes lower. On the other hand, when the variance δ decreases, the average quantity demanded in the initial stage will become less, and the average quantity demanded in the growing and maturing stages will become higher. At the same time, the average demand growth rate will change in a similar way to the average quantity demanded when the variance is altered.

The alterations of average quantity demanded and growth rate resulting from the change of variance imply that income equality is beneficial to the development of entrepreneurs whose products are in the growing and maturing stages, because more equal distribution of income will induce higher demand for the entrepreneurs in those stages. But income equality can undermine the development of entrepreneurs whose products are in the initial stage, because demand for those products decreases as income distribution becomes more equal. On the other hand, income inequality could enhance the development of entrepreneurs in the initial stage by creating more demand, and depress the development of entrepreneurs in the growing and maturing stages by reducing demand.

The demonstration of the impact of income inequality on the average demand for durable goods

In order to demonstrate the influence of income inequality, we compare three scenarios in which income is distributed with the same means of 4 but with different variances of 2, 1 and 0.5.

First, let us see the impact of income inequality on the average quantity demanded in different development stages. As we have seen, the alteration of variance could change the average quantity demanded by altering the length of different development stages, as shown in Figure 3.6.

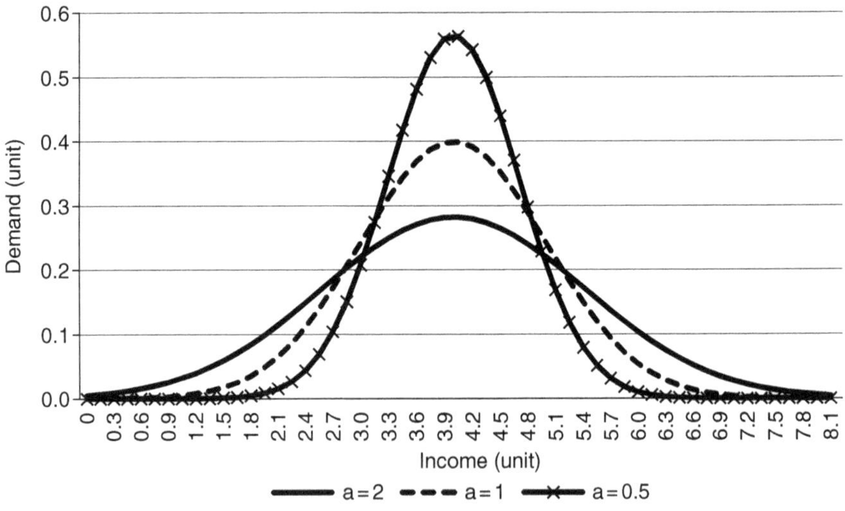

Figure 3.6 The influence of income inequality on the scale of demand for durables at different stages.

1 In the initial stage, the bigger the variance, the higher the average quantity demanded. While the variance is reduced from 2 to 1 and 0.5, the average quantity demanded decreases from 2.7 units to 1.84 units and 1.51 units, as expressed in Figure 3.6 and Table 3.1.
2 In the growing and maturing stage, the smaller the variance, the higher the average quantity demanded. While the variance decreases from 2 to 1 and 0.5, the average quantity demanded increases from 11.35 units to 16.01 units and 22.48 units in the growing stage, and increases from 24.04 units to 34.13 units and 48.07 units in the maturing stage.
3 When the variance declines from 2 to 1 and 0.5, the maximum of quantity demanded rises from 28.21 units to 39.89 units and 56.42 units.

The demonstration of the impact of income inequality on the average growth rate of demand for durables

The alteration of variance will change the shape of the demand curve as well as the shape of the demand growth rate curve. The bigger the variance is, the flatter the demand growth rate curve is, or the less the extrema and amplitude of the growth rate function are. In contrast, the smaller the variance, the bigger the extrema and amplitude of the growth rate function. Just as shown in Figure 3.7, when the variance is 2, 1 and 0.5, the maximum of growth rate is 12.1 percent, 24.2 percent and 48.4 percent, respectively.

As for the average growth rate in different stages, the bigger the variance is, the lower the average growth rate is. When the variance decreases from 2 to 1 and 0.5, the average growth rate rises from 3.88 percent to 4.09 percent and 4.64 percent in the initial stage, and rises from 10.45 percent to 20.81 percent and

Table 3.1 The influence of income inequality on the average scale and growth rate of demand for durables in different stages

Variance	*Development stage*	*The initial stage*	*The growing stage*	*The maturing stage*
	The cumulative demand	4.18	11.69	34.13
$\delta^2=2$	Interval	[0,1.55]	[1.55,2.58]	[2.58,4]
	The length of development stage	1.55	1.03	1.42
	The average demand	**2.70**	**11.35**	**24.04**
	The average growth rate	3.88	10.45	7.78
$\delta^2=1$	Interval	[0,2.27]	[2.27,3]	[3,4]
	The length of development stage	2.27	0.73	1
	The average demand	**1.84**	**16.01**	**34.13**
	The average growth rate	4.09	20.81	17.76
$\delta^2=0.5$	Interval	[0,2.77]	[2.77,3.29]	[3.29,4]
	The length of development stage	2.77	0.52	0.71
	The average demand	**1.51**	**22.48**	**48.07**
	The average growth rate	4.64	41.21	31.49

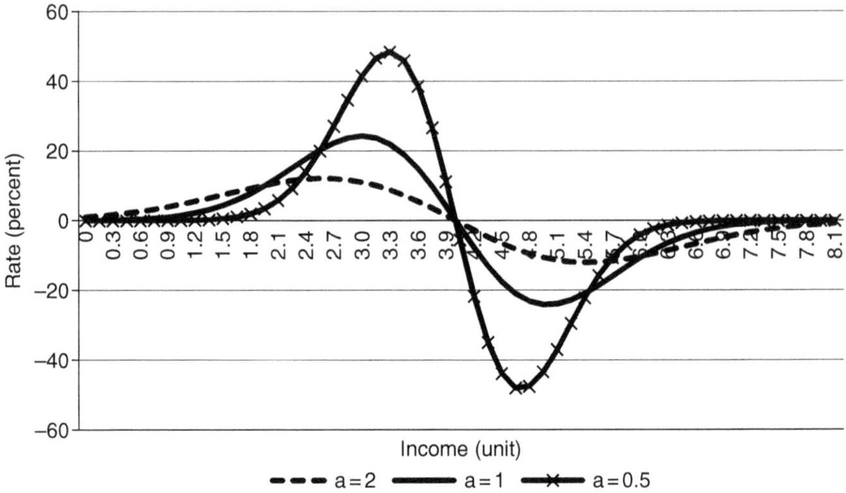

Figure 3.7 The influence of income inequality on the growth rate of demand for durables at different stage.

41.21 percent in the growing stage, and will rise from 7.78 percent to 17.76 percent and 31.49 percent in the maturing stage.

There is a conflict between the average quantity demanded and the average growth rate in the initial stage. When the variance decreases from 2 to 1 and 0.5, the average quantity demanded declines from 2.7 units to 1.84 units and 1.51 units, but the average growth rate, contrarily, rises from 3.88 percent to 4.09 percent and 4.64 percent. The reason is that the interval for the initial stage becomes much longer when variance decreases, and a greater proportion of interval with higher growth rates are included in the initial stage.

The demonstration of the impact of income inequality on the average demand and growth rate in fixed intervals

Due to the changes of the interval lengths of different stages caused by the alteration of variance, the above conclusions on the impact of income inequality are only comparable to some extent. One such instance is the conflict between the average demand and the average growth rate in the initial stage. In order to compare the impact, we fix the intervals, hence various stages of development, using a distribution with a variance of 1, and then compare the impact of income inequality on the average quantity demanded and growth rate over the same interval. The result is reported on Table 3.2.

In the fixed interval of [0, 2.27], which is the initial stage when the variance is 1, by reducing variance from 2 to 1 and then from 1 to 0.5, the average quantity demanded and the average growth rate initially declines from 4.94 units and 5.84

Table 3.2 The impact of income inequality on the average scale and growth rate of demand for durables in the fixed interval

Fixed interval of income-price ratio		*[0,2.27]*	*[2.27,3]*	*[3,4]*
$\delta^2=2$	Average demand	4.94	17.63	22.44
	Average growth rate	**5.84**	**11.79**	**8.57**
$\delta^2=1$	Average demand	1.92	15.92	26.36
	Average growth rate	**4.09**	**20.81**	**17.76**
$\delta^2=0.5$	Average demand	0.33	9.75	28.35
	Average growth rate	**1.30**	**24.39**	**30.56**

percent to 1.92 units and 4.09 percent, and then to 0.33 units and 1.3 percent. This result shows that rising income inequality is beneficial to the development of entrepreneurs whose product is in the initial stage, because inequality leads to higher demand.

In the fixed interval of [2.27, 3], which is the growing stage when the variance is 1, by reducing variance from 2 to 1 and then from 1 to 0.5, the average quantity demanded declines from 17.63 units to 15.92 units and 9.75 units, but the average growth rate increases from 11.79 percent to 20.81 percent and 24.39 percent. This contradictory result shows that the impact of income inequality is ambiguous in this special interval. There is a turning point for the impact of inequality in this interval – for the part of the interval near the initial stage, rising income inequality is beneficial to the development of entrepreneurs in the growing stage, but the effect is reversed in the part of the interval near the maturing stage.

In the fixed interval of [3, 4], which is the maturing stage when the variance is 1, by reducing variance from 2 to 1 and from 1 to 0.5, both average quantity demanded and the average growth rate initially increases from 22.44 units and 8.57 percent to 26.36 units and 17.76 percent, and then to 28.35 units and 30.56 percent. This result shows that declining income inequality is beneficial to the development of entrepreneurs whose product is in the maturing stage, because now equality leads to higher demand.

The conclusion on the impact of income inequality on durable goods demand and its growth rate

From the above analysis, we could conclude that the impact of rising income inequality is beneficial to entrepreneurs in the initial stage, and undermines entrepreneurs in the maturing stage. Thus, moderate inequality is beneficial to both the initial and maturing enterprises.

The influence of income inequality on the scale and growth rate of demand for non-durable goods

The impact of income inequality on the demand for non-durables is similar to that of durables. When the mean remains unchanged, the shape of demand distribution for non-durables is solely determined by the variance. The bigger the variance is, the flatter the demand curve for non-durables is, and vice versa. When the alteration of variance changes the shape of the demand curve, it changes the average demand as well as its growth rate, and brings about important effects on the entrepreneurs' development by altering the demand for products in different development stages.

The mechanism of the impact of income inequality on the scale and growth rate of demand for non-durables

While income distribution is assumed to be a normal with a mean of u and variance of δ, by using the two inflexion points and one maximum of the growth rate of demand for non-durables, we can divide the lifespan of non-durables into four stages, which are the initial stage in the income–price ratio interval of $[0, u-\delta]$, the blooming stage in the income–price ratio interval of $[u-\delta, u]$, the shrinking stage in the income–price ratio interval of $[u, u+\delta]$ and the saturation stage in the income–price ratio interval of $[u+\delta, +\infty]$ respectively. According to the features of normal distribution, no matter how the mean u and variance δ change, the cumulative density from zero to the turning point of growth rate, which occurs when the income–price ratio is equal to $(u-\delta)$, and to the turning point of quantity demanded, which occurs when the income–price ratio is equal to u, do not change and remain as 15.37 percent and 50 percent, respectively. But the length of interval in different stages will change when variance is altered. For instance, the bigger the variance, the shorter the length of the interval of the initial stage, and the longer the length of the blooming stage. And then we can draw one important conclusion: The average demand will rise in the initial stage and decrease in the blooming stage when variance rises.

At the same time, we could find that the maximum of growth rate, $\frac{1}{\sigma\sqrt{2\pi}}$, depends only on the standard variance. The bigger the variance, the lower the maximum is. Thus, an increase in variance will lead to an increase in the average growth rate in the initial stage and a decline for the blooming stage.

In general, increase in variance could enhance the development of entrepreneurs by creating more demand in the initial stage, but also undermine the development of entrepreneurs in the blooming stage by reducing the average scale and growth rate of demand for non-durables. On the contrary, decrease in variance is beneficial to the development of entrepreneurs in the blooming stage, but unfavorable to the development of entrepreneurs in the initial stage.

The demonstration of the influence of income inequality on the average scale and growth rate of demand for non-durables in different stage

In order to compare the different effects of income inequality on the demand in different stages, we choose three scenarios, with the same mean of 4, but different variances of 2, 1 and 0.5, respectively. This is shown in Figure 3.8. The bigger the variance is, the flatter the curve of demand for non-durables is. And no matter how variance changes, the interval of demand is [0, 15.37] in the initial stage, and [15.37, 50] in the blooming stage. However, the average scale and growth rate of demand in different stage changes with variance, because the length of stage changes with variance, shown in the Table 3.3.

In the initial stage, if variance decreases from 2 to 1 and 0.5, the interval length increases from 2.59 to 3 and 3.29, the average quantity demanded decreases from 4.58 units to 3.01 units and 2.11 units, and the average growth rate decreases from 6.05 percent to 5.63 percent and 5.45 percent.

In the blooming stage, if the variance reduces from 2 to 1 and 0.5, the interval length decreases from 1.41 to 1 and 0.71, the average scale of demand increases from 33.66 units to 35.1 units and 36.78 units, and the average growth rate increases from 24.66 percent to 35.48 percent and 50.98 percent (Figure 3.9).

In general, increase in variance will promote entrepreneurs' development in the initial stage through raising the average scale and growth rate of demand for non-durables. On the other hand, decrease in variance will affect entrepreneurs' development in the blooming stage in the same way.

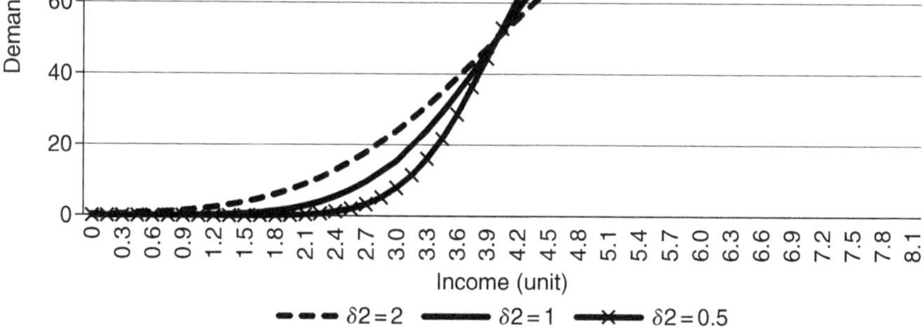

Figure 3.8 The influence of income inequality on demand for non-durables.

Table 3.3 The influence of income inequality on the average scale and growth rate of demand for non-durables

Variance	*Indicator*	*The initial stage*	*The blooming stage*
$\delta^2=2$	Interval of demand	[0,15.37]	[15.37,50]
	Interval of growth rate	[0,17.11]	[17.11,28.21]
	Interval of income–price ratio	[0,2.59]	[2.59,4]
	Interval length of stage	2.59	1.414
	Average scale of demand	4.58	33.66
	Average growth rate	6.05	24.66
$\delta^2=1$	Interval of demand	[0,15.37]	[15.37,50]
	Interval of growth rate	[0,24.2]	[24.2,39.89]
	Interval of income–price ratio	[0,3]	[3,4]
	Interval length of stage	3	1
	Average scale of demand	**3.01**	**35.10**
	Average growth rate	**5.63**	**35.48**
$\delta^2=0.5$	Interval of demand	[0,15.37]	[15.37,50]
	Interval of growth rate	[0,34.22]	[34.22,56.42]
	Interval of income–price ratio	[0,3.29]	[3.29,4]
	Interval length of stage	3.29	0.71
	Average scale of demand	2.11	36.78
	Average growth rate	5.45	50.98

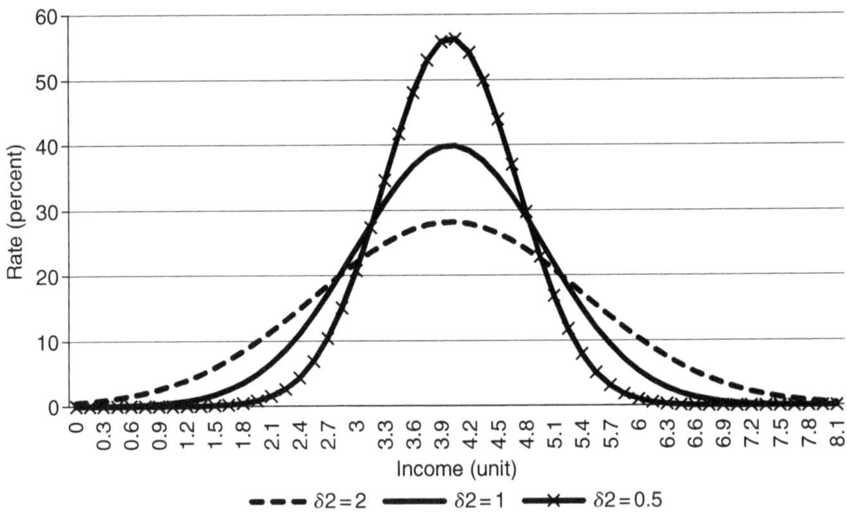

Figure 3.9 The influence of income inequality on growth rate of demand for non-durables.

The transmission mechanism from cycle of consumer goods to cycle of industry: the role of the industrial multiplier

Consumer goods are the final products of the industrial production chain. Many firms use other firms' output as inputs to produce consumer goods. Such firms include raw materials suppliers in the upstream industry and many manufacturing firms in the downstream industry. Every consumer good has a chain of production, the length of which varies. Since the demand for consumer goods exhibits an endogenous cycle caused by the normality of household income, the output of firms in the production chain of consumer goods inevitably exhibit a similar cycle, and the total output of all firms in the production chain must also exhibit a similar cycle. The length of the chain determines the industrial multiplier as well as the amplitude of the industry cycle resulting from the cycle of demand for consumer goods.

Assume the number of firms in the production chain of durable good A is n, the investment multiplier for production of durable A, i.e., the amount of investment required to produce an extra unit of A, is $\beta(0<\beta<1)$, that is, $\Delta I_1=\beta\Delta C$. Moreover, we assume that investment required for going up the supply chain increases by a factor of β. In other words, the firm that is the supplier for the producer of good A needs β^2 units of investment. Then we can see the total investments of the industry ΔI required for producing an extra unit of A is $\Delta I = \sum_1^n \beta^n \times \Delta C$. According to the formula of industrial output, $Y=I+C$, the marginal increase in output i resulting from a marginal increase in demand ΔC is $\Delta Y = \Delta I + \Delta C = (\sum_1^n \beta^n + 1)\Delta C$. This formula gives a relationship between the growth rate of demand for durables A and the growth rate of industry output, which is expressed as: $n_y = \frac{\Delta Y}{Y}(\sum_1^n \beta^n + 1) \times \frac{C}{Y} \times n_C, n_C = \frac{\Delta C}{C}$. The coefficient, $(\sum_1^n \beta^n + 1)$, is called the industrial multiplier of durable A. According to the formula of the industrial growth rate, when the consumption ratio C/Y remains unchanged, the cyclical fluctuation of the growth rate n_c of demand for durable A will inevitably result in cyclic fluctuation of growth rate of industrial output n_y. Thus, the industrial cycle is also determined by household income distribution. Since the industrial multiplier $(\sum_1^n \beta^n + 1)$ is bigger than 1, the amplitude of the industrial cycle must be larger than that of the cycle of demand for durable A. The amplitude of the industrial cycle is determined by the scale of the industrial multiplier, $(\sum_1^n \beta^n + 1)$, whose size is determined by the investment accelerator β and the length of the production chain. The longer the production chain and the bigger the investment accelerator are, *ceteris paribus*, the larger the industrial multiplier and the larger the amplitude of the industry cycle are. If the length of the chain is infinite, the industry multiplier will be $\frac{1}{1-\beta}$, which is the maximum of the industry multiplier.

The transmission mechanism from the industry cycle to the economy cycle: the impact of industrial restructuring

An economy is composed of multiple industries, and the amplitude of the whole economic cycle is also composed of several industrial cycles. Assuming that the economy consists of n industries with output Y_n, then total output of the economy would be the sum of n industries, $Y = \sum_1^n Y_n$, and the growth rate of the economy can be expressed as the weighted average of industrial growth rates, $N = \sum_1^n \frac{Y_n}{Y} \times N_{y_n}$. The growth rate of the whole economy, N, is determined by the share of each industrial output in the total output of the whole economy, $\frac{Y_n}{Y}$, and the growth rate of the industry, N_{y_n}. Since every industry has its own endogenous cycle caused by the normality of household income distribution, the growth rate of the whole economy N naturally exhibits the same endogenous cycle caused by the normality of household income distribution. The influence of each industrial cycle on the whole economic cycle depends on its proportion in the whole output and the amplitude of its cycle.

Basic conclusion

As the above analysis has shown, as long as household income is normally distributed, the growth rate of demand for consumer goods must exhibit an endogenous cycle through its lifespan. And then every industry as well as the whole economy have their own endogenous cycles induced by the endogenous cycle of consumer demand, which is in turn caused by the normality of household income distribution.

Since the accelerator from the consumer demand cycle to the industrial cycle is greater than 1, the amplitude of the industrial cycle must be larger than that of the consumer demand cycle, and is determined by the length of the industrial production chain and the size of the investment multiplier. The longer the production chain is and the bigger the investment accelerator is, the bigger the multiplier and the amplitude of industrial cycle are.

Only when the product generated by entrepreneurial innovation is new demand instead of substitution of the original product can the new products change the shape of the consumer demand cycle as well as the whole economic cycle. More importantly, the cycle of demand for non-durables transforms from a half-cycle into a complete continuous fluctuation when the new product emerges.

The impact of each industrial cycle on the whole economic cycle is determined by the ratio of output from that industry to total GDP and the amplitude of the industrial cycle. Therefore, industrial restructuring will inevitably change the shape of the whole economic cycle. The impact of emerging industry on the whole economic cycle increases through time when its output starts to account for a bigger proportion of GDP.

More equal distribution of income will enhance the development of industries in the growing stage and the maturing stage or blooming stage through speeding up the growth of demand for consumer goods or generating more demand, and thus will improve the present economic development. On the other hand, decline in income inequality may reduce the demand in emerging industries in the initial stage of development, which is detrimental to long-term economy development. On the contrary, rising income inequality would reduce demand in the industries in growing and maturing stages or the blooming stage, which is detrimental to present economy growth. But rising income inequality may enhance the development of emerging industries by generating more demand, and so enhancing growth capacity in the future. Since there is a tradeoff in the impact of income inequality, keeping income inequality at a moderate level is essential for maintaining long-lasting rapid economic growth.

Notes

1 See Chapter 2.
2 See Chapter 4.

4 In global perspective

The normal distribution of household income and the endogenous mechanism of the cycle of demand for consumer goods

Normal estimation of household income distribution in other countries, with the US and Japan as examples

Household income distributions in other countries also have bell-shaped features but are different in form due to different degrees of income inequality. For example, household income inequality is small in Japan, with a high proportion of middle-income households and a typical bell-shaped income distribution. Income inequality in the US is high, with a large proportion of low-income households and a half bell-shaped income distribution. We conducted simulative normal estimations of American household income distribution in 2011 and Japanese worker household income distribution in 2004. The results show that income distributions in America and Japan are normally distributed with the mean of the income group of the highest household proportion as the expected value.

Normal estimation of American household income distribution in 2011

In the US, household income inequality is greater, with low-income households and high-income households accounting for large proportions of the population, and a half bell-shaped income distribution. The average income of American households in 2011 was \$69,677. According to group data with \$5,000 as the interval, the group with the highest household proportion (5.88 percent) is \$10,000–\$15,000, with an average income of \$12,414. This is a large deviation from the average household income of the entire population. Thus, we take the average income (\$32,034) of another group with a household proportion of 5.5 percent as the expected value for the normal estimation and average income of each income group as sampling value x. The variance of income distribution is estimated to be 24.85. Therefore, the normal distribution function of American household income distribution in 2011 can be expressed as: $f(x)=\frac{1}{4.98\sqrt{2\pi}}e^{-\frac{(x-3.2)^2}{49.71}}$, where $f(x)$ is the household density function and x is the average income of each income group. We integrate the simulative normal density function over the interval of income groups, i.e., from the highest to the lowest income for each group, and present the estimated density of American household income distribution in 2011 in Figures 4.1 and 4.2. The regression result of estimated density for each income group on actual density shows a remarkable correlation, with goodness-of-fit at 0.975428. This confirms that American household income distribution in 2011 is normal, with $32,000 as the expected value and 24.85 as the variance.

The regression equation of the estimated density of American household income distribution (USFBG) and the actual density (USFBA) in 2011 is as follows:

$$\underset{}{\text{USFBA}} = \underset{(16.14)}{1.2175} \times \text{USFBG} + \underset{(0.68)}{0.0009} + [\text{MA}(1) = \underset{(10.48)}{0.9192}, \text{MA}(2) = \underset{(45.11)}{0.9912}]$$

$R^2=0.95428$; adjusted $R^2=0.97326$; DW=2.02. MA(1) is the moving average of the first-order residual component; the numerical values in parentheses beneath the variables are the *t*-statistics, indicating the level of significance of variables.

Normal estimation of Japanese household income distribution in 2004

Income inequality in Japan is lower, resulting in a typical bell-shaped income distribution that is remarkably different from that of the US. The average cash income of workers' households was 466,039 yen in 2004 (distribution of house-

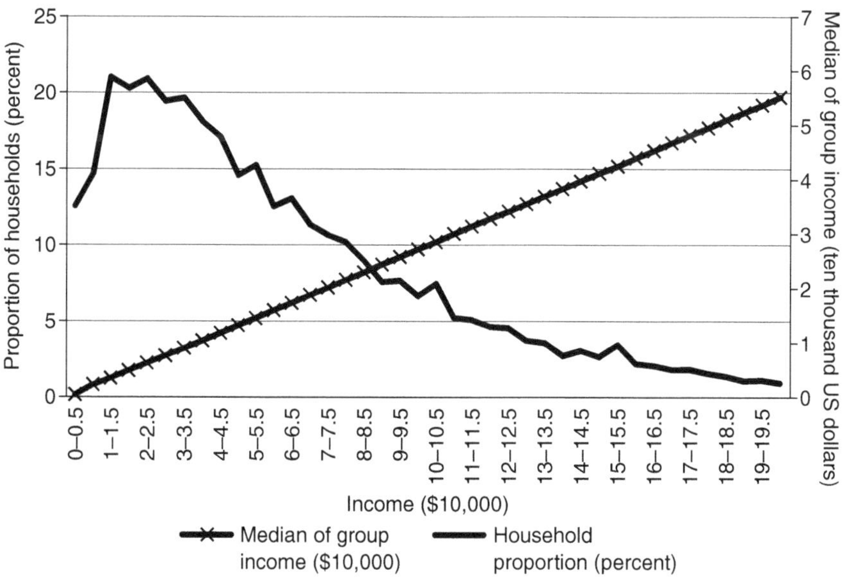

Figure 4.1 American household income distribution and median of group income.

Source: US Census Bureau, Income, Poverty, and Health Insurance Coverage in the United States 2011.

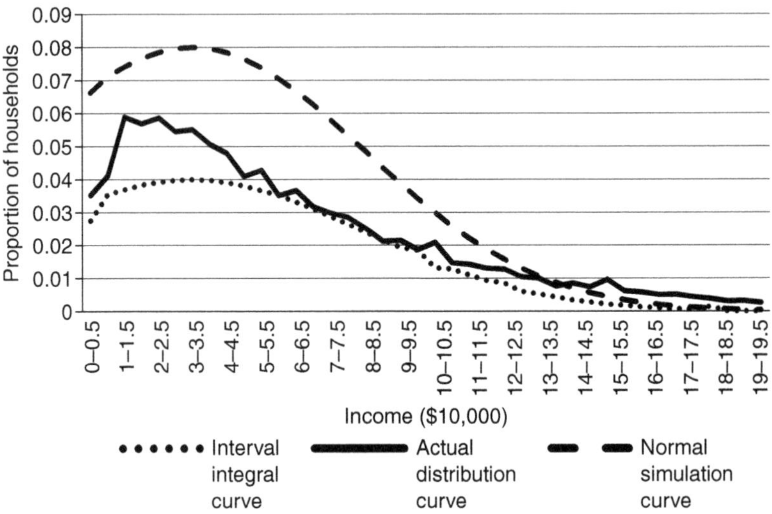

Figure 4.2 Normal estimation of American household income normal distribution in 2011.

Source: based on Figure 4.1.

hold by class of cash income). According to the group data with 50,000 yen as the interval, the household income of the group with the highest household proportion (10.8 percent) is 400,000–450,000 yen, which is close to the average household income of the whole country. On this basis, we take average cash income of workers' households in 2004 (466,000 yen) as the expected value and the median of each income group as the sampling value, denoted as *x*; for our normal estimation, the estimated income variance is 4.93 and the estimated normal distribution function of Japanese workers' household income can be expressed as: $f(x) = \frac{1}{2.22\sqrt{2\pi}} e^{-\frac{(x-4.66)^2}{9.86}}$, where *f*(*x*) is the household proportion and *x* is the median of each income group (Figure 4.3). We integrated this estimated normal distribution function over the intervals between the upper and lower limits of each income group to obtain the estimated density of households in each income group. The results are reported in Figure 4.4. Regression of the estimated density on the actual household density shows a remarkable correlation, with goodness-of-fit at 0.973787. This confirms that the cash income of Japanese worker households in 2004 is basically normally distributed with the expected value of 466,000 yen and variance of 4.93.

The regression equation of the estimated density (JPFBG) on the actual household density (JPFBA) in 2004 is as follows:

$$\underset{}{\mathrm{JPFBA}} = \underset{(12.19)}{0.8811} \times \mathrm{JPFBG} + \underset{(2.82)}{0.0078} + [\mathrm{MA}(1) = \underset{(5.22)}{1.3813},\ \mathrm{MA}(2) = \underset{(4.54)}{0.9997}]$$

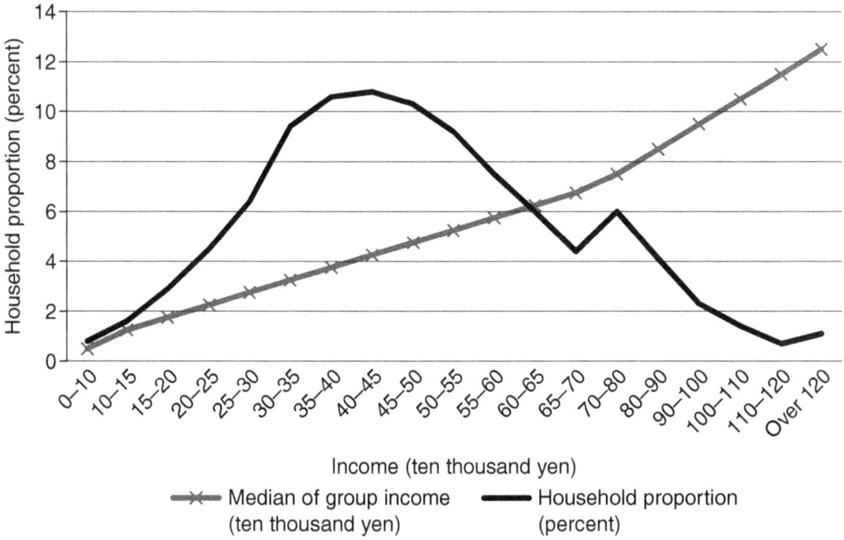

Figure 4.3 Japanese household cash income distribution and median of income group in 2004.

Source: www.stat.go.jp/english/data/zensho/2004/hutari/gaiyo14.htm.

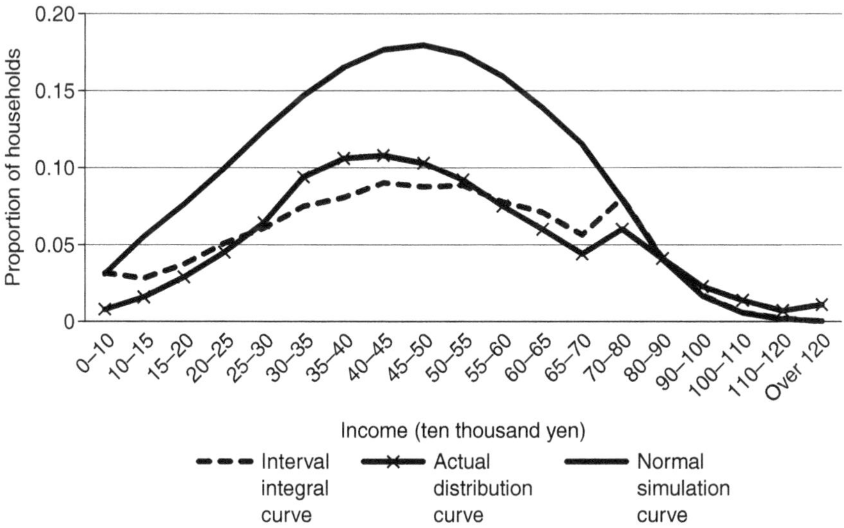

Figure 4.4 Normal estimation of Japanese household income normal distribution in 2004.

Source: calculated based on Figure 4.3.

R^2=0.973787; adjusted R^2=0.968545; DW=1.68. MA(1) is the moving average of the first-order residual component; the numerical values in parentheses beneath the variables are the *t*-statistics, indicating the level of significance for each variable.

Cycle of demand for consumer goods from a global perspective

An important feature of normal distribution is that the linear combination of multiple normal distributions is also normally distributed. Since the annual household income of a country is subject to normal distribution, the cross-time income is inevitably normally distributed, and the global annual and cross-time household income distributions are also normal. Thus, under the assumption that consumer goods can flow freely, both durable consumer goods and non-durable consumer goods have endogenous cycles induced by the normally distributed global household income.

Cycle of durable consumer goods from a global perspective

First, we assume the world household income distribution is normal, with u as the expected value and δ as the standard variance, namely: $F(x) = \frac{1}{\sigma\sqrt{2\pi}} e^{-\frac{(x-u)^2}{2\sigma^2}}$.

In this equation, x is the proportion of the population or households at different income levels. Under the condition that there exists a saturation point for consumer durable goods demand, the global demand for consumer durable goods is inevitably subject to normal distribution. The ratio of consumer durable goods demand to total demand will also be subject to the normal distribution, with u as the expected value and δ as the standard variance, namely: $Q(z) = \frac{1}{\sigma\sqrt{2\pi}} e^{-\frac{(z-u)^2}{2\sigma^2}}$,

where z is the ratio of the global household income level y to the price of durable consumer goods p, namely y/p (hereinafter referred to as the income–price ratio). After normalizing the world population or household to be 1, $Q(z)$ is the demand function for durable consumer goods.

According to the property of normal distribution, the growth of durables demand has complete cyclic fluctuation: The growth rate of durables demand, n, is the first-order derivative of the total demand function, namely, $n = Q'(z) = \frac{1}{\sigma\sqrt{2\pi}} e^{-\frac{(z-u)^2}{2\sigma^2}} \times \frac{(u-z)}{\delta^2}$, and the first-order derivative of the growth of durables demand (i.e., second-order derivative of the total demand function), which reflects the characteristics of growth fluctuation, is $n' = Q''(z) = \frac{1}{\sigma^3\sqrt{2\pi}} e^{-\frac{(z-u)^2}{2\sigma^2}} \times \left(\frac{(z-u)^2}{\delta^2} - 1\right)$. From the growth rate of durables demand and its first-order derivative, it can be seen that the growth rate of durables demand has two extreme values: when $z=u-\delta$, the growth rate of demand n reaches its maximum; when $z=u$, the growth rate of demand is 0 and quantity of demand reaches its maximum; when $z=u+\delta$, growth rate of demand reaches its minimum. Moreover, according to the second-order derivative of the growth of durable consumer good demand (the third-order derivative of the total demand function) $n''=Q'''(z)=\frac{1}{\sqrt{2\pi\delta^5}}e^{-\frac{(z-u)^2}{2\sigma^2}}\times(u-z)\times\left(\frac{(z-u)^2}{\delta^2}-3\right)$, growth rate of durables demand has three turning points, at $z=u-\sqrt{3}\delta$, $z=u$ and $z=u+\sqrt{3}$, respectively. As expressed in Figure 4.5, under the assumption that demand function for durables is normal distribution with a mean of 4 and variance of 1, quantity demanded for durables will reach its maximum when income–price ratio is equal to 4, and the growth rate of durable consumer goods demand will reach its maximum and minimum when the income–price ratio reaches 3 and 5, respectively. In conclusion, under the condition that the world household income is normally distributed, the quantity of demand for durables is also normally distributed, and the growth rate of durables demand will exhibit cyclic fluctuation induced by the normality of income distribution.

Continuous cyclical fluctuation of growth rate of demand for durable consumer goods caused by replacement demand and product innovation

All durables have a fixed service life, after which consumers will have to buy new ones. This will create replacement demand for durables. Since replacement

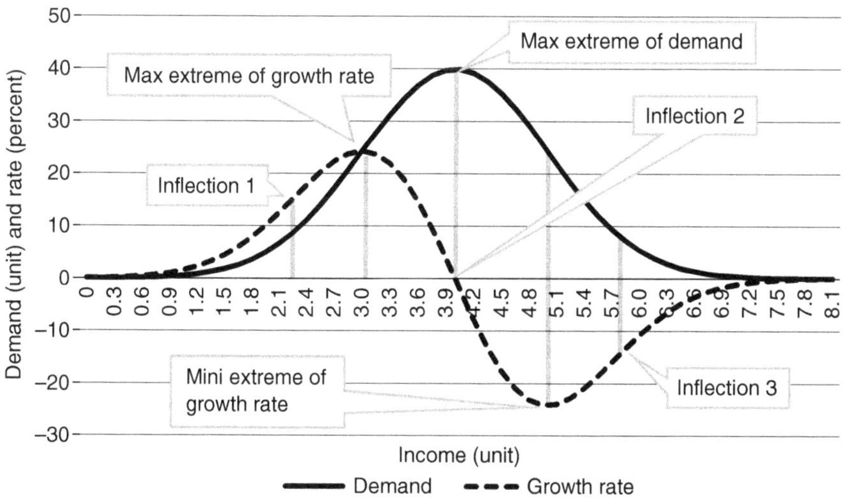

Figure 4.5 Simulation of the cycle of demand for durables determined by normal distribution of household income from a global perspective.

Source: calculated on assumed conditions.

demand is also subject to normal distribution, the growth rate of replacement demand will be the same as that of the initial demand and will also exhibit an endogenous cycle induced by income distribution. After replacement demand appears, the actual demand will be composed of replacement demand and initial demand. Because initial and replacement demand are both subject to normal distribution, their linear combination is also normally distributed. Therefore, the actual demand, which is the linear combination of initial demand and replacement demand, is still normal distributed, and the growth rate of actual demand still exhibits cyclical fluctuation. Affected by replacement demand, the growth of durables demand will exhibit continuous cyclical fluctuation. As shown in Figure 4.6, assuming both initial demand and replacement are subject to normal distribution with an expected value of 4 and variance of 1, the "growth rate 1 of total demand," after taking into account initial demand and replacement demand, also exhibits continuous cyclical fluctuation. However, the wavelength of total demand fluctuation is longer than that of the initial demand fluctuation due to the timing with which replacement demand occurs. For example, if replacement demand appears after initial demand reaches its maximum (e.g., when income–price rate rises to 6.5), the wavelength of replacement demand growth rate will be remarkably larger.

Like replacement demand, demand for new products brought about by entrepreneurial innovation (hereinafter referred to as innovation demand) can also change the cyclical properties of the growth of durables demand. As shown in Figure 4.6, if innovation demand replaces original products, just like replacement

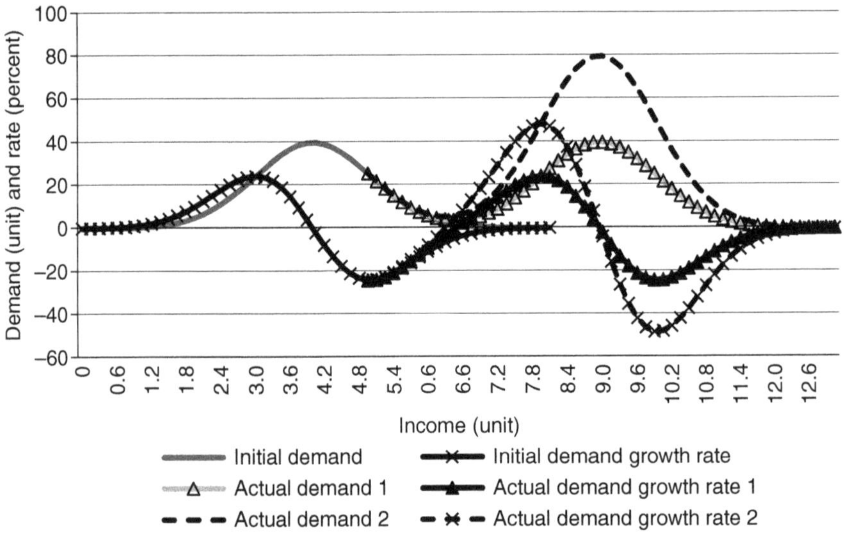

Figure 4.6 Influence of replacement demand and enterprise innovation on quantity and growth rate of demand for durables.

Source: calculated on assumed conditions.

demand, total demand will exhibit continuous cyclical fluctuation, and the fluctuation of total demand growth will be exactly the same as with replacement demand. However, if innovation demand does not replace initial demand but is simply added to total demand, then the magnitude of fluctuation of total demand growth with innovation demand, "actual demand growth rate 2," will be substantially larger than that only with replacement demand (actual demand growth rate 1). Moreover, different timing of innovation demand occurrence remarkably lengthens or shortens the wavelength of the total demand cycle. In this example, we assume that innovation demand and replacement demand appear at the same time.

The cycle of demand for non-durables from a global perspective

Unlike the demand for durables with longer service lives, consumers' demand for non-durables is continuous. Under the conditions that global household income is normally distributed with u as the expected value and δ as the standard variance, and that non-durables can flow freely, the property of continuous consumption demand implies that the distribution of global demand for non-durables is the integral of the income density function, namely: $Q(z) = \frac{1}{\sigma\sqrt{2\pi}} \int_0^z e^{-\frac{(z-u)^2}{2\sigma^2}} dz.$

Growth rate of demand for non-durables is also normally distributed, namely: $n = Q'(z) = f(z) = \frac{1}{\sigma\sqrt{2\pi}} e^{-\frac{(z-u)^2}{2\sigma^2}}$, with the fluctuating shape of a half-cycle. As shown in Figure 4.7, assuming the global household income is normally distributed with the expected value of 4 and variance of 1, the demand curve for

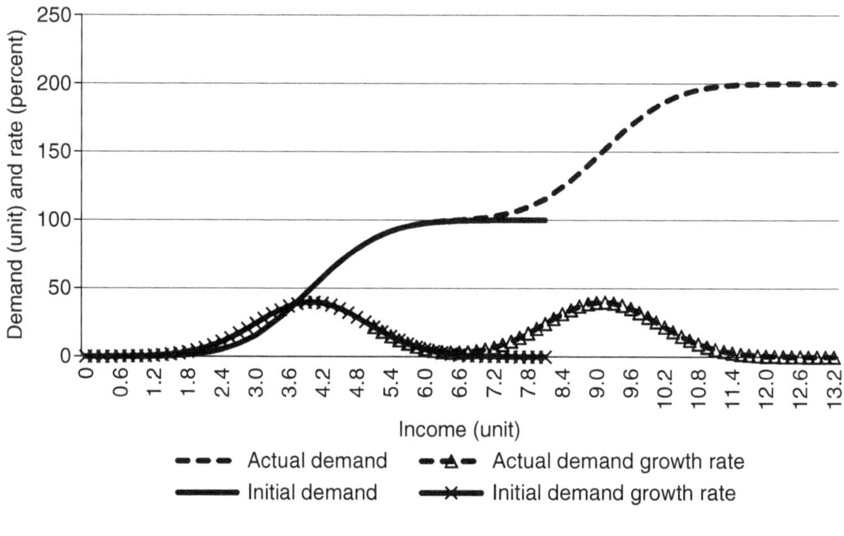

Figure 4.7 Quantity and growth rate of demand for non-durables from the global perspective.

non-durables is S-shaped (initial demand curve), and the fluctuation of the growth rate (growth rate of initial demand) will be a half-cycle of normal distribution.

Since the consumption of non-durables is instantaneous, they do not have the cycle of replacement demand. But innovation demand, in the form of additional demand, would still cause the growth of total demand for non-durables to exhibit continuous cyclical fluctuation. This can be seen from the following. (1) If new products are just replacements of the original ones, then the demand for non-durables will not change, and the cycle will still exhibit the feature of the half-cycle. (2) If new products come about in the form of additional demands, namely that the new products would not replace (or partly replace) the demand for the original products, the total demand for non-durables will increase. With the growth rate of innovation demand in a half-cycle, the growth of total non-durables demand exhibits continuous full-cycle fluctuation. As shown in Figure 4.7, assuming global household income is normally distributed with the expected value of 4 and variance of 1, the appearance of new products as additional demand will result in the expansion of total non-durable consumer good demand (actual demand curve), and the growth of non-durables demand (actual demand growth rate) will exhibit continuous cyclical fluctuation.

Influence of international market demand on individual country's cycle of demand for durables

In a closed economy, growth of durables, and thus economic growth, is always subject to endogenous cyclical fluctuation induced by the normality of household income distribution. Along with the continuous improvement of global economic integration, the fluctuation of durables demand, and thus economic fluctuation in one country, are more and more influenced by the global economic fluctuation through flow of factors of production and international trade. As we have previously shown that global household income is normally distributed, and the growth of durables demand has cyclical fluctuation induced by the normality of income distribution, then after taking into consideration the import and export of durables, demand for each country's durables is normally distributed, and the growth rate of that demand is subject to cyclic fluctuation. But international demand would lead to increases in the expected value and variance of the demand distribution. As a result, the distribution curve of demand for durables will shift toward the right and become flatter. By the same token, the magnitude of growth rate fluctuation will decrease.

Assume that a country is one of the global suppliers for durable consumer goods, the demand for durables in this country will be composed of domestic demand and international market demand (export). We normalize population size (the number of households) and the total demand for durable consumer goods both to be 1. Then the proportion of households can also represent the demand for durables under each income–price ratio. In an open economy, each country's total demand for durables needs to take the effect of saturation into account. We define domestic and foreign saturated demand as the quantity of demand such that all consumers in domestic markets and foreign markets respectively have reached their own saturation points, i.e., additional unit of durables will not bring positive utility to that individual. Under the assumption that saturated demand of each consumer is 1, domestic saturated demand is equal to the total number of domestic households or population in that country and global saturated demand is equal to the total number of households or population in the whole world.

Assume that domestic saturated demand for durable consumer goods, which also equals the number of households or population size in a country, is A instead of 1, as assumed before, and household income is normally distributed with u_1 as the expected value and δ_1 as the standard variance, the scale of domestic durable consumer good demand $Q_n(x)$ will be the product of the domestic saturated demand and the density function of demand distribution (household income distribution), namely, $Q_n(x) = \frac{A}{\delta_1\sqrt{2\pi}} e^{-\frac{(x-u_1)^2}{2\delta_1^2}}$.

For the same reason, if we assume that the global saturated demand for durables (number of households or population size in the rest of the world) is B, and the global household income is normally distributed with u_2 as the expected value and δ_2 as the standard variance, the scale of global demand for durables $Q_f(x)$ will be the product of the global saturated demand and the density function of global household income distribution, namely, $Q_f(x) = \frac{B}{\delta_2\sqrt{2\pi}} e^{-\frac{(x-u_2)^2}{2\delta_2^2}}$.

Assume that the ratio of a country's export of durables to global total demand for durables is β, as well as that per domestic household demand is equal to per global household demand at the same income–price ratio, the total scale of demand for durable consumer goods produced in that country is:

$$Q(x) = Qn(x) + \beta \times Qf(x) = \frac{A}{\delta_1\sqrt{2\pi}} e^{-\frac{(x-u_1)^2}{2\delta_1^2}} + \frac{\beta * B}{\delta_2\sqrt{2\pi}} e^{-\frac{(x-u_2)^2}{2\delta_2^2}}$$

Since the linear combination of multiple independent normal variables is still normally distributed,[1] the distribution of total demand for durables in a country, $Q(x)$, which is the linear combination of domestic demand and foreign demand, should still be normally distributed with expected value $\Phi = Au_1 + \beta Bu_2$ and variance $\Omega^2 = (A\delta_1)^2 + (\beta B\delta_2)^2$. The density function of the total demand distribution is: $P(z) = \frac{1}{\sqrt{2\pi} * \Omega} e^{-\frac{(z-\Phi)^2}{2\Omega^2}}$, where variable z is the sum of domestic demand A and foreign demand for domestic product $B \times \beta$, namely $A + B\beta$; z represents the income–price ratio, and the density function $P(z)$ represents the proportion of durables demand to total demand at each integrated income–price ratio z. In the case in which total saturated demand is normalized to 1, the density function $P(z)$ represents the demand for durable consumer goods at each integrated income–price ratio. The first-order derivative of $P(z)$ with respect to time is the growth rate of durable consumer good demand, which is expressed as: $n = P'(z) = \frac{1}{\Omega\sqrt{2\pi}} e^{-\frac{(z-\Phi)^2}{2\Omega^2}} \times \frac{(\Phi - z)}{\Omega^2}$. The first-order derivative of growth rate of durables demand can be expressed as: $n' = p''(z) = \frac{1}{\Omega^3\sqrt{2\pi}} e^{-\frac{(z-\Phi)^2}{2\Omega^2}} \times \left(\frac{(z-\Phi)^2}{\Omega^2} - 1\right)$.

According to the demand function and growth function of durables, we come to six important conclusions.

Conclusion 1: After taking global trade into consideration, the total demand for durables in one country (sum of domestic and foreign demand) is still normally distributed and the growth rate of demand is still subject to cyclical fluctuation.

Conclusion 2: After taking into account international demand, total demand for durable goods produced in a single country is determined by five factors: the size of domestic population, domestic income distribution, the size of the global population, global income distribution and the ratio of a country's export of durables to global total demand.

Conclusion 3: The growth of demand for durables and the properties of its fluctuation are determined by the same five factors.

Conclusion 4: When export ratio remains constant, increase in export could raise the expected value of the density function of durables demand, and the maximum value of its density function would shift toward the right $[(Au_1 + \beta Bu_2) > Au_1]$, which implies that export would increase the period of durables fluctuation.

Conclusion 5: Export can lead to an increase in the variance of the demand distribution for durables $[(A\delta_1)^2 + (\beta B\delta_2)^2 > (A\delta_1)^2]$, and flatten the density function, which implies that increase in exports would reduce the amplitude of the fluctuation of durables demand, because the maximum value of the growth rate of durables demand n_b is $n_b = \frac{1}{\Omega^2\sqrt{2\pi e}}$, the minimum value n_s is $n_s = \frac{-1}{\Omega^2\sqrt{2\pi e}}$ and the difference between the maximum and the minimum is $n_b - n_s = \frac{2}{\Omega^2\sqrt{2\pi e}}$. The larger the variance Ω^2, the smaller the difference will be.

Conclusion 6: With a gradual increase in export ratio, the expected value and variance of the density function for durable consumer goods demand will also gradually increase and the density function will gradually flatten out.

In order to illustrate the influence of exports on the growth rate of durables demand, we assume that the domestic saturated demand for durable A is 1 and the expected value u_1 and variance δ_1^2 of the domestic income distribution are 4 and 2, respectively, the global saturated demand B is 4 and the expected value u_2 and variance δ_2^2 of global income distribution are 4 and 1, respectively; and there are two scenarios for the export ratio β: remains unchanged at 10 percent or rises at a rate of 0.2 percent per year starting from 5 percent. Under these conditions, we work out three curves associated with demands for domestic durables: the distribution of demand function, the growth rate function and the scale of demands under different assumed conditions. The results are reported in Figures 4.8 and 4.9. We investigate the property of the density function, the demand function and the growth rate function in three different scenarios.

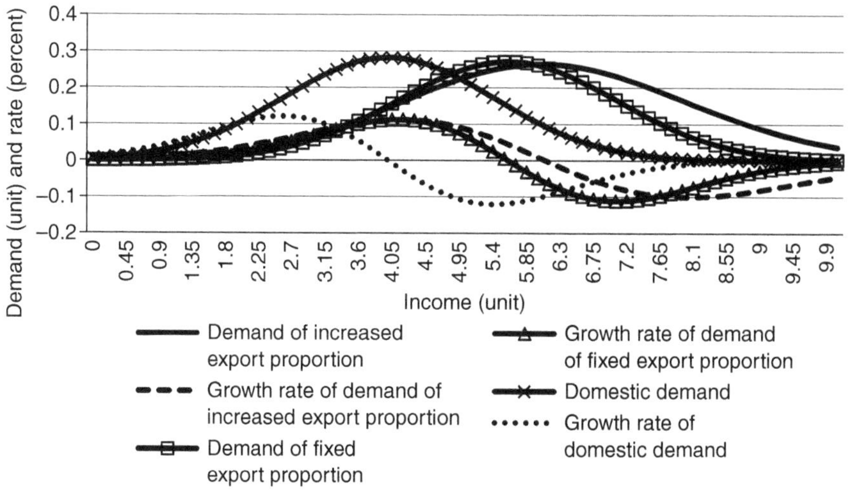

Figure 4.8 Influence of export on demand probability distribution and demand growth rate of durable consumer goods.

Source: calculated on assumed conditions.

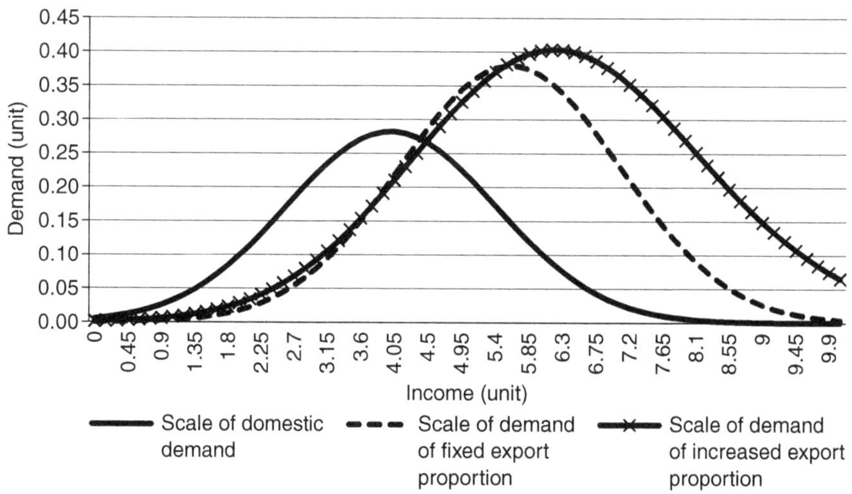

Figure 4.9 Influence of export on the scale of demand for durables.

Source: calculated on assumed conditions.

Only considering domestic demand as a benchmark

Without export, total demand is domestic demand. Thus the expected value of total demand probability distribution density function is 4 and the variance is 2; when income–price ratio reaches 4, the probability distribution density function (demand proportion) is at its maximum value of –28.21 percent. Because the total amount of domestic saturated demand is 1, then the maximal domestic demand is 0.2821. The growth rate of domestic demand is at its maximum value of 12.1 percent and minimal value of –12.1 percent when the income–price ratio reaches 2.5858 and 5.4142, respectively, and the amplitude of growth rate fluctuation is 24.2 percent.

Export proportion is fixed at 10 percent

When the ratio of export to global saturated demand is 10 percent, the density function of durables demand shifts rightwards from its original position when there is only domestic demand. The expected value and variance rise up to 5.6 and 2.16 respectively. When the income–price ratio is equal to 5.6, the density function (proportion of demand) reaches its maximum value of 27.14 percent. The total amount of saturated demand rises to 1.4, of which 1 unit comes domestically and 0.4 units comes from foreign saturated demand (the product of global households (4) multiplied by the export–demand ratio of 10 percent). The total demand for domestic durable consumer goods has a maximum value of 0.38, which is 1.35 times the maximum value of domestic demand. The growth rate of durable consumer goods demand reaches its maximal value of 11.2 percent and minimal value of –11.2 percent when the income–price ratio is at 4.1303 and 7.0697 respectively. The amplitude of growth rate fluctuation is 22.4 percent, 1.8 percent lower than in the scenario without export.

Progressive increase in export proportion

When the proportion of export to global demand increases at a rate of 0.2 percent from 5 percent, the expected value and variance of the distribution of durables demand will gradually increase along with the rise of export proportion. But the demand is still normally distributed, with an expected value of 6.11 and variance of 2.278, according to the simulation results shown in Figure 4.8. Increase in export proportion leads to a rightwards shift of the demand distribution curve. When income–price ratio reaches 6.11, the density function (proportion of demand) reaches its maximum value of 26.43 percent, and the total demand for durable consumer goods reaches its maximum value of 0.4037, which is equivalent to 1.43 times the maximum value of domestic demand, and 6.2 percent higher than the maximum value of total demand with a fixed export ratio. The growth rate of durables demand reaches its maximal value of 10.62 percent and minimal value of –10.62 percent when the income–price ratio is at 4.5733 and 7.5867 respectively. The amplitude of growth rate fluctuation is 21.24 percent,

Table 4.1 Simulation of distribution density function, demand and demand growth rate of durables under different conditions

Conditions	*Maximal value of demand distribution (%)*	*Maximal value of demand*	*Maximal value of growth rate (%)*	*Minimal value of growth rate (%)*	*Amplitude of growth rate fluctuation (%)*
Domestic demand	28.21	0.2821	12.10	−12.10	24.20
Demand of fixed export proportion	27.14	0.3800	11.20	−11.20	22.40
Demand of increased export proportion	26.43	0.4037	10.62	−10.62	21.24

Source: calculated on assumed conditions.

which is 1.16 percent lower than that with export–demand ratio fixed at 10 percent. Table 4.1 offers a summary.

The influence of international market demand on the cycle of demand for non-durables in individual countries

Similar to the effects of international demand on a country's cycle of durables demand, export also has significant influence on a country's cycle of non-durables demand. Export would increase the demand for domestic non-durables; total demand (domestic plus foreign) is still S-shaped, and the growth rate of total demand exhibits a half-cycle with a rate between the domestic demand growth rate and export growth rate.

We still assume that domestic household income is normally distributed with u_1 as the expected value and δ_1 as the standard variance; total domestic saturated demand is A; global household income is normally distributed with u_2 as the expected value and δ_2 as the standard variance; global saturated demand is B; the ratio of non-durables export to global saturated demand is β; and non-durables can flow freely around the world. Under these conditions, domestic demand for non-durables $Q_n(x)$ is the product of domestic saturated demand A and domestic demand density function (integral of domestic household income density function), namely, $Q_n(x) = \frac{A}{\delta_1\sqrt{2\pi}}\int_0^x e^{-\frac{(x-u_1)^2}{2\delta_1^2}}dx$. Export of non-durables $Q_f(x)$ is the product of export proportion β, global saturated demand B and global demand density function (integral of global household income density function), namely, $Q_f(x) = \frac{\beta B}{\delta_2\sqrt{2\pi}}\int_0^x e^{-\frac{(x-u_2)^2}{2\delta_2^2}}dx$. The total demand for non-durables $Q(x)$ is the sum of domestic demand and export, namely

$$Q(x) = Q_n(x) + Q_f(x) = \int_0^x \left(\frac{A}{\delta_1\sqrt{2\pi}} e^{-\frac{(x-u_1)^2}{2\delta_1^2}} + \frac{\beta B}{\delta_2\sqrt{2\pi}} e^{-\frac{(x-u_2)^2}{2\delta_2^2}} \right) dx.$$

According to the property of normal distribution, the distribution of total demand for non-durables is still S-shaped and its integral is still normally distributed, with the expected value $\Phi(\Phi = Au_1 + \beta Bu_2)$ and variance $\Omega^2(\Omega^2 = (A\delta_1)^2 + (\beta B\delta_2)^2)$, namely $P(z) = \frac{1}{\sqrt{2\pi} \times \Omega} \int_0^z e^{-\frac{(z-\Phi)^2}{2\Omega^2}} dz$, and the growth rate of total demand is $n = P'(z) = \frac{1}{\sqrt{2\pi} \times \Omega} e^{-\frac{(z-\Phi)^2}{2\Omega^2}}$. Since both the expected value and variance of total demand distribution are bigger than those of domestic demand distribution, the curves of demand distribution and growth rate of total demand are also flatter than those of domestic demand.

In order to illustrate the influence of export on the growth rate of non-durables demand, we assume that the domestic saturated demand for non-durable consumer goods A is 1, and the expected value u_1 and variance δ_1^2 of the domestic income distribution are 4 and 2 respectively; the global saturated demand B is 4; the expected value u_2 and variance δ_2^2 of global income distribution are 4 and 1 respectively; and the export proportion β remains unchanged at 10 percent. Under these conditions, we first estimate domestic demand, export demand and total demand, and all three types of demands are S-shaped. The maximum value of total demand rises to 1.4, which is the sum of the maximum value of domestic demand 1 and the maximum value of export 0.4. The simulation result is reported in Figure 4.10.

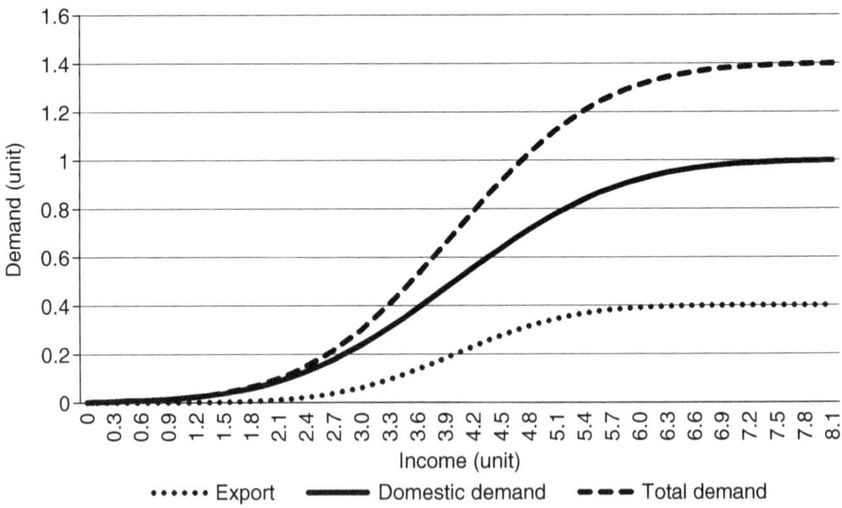

Figure 4.10 Influence of export on demand for non-durable consumer goods.

Source: calculated on assumed conditions.

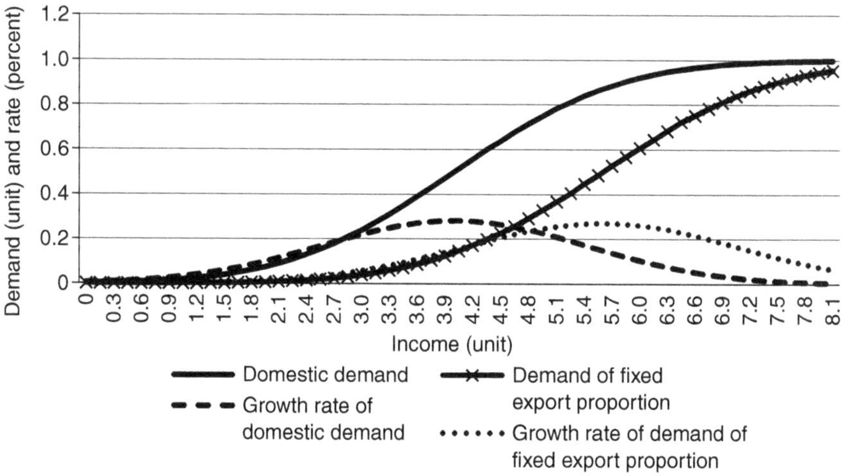

Figure 4.11 Influence of export on the distribution and growth rate of demand for non-durables.

Source: calculated on assumed conditions.

Second, we calculate the curves of total demand distribution and growth rate, as shown in Figure 4.11. The curve of total demand distribution (demand under fixed export–demand ratio) is still S-shaped, but it is flatter than the curve of domestic demand distribution. The curve of growth rate also exhibits a half-cycle fluctuation, but it is also flatter than the growth rate curve of domestic demand, and its maximum value is only 27.15 percent, which is lower than the maximum value of growth rate of domestic demand (28.22 percent).

Note

1 With $X \sim N(u_1, \delta^2_1)$, $Y \sim N(u_2, \delta^2_2)$, and the linear combination U of X and Y is still normally distributed distribution, namely, $U = aX + bY \sim N(au_1 + bu_2, a^2\delta^2_1 + b^2\delta^2_2)$, in which a and b are real numbers.

5 Categories of economic cycles and analysis of the factors affecting their periods

Traditional Western business cycle theories divide business cycles into short cycle, mid cycle, mid-to-long cycles and long cycles according to the period of the business cycle. The business cycles can also be classified into agricultural cycle, inventory cycle, equipment investment cycle, construction cycle and technological cycle, according to the determining factors of the business cycles. In reality, the periodic changes of economic indicators are often irregular. The duration and magnitude of the fluctuation of a single economic indicator can be very different in different time periods, making it difficult for traditional business cycle theories to explain. The analysis in this chapter shows that the growth of consumer demand and the economy as a whole embodies a type of endogenous cycle, namely the income distribution cycle, which is determined by the normality of household income distribution. The basic factors determining the period of the income distribution cycle are household income and consumer price level. Greater household income, higher household income growth rate, less income inequality, lower consumer price level and larger decline in price will shorten the period of the income distribution cycle. In addition, there are also actual demand cycles. Supply lag, replacement demand, product innovation and export can also give rise to the price adjustment cycle, replacement demand cycle, innovation demand cycle, export cycle and other actual demand cycles. The periods of these cycles depend on the length of supply lag period, the service lives of durable consumer goods, the frequency of product innovation, the distribution of foreign household income, export competitiveness and other factors. Through its impacts on household income and consumer price level, actual demand cycles affect the period of the income distribution cycle. With the higher household income, the transformation of industrial structure induced by the upgrading of the household consumption structure will inevitably change the period of the cycle. If the household consumption demand shifts from the consumer goods produced in light industries (with relatively lower value and shorter demand cycle periods) to the consumer goods produced in the heavy industries (with relatively higher value and longer demand cycle periods), then the period of both income distribution cycle and actual demand cycle would be extended. But in the later stage, the improvement of household income growth rate caused by rapid economic development can shorten the period of the income distribution cycle of consumer goods and the whole economy.

Household income and consumer prices are two basic factors that determine the period of the income distribution cycle

In Chapter 3 we proved that the consumption of both durable and non-durable consumer goods reflect the cycles that are determined by the normality of the household income distribution (hereinafter referred to as the "income distribution cycle"). According to the consumer goods demand growth function, the periods of income distribution cycle for durables and non-durables are both equal to twice the time needed to increase the income–price ratio from its initial level to its expected value. Therefore, the household income conditions (income level, growth rate and distribution) and the consumer price conditions (the current price level and its growth rate) are the two primary types of factors determining the period of income distribution cycle of consumer demand. A higher household income, a higher income growth rate or a smaller income inequality can lead to a shorter income distribution cycle. The more a consumer good costs when it is first produced and introduced to the market, and the smaller the subsequent price decline is, the longer it will take for the average consumer to reach the income level that makes such a good affordable, and the longer the income distribution cycle will be.

The function of the period of income distribution cycle of durables

Assume the household income is normally distributed, and let the saturation demand of durables be equal to 1. The demand for durables will also be normally distributed and the probability distribution density function of demand (hereinafter referred to as "demand function") can be expressed as $Q(x)=\frac{1}{\sigma\sqrt{2\pi}}e^{-\frac{(x-u)^2}{2\sigma^2}}$, where x is the ratio of the household income level y to the product price p (hereinafter referred to as the "income–price ratio"), u is the expected value of x and δ^2 is the variance of x. Here the household income level y is set to be the average household income of that year, and the product price p equals the price level of durables that year. The following can be inferred from this demand function: as the price of durable consumer goods p is very high when they are first produced, the income–price ratio x is very low; initially only the high-income households can afford such consumer goods. As price decreases or household income increases, the middle-income households and even low-income households will be able to afford these durables. Because household income is normally distributed, in the previous process of a rising income–price ratio, the group with demand for durables expands from high-income households to low-income households, and the demand for durables will also show features of normal distribution, like the household income distribution.

The growth function of the demand for durables is first-order derivative of the demand function, expressed as $n = Q'(x) = \frac{1}{\sigma\sqrt{2\pi}} e^{-\frac{(x-u)^2}{2\sigma^2}} \times \frac{(x-u)}{\delta^2}$. The function has the following characteristics: when the income–price ratio x is equal to $u-\delta$, the growth rate reaches its maximum value; when the income–price ratio x is equal to u, the growth rate reaches 0; when $x=u+\delta$, the growth rate reaches its minimum value. Therefore, its cycle length shall equal twice the time needed to increase the income–price ratio x from its initial level to its expected value u. Accordingly, we can express the period of the income distribution cycle of the demand for durables as $L = 2 \times \left[\log\left(\frac{u}{x_0} \right) \right] / \log N$, of which L is the period of the income distribution cycle of the demand for durables, N is the average growth rate of income–price ratio, and x_0 is the initial value of income–price ratio of durables.

We can set y_0 and p_0 as the initial values of household income and consumer price level, y_u and p_u as the expected values of household income and consumer price level, and N_y and N_p as the average growth rate of household income and the average growth rate of consumer price. As the income–price ratio increases from its initial value to its expected value, the period of the income distribution cycle of the demand for durables can be calculated as:

$$L = 2\left[\log\left(\frac{y_u}{y_0} \right) - \log\left(\frac{p_u}{p_0} \right) \right] / [\log N_y - \log N_p]$$

of which

$$x_0 = \frac{y_0}{p_0}, 0, N = \frac{N_y}{N_p}$$

The function of the period of income distribution cycle of non-durables

Assume the household income is normally distributed, and let the saturation demand of non-durables be equal to 1; thus the demand function of non-durables will be the integral of the distribution density function of household income, and can be expressed as $Q(x) = \int_0^x \frac{1}{\sigma\sqrt{2\pi}} e^{-\frac{(x-u)^2}{2\sigma^2}} dx$, of which x is the income–price ratio (the ratio of household income level y to the product price p, namely y/p), u is the expected value of x, δ^2 is the variance of x. We still set the household income level y to equal the average household income that every year and the product price p as the price level of non-durables. The following can be inferred from the demand function of non-durables: in the initial production period of non-durables, its price p is very high, the income–price ratio x is very low; initially only high-income households can afford such consumer goods. As price drops or household income increase, middle-income households and even low-income households will gradually be able to afford such goods. Due to the short service life of non-durables, the demand for them is continuous. The demand for non-durables expands with the growth of its consumer groups. The demand curve of non-durables is an S-shaped curve of the integral value of normal distribution density function.

The demand growth function of non-durables is the first-order derivative equation of the demand function, $n = Q'(x) = \frac{1}{\sigma\sqrt{2\pi}} e^{-\frac{(x-u)^2}{2\sigma^2}}$. The function has the following characteristics: When the income–price ratio increases to u, the growth rate reaches its maximum value. Its cycle length shall be twice the time needed to increase the income–price ratio from its initial level to its expected value u. Just like the period formula of the durables demand cycle, the period of the income distribution cycle of the demand for non-durables can be expressed as:

$$L = 2\log\left(\frac{u}{x_0}\right) / \log N = 2\left[\log\left(\frac{y_u}{y_0}\right) - \log\left(\frac{p_u}{p_0}\right)\right] / [\log N_y - \log N_p]$$

In the above formula, L is the period of the income distribution cycle of the demand for non-durables, N is the average growth rate of the income–price ratio, x_0 is the initial value of the income–price ratio of non-durables, y_0 and p_0 are the initial values of household income and consumer price level, y_u and p_u are the expected values of household income and consumer price level, and N_y and N_p are the average growth rate of household income and the average growth rate of consumer price level as the income–price ratio increases from its initial value to its expected value.

Basic factors affecting the period of income distribution cycle of consumer goods

Based on the period functions of durables demand cycle and non-durables demand growth half-cycle, we can classify the factors that affect the period of income distribution cycle of consumer goods into two fundamental groups, namely household income factors and consumer price factors. Specifically, to analyze the effects of these two on the period of the income distribution cycle, we can start with the following five aspects: household income and its growth rate, income inequality or income distribution, consumer price level, the interaction between household income and consumer price:

1 *The higher average growth rate of household income is, the shorter the period of income distribution cycle will be.* If the initial household income is relatively high, accordingly the ratio of the expected value of household income to the initial value of household income will be relatively low, which means it will take less time for the household income to increase from its initial level to its expected value, then the period of income distribution

cycle of consumer goods will be shorter. Similarly, if the average growth rate of household income N_y is relatively high, less time is needed for the household income to increase from its initial level to its expected value, and the period of the income distribution cycle of consumer goods will be shorter. Under the condition of fixed consumer price, the period of the income distribution cycle of consumer goods shall be twice the time needed to increase the household income from its initial income level to its expected value. Considering that household income growth rate depends on economic growth rate, the period of income distribution cycle of consumer goods shall be shorter during a period of accelerated economic growth.

2 *The smaller income inequality is, the shorter the period of income distribution cycle will be.* Given the expected value of household income, greater income inequality between households – greater variance – leads to slower household income growth (log N_y is smaller), flatter function curves of household income distribution, demand for durable consumer goods and growth rate of the demand for non-durable consumer goods, and a longer income distribution cycle. Conversely, if the income inequality between households is smaller, the household income growth rate will be higher (log N_y is greater). The period of income distribution cycle of consumer goods will also be shorter.[1]

3 *The higher the initial consumer price, the longer the period of the income distribution cycle will be.* According to the period function of the consumer demand cycle, it can be concluded that, given the expected value of price P_u, if the initial consumer price P_0 is higher, $\log(P_u / P_0)$ will be smaller, and the period of income distribution cycle of consumer goods will be longer. From the perspective of consumer purchasing power, higher initial consumer price means that it will take longer for the majority of consumers to accumulate enough purchasing power to purchase consumer goods, and the period of the demand cycle will also be longer.

4 *The greater the average decline in consumer price is, the shorter the period of the income distribution cycle will be.* In the context that the ratio of the initial consumer price to the expected consumer price P_u / P_0 is unchanged, if the average decline in consumer price is greater, then the time for the price to drop from the initial price to its expected value will be shorter, and the period of the income distribution cycle of consumer goods will also be shorter.

5 *Accelerated household income growth and the sharp decline in consumer price will greatly shorten the period of the consumer demand cycle.* Both accelerated household income growth and sharp decline in consumer price can shorten the consumer demand cycle. Before the demand for durables reaches its maximum or the non-durables reaches the demand saturation point, the acceleration of household income growth and drastic decline in consumer price often occur at the same time because income growth acceleration can shorten the income distribution cycle and increase demand at the same time. Demand increase usually leads to production expansion and cost

reduction, and the consumer price will also decrease as a result of lower production costs. Meanwhile, the expansion of consumer good production means the expansion of the entire industrial chain; economic growth and household income growth will be increased. Through a combination of consumer price decline and accelerated household income growth, the period of the income distribution cycle of consumer goods will be greatly shortened.

The consumer price adjustment cycle induced by supply lag and its influence on the period of the income distribution cycle

In the above analysis, we have assumed that there is no supply problem – the consumer goods supply can be adjusted in a timely manner as demand changes. This assumption does apply to consumer goods with relatively shorter production cycles. But for consumer goods with relatively longer production cycles, supply lag will make it difficult for supply–demand imbalance to be corrected promptly. The supply–demand imbalance will lead to a wide range of consumer price fluctuations, and the fluctuations in price can affect the future supply and change the future price trend, thus forming the consumer price adjustment cycle. The consumer price adjustment cycle induced by supply lag can change the price of consumer goods and affect the level and distribution of household income, and thus affect the duration of the income distribution cycle. The extent of its impact ultimately depends on the influence of the price adjustment cycle on consumer price level and household income.

A typical consumer price adjustment cycle is the price cycle of agricultural products. Agricultural products have the features of concentrated supply, seasonal output, long production cycle, relatively low demand–price elasticity, and so on. Once the supply–demand imbalance appears, such as an oversupply of products, the price of agricultural products will drop significantly. Because of asymmetric information, producers may reduce their scale of production, which will lead to insufficient supply in the future and a large rebounce in price, thus forming the price adjustment cycle of agricultural products. With regard to the price adjustment cycle of agricultural products, the cobweb model theory of British economist Kaldor in 1934 gives a perfect explanation. Using the model, we can generalize all the price adjustment cycles that have product supply lag. Assume that the current product demand D_t has a liner relationship with the current price P_t, or $D_t = \alpha - \beta \times P_t$, and the current product supply S_t is determined by the previous price P_{t-1}, or $S_t = \delta + \varphi \times P_{t-1}$. There exists a balance between current supply and demand, $D_t = S_t$. The first-order conditions can be obtained, $\beta \times P_t + \varphi \times P_{t-1} + \delta - \alpha = 0$, of which α, β, δ and φ are constant. The product price will have cyclical fluctuations when α, β, δ and φ meet certain conditions. If $\varphi > \beta$, the price P_t will exhibit a trend of amplified oscillation. If $\varphi = \beta$, the price P_t will show a trend of unit oscillation; if $\varphi < \beta$, the price P_t will show a trend of damped oscillation.[2]

The cobweb model only describes the fluctuations of price adjustment cycle based on one-period-lag supply. If the current supply is influenced by the multiple period lag prices, then the product price adjustment equation will be converted into a higher-order differential equation. For example, assuming that the current supply is determined by previous prices P_{t-1} and P_{t-2}, or $S_t=\delta+\varphi\times P_{t-1}+\theta\times P_{t-2}$, then the product price adjustment equation will be converted into a second-order differential equation, i.e., $\beta\times P_t+\varphi\times P_{t-1}+\theta\times P_{t-2}+\delta-\alpha=0$. The product price will show a trend of cyclical fluctuations when α, β, δ, φ and θ meet certain conditions. That is to say, as long as there is a certain lag period in the product supply, and the current price can affect the future supply, the product price will have an endogenous fluctuation cycle induced by supply lag, a phenomenon we can call the price adjustment cycle. The period and amplitude of the price adjustment cycle depend on the length of the lag period and the price elasticity of demand and supply. The inventory cycle of industrial products can be regarded as the inventory changes induced by the price adjustment cycle. In other words, the inventory cycle can be regarded as a translation of the price adjustment cycle into the quantity adjustment of product supply.

Returning to the example of agricultural products, we can now further analyze the effects of the price adjustment cycle on the income distribution cycle. The government's intervention in the agricultural product market makes the price cycle of agricultural products disappear or its degree of fluctuations are reduced. Consequently, the influence of the price cycle of agricultural products on the income distribution cycle will also disappear or be weakened significantly. Therefore, we only discuss the influence of price fluctuations on the period of the income distribution cycle in the case that there exists a price adjustment cycle. (1) Wide fluctuations in agricultural product prices in the short run can influence the period of the income distribution cycle in multiple ways. Insufficient supply will lead to price rise and exit of buyers, thus extending the income distribution cycle by increasing price. Surplus supply, on the other hand, will depress price and make the goods affordable to lower-income households, and the period of the income distribution cycle will be shortened as price is reduced. In the long run, the price cycle's effects on the period of income distribution cycle – extending the cycle in periods of rising prices and shortening the cycle in periods of decreasing prices – would offset each other. The ultimate impact of consumer price changes on the period of the income distribution cycle should be determined by the average change of consumer price during that period. (2) The fluctuations of the price of agricultural products can affect producer income, especially in countries or regions where agricultural products are the primary output of the economy. Agricultural product price rises can increase producers' income and increase household income growth, thus shortening the income distribution cycle. In periods of dropping prices, the reduction of producer income and the slowing down of household income growth will prolong the income distribution cycle. In the long run, the ultimate impact of income fluctuations induced by price fluctuations on the period of the income distribution cycle depends on the average growth rate of household income.

The replacement demand cycle of durables induced by replacement demand and its influence on the period of the income distribution cycle

Each consumer durable has its own service life, and consumers will repurchase the goods by the end of the product's service life. This constitutes the replacement demand for durable consumer goods. The actual demand for durables consists of the replacement demand and the initial demand. The durables demand cycle consists of two types of cycles. One type is the initial demand cycle determined by the income distribution and the income–price ratio, namely the income distribution cycle. The other type is the actual demand cycle, with the service lives of durables as its period, namely the replacement demand cycle. The effects of replacement demand cycle on income distribution cycle depend on the influence of replacement demand on the price of durables and household income.

The replacement demand cycle of durables

Considering that the service life of durable consumer goods is shorter than the period of the income distribution cycle, the actual demand for durables will include the initial demand and the replacement demand, and as the replacement demand is derived from the initial demand, if the initial demand is normally distributed, the replacement demand will also be normally distributed. The linear combination of multiple normal distributions will be normally distributed, so the actual demand, which consists of the replacement demand and the initial demand, will still be in conformity with normal distribution. The actual demand cycle will be jointly determined by the income distribution cycle and the replacement demand cycle. But the period of the actual demand cycle will be determined by the time of inception of replacement demand, or by the service life of durable consumer goods. This is because, given that the total saturation demand and individual saturation demand are fixed, before completely fulfilling the initial demand, the actual demand will be the sum of both initial demand and replacement demand; and after the fulfillment of the initial demand, the actual demand will be the sum of the first replacement demand and the second replacement demand (the second replacement demand occurs with the end of the service life of the first replacement). The actual demand will have cyclical fluctuations with the service lives of durables as its period, and the cycle of actual demand will also have continuous cyclical fluctuations with the service lives of durables as its period. Hence the actual demand cycle that is determined by the replacement demand can be called the replacement demand cycle.

In order to illustrate the impact of replacement demand on the actual demand cycle, here we take a consumer durable with normally distributed initial demand, expected income–price ratio of 4 and variance of 1, as an example to discuss the characteristics of the replacement demand cycle. Consider the following two scenarios.

Scenario 1: The service life of durables is greater than half of the period of the income distribution cycle, but smaller than the period of the income distribution cycle. In this scenario, the replacement demand occurs after the initial demand peaks, and the occurrence of replacement demand will not change the period when initial demand peaks. However, it puts the endpoint of the actual demand cycle ahead of the end point of the income distribution cycle, making the period of the actual demand cycle shorter than the period of the income distribution cycle. Specifically, assuming income–price ratio grows by 0.15 each unit period, and the initial demand is in conformity with normal distribution with the expected value of 4 and variance of 1, the period length of the income distribution cycle of consumer durables shall be 55 unit periods. Assuming that the replacement demand occurs when the income–price ratio is 6.45 (the 44th unit period), the replacement demand will cause the actual demand growth (see Figure 5.2 – the actual demand growth rate is 1) to change from negative to positive after the 50th unit period. The actual demand growth rate will change from negative to positive again at the 93rd unit period. With the influence of replacement demand, the period of actual demand cycle will decrease from 55 unit periods to 43 unit periods, which is close to the service life of the durable consumer goods.

Scenario 2: The service life of durable consumer goods is shorter than half of the period of the income distribution cycle. In this scenario, at least two rounds of replacement demand for durables will take place before the end of the first income distribution cycle. This means that if the replacement demand occurs after the turning point (the first inflexion) of initial demand (the maximum value of initial demand growth), then another round of replacement demand will take place before the end of this income distribution cycle period; and if the replacement demand occurs before the turning point of initial demand, then at least three rounds of replacement demand will occur afterwards. Here, we have only discussed the scenario in which the replacement demand occurs after the turning point of initial demand and before the peak point of initial demand. In this scenario, the replacement demand will make the maximum value of actual demand greater than the maximum value of initial demand, because the replacement demand is still increasing when the initial demand reaches its maximum value. The replacement demand will not change the period when the maximum demand occurs, but it will prevent the actual demand curve developing a downward trend after the actual demand reaches its maximum value, as the initial demand curve goes downward after such a point. Instead, the actual demand will exhibit a growth pattern of cyclical fluctuations that is not downward trending because the replacement demand will offset the downward trend of initial demand. The actual demand cycle develops a cyclical pattern after this point, which has a period that is equal to the service life of durable consumer goods, far shorter than the period of the income distribution cycle. As shown in Figures 5.1 and 5.2, we assume that the first round of replacement demand occurs when the income–price ratio reaches 3.15 (the 22nd unit period, when the initial demand growth rate reaches its maximum value at an income–price ratio of 3), and the

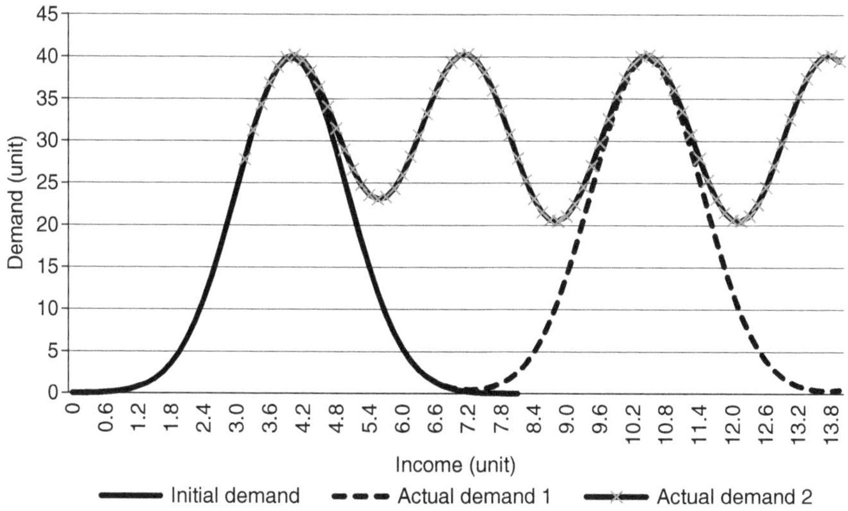

Figure 5.1 The influence of replacement demand on the actual demand for durable consumer goods (%).

Data source: the data are obtained through the simulated calculation based on the assumed conditions of income-to-price ratio 4 and variance 1.

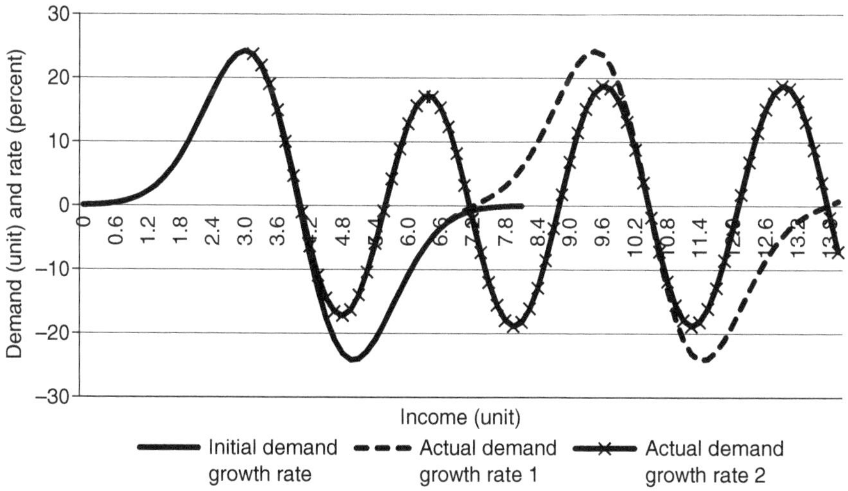

Figure 5.2 The influence of replacement demand on the actual demand cycle of durable consumer goods (%).

Data source: the data are obtained through the simulated calculation based on the assumed conditions of income-to-price ratio 4 and variance 1.

second round of replacement demand occurs during the 44th unit period (still within the income distribution cycle). The new rounds of replacement demand occur every 22 unit periods. In this scenario, the actual demand (the actual demand growth is 2 in Figure 5.1) no longer returns to the level of zero, but fluctuates between 20 and 40 units. The period of actual demand growth (the actual demand growth is 2 in Figure 5.2) is greatly shortened: 22 periods by trough-to-trough counting. In other words, the period of actual demand cycle is shortened to the service life of durable consumer goods.

The influence of replacement demand cycle on the period of the income distribution cycle

The replacement demand will convert the actual demand cycle for durables into the replacement demand cycle with a period equal to the service life of durables. The impact of replacement demand on the income distribution cycle is mainly manifested in the former's influence on consumer price and household income: The replacement demand is the repurchase behavior derived from the initial demand, given that the replacement demand does not change saturation demand or the income–price ratio, the initial demand distribution and its income distribution cycle – determined by the income distribution and the income–price ratio – will not change. However, replacement demand, as demand beyond the initial demand, will inevitably affect the price of durable consumer goods, the household income level and the period of the income distribution cycle. The replacement demand leads to the expansion of actual demand scale. The expansion of actual demand scale will increase the scale of production, and the production cost of durables will be reduced due to economies of scale, thus resulting in a decrease in product price. On the other hand, the expansion of production scale means a higher economic growth rate, and household income level and growth rate will increase accordingly. The product price decrease and household income increase induced by the replacement demand will shorten the income distribution cycle.

In addition, as for the cumulative demand for durable consumer goods, because the replacement demand is merely the repurchase behavior derived from initial demand or earlier demand, the cumulative demand for durable consumer goods is still the integral of the initial demand with a bell-shaped distribution. It is S-shaped. But the drop in product price and the improvement of household income level induced by the replacement demand can shorten the S-shape. The period of the income distribution cycle of durable consumer goods will be shortened.

The innovation demand cycle induced by product innovation and its influence on the period of income distribution cycle of consumer goods

In traditional business cycle theories, technological progress is the decisive factor for cycles of periods longer than 20 years. It refers to the revolutionary technological innovation that can result in a significant change in industrial structure. However, product innovation induced by smaller technological progress can also affect the consumer demand cycle. The new consumer demand cycle induced by a significant technological innovation also obeys the rules of the income distribution cycle of general consumer goods. In this section, we focus on the influence of product innovation on the actual consumer demand cycle. The analysis shows that if the new product totally replaces the old one, the cycle of consumer goods will become the cycle of the demand for new products. When the new products only partially replace the original products, especially when the replacement renewal demand or product innovation leads to replacement demand, the actual demand cycle will become the innovation demand cycle, with the innovation duration as its period. The shorter the innovation duration is, the shorter the period of innovation demand cycle will be, and the smaller the amplitude. When innovation can change household income and consumer price level, the period of the income distribution cycle of consumer goods will be altered.

Usually, entrepreneurial innovations give rise to new products that are superior to the original product. The new product has a big influence on the replacement demand and on the original product price. Here, we will discuss the influence of product innovation on the consumer demand cycle according to different levels of substitution of new products to the original ones.

Demand for new products fully replaces demand for original products

In this case, the cycle of the demand for original products will become the cycle of the demand for new products. In general, the price of the new products is higher than that of the original ones. Assuming that demand for the new products will fully replace the demand for the original products, saturation demand will be unchanged. But based on the period formula of the consumer demand cycle, we know that the period of the income distribution cycle of consumer goods will be extended because of the rise in prices of new products.

Demand for new products only replaces the replacement demand for original products

Normally, the emergence of new products will replace part of the demand for original products. In particular, the replacement demand for original products will be replaced by demand for new products. When the replacement demand is replaced by demand for new products, there may be two scenarios: First, the original products are replaced by demand for new products when the replacement demand occurs, then the replacement demand will turn into part of the demand for new products. Hence the actual demand will be composed of the initial demand and the replacement demand or the demand for new products. The influence of new products on the actual demand cycle is the same as the influence of replacement demand on the actual demand cycle. With regard to durable consumer goods, the

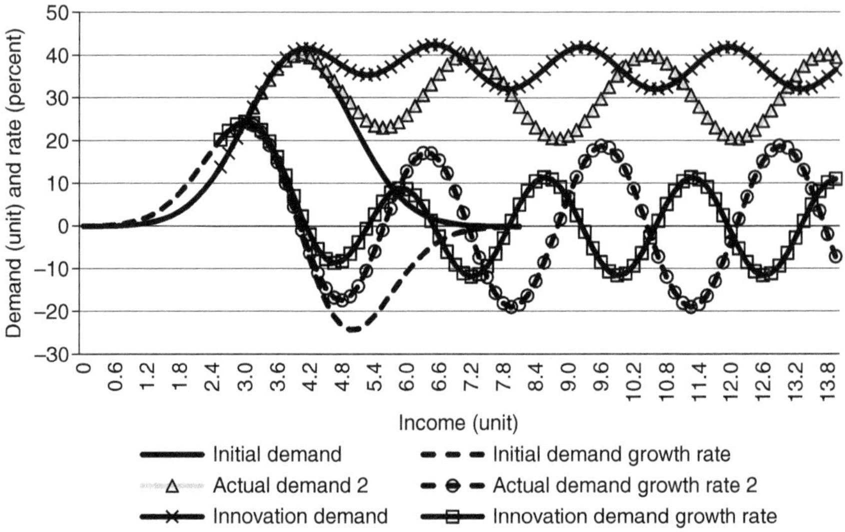

Figure 5.3 The influence of product innovation on the actual demand cycle (%).

Data source: the data are obtained through the simulated calculation based on the assumed conditions of income-to-price ratio 4 and variance 1.

period of the actual demand cycle will be equivalent to the service life of the product, as shown in Figure 5.3. The second scenario is one in which product innovation caused the replacement demand to occur earlier than usual. The period of product innovation is less than the service life of products. The period of the actual demand cycle will be transformed into the period of product innovation, and the amplitude of actual demand cycle will decrease, as shown in Figure 5.3. In both scenarios, the influence of new products on the income distribution cycle of the initial demand depends on whether the household income level and the original product price have been altered by the coming of new products. Normally, the emergence of new products can result in a decline in the original product price, thus shortening the period of income distribution cycle. If new products can also lead to an increase in the household income growth rate, then the period of the income distribution cycle of original products will be further shortened.

Innovation demand partly replaces the demand for original products and the replacement demand

In this scenario, the actual demand for products consists of part of the demand for original products and the demand for new products. The period of the actual demand cycle will be between the period of the income distribution cycle of the demand for original products and the period of the income distribution cycle of the demand for new products.

Simulation analysis of the replacement demand induced by product innovation

In order to illustrate the influence of technological innovation on the actual demand cycle, here we still take as an example the durables with the initial demand that obeys the normal distribution with the expected income–price ratio 4 and variance 1. Assuming that: (a) the product innovation occurs at the 18th period when the income–price ratio equals 2.55; (b) is four periods ahead of the replacement demand (meaning that the product innovation causes the replacement demand to occur earlier); and (c) the frequency of product innovation remains the same as 18 periods, then the actual demand (the innovation demand shown in Figure 5.3) will be the sum of the initial demand and the demand for new products, and the range of its fluctuations is between 32 to 42 units, the period of the actual demand cycle (the innovation demand growth rate shown in Figure 5.3) will be 18 periods, and the amplitude of fluctuations will be between 11 and 9 percent. Compared to the changes of the actual demand cycle induced by the replacement demand, because we assume that the period of product innovation is less than the period of replacement demand (the service life of products), product innovation will shorten the period of the actual demand cycle and decrease its amplitude.

The influence of export on the period of the income distribution cycle of consumer goods

The period formulas of the durable consumer goods demand cycle and the non-durable consumer goods demand cycle are the same. Taking durable consumer goods as an example, we analyze the influence of export on the period of the consumer demand cycle. In Chapter 4 we confirmed that even taking into consideration the international market demand, a country's total demand for durable consumer goods will still be normally distributed. The probability distribution density function of its demand depends on five major factors: domestic population scale, domestic income distribution, global population scale, global income distribution and the share of a country's exports in global demand. These five major factors can also affect the period of the cycle of durable consumer goods demand. The export of consumer goods increases the expected value of income–price ratio and extends the period of the demand cycle. Gradually increasing export share can also raise the expected value of the income–price ratio and extend the period of the durable consumer goods demand cycle. The export of consumer goods can affect the growth rates of consumer price and household income, thus changing the period of the cycle. Foreign household income growth and population size can also affect the period of consumer demand cycle.

In the case that domestic and foreign household income distributions are normally distributed, let domestic demand distribution be $X \sim N(\mu_1, \delta^2{}_1)$, and international demand distribution be $Y \sim N(u_2, \delta^2{}_2)$. Assuming that domestic population size is A, international population size is B, and the export share in the international market is β, then a country's total demand for durable consumer goods shall still be in conformity with the normal distribution. Its probability distribution density function shall be $P(z)=\frac{1}{\sqrt{2\pi}\times\Omega}e^{\frac{(z-\Phi)^2}{2\Omega^2}}$, of which the expected value $\varphi=Au_1+\beta Bu_2$, and the variance $\Omega^2=(A\delta_1)^2+(\beta B\delta_2)^2$. On this basis, assuming that price is the same at home and abroad, then the period formula of the durable consumer goods demand cycle can be converted into:

$$L=2\left[\log\left(\frac{\Phi}{z_0}\right)/\log N\right]=2\left[\log\left(\frac{u_0}{x_0}\right)-\log\left(\frac{p_u}{p_0}\right)\right]/[\log N_y-\log N_p]$$

In the above formulas, the initial value X_0 and the expected value X_u of income distribution are the weighted values of the initial values and expected values of domestic and foreign household income distribution with domestic and foreign population sizes as the weights. $X_0=AY_{10}+\beta BY_{20}$, $X_u=AY_{1u}+\beta BY_{2u}$, of which Y_1 and Y_2 are domestic household income and foreign household income respectively.

Based on the probability distribution density function of the demand for durable consumer goods and the period formula of the demand cycle, we can come to the following five conclusions. Considering that the period formula of non-durable consumer goods demand cycle is similar to that of the durable consumer goods demand cycle, when analyzing influence of export on the period of non-durable consumer goods demand cycle, these conclusions also apply:

1 The export of consumer goods increases the expected value of the income–price ratio. Given a constant growth rate of the income–price ratio, the time needed to increase the income–price ratio from the initial value to the expected value will be extended, and the period of the durable consumer goods demand cycle will also be extended.
2 The rising export share β can increase the expected value of the income–price ratio and extend the rise phase and period of durable consumer goods demand cycle.
3 The export of durable consumer goods can also affect consumer price and domestic household income growth rate, thus changing the period of the demand cycle. If the accelerated expansion of production scale induced by export causes a drastic decline in average price, then the period of the demand cycle will be shortened. The export of consumer goods can increase domestic household income, thus the rise in domestic household income growth rate leads to the increase of household average income growth rate N_y, and the period of the demand cycle will also be shortened.
4 The growth of foreign household income will also change the period of the demand cycle. If foreign household income growth rate increase, then the weighted income growth rate N_y will also increase, thus shortening the period of the durable consumer goods demand cycle.
5 Population size can also affect the period of the consumer demand cycle. A country's population size relative to global population size determines the

relative size of its domestic market to the international market. When domestic population size is relatively large, the period of the demand cycle mainly depends on the period of the domestic demand cycle. Conversely, in a country with a relatively small population size, the period of the consumer demand cycle mainly depends on the period of the international market demand cycle.

The period of the consumer demand cycle and the period of the economic cycle

In the context that the production chain of consumer goods fluctuates synchronously with consumer demand, the amplitude of the whole industrial cycle is greater than the amplitude of the consumer demand cycle, but the period is the same. The influence of the industrial cycle on the economic cycle depends on the status of the industry in the whole economy, or the weight of its industrial added-value to GDP. The period of the cycle of the entire economy is determined by the periods of the cycle of its dominant industries.

In Chapter 3 we analyzed the internal relations among the consumer demand cycle, the industrial cycle and the economic cycle. The relationship is captured by the functions $N_y = (\sum_1^N \beta^n + 1) \times \frac{c}{y} \times N_c$ and $N = \sum_1^n \frac{y_n}{Y} \times N_{y_n}$, of which N_y, N_c and N are the industrial growth rate, the consumer demand growth rate and the economic growth rate, y, c and Y are the industry's output, the consumer demand and GDP, $\beta(0<\beta<1)$ is the accelerator of consumer demand (the investment expansion effect of one unit increase in consumer demand on the supply chain) and the coefficient $(\Sigma^N{}_1\beta^n+1)$ is the industry multiplier of consumer goods. As for the relationship between the industrial output growth rate N_y and the consumer demand growth rate, given that the upstream enterprises' output fluctuates synchronously with the consumer demand, the output growth rate of any consumer goods industry will fluctuate synchronously with the consumer demand growth rate. The period of the industrial cycle will be the same as the period of the consumer demand cycle. But from the consumer demand growth rate to the industry output growth rate, the industry multiplier is greater than 1, so the amplitude of the industrial cycle is greater than that of the consumer demand cycle. For the relationship between the industrial growth rate N_{y_n} and the economic growth rate N, the economic growth rate and its fluctuation trend are jointly determined by various industries' output growth rates and the share of their outputs in the total output. But the period of the output cycle of the industry that accounts for the highest share in the total output plays a decisive role in the period of the whole economic cycle.

The previous analysis has shown that there exist two categories of cycle, one being the income distribution cycle, which is determined by the normality of household income distribution, and the other being the actual demand cycle, which is caused by supply lag, replacement demand, innovation demand and export. From the perspective of the relations among the consumer demand cycle, the industrial cycle and the economic cycle, the industrial cycle and the economic cycle each will also inevitably have two categories of cycles, namely the income distribution cycle determined by the household income distribution and the actual demand cycle. Among them, the period of the income distribution cycle of the industry and the economy is relatively longer, and the basic factors that determine its period are household income level and consumer price. The actual demand cycle of the industry and the economy can also be divided into the price adjustment cycle, the replacement demand cycle, the innovation demand cycle and the export cycle. The periods of these cycles also depend on the supply lag of consumer goods, the service life of durable consumer goods, the period of product innovation and the export growth. The actual demand cycle of consumer goods can change consumer price level and household income, thus changing the period of the income distribution cycle of consumer goods, which can also inevitably lead to changes in the period of the income distribution cycle of industry and the economy.

According to the relationship between the consumer demand cycle and the economic cycle, we can further infer that the consumption structure determines the fluctuation pattern of the economic cycle by shaping the industrial structure. Unchanged consumption structure means unchanged industrial structure, and the fluctuation patterns of the economic cycle will not change. The upgrading of the consumption structure can change the period and the amplitude of the economic cycle. When consumer demand shifts from non-durable consumer goods with relatively lower value and a shorter demand cycle period to durable consumer goods with relatively higher value and a longer demand cycle period, the period of the economic cycle will extend, and its amplitude will increase. It is worth mentioning here that the process of consumption structure upgrading from electric appliances and other light industrial consumer goods to automobiles, houses and other heavy industrial consumer goods also corresponds with an accelerating phase of economic growth. Household income is increasing rapidly along with the accelerating economic growth, which will shorten the period of the consumer demand cycle and partially offset the lengthening effect of consumption structure upgrading on the period of the economic cycle.

Notes

1 In this scenario, household income shall obey the normal distribution with expected value u and standard variance δ, so the household income growth rate shall be the first-order derivative of the normal density function of income distribution, i.e., $n = \frac{1}{\sigma\sqrt{2\pi}} e^{-\frac{(x-u)^2}{2\sigma^2}} \times \frac{(u-x)}{\delta^2}$; under the condition of an invariable expected value of income u, if the income inequality is greater, then the variance of income δ^2 will be greater, and the income growth rate n will be smaller.

2 See Jiang Zhongyi (1999: 734–737).

6 Factors affecting the amplitude of the economic cycle

In the real economy, multiple types of cyclical fluctuation can occur in the courses of consumer demand growth and economic growth. For instance, there are the income distribution cycle, the price adjustment cycle, the replacement demand cycle, innovation demand cycle and export cycle, induced respectively by the normality of household income distribution, supply lag, replacement demand, product innovation and export. Produced by distinctive causes, different economic cycles have different amplitudes. Significant amplitude differences also exist in different periods of the same cycle. Income–price ratio variance shapes consumption and income distribution cycles. Less income inequality, higher consumer prices and more rapid consumption and economic growth lead to a greater amplitude of the income distribution cycle. The price elasticity of supply and demand for consumer goods determines the amplitude of the price adjustment cycle. An increase in price elasticity of supply or a decrease in price elasticity of demand can increase the amplitude of the price adjustment cycle. Longer service lives of consumer durables result in a higher amplitude of the consumer goods replacement demand cycle, and higher amplitude of the replacement demand cycle of industrial output and economy. More frequent product innovations reduce the amplitude of the innovation demand cycle of consumer goods and lower the amplitude of the innovation demand cycle of industrial output and economy. Expanding export raises the variance of the income–price ratio and lessens the amplitude of consumer demand and the economic cycle. The industry multiplier for consumer goods measures the degree of amplification from consumption to industrial output. A greater industry multiplier for consumer goods also causes the amplitude of the economic cycle to be greater. For consumer goods with a long industry production chain and a great industry accelerator β, its industry multiplier would also be great. A greater industry multiplier means the same consumer demand growth rate will result in a higher industrial output growth rate. The share of consumption in GDP is indicative of the potential impact of consumer demand structure and industrial structure on the amplitude of the economic cycle. The amplitude of the economic cycle increases with a rising share of consumer goods of the demand cycle that have relatively great amplitude – heavy industrial consumer durables, for instance. The amplitude of the economic cycle decreases with a rising share of consumer goods of the demand cycle that have relatively smaller amplitude – consumer non-durables, for instance.

Factors influencing the amplitude of the income distribution cycle of consumer goods

According to the growth function of consumer demand, the variance of the income–price ratio determines the amplitudes of the income distribution cycles of both consumer durables and consumer non-durables. A greater variance of the income–price ratio corresponds to a lower amplitude of the income distribution cycle of consumer goods. The income–price ratio is the ratio of household income level to consumer price level. Higher household income level, greater income inequality and lower consumer price level give rise to a higher variance of the income–price ratio, which will reduce the amplitude of the income distribution cycle of consumer goods. The growth function of durable consumer goods differs from that of non-durables. The variance of the income–price ratio has a greater impact on the amplitude of the former. Reducing income–price ratio will lower the amplitude of the consumer goods income distribution cycle. If we hold household income and consumer prices constant, reductions in income inequality can effectively boost consumption demand growth.

Given that household income is normally distributed, and letting the saturation demand for consumer goods be 1, the demand for consumer durables will also be normally distributed. The demand for consumer non-durables shall be the integral of the probability density function of household income distribution. In such a case, the probability density functions of the demand for consumer durables and non-durables shall be $Q(x)=\frac{1}{\sigma\sqrt{2\pi}}e^{-\frac{(x-u)^2}{2\sigma^2}}$ and $Q(x)=\int_0^x \frac{1}{\sigma\sqrt{2\pi}}e^{-\frac{(x-u)^2}{2\sigma^2}}dx$, where x is the ratio of household income level y to product price p, namely y/p, u is the expected value of x and σ^2 is the variance of x.

In the equation below, the asterisk should be a multi - the equation changes when I attempt to edit it

According to the properties of the derivative function, the growth rate of the demand for consumer durables shall be the first-order derivative of the demand function, i.e., $n=Q'(x)=\frac{1}{\sigma\sqrt{2\pi}}e^{-\frac{(x-u)^2}{2\sigma^2}}\times\frac{(u-x)}{\delta^2}$. The demand growth rate reaches the maximum value when the income–price ratio equals to $u-\delta$, 0 when the income–price ratio equals u, and the minimum value when the income–price ratio equals $u+\delta$. The amplitude of the income distribution cycle of consumer durables, H, is the magnitude of fluctuation as demand growth decelerates from the maximum value to the minimum value, i.e., $H=\frac{2e^{-\frac{1}{2}}}{\sigma^2\sqrt{2\pi}}$.

According to the properties of the derivative function, the growth rate of the demand for consumer non-durables shall be the first-order derivative of the demand function, i.e., $n = \frac{1}{\sigma\sqrt{2\pi}} e^{-\frac{(x-u)^2}{2\sigma^2}}$. Its shape is a normal distribution curve. The demand growth rate reaches the maximum value when the income–price ratio is equal to u. The amplitude of consumer non-durables income distribution cycle, H, equals the maximum value of demand growth, i.e., $H = \frac{1}{\sigma\sqrt{2\pi}}$.

From the amplitude formulas of the income distribution cycles of consumer durables and non-durables, it can be inferred that the amplitude of the income distribution cycle of consumer demand depends on the standard deviation of income–price ratio δ. The greater the standard deviation is, the lower the amplitude will be. The factors that determine the standard deviation of the income–price ratio are the same ones that determine the amplitude of the income distribution cycle of consumer goods. The variance of income–price ratio is the sum of squared deviations between the actual values and expected value of income–price ratio, or $\delta^2 = \sum_{i=1}^{n}(x_i - u)^2 = \sum_{i=1}^{n}\left(\frac{y_i}{p_i} - \frac{y_u}{p_u}\right)^2$, where y_u and p_u are the expected values of household income and consumer price. Based on the variance formulas of the income–price ratio, it can be inferred that household income and consumer price are the basic factors affecting the amplitude of the income distribution cycle of consumer goods:

1 *Higher household income level leads to a greater variance of income–price ratio and a lower amplitude of the income distribution cycle of consumer goods.* Given a constant household income gap, a higher household income results in a greater income–price ratio, a greater variance of income–price ratio and a lower amplitude of the consumer goods income distribution cycle.
2 *Greater income inequality leads to a greater variance of income–price ratio and a lower amplitude of the income distribution cycle of consumer goods.* Without considering the impact of household income changes on consumer price, widening inequality can directly increase the variance of the income–price ratio and decrease the amplitude of the income distribution cycle.
3 *Higher consumer price level leads to a smaller variance of income–price ratio and a greater amplitude of the income distribution cycle of consumer goods.* Under the condition of unchanging household income and income inequality, a higher consumer price level results in a lower income–price ratio and a smaller variance of income–price ratio. Consequently, the amplitude of the income distribution cycle of consumer goods will be larger.
4 *A change in household income or consumer price will have a much greater impact on the amplitude of the income distribution cycle of consumer durables than that of consumer non-durables.* Starting with the same variance

of income–price ratio, a marginal reduction in the variance of the income–price ratio will result in a much greater increase in the amplitude of the income distribution cycle of consumer durables than that of consumer non-durables. In the acceleration phase of consumer demand growth, the same rule dictates that a reduction in the variance of income–price ratio will result in much greater growth acceleration in the demand for consumer durables than consumer non-durables.

Factors influencing the amplitude of the price adjustment cycle of consumer goods

Supply lags give rise to cyclical price adjustments in consumption demand. The duration of supply lag determines the period of the price adjustment cycle. The demand fluctuation's shape and amplitude depend on the price elasticity of supply and demand for consumer goods. For consumer goods, a greater price elasticity of supply or a smaller price elasticity of demand can result in a greater amplitude of demand. When the price elasticity of supply and demand are the same, the amplitude of demand will be unchanged. When the price elasticity of demand is greater, the amplitude of demand will decrease continuously. When the price elasticity of supply is greater, the amplitude of demand will increase continuously.

Assuming that the supply lags by one period, demand is determined by the spot price ($D_t=\alpha-\beta\times P_t$), supply is determined by the last period's price ($S_t+\delta+\varphi\times P_{t-1}$), and there exists a equilibrium between current supply and demand ($D_t=S_t$). The fluctuation equation of consumer price shall be $\beta\times P_t+\varphi\times P_{t-1}+\delta-\alpha=0$, where β is the price elasticity of demand for consumer goods, φ is the price elasticity of supply for consumer goods and α and δ are constants. Given the assumption of a current equilibrium, the equation of the price adjustment cycle can be converted into the demand adjustment equation $\beta\times D_t+\varphi\times D_{t-1}=\delta\times\beta+\alpha\times\varphi$, and the time series function of demand shall be $D_t=\left(D_0-\dfrac{\alpha\times\varphi-\delta\times\beta}{\beta+\varphi}\right)\times\left(-\dfrac{\varphi}{\beta}\right)^t+\dfrac{\alpha\times\varphi-\delta\times\beta}{\beta+\varphi}$ (Jiang Zhongyi 1999). From the time series function of demand, it can be inferred that the constant term $\dfrac{\alpha\times\varphi-\delta\times\beta}{\beta+\varphi}$ is the equilibrium value of demand, and the fluctuating term $\left(D_0-\dfrac{\alpha\times\varphi-\delta\times\beta}{\beta+\varphi}\right)\times\left(-\dfrac{\varphi}{\beta}\right)^t$ is jointly determined by three factors. The first factor is the deviation of the initial value of demand D_0 from its equilibrium value. The second factor is the ratio of the price elasticity of supply to that of demand φ/β. The third factor is time t. The deviation of initial demand value from equilibrium determines the base fluctuation range of demand. The ratio between supply and demand price elasticities, together with time, determines the fluctuation state of demand and the trend of fluctuation range. Specifically, it can be divided into three situations: (1) When the price elasticities of consumer goods supply and demand are equal, or $\varphi=\beta$, the demand will exhibit a trend of unit oscillation. The amplitude will be twice the deviation of the initial demand value from its equilibrium value. The deviation of initial demand from its equilibrium value depends on the price elasticities of supply and demand. Greater price elasticities create greater deviation and greater amplitude of demand fluctuation. Contrariwise, the smaller price elasticities create smaller deviation and a lower amplitude of demand fluctuation. (2) When the price elasticity of supply of consumer goods is greater than that of demand, meaning $\beta>\varphi$ or $\varphi/\beta<1$, the demand will exhibit a trend of damped oscillation with its equilibrium value as the center. As time progresses, the amplitude of demand fluctuation decreases continuously from the initial value, which equals the deviation of initial demand from the equilibrium value. The price elasticities of supply and demand can also affect the amplitude of demand fluctuation. When the difference between the price elasticity of demand and the price elasticity of supply increases, the amplitude of demand fluctuation will be smaller and will converge to zero faster. Conversely, if such difference decreases, the amplitude of demand fluctuation will be greater, and the convergence speed will be slower. (3) When the price elasticity of supply of consumer goods is less than that of demand, meaning $\beta<\varphi$ or $\varphi/\beta>1$, the demand will exhibit a trend of amplifying oscillation with its equilibrium value as the center. The amplitude of demand increases continuously from its initial value, which equals the deviation of initial demand from the equilibrium value. When the difference between the price elasticity of supply and the price elasticity of demand increases, the amplitude of demand will be larger, and the amplification of the amplitude of demand fluctuation will be greater. Conversely, when the difference between the price elasticity of supply and the price elasticity of demand diminishes, the amplitude of demand will be smaller, and the amplification will be weaker. *In general, the amplitude of the price adjustment cycle depends on the price elasticities of supply and demand. When price elasticities of supply and demand differ, a greater price elasticity of supply or a smaller price elasticity of demand will make the amplitude of the price adjustment cycle greater.*

Factors influencing the amplitude of the replacement demand cycle of consumer goods

Replacement demand puts replacement demand cycles into the actual demand for consumer durables. The service life of consumer durables determines the period of the replacement demand cycle. When the service life of consumer durables, or the period of the replacement demand cycle, is shorter than the period of the income distribution cycle, the actual demand for consumer durables will include both the replacement demand and the initial demand. In addition, the actual demand will still be normally distributed, but the fluctuation range of actual demand will be narrower than that of the demand of the income distribution demand cycle. The amplitude of actual demand growth rate fluctuations still depends on income–price ratio changes. However, the amplitude will be significantly lower than the amplitude of the income distribution cycle. A shorter period of the replacement demand cycle results in a lower amplitude.

When the service life of consumer durables, or the period of the replacement demand cycle, is shorter than the period of the income distribution cycle, the actual demand for consumer durables will consist both of the replacement demand and the initial demand. Considering that the replacement demand is the repurchase behavior derived from initial demand, the replacement demand will still be normally distributed. The actual demand, which includes the replacement demand and the initial demand, will also be normally distributed. The period of the replacement demand cycle is determined by the service life of consumer durables, and its amplitude depends on income–price ratio changes. *However, as the replacement demand shortens the period of the actual demand cycle, making it shorter than the period of the income distribution cycle, the amplitude of the replacement demand cycle will be significantly lower than that of the income distribution cycle. The shorter the period of the replacement demand cycle is, the lower its amplitude will be.* (1) Upon the inception of replacement demand, actual demand will deviate from initial demand. Regardless of the inception point of replacement demand, the value of actual demand will always be above the value of initial demand, and the minimum value of actual demand will also be greater than that of initial demand. This means that the initial demand and the endpoint demand of the replacement demand cycle are both greater than those of the income distribution cycle. The inception point of the replacement demand cycle appears after the inception point of the income distribution cycle. However, its endpoint occurs before the endpoint of the income distribution cycle. (2) If the replacement demand occurs before the peak of initial demand, then before the initial demand reaches its maximum value, both the replacement demand and the initial demand will be rising, and therefore the actual demand will continue to rise as well. After the initial demand passes its maximum value and starts a gradual decline, the replacement demand will continue to rise. Only when the increase in replacement demand exceeds the decrease in initial demand will actual demand rebound and enter the rising phase of the replacement demand cycle. In other words, the replacement demand cycle occurs after the initial demand reaches its maximum. (3) A shorter service life of consumer durables means the replacement demand occurs earlier. It also means that the lower bound of actual demand will be greater after initial demand peaks and that the difference between the maximum value and the minimum value of actual demand will be smaller. In other words, under the influence of continuous replacement demand, a lower amplitude of actual demand's cyclical fluctuation results in a narrower fluctuation range of actual demand growth rate and lower amplitude of the replacement demand cycle.

We can use a hypothetical consumer durable to illustrate the impact of consumer durables' service lives, or the period of the replacement demand cycle, on the amplitude of the replacement demand cycle. Assuming the consumer durable has an initial demand that is normally distributed, with expected income–price ratio 4 and variance 1, the following two scenarios can take place:

Scenario 1: The service life of the consumer durable is greater than the half period of the income distribution cycle but less than the period of the income distribution of cycle. In the case that the initial demand is normally distributed with expected income–price ratio of 4 and variance of 1, the maximum value of the initial demand for consumer durables will be 39.89 units (the total demand is 100 units), and the amplitude of the income distribution cycle will be 48.4 percent (the highest growth rate is 24.2 percent). Assuming the income–price ratio increases by 0.15 every unit period, the length of the income distribution cycle will be 55 unit periods. The replacement demand will occur when the income–price ratio reaches 6.45, or in the 44th unit period. The replacement demand will cause the fluctuation range of actual demand to decrease from 40 units, which is the fluctuation range of the income distribution cycle, to 39.4 units. The fluctuation range of actual demand growth rate shall be 48.27 percent (see *Actual Demand Growth Rate 1* in Figure 6.2), which is only 0.13 percent less than the amplitude of the income distribution cycle. This is to say, when the service life of a consumer durable or the period of the replacement demand cycle is very long, replacement demand will only have a small impact on the amplitude of the actual demand cycle.

Scenario 2: The service life of the consumer durable is shorter than the half period of the income distribution cycle. In this scenario, the replacement demand will cause the maximum value of actual demand to exceed the maximum value of initial demand. Because the replacement demand is still increasing when the initial demand reaches its maximum value, the introduction of replacement demand will not change the time when the maximum demand occurs. However, after reaching its maximum value, the actual demand will behave differently from the initial demand, which is decreasing. Instead, the actual demand will exhibit cyclical fluctuations because the introduction of replacement demand offsets the fall in initial demand. The period of the actual demand cycle will also become equal to the service life of the consumer durable, which is far shorter than the period of the income distribution cycle. As shown in Figures 6.1 and 6.2, we assume that the first replacement demand occurs when the income–price ratio reaches 3.15 during the 22nd unit period, and that the second replacement demand occurs during the 44th unit period (still within the income distribution cycle); then a new round of replacement demand would occur every 22 unit periods. Affected by the replacement demand, the actual demand (see *Actual Demand 2* in Figure 6.1) no longer falls back to the level near zero, but fluctuates between 20 and 40 units. The period of the actual demand cycle (see *Actual Demand Growth Rate 2*, as shown in Figure 6.2) is greatly reduced to the service life of consumer durables (22 unit periods). The amplitude of the actual demand cycle decreases to 37.72 percent, which is far less than 48.27 percent – the amplitude of replacement demand growth in the 44th unit period.

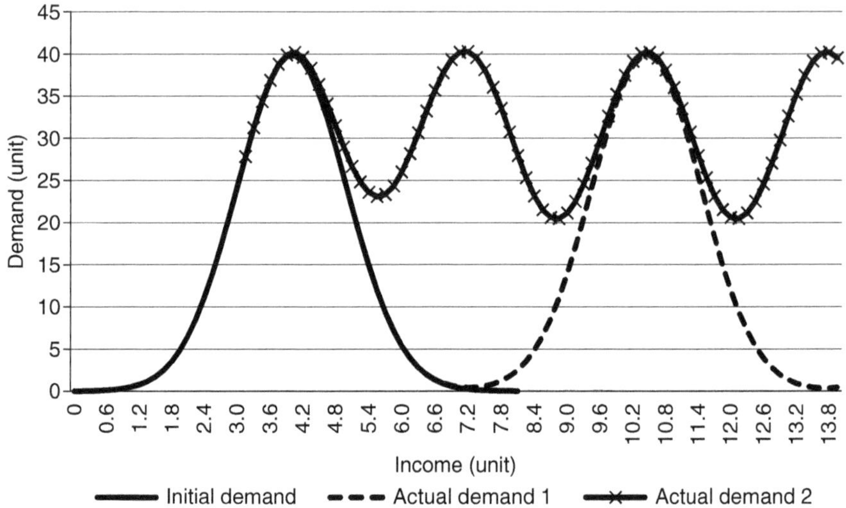

Figure 6.1 The influence of replacement demand on the actual demand for consumer durables (%).

Data source: the data are obtained through the simulation based on the assumed conditions of income-to-price ratio 4 and variance 1.

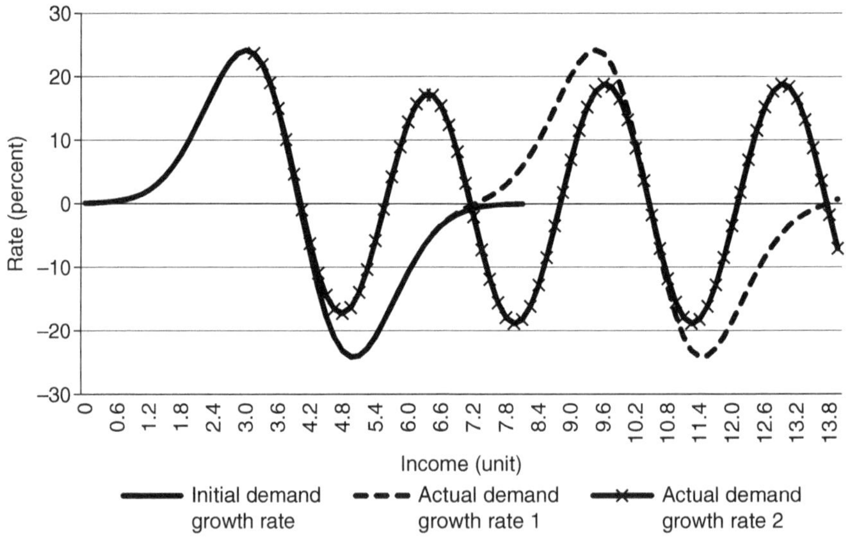

Figure 6.2 The influence of replacement demand on the actual demand cycle of consumer durables (%).

Data source: the data are obtained through the simulated calculation based on the assumed conditions of income-to-price ratio 4 and variance 1.

Factors influencing the amplitude of the innovation demand cycle of consumer goods

Product innovation has a strong substitution effect on the demand for original products and will make the replacement demand occur earlier. If the demand for innovative products completely replaces the demand for original products, the consumption cycle will transform into the cycle of demand for innovative products. The variance of the income–price ratio of the innovative products will determine the amplitude of the new cycle. If the demand for the innovative products only partially replaces the demand for original products, especially when it replaces the original replacement demand, or when the product innovation itself creates new replacement demand, the actual demand cycle will transform into the innovation demand cycle with the length of the innovation cycle as its period. More frequent innovations lead to a shorter period and a lower amplitude of the innovation demand cycle.

In the case that the innovation demand replaces the replacement demand, product innovation will affect the amplitude of the actual demand cycle in two ways. First, the innovative products affect the amplitude of the cycle of consumer goods by changing the consumer price. The price of innovative products is often higher than that of the original products. If the demand for innovative products supersede the original replacement demand, the rise in product price will reduce the variance of income–price ratio and increase the amplitude of the replacement demand cycle. The rise of innovative products often brings down the price of original products. The decline in the price of original products can increase the variance of the income–price ratio of original products and reduce the amplitude of the income distribution cycle of initial demand. Second, the innovation products affect the amplitude of the actual demand cycle by changing the frequency of demand replacement. If the innovation period is shorter than the service life of the consumer durable, the product innovation will cause the replacement demand to occur earlier. The period of the actual demand cycle will be shortened, and the amplitude of the actual demand cycle will also decrease.

To illustrate the influence on the amplitude of the actual demand cycle when the innovation frequency is shorter than the service life of consumer durables, here we return to the previous example. Again, the consumer durable has an initial demand that is normally distributed with an expected income–price ratio of 4 and variance of 1. Assume that the product innovation takes place during the 18th unit period, when the income–price ratio is 2.55 and is four unit periods ahead of the original replacement demand. In other words, product innovation causes the replacement demand to occur earlier, and the period of product innovation remains 18 unit periods. In this scenario, the actual demand (see *Innovation Demand* in Figure 6.3) is the sum of the initial demand and the demand for innovative products, and it fluctuates between 32 units and 42 units. The fluctuation of actual demand growth rate (see *Innovation Demand Growth Rate* in Figure 6.3) is between –11.48 and 11.48 percent. In other words, the amplitude of the actual growth rate cycle has decreased to 22.96 percent, which

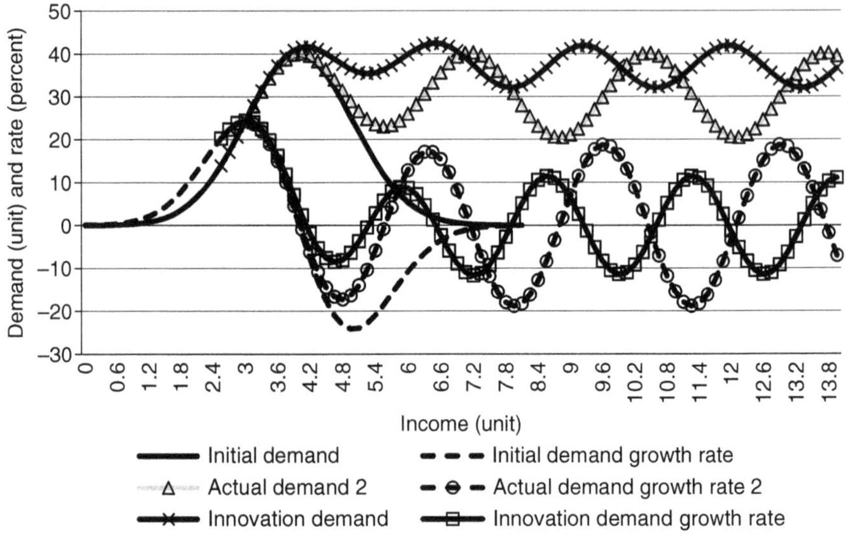

Figure 6.3 The influence of product innovation on the actual demand cycle (%).

Data source: the data are obtained through the simulated calculation based on the assumed conditions of income-to-price ratio 4 and variance 1.

is far lower than 37.72 percent – the amplitude of the replacement demand cycle whose period is 22 unit periods.

The influence of export on the amplitude of the consumer demand cycle

Taking demand from international markets into consideration, the actual demand for consumer goods consists of domestic demand and export. The actual demand cycle is jointly determined by both the domestic demand cycle and the export cycle. The amplitude of the actual demand cycle still depends on the variance of the income–price ratio. The influence of export on the amplitude of the actual demand cycle is mainly manifested in five ways. First, with export, the variance of income–price ratio will increase, and the amplitude of the cycle of consumer demand will decrease. Second, growth in export share will directly increase the variance of the income–price ratio and reduce the amplitude of the actual demand cycle. Third, the acceleration of domestic household income growth induced by export can reduce the amplitude of the actual demand cycle of consumer goods. Fourth, exports will influence consumer prices, thus indirectly changing the amplitude of the actual demand cycle of consumer goods. Fifth, the instability of export share induced by non-market factors can intensify the fluctuations of the consumer demand cycle.

Both domestic and foreign household income distributions are normally distributed. The actual consumer demand consists of domestic demand and export.

The actual demand for consumer durables, also made of domestic and export demands, will be normally distributed as well. The growth rate of the actual demand for consumer non-durables will also be normally distributed. Assuming that the domestic demand for consumer durables obeys $X \sim N(\mu_1, \delta_1^2)$, the international demand obeys $Y \sim N(u_2, \delta_2^2)$, the domestic population size is A, the population size of the international market is B and the export share in the international market is β, then a country's actual demand for consumer durables shall still be normally distributed, and its probability density function shall be $P(z) = \frac{1}{\sqrt{2\pi} \times \Omega} e^{-\frac{(z-\varphi)^2}{2\Omega^2}}$, and the actual demand growth rate shall be $n = p'(z) = \frac{1}{\Omega\sqrt{2\pi}} e^{-\frac{(z-\varphi)^2}{2\Omega^2}} \times \frac{(\varphi - z)}{\Omega^2}$, where the expected value is $\varphi = Au_1 + \beta Bu_2$, and the variance is $\Omega^2 = (A\delta_1)^2 + (\beta B\delta_2)^2$. Based on the fact that demand for consumer non-durables is equivalent to the cumulative demand for consumer durables, the demand for consumer non-durables shall be the integral of the density function of domestic and foreign household income. The demand growth rate shall be the normal distribution function with the domestic and foreign household income–price ratios as the explanatory variables, i.e., $n = \frac{1}{\sqrt{2\pi} \times \Omega} e^{-\frac{(z-\varphi)^2}{2\Omega^2}}$. On this basis, it can be inferred that, in consideration of consumer goods exports, the amplitude of the actual demand cycle of consumer durables shall be $H = \frac{2e^{-\frac{1}{2}}}{\Omega^2\sqrt{2\pi}}$, the amplitude of the actual demand cycle of consumer non-durables shall be $H = \frac{1}{\Omega\sqrt{2\pi}}$ and the variance of the income–price ratio of consumer goods shall be $\Omega^2 = \sum_{i=1}^{n}(z_i - \Phi)^2 = \sum_{i=1}^{n}\left(\frac{y_i}{p_i} - \frac{y_\varphi}{p_\varphi}\right)^2$.

According to the above amplitude formula of the actual demand cycle of consumer goods, the amplitude of the actual demand cycle of consumer goods still depends on the variance of the income–price ratio. Higher income levels mean greater income gaps, lower consumer prices, greater variance of the income–price ratio and lower amplitude of the actual demand cycle of consumer durables. However, due to international demand, the change of the variance of the income–price ratio will be affected by various factors, such as the variance of the income–price ratio of domestic demand, the variance of the income–price ratio of foreign demand, and export. Therefore, factors affecting the amplitude of the actual demand cycle of consumer goods are more complex. Specifically, export affects the amplitude of the actual demand cycle of consumer goods in five ways:

1 *Export will reduce the amplitude of the actual demand cycle of consumer goods.* The involvement of international factors will cause the expected

value of income–price ratio and the variance to increase. The consumer demand curve will flatten out. The amplitude of the actual demand cycle will decrease due to the increase in the variance of income–price ratio.

2 *The increase in export share will directly increase the variance of income–price ratio and reduce the amplitude of the actual demand cycle.* Under the condition of constant domestic demand and international market demand, an increase in the export share indicates an expansion of a country's export. Export will have a greater influence on the actual demand cycle of consumer goods as a result. The increase in the variance of income–price ratio, induced by growing export share, will reduce the amplitude of the actual demand cycle.

3 *Export-led acceleration of domestic household income growth reduces the amplitude of the actual demand cycle of consumer goods.* The demand growth induced by the expansion of export can stimulate economic growth and domestic household income growth. This will increase the variance of the income–price ratio and reduce the amplitude of the actual demand cycle of consumer goods.

4 *Export can influence consumer prices, thereby indirectly changing the amplitude of the actual demand cycle of consumer goods.* As additional demand over domestic demand, export expansion lends strong demand-side support to consumer prices. The resulting increase, or the slowing down of decrease, in consumer price will reduce the variance of the income–price ratio and increase the amplitude of the actual demand cycle of consumer goods. However, the total consumer demand expansion, induced by export, will also lead to the expansion of production and the reduction of production cost. This will indirectly cause consumer prices to drop, variance of income–price ratio to rise, and the amplitude of the actual demand cycle to fall.

5 *The instability of export share can intensify fluctuations of the consumer demand cycle.* A country's export is not totally determined by the market. External interventions, such as export quota, trade protection and other non-market factors can directly affect export and destabilize it. When export share swings, it will cause the actual demand cycle of consumer goods to exhibit irregular changes.

Factors influencing the amplitude of the industrial cycle

Each type of consumer good has its own production chain that converts various raw materials into final products. The production chain constitutes the production industry of such consumer goods. The consumer demand comprises multiple cycles, including the income distribution cycle determined by the normality of household income distribution, the price adjustment cycle determined by supply lag, the replacement demand cycle determined by the service lives of consumer durables, the innovation demand cycle determined by the frequency of product innovation, as well as the export cycle. The industrial output of consumer goods also comprises multiple corresponding cycles, including the income distribution cycle, the price adjustment cycle, the replacement demand cycle, the innovation demand cycle and the export cycle. The period of any industrial output cycle is determined by the period of the corresponding consumer demand cycle. Factors affecting the amplitude of the consumer demand cycle will also affect the amplitude of the industrial output cycle. For example, higher consumer price results in lower price elasticity of demand for consumer goods, longer service lives of consumer durables and less frequent product innovation, greater amplitude of the consumer demand cycle and greater amplitude of the industry cycle of consumer goods. In addition to factors affecting the amplitude of the consumer demand cycle, the amplitudes of the industrial output cycles also depend on the industry multiplier and the industry consumption rate. A greater industry multiplier or a higher consumption rate leads to greater amplitude of the industrial output cycle from the amplitude of the consumer demand cycle.

Assume a unit increase in the output of consumer goods leads to $\beta(0<\beta<1)$ units of output increase in the upstream supportive production enterprises. β will be referred to as the industry accelerator hereinafter. The consumer demand growth rate and the industrial output growth rate of consumer goods will have the following relationship: $N_y = \left(\sum_1^n \beta^n + 1\right) \times \frac{c}{y} \times N_c$, where N_y and N_c are the industrial output growth rate of consumer goods and the consumer demand growth rate, C and y are the consumer demand and the industrial output of consumer goods. The coefficient $\left(\sum_1^n \beta^n + 1\right)$ is the industry multiplier for consumer goods, and C/y is the ratio of consumer demand to industrial output (hereinafter referred to as the industry consumption rate).

From the relationship between consumer demand growth rate and industrial output growth rate, we can derive the relationship between the amplitude of the industrial output cycle and the amplitude of the consumer demand cycle. Taking as an example the relationship between the amplitudes of the consumer goods income distribution cycle and the industrial output income distribution cycle, the relationship between the amplitude of the income distribution cycle of consumer durables and the amplitude of the income distribution cycle of industrial output can be expressed as $H_y = \left(\sum_1^n \beta^n + 1\right) \times \frac{c}{y} \times H_c = \left(\sum_1^n \beta^n + 1\right) \times \frac{c}{y} \times \frac{2e^{-\frac{1}{2}}}{\delta^2\sqrt{2\pi}}$. The relationship between the amplitude of the income distribution cycle of consumer non-durables and the amplitude of the income distribution cycle of industrial output can be expressed as $H_y = \left(\sum_1^n \beta^n + 1\right) \times \frac{c}{y} \times H_c = \left(\sum_1^n \beta^n + 1\right) \times \frac{c}{y} \times \frac{1}{\sigma\sqrt{2\pi}}$.

From the relationship between the consumer demand growth rate and the industrial output growth rate, it can be inferred that the industrial output growth rate and the amplitude of its cycle depend on three major factors:

The first is consumer demand growth rate and its amplitude. Higher consumer demand growth rate give rise to a higher industrial output growth rate, a greater amplitude of the consumer demand cycle, and a greater amplitude of the industrial output cycle. From the factors affecting the amplitude of the consumer demand cycle, it can be inferred that higher consumer price level results in a greater amplitude of the income distribution cycle of consumer goods, and a greater amplitude of the industrial output cycle of consumer goods. Lower price elasticity of demand for consumer goods results in a greater amplitude of the price adjustment cycle of consumer goods and a greater amplitude of the price adjustment cycle. A longer service life of consumer durables results in a greater amplitude of the replacement demand cycle of consumer goods and a greater amplitude of the replacement demand cycle of industrial output. More frequent product innovations result in a lower amplitude of the innovation demand cycle of consumer goods and a lower amplitude of the innovation demand cycle of industrial output. A greater rise in export share results in a greater variance of income–price ratio, a lower amplitude of the actual demand cycle of consumer goods and a lower amplitude of the industrial output cycle.

The second is industry multiplier. The industry multiplier $\left(\sum_{1}^{n}\beta^{n}+1\right)$ is greater than 1. Its value depends on the length of the corresponding industrial chain and the value of the accelerator β. The longer industrial chain and greater accelerator corresponds to a greater industry multiplier, meaning the augmentation from the consumer demand growth to the industrial output growth will be greater. Compared to consumer non-durables, consumer durables have higher prices, longer production chains, greater industry multipliers and greater industrial output cycle amplitudes. The price of heavy industrial consumer goods is higher than that of light industrial consumer goods; the industrial chain of heavy industrial consumer goods is longer than that of light industrial consumer goods. The industry multiplier for heavy industrial consumer goods is greater than that for light industrial consumer goods. Also, the amplitude of the heavy industry output cycle is obviously larger than that of light industry's output cycle.

The third is the industry consumption rate. With the industry multiplier fixed, a higher industry consumption rate translates into greater augmentation from the amplitude of the consumer demand cycle to the amplitude of the industrial cycle. In general, the consumer goods with a relatively long industrial chain have relatively low industry consumption rates. The industry consumption rate of consumer durables is lower than that of consumer non-durables. For example, in 2007 final consumption and export accounted for 44.51 percent of the total industry output of China's food and beverage manufacturing and tobacco industry. The final consumption and export accounted for 46.23 percent of the total output of the clothing, garment and leather products manufacturing industry. Beyond these two industries, final consumption and export of the rest of the manufacturing industries accounted for 22.9 percent of total output. A relatively low industry consumption rate of consumer durables will lower the amplitude of the industrial output cycle. However, because the industrial chain of consumer durables is much longer than that of consumer non-durables, the industry multiplier for consumer durables will be much greater than that of consumer non-durables, and in general the amplitude of the industrial cycle of consumer durables will be larger than that of consumer non-durables. For consumer durables industries with exceptionally long industrial chains and exceptionally high industrial consumption rates, the amplitude of its industrial cycle can be very high. For example, in 2007, final consumption and export of the machinery and equipment manufacturing industry accounted for 32.28 percent of total output, which was far greater than the industry consumption rate of other manufacturing industries. Also, the amplitude of the output growth rate fluctuations of the machinery and equipment manufacturing industry was significantly greater than those of light industries. See Figures 6.4 and 6.5 for comparison.

Factors influencing the amplitude of the economic cycle

If the production chain of consumer goods fluctuates synchronously with the consumption demand, the amplitude of the whole industrial cycle will be greater than the amplitude of the consumer demand cycle. However, the periods of the two will be equal. The influence of the industrial cycle on the economic cycle

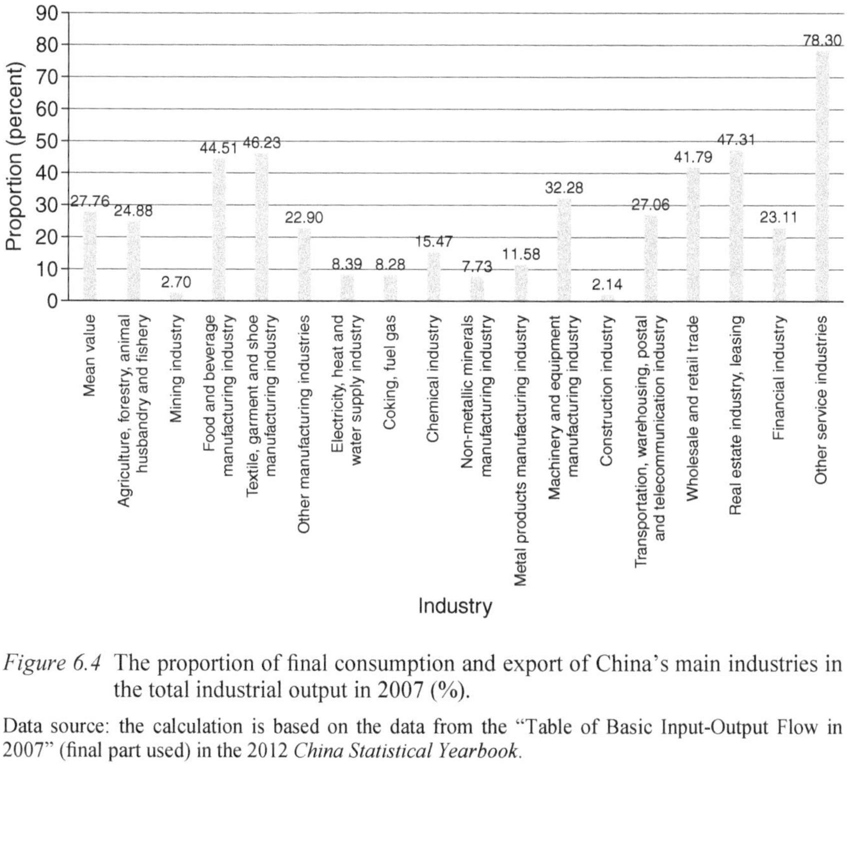

Figure 6.4 The proportion of final consumption and export of China's main industries in the total industrial output in 2007 (%).

Data source: the calculation is based on the data from the "Table of Basic Input-Output Flow in 2007" (final part used) in the 2012 *China Statistical Yearbook*.

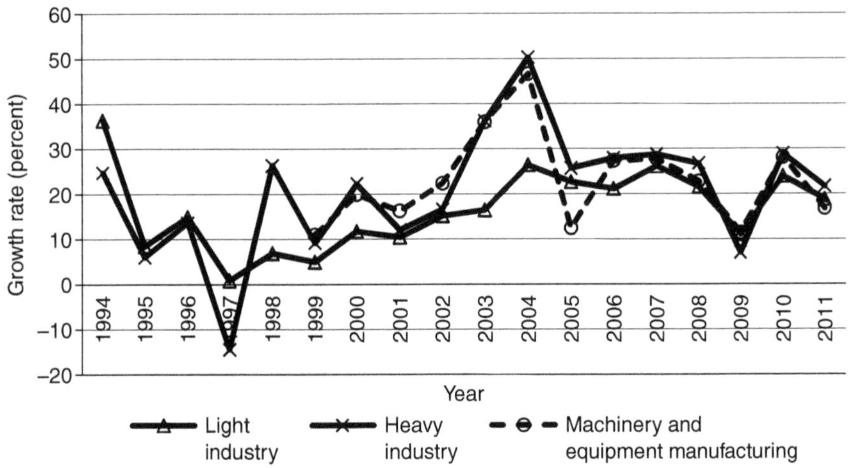

Figure 6.5 The growth rate of China's total industrial output value during 1994–2011 (%).
Data source: the calculation is based on the data from China Macroeconomic Database of WIND.

will be determined by the position of the industry in the whole economy or the share of its industrial value-added in GDP. The period of the economic cycle will be determined by the period of the dominant industry's cycle.

Assuming that the economy is composed of n industries, the relationship between the industrial output growth rate N_y and the economic growth rate N shall be $N = \sum_{1}^{n} \frac{y_n}{Y} \times N_{y_n}$. If the industry multiplier for the nth consumer good is $\alpha_n \left[\alpha_n = \left(\sum_{1}^{n} \beta^n + 1 \right) \right]$, then the relationship between the growth rate of consumer good N_{cn} and the economic growth rate N shall be $N = \sum_{1}^{n} \frac{c_n}{Y} \times \alpha_n \times N_{c_n}$.

From the relationship between industrial output growth rate and economic growth rate, it can be inferred that the economic growth rate is determined by the growth rate of each industrial output and the share of each industry's industrial output in GDP. The period and amplitude of the economic cycle depends on the period and amplitude of the output cycle of the dominant industry, which has the highest output share in GDP. The transformation of the industrial structure changes not only the period but also the amplitude of the economic cycle. When the industry with a relatively lower output cycle amplitude is dominant, the amplitude of the economic cycle will be relatively lower. On the other hand, if the industry with a relatively large output cycle amplitude expands its output and increases its share of GDP continuously, the industry with a relatively large amplitude will contribute more and more to the amplitude of the economic cycle, making it greater over time. Once the industry with a relatively large amplitude becomes dominant, the amplitude of the economic cycle will be determined by the amplitude of the cycle of that industry.

From the relationship between economic growth rate and consumer demand growth rate, it can be inferred that the amplitude of the economic cycle is determined by three major factors: the share of consumer demand in GDP, the industry multiplier for consumer goods and the amplitude of the consumer demand cycle. A higher share of consumer demand, a greater industry multiplier and a larger amplitude can make the influence of a particular consumer good industry greater on economic growth rate and the economic cycle. Similar to the influence of the consumer demand cycle on industrial output, we can summarize the influence of the consumer demand growth rate and the amplitude of the demand cycle on economic growth and the amplitude of the economic cycle into the following three points.

Consumer demand growth rate and the amplitude of demand cycle

All the factors affecting the growth rate of consumer demand and the amplitude of the demand cycle also affect the economic growth rate and the amplitude of the economic cycle. Higher consumer demand growth rate, larger amplitude of the demand cycle and higher economic growth rate will make the amplitude of the economic cycle greater. There are seven ways consumer demand growth rate and amplitude of demand cycle are affected:

1 *During periods of relatively low levels of economic development and household income, higher economic growth rate leads to greater amplitude of economic fluctuations.* Higher household income level means a greater variance of the income–price ratio of consumer goods, and a greater variance of the income–price ratio of consumer goods means a lower consumer demand growth rate and a lower amplitude of demand cycle. These will make economic growth slower and the amplitude of economic cycle smaller.
2 *The narrowing of income inequality can increase both economic growth rate and the amplitude of the economic cycle.* Less inequality means a smaller variance of the income–price ratio of consumer goods, which will result in a higher consumer demand growth rate and a larger amplitude of the demand cycle. These will make the economic growth rate higher and the amplitude of the economic cycle greater.
3 *The expansion of the scale of the demand for consumer goods with high value can improve the economic growth rate and increase the amplitude of the economic cycle.* The higher consumer price means smaller variance of the income–price ratio of consumer goods, which will result in higher growth rate of consumer demand and larger amplitude of the demand cycle, and a higher economic growth rate and larger amplitude of the economic cycle.

4 *The supply lag can cause the growth rate of products with an inelastic demand to fluctuate sharply and increase the amplitude of the economic cycle.* If the price elasticity of demand for consumer goods is small, and the price elasticity of supply of consumer goods is large, then the amplitude of the price adjustment cycle of consumer goods will be great, and the amplitude of the price adjustment cycle of the whole economy will be great too.
5 *Replacement demand can change the fluctuation state of the durable consumer goods demand cycle and cause the economy to maintain cyclical growth.* Without replacement demand, the demand for consumer durables will decline continuously after its peak. The addition of replacement demand will cause the actual demand for consumer durables to maintain the state of cyclical growth after the initial demand reaches its maximum value. Industrial output and the whole economy will therefore maintain cyclical growth. A longer service life of consumer durables means its amplitude of replacement demand cycle will be larger, and the amplitude of the replacement demand cycle of industrial output and the whole economy will be larger too.
6 *More frequent product innovations lead to a smaller amplitude of the economic cycle.* Similar to replacement demand, the innovation demand induced by product innovation can cause consumer demand to maintain the state of cyclical growth after it reaches its maximum point. Industrial output and the economy will also develop innovation demand cycles. More frequent product innovations are associated with a lower amplitude of the innovation demand cycle of consumer goods, and a lower amplitude of the innovation demand cycle of industrial output and the whole economy.
7 *The spread of export will cause the amplitude of the economic cycle to be smaller.* An increase in export share means a greater variance in the income–price ratio, which will result in a lower amplitude of the actual demand cycle of consumer goods and a lower amplitude of the cycle of industrial output and the whole economy.

Industry multiplier for consumer goods

The industry multiplier for consumer goods $\left(\sum_{1}^{n}\beta^{n}+1\right)$ is greater than 1.

A longer industry production chain or a greater accelerator β results in a greater industry multiplier. The amplification from the growth rate of consumer demand to the industrial output growth rate will be enlarged as well. The influence of consumer goods on the amplitude of the economic cycle will also increase. Because the industry multiplier of consumer durables is greater than that of consumer non-durables, the industry multiplier of heavy industrial consumer goods will be greater than that of light industrial consumer goods. The amplitude of the demand cycle of heavy industrial consumer durables will have a greater influence on the amplitude of the economic cycle than that of light industrial consumer durables.

Consumption structure and the share of consumer demand

The share of the demand for a certain kind of consumer good in GDP reflects the position of consumer goods in the whole economy. The higher the share, the greater influence such consumer goods will have on the economic growth rate and the amplitude of the economic cycle. The share of consumer demand also indirectly reflects the level of industry consumption rate of consumer goods. If the industry consumption rate of consumer goods is high, then the share of consumer demand in GDP will be high, and the influence of the consumer demand growth and the amplitude of the demand cycle on the economic growth rate and the amplitude of the economic cycle will also be great. Changing shares of consumer demand in GDP reflect a transformation of the consumption structure. When the share of the consumer goods with relatively large demand cycle amplitudes (e.g., heavy industrial consumer durables) increase, the amplitude of the economic cycle will also increase. When the share of consumer goods with relatively small demand cycle amplitudes (e.g., consumer non-durables) rise, the amplitude of the economic cycle will decrease.

7 The dynamic equilibrium growth process of the economic cycle

There are two major schools of modern economic growth theories – Keynesian disequilibrium growth theory and neoclassical equilibrium growth theory. Based on their distinct theories of economic growth, the two schools disagree sharply over the endogeneity of the economic cycle and the effectiveness of macroeconomic policies. The neoclassical school believes that the economic cycle is exogenous, and government's policy interventions are invalid and even destructive. The Keynesian school affirms the endogeneity of the economic cycle and points out that government policy interventions are effective in stimulating economic growth. This chapter supports the view that cyclical fluctuations are the endogenous phenomenon of economic growth and the normal state of economic activities. At any stage in the cyclical fluctuations of economic growth, there always exists an instantaneous equilibrium value, which evolves with the economic structure and external conditions. The neoclassical stable equilibrium growth model (Solow model) is a static model of equilibrium growth. By integrating the time variable into the Solow model, the dynamic Solow model itself becomes a model of cyclical endogenous growth, and its instantaneous equilibrium growth process becomes the stable equilibrium growth process under static conditions. Thus, we can see that neoclassical stable equilibrium growth theory is consistent with the dynamic equilibrium growth process of the economic cycle in essence. In real economic activities, short-term fluctuations may affect the shape of long-term fluctuations and the process of dynamic equilibrium, but the short-term fluctuation always centers on long-term fluctuation and takes the long-term fluctuation as its dynamic equilibrium value. An important policy implication of this study is that moderate short-term policy interventions can be effective in maintaining steady economic growth, but such policy interventions should be in compliance with the dynamic equilibrium growth trend of economic growth. Furthermore, export plays a prominent role in increasing the dynamic equilibrium value of economic growth.

Cyclical fluctuations are the basic rule of economic activity

Since the discovery of a variety of regular cyclical fluctuations in economic activities in the nineteenth century, economists have conducted numerous studies on the subject. These studies mainly focused on two fields: the statistical analysis on the characteristics of cyclical fluctuations and the causes of cyclical fluctuations. There were few controversies about the statistical characteristics of cyclical fluctuations, and economic cycles were categorized as a short-term cycle, mid-term cycle, mid-to-long-term cycle and long-term cycle according to their different periods. However, there have been many controversial issues surrounding the causes of economic cycles. For instance, the earlier classical cycle theories attribute different cycles to various single factors, but later studies were more complex. Later researchers' theories were categorized into two schools, which are Keynesian cycle theory and neoclassical cycle theory. The debating between these two schools is on the endogeneity of the economic cycle. Based on its economic equilibrium growth theory, the neoclassical school asserts that economic growth is an equilibrium process, and the fluctuations of the economic cycle are exogenous due to temporary deviations from the equilibrium growth path caused by external shocks. Hence the economy will automatically return to the equilibrium growth path. The Keynesian school's cycle theory denies the viewpoint of the economy's equilibrium growth path; this school believes that economic growth is a non-equilibrium process, and the fluctuations of the economic cycle have certain endogeneity. In the real economy, the classical cycle, which is characterized by the absolute decline of economic aggregates, has less prominent influence and even disappears at a certain stage. But economic growth rates always show a state of cyclical fluctuation, and the cyclical fluctuations of economic growth rates are the basic law of economic activities.

In 1939, Samuelson, who was one of the representative figures of New Keynesianism and the first one to conduct a rigorous theoretical analysis of the endogeneity of the economic cycle, put forward the multiplier-accelerator model that proved the endogeneity of the economic cycle for the first time (Samuelson, 1939). The model illustrated the transmission mechanism of the economic cycle, i.e., that fluctuations of consumer demand could lead to fluctuations in investment and the whole economy. Tinbergen, Schultz, Ricel and Kaldor jointly developed the cobweb model, and they used elasticity theory to explain the price fluctuations of commodities with relatively longer production cycles in the state of disequilibrium (Tinbergen, 1939).

The multiplier-accelerator model and the cobweb model explain the endogenous mechanism of the classical economic cycle (cyclical fluctuations of economic aggregates). From our studies based on the normality of household income distribution in Chapters 3 and 4, it can be inferred that both household consumption demand and its growth rate have endogenous cyclical fluctuations determined by the normality of household income. In general economic growth, there also exists endogenous cyclical fluctuations determined by the consumption demand cycle. Household income is normally distributed in various countries. Given the normality of household income distribution, the household demand for consumer durables will be normally distributed; and the demand for consumer non-durables will generate an S-shaped normal cumulative distribution (i.e., the integral of the normal distribution probability density function).

The durables consumption demand growth rate shows complete cyclical fluctuations, while the non-durables consumption demand growth rate has half-cycle fluctuations. Both durables and non-durables demand growth rates will see continued cyclical trends due to the renewal demand for durable goods and the innovation demand induced by product innovation. Meanwhile, as household income is normally distributed across various countries, growth rates of international market demand and export show a cyclical trend. Also, since both the domestic consumer demand and the export growth rate show cyclical fluctuations, the whole economy growth will inevitably develop a cyclical trend (see Chapters 3 and 4).

There are a variety of endogenous cycles in real economic activities. For example, the growth rate of the demand for every good has different cyclical fluctuations, including the consumer demand cycle determined by the household income distribution, the period of the price adjustment cycle determined by lagging supply, and the renewal demand and innovation demand cycles determined by the lifetime of consumer durables and technological progress. The periods and amplitudes of these cycles are different, and each of them has different shapes at the same stage (each peak and trough might occur in a different time). The actual cycle of one good and its related industry is the aggregate results of a variety of cyclical fluctuations.

Meanwhile, the cycles of different goods and their related industries are very different during the same period. The actual economic cycle is the comprehensive result of a variety of cycles of different consumer goods and export products and their related industries. Besides, external shocks can affect the endogenous cycles of the economy and even change the shape of cyclical fluctuations, but they cannot change the nature of the endogeneity of the cycle.

The instantaneous equilibrium value of the economic cycle and its influence factors

There exists an instantaneous equilibrium value in any cyclical fluctuation. And most equilibriums of cyclical fluctuations are non-zero. Only when the equilibrium is excluded is a single type of demand cycle seen as a cyclical fluctuation with zero equilibrium value. The whole consumption consists of many kinds of demand for durables or non-durables, and the equilibrium value of the economic cycle is jointly determined by various demand cycles. As there is a wide range of consumer goods and complex correlations among these industries, it is very difficult to identify the industrial chain of a particular consumer good. Thus, it becomes even more difficult to evaluate the influence of the cycle of demand for a single product on the whole consumer demand and economic cycle, as well as its instantaneous equilibrium value. But the factors affecting different consumer demand cycles have something in common; in some instances these factors can not only determine the fluctuation shapes of different consumer demand cycles, but also affect the fluctuation shapes of the whole consumer demand and economic cycle (see Chapters 5 and 6).

An economy can be seen as a semi-closed circulation system consisting of all interrelated economic activities. According to the correlation among consumer demand, investment demand and economic growth, we can incorporate the factors affecting the consumer demand and economic cycles into the system analysis, and turn consumption growth rate, investment growth rate and economic growth rate into the difference equation of their lagged variables. Then we can analyze the factors of the economic cycle and its instantaneous equilibrium value through the differential equations. The results of the analysis indicate that at any stage the cyclical fluctuations of consumption growth rate, investment growth rate and economic growth rate have an instantaneous equilibrium value that is developing dynamically. The equilibrium value depends on eight factors: government expenditure growth rate, government expenditure ratio, net export growth rate, net export ratio, the export accelerator of investment, the consumption accelerator of investment, consumption ratio to GDP, and the consumption elasticity of economic growth rate. Since these eight major factors vary in different periods, the instantaneous equilibrium value of economic growth rate will develop dynamically at different stages.

From the perspective of demand, economic growth is driven by five major types of demand: investment, household consumption, government expenditure, export and import demand. The investment can be seen not only as a demand factor in the short term, but also as a supply factor in the mid-to-long term; the investment scale is determined by export and consumer demand. The consumer demand depends on household income, while the household income is subject to economic growth. Import depends on domestic investment demand and consumer demand. On this basis, we can build a simple macroeconomic model with government expenditure and net export as its exogenous variables:

$$Y_t = I_t + C_t + G_t + NE_t \tag{1}$$

$$N_{Y_t} = I_{t-1} / Y_{t-1} \times N_{I_t} + C_{t-1} / Y_{t-1} \times N_{C_t} + G_{t-1} / Y_{t-1} \times N_{G_t} + NE_{t-1} / Y_{t-1} \times N_{NE_t} \tag{2}$$

or

$$N_{Y_t} = \delta_{I_t-1} \times N_{I_t} + \delta_{C_t-1} \times N_{C_t} + \delta_{G_t-1} \times N_{G_t} + \delta_{NE_t-1} \times N_{NE_t}$$

in which, Y_t, I_t, C_t, G_t and NE_t, are GDP, investment, consumption, government expenditure and net export in the tth period, respectively; N_{Y_t}, N_{I_t}, N_{C_t}, N_{G_t} and N_{NE_t}, are the growth rate of GDP, investment, consumption, government expenditure and net export in the tth period respectively; δ_{I_t-1}, δ_{C_t-1}, δ_{G_t-1} and δ_{NE_t-1} are the ratio of previous investment, consumption, government expenditure and net export to GDP ratio, respectively (hereinafter referred to as investment ratio, consumption ratio, government expenditure ratio and net export ratio).

Assuming that the investment depends on domestic consumption and net export, i.e., $I_t = \alpha \times (C_t - C_{t-1}) + \beta \times (NE_t - NE_{t-1})$, α and β are the investment accelerators of consumption and net export, which mean that the amount of investment resulting from the increased unit of consumer demand and net export growth respectively (hereinafter referred to as the consumption accelerator of investment and the export accelerator of investment, respectively).

According to Equation 2, the equation of the relationship among investment growth rate, consumption growth rate and net export growth rate can be described as:

$$N_{I_t} = \alpha \times \delta_{C_t-1} / \delta_{I_t-1} \times (N_{C_t} - 1) + \beta \times \delta_{NE_t-1} / \delta_{I_t-1} \times (N_{NE_t} - 1) \tag{3}$$

Assuming that the consumer demand growth rate in current period depends on the household income growth rate of the previous period, and the household income growth rate depends on the economic growth rate, that is:

$$N_{C_t} = \gamma \times N_{yt-1} \tag{4}$$

where γ is the elasticity coefficient of domestic consumer demand of the economic growth (hereinafter referred to as the consumption elasticity).

According to equations (2), (3) and (4), the differential equation of economic growth rate can be obtained:

$$N_{Y_t} = \delta_{C_t-1} \times \gamma * (\alpha + 1) \times N_{Y_t-1} + \delta_{G_t-1} \times N_{G_t} + (\beta + 1) \times \delta_{NE_t-1} \times N_{NE_t} - (\alpha \times \delta_{C_t-1} + \beta \times \delta_{NE_t-1}) \tag{5}$$

According to Equation 5, the equation of the instantaneous equilibrium value of economic growth rate can be deduced as follows:

$$N_Y = \frac{\{\delta_{G_t-1} \times N_{G_t} + (\beta + 1) \times \delta_{NE_t-1} \times N_{NE_t} - (\alpha \times \delta_{C_t-1} + \beta \times \delta_{NE_t-1})\}}{\{1 - \delta_{C_t-1} \times \gamma \times (\alpha + 1)\}} \tag{6}$$

therefore, the differential equations of consumer demand growth rate and investment growth rate and the equations of their instantaneous equilibrium values can be deduced through equations (3), (4) and (5).

The differential equation of consumer demand growth rate is:

$$N_{C_t-1} = \delta_{C_t-1} \times \gamma \times (\alpha + 1) \times N_{C_t} + \gamma \times \delta_{G_t-1} \times N_{G_t} + \gamma \times (\beta + 1) \times \delta_{NE_t-1} \times N_{NE_t} - \gamma \times (\alpha \times \delta_{C_t-1} + \beta \times \delta_{NE_t-1}) \tag{7}$$

The equation of the instantaneous equilibrium value of the cyclical fluctuations of consumer demand growth rate is:

$$N_C = \frac{\{\delta_{G_t-1} \times N_{G_t} + (\beta + 1) \times \delta_{NE_t-1} \times N_{NE_t} - (\alpha \times \delta_{C_t-1} + \beta \times \delta_{NE_t-1})\} \times \gamma}{\{1 - \delta_{C_t-1} \times \gamma \times (\alpha + 1)\}} \tag{8}$$

The differential equation of investment growth rate is:

$$\delta_{I_t} * N_{I_t} = (\alpha+1)\times\delta_{C_t}\times\delta_{I_t-1}\times N_{I_t} + (\alpha-\beta)\times\delta_{C_t}\times\delta_{NE_t-1}\times N_{NE_t} + \beta\times\delta_{NE_t}\times N_{NE_t+1} + \alpha\times\delta_{C_t}\times\gamma\times\delta_{G_t-1}\times N_{G_t} + \{\alpha\times\delta_{C_t}\times(\gamma\times\delta_{C_t-1}-1)+\gamma\times\beta\times\delta_{C_t}\times\delta_{NE_t-1}-\beta\times\delta_{NE_t}\} \tag{9}$$

The equation of the instantaneous equilibrium value of the cyclical fluctuations of investment growth rate is:

$$N_{I_t} = \frac{\{(\alpha-\beta)\times\delta_{C_t}\times\delta_{NE_t-1}\times N_{NE_t} + \beta\times\delta_{NE_t}\times N_{NE_t+1} + \alpha\times\delta_{C_t}\times\gamma\times\delta_{G_t-1}\times N_{G_t} + [\alpha\times\delta_{C_t}\times(\gamma\times\delta_{C_t-1}-1)+\gamma\times\beta\times\delta_{C_t}\times\delta_{NE_t-1}-\beta\times\delta_{NE_t}]\}}{\delta_{I_t}-(\alpha+1)\times\delta_{C_t}\times\delta_{I_t-1}} \tag{10}$$

According to the properties of first-order linear differential equations (Chiang, 1999), the differential equations of economic growth rate, consumer demand growth rate and investment growth rate demonstrate that the economic growth rate, the consumer demand growth rate and the investment growth rate experience endogenous cyclical fluctuations with government expenditure growth rate and net export growth rate as their exogenous variables. However, due to changes in investment ratio, consumption ratio, government expenditure ratio, net export ratio, consumption accelerator, export accelerator and consumption elasticity, the shapes of cyclical fluctuations of consumption growth rate, investment growth rate and economic growth rate will vary in different periods. This is consistent with the conclusion of Chapter 3, which says that there exist endogenous cycles in the economy.

From the equations (6), (8) and (10), we can see instantaneous equilibrium values exist in the cyclical fluctuations of the economic growth rate, consumption growth rate and investment growth rate at any period. The instantaneous equilibrium value of cyclical fluctuations depends on multiple factors, such as government expenditure growth rate, government expenditure ratio, net export growth rate, net export ratio, the export accelerator of investment β, the consumption accelerator of investment α, consumption ratio and the consumption elasticity of economic growth rate Y. Only when all eight factors stay unchanged will the instantaneous equilibrium value of cyclical fluctuation be stable. But government expenditure growth rate and export growth rate are dynamic in the real economy, so government expenditure and exports ratios will vary. Therefore, the instantaneous equilibrium value of the cyclical economic fluctuations varies with the changes of government expenditure and export growth rates and their ratios. Furthermore, even if government expenditure growth rate and export growth rate and their ratios remain unchanged, the other four factors may vary with economic development. For instance, income improvement will change the consumption expenditure structure, such as shifting from food consumption to consumer durables, and this change will affect the industrial structure such as switching to a non-agricultural industry from an agricultural industry. Only if the durables industrial chain is longer than the food industrial chain will the consumption accelerator of investment increase, and the consumption ratio and the consumption elasticity of economic growth rate would be adjusted accordingly. Also, adjustment of the export structure can lead to a change of the export accelerator of investment. Due to the constantly changing consumption ratio, consumption elasticity, consumption accelerator and export accelerator, instantaneous equilibrium values of the cyclical fluctuations of consumption, investment and economic growth rates develop dynamically with the change of economic structure. Therefore, the instantaneous equilibrium growth process of the cyclical fluctuations of consumption, investment and economic growth rates is dynamic.

Consistency between neoclassical stable growth theory and dynamic equilibrium growth process of the economic cycle

In the studies of the economic cycle, the neoclassical school, which is based on the Solow stable growth theory (hereinafter referred to as the Solow model), denies the endogeneity of the economic cycle. The question is whether the Solow stable growth theory can be grounded in the rejection of the endogeneity of the cyclical fluctuations of economic growth. And can we find any connection between the Solow stable growth process and the dynamic equilibrium growth process of the cyclical fluctuations of economic growth in our analysis? Our analysis says that the Solow model as a static stable growth model only proves the existence of a stable growth process of economic growth under static conditions, rather than excluding the endogeneity of the cyclical fluctuations of economic activities under dynamic conditions. After introducing the time variable to the Solow model, the dynamic Solow model itself becomes a model of the endogenous economic cycle, and the conditions for the cyclical fluctuations of the Solow model to reach the instantaneous equilibrium growth process under dynamic conditions coincide with the conditions for its cyclical fluctuations to reach steady growth under static conditions. Meanwhile, the Solow model discovered the cyclical fluctuations of capital-to-labor ratio under dynamic conditions – the cyclical fluctuations mainly depend on the cyclical fluctuations of the investment growth rate and can be seen as the manifestation of cyclical fluctuations of economic activities in the field of supply, and its equilibrium growth process is consistent with the dynamic equilibrium growth process of the cyclical fluctuations of the economy in essence.

Basic architecture of the Solow stable growth model

On the premise that demand is determined by supply, the Solow stable growth model comes to the conclusion that a stable growth process of the economy exists by giving a series of strict assumptions. The assumptions of this model include constant return to scale, full employment, homogeneous linear production function, diminishing marginal product, capital–labor substitution, savings–investment transformation and so on. The basic structure of the model is: $Y=F(K,L)$, $K'=s\times F(K,L)$, $L'/L=n$, $Y/L=F(K/L,1)=f(r,1)$, where Y, K, L and

$f(r, 1)$ are output, capital, labor force and output per capita respectively, and K' is investment, s is saving ratio, n is labor force growth rate and r is capital-to-labor ratio. The basic equation of the Solow stable growth model is $r' = s \times f(r, 1) - n \times r$, which shows that a stable capital-to-labor ratio enables economic growth to be in a state of steady growth. More specifically, when $s \times f(r, 1) + n \times r$, the first-order derivative of capital-to-labor ratio r will be as $r' = 0$, and r will be a specific ratio R here. When $s \times f(r, 1) > nr$, $r' > 0$, r will continue to rise. When $s \times f(r, 1) < nr$, $r' < 0$, r will continue to decline, thus the capital-to-labor ratio r will stay at R ultimately – the economy (output) will be in a state of steady growth when r reaches R. Either the economic (output) growth rate or the capital growth rate will be the labor force growth rate n (Solow, 1969).

Cyclical fluctuation characteristic of the dynamic Solow stable growth model

The Solow stable growth model is a static equilibrium growth model, whose basic equation has proved that there exists a static stable equilibrium growth process in economic growth. But the static stable equilibrium growth process cannot reject the endogenous cyclical fluctuations of dynamic economic growth. Dynamically, the capital-to-labor ratio in the Solow model will regress to its equilibrium value when it deviates from the equilibrium value, which is exactly the trait of endogenous cyclical fluctuations in economic growth.

In order to examine the dynamic characteristic of the Solow model and hold the other assumptions constant in the Solow model, we introduce the time variable to the Solow stable growth model, i.e., the current output depends on the current capital and labor, $Y_t = F(K_t, L_t)$ or $Y_t / L_t = f(r_t, 1)$; and the current investment is equal to the previous savings, $K'_t = K_t - K_{t-1} = sY_{t-1}$.

The differential equation of capital-to-labor ratio can be derived by new investment equations, such as $K_t / L_t - (L_{t-1} / L_t) \times K_{t-1}/L_{t-1} = sY_{t-1}/L_{t-1} \times L_{t-1} / L_t$, and $n \times r_t - r_{t-1} - s \times f(r_{t-1}, 1) = 0$. Based on the properties of differential equation (Chiang, 1999), the capital-to-labor ratio r has endogenous cyclical fluctuations, and the shape of its cyclical fluctuations depends on both the labor force growth rate n and the saving ratio s. The cyclical fluctuations have an instantaneous equilibrium value, and when the capital-to-labor ratio reaches the equilibrium value R, the following equation can be satisfied: $s \times f(R, 1) = (n - 1) \times R$; and this equation is fundamentally the same as the equation $s \times f(R, 1) = n \times R$, which can be satisfied when the capital-to-labor ratio reaches the equilibrium value under static conditions. The only difference between these two equations is the coefficient on the right-hand side of the equations; the former is the labor force growth range $(n - 1)$ while the latter is the labor force growth rate index n. The difference between these two equations is because the investment equation under static conditions does not take into account the dynamic factor, which means that the current investment under dynamic conditions is equal to the previous savings. Meanwhile, because we have assumed that the saving ratio s and the labor force growth rate n remain the same, the instantaneous equilibrium value R of the capital-to-labor ratio r also remains unchanged according to the equation $s \times f(R,1) = (n-1) \times R$. But in the real economy, even if the labor force growth rate remains the same, the saving ratio s may vary with the change of economic structure, so the instantaneous equilibrium value of the cyclical fluctuations of capital-to-labor ratio also develops dynamically.

As the per capita output function $f(r,1)$ in the Solow model is a monotonic increasing convex function of r, where the first derivative of per capita output function $f'(r,1)$ is greater than or equal to 0, and its second derivative $f''(r,1)$ is less than 0. The per capita output $f(r_t,1)$ and its growth rate must see inevitable cyclical fluctuations under the situation in which the capital-to-labor ratio r shows cyclical fluctuations. According to the output function $Y_t/L_t = f(r_t,1)$, the output growth rate N_t is the product of the labor force growth rate n and the growth rate of per capita output, i.e., $N_t = n \times f(r_t,1) f(r_{t-1},1)$. Due to the cyclical fluctuations of the per capita output growth rate, the output (economic) growth rate also shows inevitable cyclical fluctuations, and the instantaneous equilibrium value of the cyclical fluctuations of output (economic) growth rate depends on the equilibrium value of the capital-to-labor ratio R. The per capita output is equal to its equilibrium value when r stays in its equilibrium value. When labor force growth rate n and the saving ratio s remain unchanged, the equilibrium values of per capital output at different stages will be identical, and the instantaneous equilibrium value of the cyclical fluctuations of output (economic) growth rate will be equal to the labor force growth rate n. Hold labor force growth rate n constant, the instantaneous equilibrium value of the cyclical fluctuations of economic growth rate will remain unchanged in the dynamic Solow model. In other words, there is a stable equilibrium growth process in an economy – the same conclusion of the Solow model under static conditions. If the labor force growth rate or saving ratio changes, the instantaneous equilibrium value of the output growth rate in the dynamic Solow model will develop dynamically.

According to the analysis above, the Solow stable growth model under static conditions has only proved the existence of a steady-state of instantaneous equilibrium growth in economic growth at a certain time point. Under dynamic conditions, the cyclical fluctuations of the capital-to-labor ratio and the output are the normal state of the economy. The instantaneous equilibrium values of the cyclical fluctuations of both the capital-to-labor ratio and the output growth rate will stay unchanged only if the labor force growth rate n and the saving ratio s remain the same. In real economic activities, instantaneous equilibrium values of capital-to-labor ratio and the output growth rate may vary with the change of the labor force growth rate or the saving ratio.

Consistency between equilibrium growth process of the dynamic Solow stable growth model and dynamic equilibrium growth process of the economic cycle

Actual economic growth is subject to both supply and demand factors. The Solow stable growth model only considers two supply factors, capital and labor, and the expanded model only adds the technological progress factor (Solow, 1969). A series of derivative neoclassical growth models can be seen as variations of the Solow model. For example, transforming capital and labor force into aggregate social capital and human capital does not make a breakthrough in the basic architecture of the Solow model. The limitation of this theory is that only the impact of supply factors on economic growth is considered, and the influence of effective demand on economic growth is ignored. After we incorporate the time factor in the Solow model, the cyclical fluctuations of the capital-to-labor ratio in the dynamic Solow model only represent the cyclical fluctuations of economic activities in the field of supply. Observing the relationship between the cyclical fluctuations of overall economic performance and various economic activities, given that labor force growth rate depends on the population growth rate, the trend of labor supply over a certain period is established. Based on the assumption of full employment (one of the assumptions of the Solow model), the cyclical fluctuations of the capital-to-labor ratio largely depend on the cyclical fluctuations of the capital growth rate, while the cyclical fluctuations of the capital growth rate are determined by the cyclical fluctuations of investment growth rate. On the demand side, investment acts as one of the factors that determines supply, and the cyclical fluctuations of its growth rate ultimately depend on the cyclical fluctuations of consumer demand and export growth rates. So far, we have clarified the relations between the dynamic equilibrium growth process of the cyclical fluctuations in economic growth and the stable growth process of the Solow stable growth model. More specifically, the cyclical fluctuations of the capital-to-labor ratio reflected by the dynamic Solow model are induced by the cyclical fluctuations of the investment growth rate, representing cyclical fluctuations of the capital-to-labor ratio in the whole economy. There is consistency between the equilibrium growth progress (determined by the cyclical fluctuations of the capital-to-labor ratio) and the dynamic equilibrium growth progress (determined by the cyclical fluctuations of economic operation), and the two types of equilibrium growth progress are determined by different factors that induce cyclical fluctuations of consumer demand and export growth rates.

The stable growth process in the Solow model is specified under the full employment assumption, and therefore the stable growth rate is seen as the potential growth rate. Yet full employment is not a necessary condition of the Solow model, and the static growth Solow model assumes there is a capital–labor substitution, and this suggests that the quantities of capital and labor can be adjusted. The capital-to-labor ratio will stay below or above the steady-state of the capital-to-labor ratio before reaching the state steady, and thus there are two possibilities – either it does not reach full employment or the capital stock does not reach the level required for full employment. Based on the differential equation of the dynamic Solow model above, there exists an instantaneous equilibrium growth process at any stage of economic growth, even in the case of non-full employment or varying labor growth rates at different stages of economic growth. But we will see the dynamic non-stationary equilibrium growth process as the instantaneous equilibrium value varies at different stages of economic growth. In the real economy, non-full employment is normal, and the dynamic equilibrium value of the cyclical fluctuations is inherent in real economic growth, instead of the potential output growth rate under full employment.

Empirical test: the impact of short-term fluctuations on long-term fluctuations and the dynamic equilibrium growth process

The cyclical fluctuations in economic growth and the dynamic equilibrium growth process is a comprehensive result of cyclical fluctuations based on a variety of products and different industries. Different cyclical fluctuations have dynamic equilibrium processes. The factors that affect the cyclical fluctuation and its dynamic equilibrium growth process can change the cyclical fluctuations of other economic indicators and their dynamic equilibrium growth process because of the interactions among economic activities. In this chapter, we focus on analyzing the influence of the short-term fluctuations of consumption growth rate on the long-term fluctuations by using the relationship among three major types of demand and economic growth, to clarify the internal mechanism by which the longer-term fluctuation is the dynamic equilibrium value of the shorter-term fluctuation.

In Chapter 5, we have proposed that there will be two categories of each consumer goods demand cycle. One is the distribution of the income cycle characterized by the normally distributed household income, and of the fluctuations depending on the household income level, income distribution structure and consumer prices. When the income growth is higher, the smaller the income gap, the lower consumer prices and the greater the decline of the price. Also, the periods of the income distribution cycles of the whole economy and consumer goods growth will be shorter. The other category refers to short cycles, including the price adjustment cycle, the renewal demand cycle, the innovation demand cycle and the export cycle; the periods of these cycles are determined by the period of supply lag, the lifecycle of products, the frequency of product innovation and export. The income distribution cycle has the longest period. For example, the period of the income distribution cycle on color TV sets, refrigerators, washing machines and family passenger vehicles in China's urban households were 27 years, 32 years, 32 years and 64 years respectively (see Chapter 8). But the actual consumer demand cycle, including the price adjustment cycle, the renewal demand cycle, the product innovation demand cycle and other cyclical fluctuations, have relatively shorter periods. For instance, from 1978 to 2012, the average period of the actual consumer demand cycle of color TV sets, refrigerators, washing machines and family passenger vehicles in China were six years, 6.2 years, eight years and 12 years, respectively (see Chapter 8).

Based on the relationship between short-term and long-term fluctuations, the consumer price and the household income level will be changed after the short-term fluctuation occurs. This is because the frequency of occurrence of short-term fluctuation is higher than that of long-term fluctuations. So can the fluctuations of price and income level induced by short-term fluctuations affect the shape of long-term fluctuations?

First, the price change caused by the short-term fluctuation of consumer demand growth rate will not change the shape of its long-term fluctuation. Price variation is one of the main factors that affects long-term fluctuations. The lower the consumer price, and the greater the price decline, the shorter the period of the income distribution cycle of consumer goods and the greater its amplitude. But as regular short-term fluctuations are always symmetrical, the price variation arising from short-term fluctuations will not affect the long-term trend in consumer price. So the price fluctuations caused by short-term fluctuations will not distort the shape of long-term fluctuations in the long run. For example, the price adjustment cycle will have an impact on the income distribution cycle. Price increase caused by being in the price adjustment rising period or supply shortages would push some consumers out of the market, and thus the period of income distribution growth is extended as the increase in average consumer price. Price reduction arising from the falling stage of the price adjustment cycle or cases of oversupply mean the lower-income group will join the groups of buyers earlier, and thus the period of the income distribution cycle is shorter due to the reduction in average consumer price. In the long run, the extending and shrinking period of the income distribution cycle caused by the price adjustment cycle will cancel each other out (see Chapter 5). The amplitude of the household income distribution cycle depends on the variance of the ratio of income to price for households. When the variance is greater, the smaller the amplitude of the cycle and the larger the range of price fluctuations caused by short-term fluctuations. Hence, it will decrease the variance of the ratio of income to price for households and will increase the fluctuation range of long-term fluctuations in the short term. But in the long run, as long as the price fluctuations induced by short-term fluctuations are symmetrical, the long-term trend of price will be the same, and the price fluctuations induced by short-term fluctuations will not change the amplitude of long-term fluctuation. Other short-term fluctuations, such as the price fluctuations induced by the renewal demand cycle, the innovation demand cycle and the export cycle, will not affect the fluctuation shape of the income distribution cycle of consumer goods if they are symmetrical.

Second, the short-term fluctuations that persistently change income growth rate will affect the shape of long-term fluctuations. Income growth rate and income gap are two major factors that determine the fluctuation shape of the income distribution cycle in consumer goods. For instance, the higher the income growth rate, the larger the income gap will be. The shorter the period of the income distribution cycle is, the smaller its amplitude will be. In the long run, the symmetrical price fluctuations of the price adjustment cycle have no persistent influence on the income growth rate, but they can change the income level or income distribution structure. For example, rising agricultural product prices will increase the incomes of farmers and agricultural product marketers while reducing urban household income accordingly (their expenditure on agricultural products will increase). The incomes of farmers and the expenditure of urban household will decrease with a falling price of agricultural products, but the income of marketers may not decline. As a result, this directs a change in the income structure within a price adjustment cycle, and the expansion of the income gap will decrease the period and amplitude of the income distribution cycle. Renewal demand, innovation demand and export are new demand factors that can improve household income and increase the household income growth rate. Accordingly, the period of the household income distribution cycle becomes shorter.

Furthermore, since short-term fluctuations always move around the long-term fluctuation, the longer-term fluctuation could be treated as the equilibrium value of the shorter-term fluctuation. The period of short-term fluctuation is relatively shorter than that of long-term fluctuations, and a long-term fluctuation contains several short-term fluctuations. Consequently, the short-term fluctuations are always covered by the long-term fluctuation, no matter whether short-term fluctuations change the shape of the long-term fluctuation. In other words, short-term fluctuations always center on the long-term fluctuation, and the long-term fluctuation is the mean value or the dynamic equilibrium value of short-term fluctuations.

Moreover, given the relationship between the short-term fluctuation and the long-term fluctuation of consumer demand growth rate, the shorter-term fluctuations in overall economic performance also concentrate on the longer-term fluctuations, according to the correlation among three major demands and economic growth. From the demand-determined perspective, the short-term economic growth is subject to three major types of demand: consumption, investment and export. In the long run, consumption and export are the decisive demand factors. Also, investment as a supply factor depends on consumption and export while consumption depends on the income level determined by economic growth. Therefore, the economy can be seen as a semi-closed circulation system, with consumption as its starting point and export as an exogenous variable. Similarly, the cyclical fluctuations of an economy can be seen as a semi-closed circulation system with the cyclical fluctuations of consumer demand growth rate as the starting point and the cyclical fluctuations of export growth rate as an exogenous variable. More specifically, the dynamic equilibrium growth process of the consumption growth and export become the fundamental factor of the dynamic equilibrium growth process of the growth rate of investment and the whole economy, while the dynamic equilibrium growth process of economic growth rate become the decisive factor affecting the dynamic equilibrium growth process of consumption growth rate. Since the short-term fluctuations of consumption growth rate always center on its long-term fluctuation and take the long-term fluctuation as the dynamic equilibrium value, the short-term fluctuations of the growth rate of investment and the whole economy, which is determined by consumption growth rate, will inevitably move around the long-term fluctuation of the growth rate of investment and economy and take the long-term fluctuation as their dynamic equilibrium value.

Lastly, the cyclical fluctuations of China's economic growth rate provide empirical support for our analysis. By using BP filtering and HP filtering to separate the cycles of China's GDP growth from the first quarter of 1992 to the fourth quarter of 2014, we obtained the short-term fluctuation (GDP growth rate itself), mid-term fluctuation, mid-to-long-term fluctuation, long-term fluctuation and long-term equilibrium value of China's GDP growth (seen in Figures 7.1 and 7.2). From the cyclical fluctuations, China's GDP growth rate (short-term fluctuation) always centers on the mid-term fluctuation. Also, the mid-term fluctuation, the mid-to-long-term fluctuation and the long-term fluctuation always move around with the mid-to-long-term fluctuation, the long-term fluctuation and the long-term equilibrium value as their dynamic equilibrium values. The growth rate of the whole economy evolves with the long-term equilibrium value as its dynamic equilibrium. From 1992 to 2014, the long-term equilibrium value of China's GDP growth rate is characterized by an obvious trend of cyclical fluctuations, and the trend reflects the path of economic development in China shifting from light industrialization (1990–1999) to heavy industrialization (1999–2007), and then to late-industrialization (after 2007) (the specific analysis will be shown in Chapter 10).

Conclusion and policy implications

This chapter shows that cyclical fluctuations are the norm of economic growth, and there always exists a dynamic equilibrium growth process at any stage of the cyclical fluctuations in economic growth. The dynamic neoclassical stable

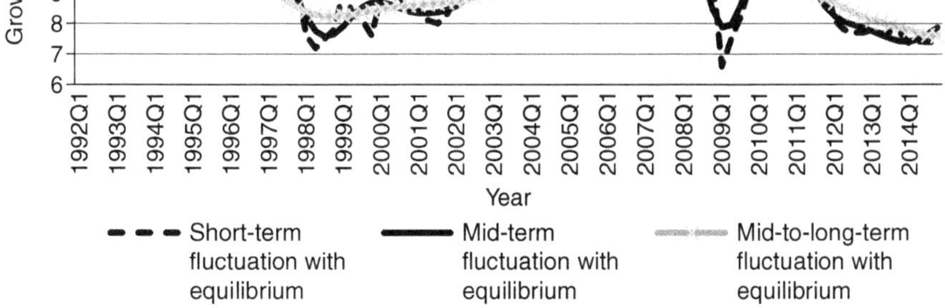

Figure 7.1 GDP growth rate and its mid-term fluctuation and mid- and long-term fluctuation during the period from the first quarter of 1992 to the fourth quarter of 2014 (%).

Source: the data filtering is based on the data on GDP growth rate provided by WIND.

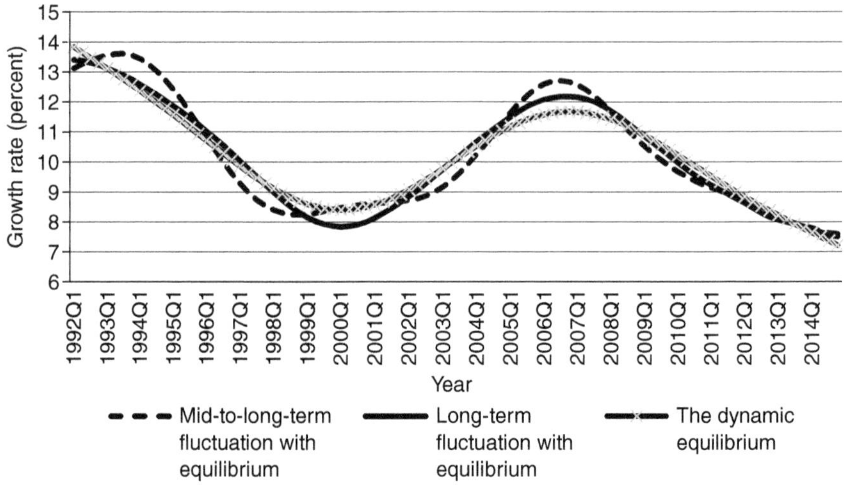

Figure 7.2 Mid-to-long-term fluctuation, long-term fluctuation and dynamic equilibrium value of GDP growth rate during the period from the first quarter of 1992 to the fourth quarter of 2014 (%).

Source: the data filtering is based on the data on GDP growth rate provided by WIND.

equilibrium growth model itself is a model of an endogenous cycle, and its stable equilibrium growth process is consistent with the dynamic equilibrium growth process of the economic cycle, and is a supply-side manifestation of the dynamic equilibrium growth process of the economic cycle. More importantly, this discovery offers an explanation of the disagreement between the Keynesian non-equilibrium growth theory and the neoclassical equilibrium growth theory. The Keynesian disequilibrium growth theory emphasizes the cyclical fluctuations of economic growth, while the neoclassical equilibrium growth theory focuses on the dynamic equilibrium growth process of the cycle fluctuations in economic growth. The two theories provide explanations of the basic characteristics of the cyclical fluctuations of economic activities from different perspectives, and they are in essence consistent. In the real economy, mid-term and short-term fluctuations always move around the long-term fluctuation and take the long-term fluctuation as their dynamic equilibrium values. The symmetrical price fluctuations caused by short-term fluctuations will not change the shape of long-term fluctuation. But the short-term fluctuation factors, which can change the income growth rate, will change the shape and the dynamic equilibrium growth process of long-term fluctuation. Thus the study helps us fully understand the effectiveness of macroeconomic policies and the importance of appropriate policy interventions.

First, short-term policy intervention is an effective instrument to maintain stable economic growth. The neoclassical view asserts that policy intervention is unnecessary, because they believe the cyclical fluctuations of economic growth rate are temporary deviations from the equilibrium growth path and the growth rate will automatically return to the steady-state of equilibrium value. In fact, the short-term economic fluctuations will affect the long-term fluctuation or the dynamic equilibrium growth trend. The short-term fluctuation interventions are effective measures to maintain stable economic growth. Especially when there is an external shock, direct policy intervention will be crucial to prevent economic growth from strong deviation from the inherent growth trend.

Second, policy interventions should be timely and apt. As the cyclical fluctuations of economic growth are highly endogenous, adaptive policy interventions can moderate the amplitude of short-term fluctuations, but policy interventions that are excessive or untimely may exacerbate economic convulsions. So it is necessary to make choices in accordance with the stage of the cyclical economic fluctuation. For instance, the current Chinese economy has fallen to the bottom of the mid-to-long-term cyclical fluctuation. Since reform measures that are effective in stimulating long-term growth may come with short-term deflationary effects, it is crucial for China to adopt appropriate policies to prevent a deep downturn in economic growth.

Additionally, policy interventions should observe the dynamic equilibrium growth trend of the economy. The dynamic equilibrium growth trend of economic growth rates reflects the inherent trend and phased development characteristics of economic growth. The effectiveness of short-term policies depends on whether they are consistent with the dynamic equilibrium growth trend. For example, given that demand for durables is saturated, policies to stimulate durables demand will be ineffective in promoting economic growth, and abusing such policies will only lead to economic stagnation. In such a scenario, only policies aimed at encouraging enterprise innovation and stimulating innovation demand can promote economic growth.

Lastly, external demand plays a prominent role in increasing the dynamic equilibrium value of economic growth. In the semi-closed circulation system with export as an exogenous variable, both investment demand and consumer demand are endogenous variables. Also, government expenditure is restricted by economic growth. So the acceleration of export growth can be seen as an important exogenous cause that could increase the dynamic equilibrium value of the economic growth rate or lift the mid-to-long-term growth trend.

8 The cycle of demand for consumer durables and its influence on the economic cycle in China

In the period of industrialization, the demand for consumer durables is the fundamental driver of economic growth. In the case that household income is normally distributed, the demand for consumer durables has an income distribution cycle that is determined by the characteristics of normally distributed household income. Meanwhile, due to supply lag, renewal demand, product innovation and export, the actual demand for consumer durables exhibits various cycles, such as the price adjustment cycle, the renewal demand cycle, the innovation demand cycle and the export cycle. Since 1978, household electrical appliances, such as color TV sets, refrigerators and washing machines, and family passenger vehicles have become the focus of urban and rural households' expenditure on consumer durables in China. The analysis shows that the periods of the income distribution cycle of color TV sets, refrigerators, washing machines and family passenger vehicles in China's urban households are 27 years, 32 years, 32 years and 64 years respectively, and the periods of the income distribution cycle of color TV sets, refrigerators and washing machines in rural households are about 27 years, 37 and 39 years respectively. Product innovation can have a strong substitution effect on original products, so rural households' demand for black-and-white TV sets has been replaced gradually by the demand for color TV sets after 1997. Renewal demand, supply lag, technological progress and other factors shorten the period of the actual demand cycle of consumer durables. During the period from 1978 to 2012, China experienced 3–5 actual demand cycles of color TV sets, refrigerators, washing machines and family passenger vehicles, and the average period of each cycle was six years, 6.2 years, eight and 12 years respectively. However, the periods of these cycles have extended over time. The shift of the priority demand for consumer durables has an important influence on the household consumption structure and the period of the economic cycle. After 1978, Chinese households' priority demand for consumer durables experienced a gradual shift from household electrical appliances to family passenger vehicles, and the period of the GDP cycle extended from six years in the first cycle (1978–1984) to eight years in the second cycle (1984–1992), and then to 15 years in the third cycle (1992–2007). After 2007, urban and rural households' demand for household electrical appliances gradually reached demand saturation in China, the actual demand cycle of household electrical appliances and family passenger vehicles has entered a period of cyclical downturn coupled with a sharp decline in the exports of household electrical appliances and automobiles; thus GDP growth rate has entered a stage of mid-to-long-term correction. In the future, domestic urban and rural households' demand for household electrical appliances will be dominated by renewal demand and innovation demand; the demand for passenger vehicles has passed the initial acceleration phase, but the actual demand for passenger vehicles, which mainly consists of high-income households' renewal demand and middle-income households' initial demand, will continue to grow rapidly, thereby providing China's heavy industry and the economy's rapid growth with an important demand support. It is necessary to encourage domestic enterprises to expand the export of consumer durables and enhance the support for enterprises' product innovation, so as to extend the period of growing demand for passenger vehicles and increase the contribution of the demand for consumer durables to economic growth.

The period of the income distribution cycle of household electrical appliances and family passenger vehicles in China's urban households

The cumulative demand for consumer durables is S-shaped, i.e., the cumulative demand for consumer durables will remain stable at a certain level when reaching a phase of saturated demand, so we can judge the period of the income distribution cycle of consumer durables on this basis. From the ownership statistics of color TV sets, refrigerators and washing machines per 100 Chinese urban households, it can be seen that Chinese urban households' demand for color TV sets reached saturation in 2007, and the period of its income distribution cycle was about 27 years. The demand for refrigerators and washing machines was close to saturation in 2012, and the periods of their income distribution cycles were about 32 years. The number of family passenger vehicles owned by every 100 urban households was only 21.5 in 2012. According to its demand function, the period of the income distribution cycle of passenger vehicles should be about 64 years. The period of the income distribution cycle of passenger vehicles is much longer than that of household electrical appliances, and the decisive cause for this is that passenger vehicles are far more expensive than household electrical appliances. The period of the income distribution cycle of color TV sets is shorter than that of washing machines and refrigerators, and an important reason for this is that the frequency of product innovation of color TV sets is higher than that of washing machines and refrigerators.

From the sample survey data on urban and rural households provided by the National Bureau of Statistics of China, it can be seen that household electrical appliances, such as color TV sets, refrigerators and washing machines, had entered urban and rural households around 1980. We can use whether every 100 households have 100 or more sets of household electrical appliances as the standard to judge whether consumer durables, such as household electrical appliances and family passenger vehicles, has reached demand saturation or not. The number of color TV sets owned by every 100 urban households was 100.48 and reached demand saturation in 1997, but it continued to rise until reaching 137.79 in 2007. We can use the year 1980 as the starting point of the cycle of urban households' demand for color TV sets, treat urban households' rising consumer demand for color TV sets after 1997 as the demand expansion induced by product innovation, and consider the year 2007, when there is a relatively stable cumulative demand, as the saturation point of the demand for color TV sets. On this basis, it can be estimated that the period of the income distribution cycle of color TV sets (including innovative products) owned by Chinese urban households was 27 years.

The number of washing machines and refrigerators owned by every 100 urban households in China increased from 48.29 sets and 6.85 sets in 1985 to 96.77 sets and 95.03 sets in 2007 respectively; then the rising range significantly narrowed to 98 sets and 98.5 sets in 2012, i.e., the urban households' demand for washing machines and refrigerators approximately reached demand saturation in 2012. China's output of household washing machines and refrigerators was only 400 sets and 28,000 sets respectively in 1978, and washing machines and refrigerators began to enter urban households around 1980; on this basis, it can be estimated that the period of the income distribution cycle of Chinese urban households' demand for washing machines and refrigerators was 32 years.

Family passenger vehicles also began to enter urban households around 1985, and there were 19,500 privately owned vehicles in China in 1985, but there were no statistics on passenger vehicles. From the sample survey data on urban households, it can be seen that every 100 urban households had 0.34 passenger vehicles in 1999, and the corresponding figure increased to 10.89 in 2009, which was followed by a further increase to 21.5 in 2012 (Figure 8.1). This means that demand for passenger vehicles has been met for the highest-income and high-income households. Together the two accounted for 20 percent of the total households. In 2011, the average disposable income of high-income urban households was 91,439 yuan, the household disposable income of middle-income urban households was 55,117 yuan, and the household disposable income of lower-middle-income urban households was 43,640 yuan. According to the inter-year average income growth rate of middle-income households during the period from 2001 to 2011, which is 10.4 percent, and that of lower-middle-income households during the same period, which is 10.1 percent, it can be estimated that it will take middle-income households and lower-middle-income households 5.1 years and 7.7 years respectively to reach the income level of high-income households in 2011. Every 100 urban households owned 18.58 passenger vehicles in 2011, i.e., when high-income households' income level increases to 55,117 yuan, 20 percent of urban households including the highest-income and high-income households can approximately meet their demand for passenger vehicles. On this basis, it can be estimated, in the case that the price of passenger vehicles remains constant and the average growth rate of middle-income households' disposable income is around 10 percent, it will take middle-income households and lower-middle-income households 5.1 years and 7.7 years

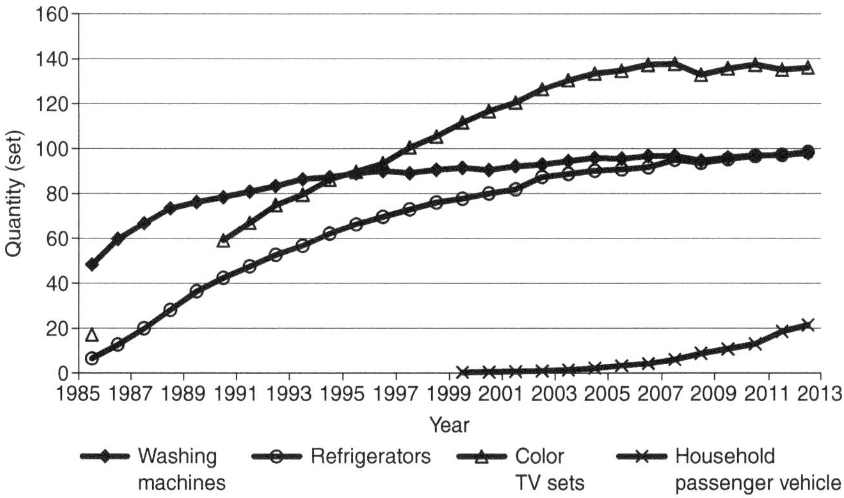

Figure 8.1 Quantities of household electrical appliances and passenger vehicles owned by every 100 urban households in China in 1985–2012 (unit: set/vehicle).

respectively to meet their demand for passenger vehicles, i.e., by 2017 and 2020 respectively. Middle-income households are the largest group among all the households in terms of total demand, and this means that urban households' demand for passenger vehicles will reach the maximum value by around 2017. Accordingly, if we regard urban households' demand for passenger vehicles in 1985 as the starting point, the period of the income distribution cycle of urban households' demand for passenger vehicles shall be about 64 years.

By comparing the period of the income distribution cycle of household electrical appliances such as color TV sets, washing machines and refrigerators with that of passenger vehicles, it can be seen that the period of the cycle of passenger vehicles is much longer than that of household electrical appliances, and the decisive factor for this is that the price of passenger vehicles is much higher than that of household electrical appliances. The period of the income distribution cycle of color TV sets is shorter than that of washing machines and refrigerators, and an important reason for this is that the frequency of product innovation of color TV sets is much higher than that of washing machines and refrigerators.

The period of the income distribution cycle of rural households' demand for household electrical appliances in China

From the quantities of color TV sets, refrigerators and washing machines owned by every 100 rural households, it can be seen that Chinese rural households' demand for color TV sets reached demand saturation in 2012; two-thirds of households had fulfilled their demand for refrigerators and washing machines (Figure 8.2). The period of the income distribution cycle of the demand for color TV sets was about 27 years, and those of the demand for refrigerators and washing machines were about 37 years and 39 years respectively.

Color TV sets entered rural households in about 1985, and the number of color TV sets owned by every 100 rural households increased from 0.8 in 1985 to 116.9 in 2012. From the trend of color TV set ownership, it can be seen that Chinese rural households' demand for color TV sets reached demand saturation in 2012, and the period of its income distribution cycle was about 27 years, which was the same as the period of the income distribution cycle of urban households' demand for color TV sets.

Refrigerators began to enter rural households in 1985, and the number of refrigerators owned by every 100 rural households increased from 0.06 sets in 1985 to 67.3 sets in 2012. Washing machines entered rural households in 1983, and the number of washing machines owned by every 100 rural households increased from 0.4 sets in 1985 to 67.2 sets in 2012. Given that consumer durables have a bell-shaped, normally distributed demand density function and consequently an S-shaped cumulative demand function, when the number of refrigerators and washing machines in rural households is more than 50 per 100 households, it means that middle-income households, which account for the largest proportion of the population, have fulfilled their demand for refrigerators and washing machines. The peak value of the initial demand for refrigerators and washing machines is the middle-income households' demand; the initial demand will decline gradually after it reaches peak value, and the rise in cumulative demand will slow down gradually. In 2011, the average net income of

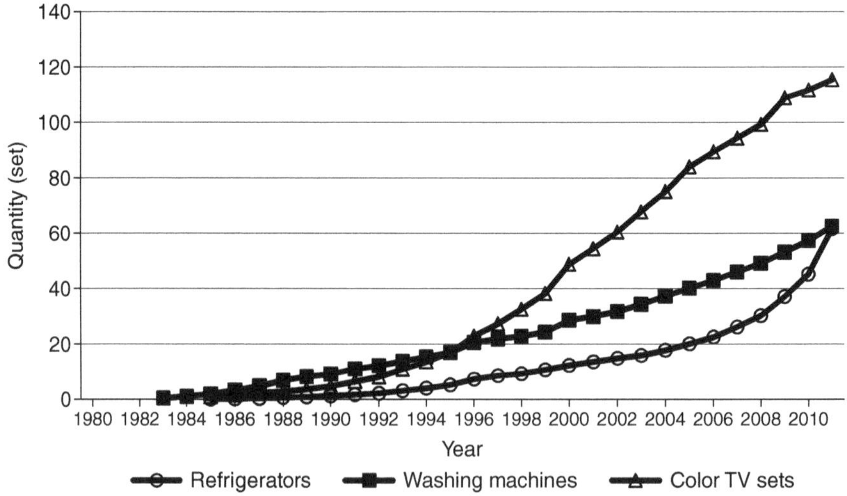

Figure 8.2 Quantity of household electrical appliances owned by every 100 rural households in China, 1983–2012 (unit: set).

middle-income rural households was 6,207.68 yuan, and every 100 rural households had 61.54 refrigerators and 62.57 washing machines; this is to say that at the income level of 6,207.68 yuan, 60 percent of rural households including high-income households, above-average households and middle-income households fully met their consumer demand for refrigerators and washing machines. Under the condition of constant income–price ratio of refrigerators and washing machines, in order to meet their consumer demand for refrigerators and washing machines, low-income households need to increase their income level to the average net income level of middle-income households in 2011. In the same year, the average net income of low-income households was 2,000.51 yuan, the average income of middle-income households was 6,207.68 yuan and the nominal growth rate of the average net income of rural households averaged 11.04 percent during the period from 2000 to 2012. Assuming that the future average net income of rural households will continue growing at this rate, it will take low-income households 10.85 years to increase their income level to the 2011 level of middle-income households. On this basis, it can be estimated that in the case that the prices of refrigerators and washing machines remain constant, rural households' demand for refrigerators and washing machines will reach demand saturation by 2022, i.e., the period of the income distribution cycle of rural households' demand for refrigerators and washing machines shall be about 37 years and 39 years respectively, which is five years and seven years longer than the period of the income distribution cycle of urban households' demand for refrigerators and washing machines, respectively. If the prices of refrigerators and washing machines fall in the future, the periods of their income distribution cycles will be shorter. However, the future growth rate of average net income of rural households may be less than its cross-year average growth rate during the period from 2000 to 2012, and the slowing down of income growth rate will extend the period of the income distribution cycle.

By comparing the periods of the income distribution cycles of color TV sets, refrigerators and washing machines in rural households, it can be seen that the period of the income distribution cycle of rural households' demand for color TV sets is also shorter than that of washing machines and refrigerators, and an important reason for this is that the frequency of product innovation of color TV sets is much higher than that of washing machines and refrigerators.

Influence of product innovation on the period of the consumer durables demand cycle: taking rural households' demand for TV sets as an example

Demand for innovative products can partly replace the demand for original products and change the period of the income distribution cycle of consumer durables. Chinese rural households' demand for TV sets is a typical example of a partial replacement of the demand for original products by innovation demand. After black-and-white TV sets entered rural households in 1980, the number of black-and-white TV sets owned by every 100 households increased continuously.

After color TV sets entered rural households in around 1985, however, its substitution effect on black-and-white TV sets was continually intensified. The rise in the number of black-and-white TV sets owned by every 100 rural households slowed gradually, and the number began to decline after rising to 65.12 in 1997, i.e., the color TV sets completely replaced rural households' renewal demand for black-and-white TV sets and partly replaced rural households' initial demand for TV sets after the year 1997, thus bringing the cycle of demand for black-and-white TV sets to an earlier end. But because color TV set ownership continued to rise, the number of TV sets owned by rural households still enabled the cumulative demand for consumer durables to show an S-shaped rising trend and reached demand saturation in 2004, and the period of its income distribution cycle was 24 years, which was shorter than the period of the income distribution cycle of color TV sets (27 years).

From the sampling survey data on rural households provided by the National Bureau of Statistics of China, it can be seen that black-and-white TV sets entered rural households in 1980, and the number of black-and-white TV sets owned by every 100 rural households increased from 0.4 sets in 1980 to 10.9 sets in 1985. During this period, color TV sets also began to enter rural households, and the number of color TV sets owned by every 100 rural households was 0.8 sets in 1985, which was equivalent to the number of black-and-white TV sets owned by every 100 rural households in 1981 (0.9 sets). But as a novel product, color TV sets had an increasing substitution effect on black-and-white TV sets after the year 1985. The number of black-and-white TV sets owned by every 100 rural households trended downward after reaching 65.12 sets in 1997, and dropped to 1.66 sets in 2011. The declining black-and-white TV set ownership in rural households shows that the income distribution cycle of rural households' black-and-white TV sets ended in 1997, and the period of the income distribution cycle of black-and-white TV sets was only 17 years. After the year 1997, rural households' renewal demand and initial demand for black-and-white TV sets has been replaced by that for color TV sets. From the number of color TV sets owned by rural households, it can be seen that color TV set ownership increased continuously after the year 1985 and rose to 116.9 sets in 2012, and the color TV set ownership showed a slowly rising trend, thus indicating that the period of the cycle of Chinese rural households' demand for color TV sets was about 27 years. From the total number of TV sets (the sum of black-and-white TV sets and color TV sets) owned by rural households (Figure 8.3), it can be seen that the curve of total ownership was still S-shaped and showed some fluctuations within a narrow range after ownership increased to 113.01 sets in 2004, and then the rising trend of ownership clearly slowed down. This is a sign indicating that rural households' demand for TV sets reached demand saturation in 2004, and the period of its income distribution cycle was about 24 years, which was between the period of the income distribution cycle of black-and-white TV sets (17 years) and that of color TV sets (27 years).

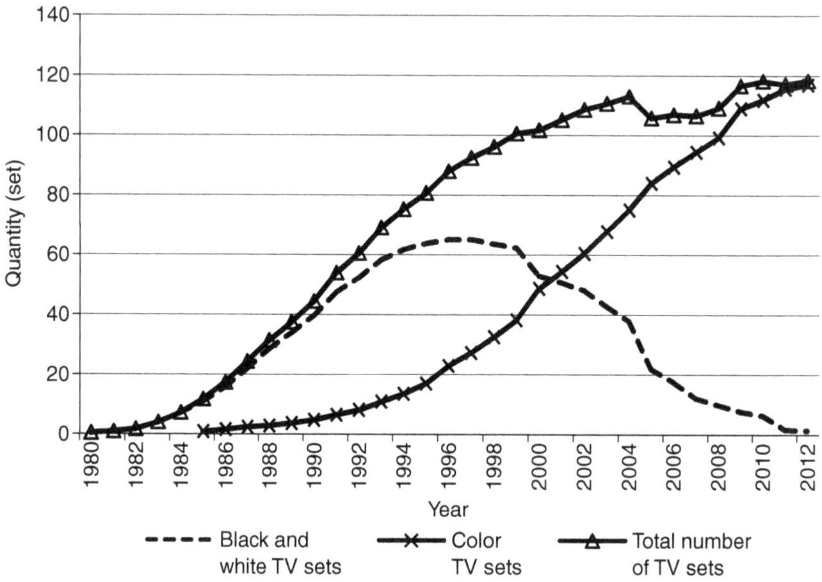

Figure 8.3 Quantity of TV sets owned by every 100 rural households in China, 1980–2012 (unit: set).

Period of actual demand cycle of household electrical appliances and passenger vehicles in China

Affected by supply lags, renewal demand, technological progress, export and other factors, the actual demand for consumer durables exhibits various cycles, such as the price adjustment cycle, the renewal demand cycle, the innovation demand cycle and the export cycle. Those cycles' periods are determined by supply lag, the product life of consumer durables, the frequency of product innovation and other factors. The periods of all kinds of actual demand cycles is shorter than the period of the income distribution cycle, and at different stages of the actual demand cycle; its period can also vary greatly with different influencing factors. In order to analyze the period of the actual demand cycle of consumer durables, we used the ownership of color TV sets, refrigerators, washing machines and the civilian passenger vehicle during the period from 1978 to 2012 as alternative indicators of the actual demand for household appliances and family passenger vehicles (Figures 8.4 and 8.5). The analysis results show that the actual demand for color TV sets, refrigerators, washing machines and passenger vehicles had 3–5 cycles during the period from 1978 to 2012; the period of each cycle tended to be longer, and their average period was six years, 6.2 years, eight years and 12 years respectively. Just like the period of the income distribution cycle of all kinds of consumer durables, due to relatively higher frequency of product innovation of color TV sets and other influencing factors, the

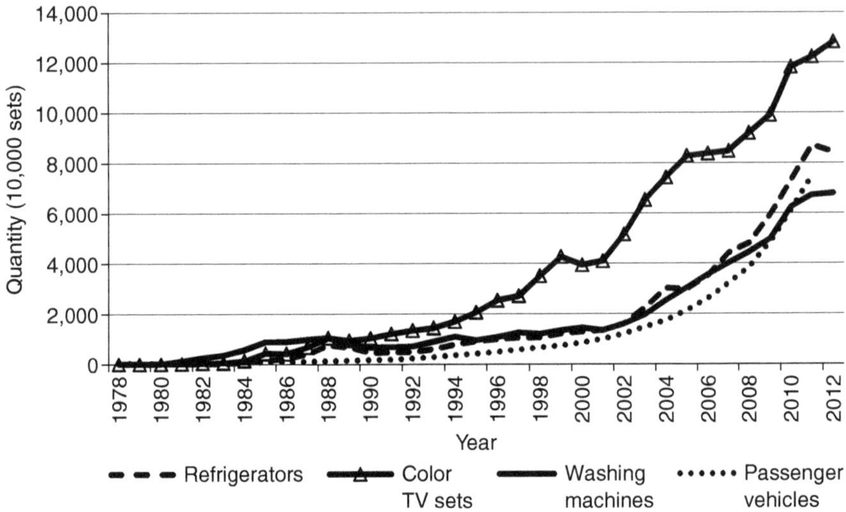

Figure 8.4 Production of household electrical appliances and ownership of civilian passenger vehicles in China, 1978–2012 (unit: 10,000 sets/vehicles).

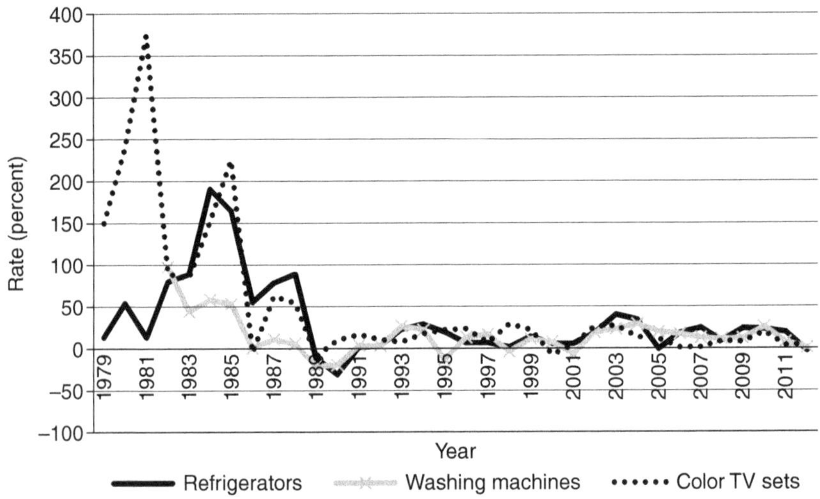

Figure 8.5 Fluctuations of growth of color TV sets, household refrigerators and washing machines in China, 1979–2012 (%).

period of the actual demand cycle of color TV sets is much shorter than that of washing machines and refrigerators, and the period of the actual demand cycle of more expensive passenger vehicles is significantly higher than that of relatively cheaper household electrical appliances.

Period of actual demand cycle of household refrigerators

Based on peak-to-peak calculation, there were four complete actual demand cycles of refrigerators during the period from 1978 to 2012 (Table 8.1): the 1984–1988 cycle with a period of four years, the 1988–1994 cycle with a period of six years, the 1994–2003 cycle with a period of nine years and the 2003–2009 cycle with a period of six years. The average period of all cycles was 6.25 years. Based on the trough-to-trough calculation, there were five actual demand cycles of refrigerators: the 1981–1986 cycle with a period of five years, the 1986–1990 cycle with a period of four years, the 1990–1998 cycle with a period of eight years, the 1998–2005 cycle with a period of seven years and the 2005–2012 cycle with a period of seven years. The average period is 6.2 years. In general, the period of actual demand cycle of refrigerators extended after the year 1978, and the average period was 6.2 years.

Period of actual demand cycle of washing machines

Based on peak-to-peak calculation, there were three complete actual demand cycles of washing machines during the period from 1978 to 2012 (Table 8.2): the 1982–1993 cycle with a period of 11 years, the 1993–2004 cycle with a

Table 8.1 Evolution characteristics of actual demand cycles of household refrigerators in China in 1978–2012 (years)

Time point of trough	*Time point of peak*	*Peak-to-peak*	*Trough-to-trough*	*Trough-to-peak*	*Peak-to-trough*
1981	1984			3	
1986	1988	4	5	2	2
1990	1994	6	4	4	2
1998	2003	9	8	5	4
2005	2009	6	7	4	2
2012			7		3

Source: calculated based on the data on refrigerator production provided by WIND.

Table 8.2 Evolution characteristics of actual demand cycles of washing machines in China in 1978–2012 (years)

Time point of trough	*Time point of peak*	*Peak-to-peak*	*Trough-to-trough*	*Trough-to-peak*	*Peak-to-trough*
	1982				
1990	1993	11		3	8
1998	2004	11	8	6	5
2008	2010	6	10	2	4

Source: calculated based on the data on washing machine production provided by WIND.

period of 11 years and the 2004–2010 cycle with a period of six years. The average period of all cycles was 9.3 years. Based on the trough-to-trough calculation, there were two actual demand cycles of washing machines, including the 1990–1998 cycle with a period of eight years and the 1998–2008 cycle with a period of ten years. The average period of all cycles was nine years; the period of the 2008–2012 cycle was only four years, but the year 2012 should not be the trough of a new round of the actual demand cycle of washing machines. In general, the average period of the actual demand cycle of washing machines was nine years.

Period of actual demand cycle of color TV sets

Based on peak-to-peak calculation, there were five complete actual demand cycles of color TV sets during the period from 1978 to 2012 (Table 8.3): the 1981–1985 cycle with a period of four years, the 1985–1991 cycle with a period of six years, the 1991–1998 cycle with a period of seven years, the 1998–2003 cycle with a period of five years and the 2005–2010 cycle with a period of five years. The average period of all cycles was 5.8 years. Based on the trough-to-trough calculation, there were five complete actual demand cycles of color TV sets: the 1979–1983 cycle with a period of four years, the 1983–1989 cycle with a period of six years, the 1989–1993 cycle with a period of four years, the 1993–2000 cycle with a period of seven years, the 2000–2007 cycle with a period of seven years and the 2007–2012 cycle with a period of five years. It has not been confirmed whether the year 2012 was the trough of a new round of the cycle. From the five previous trough-to-trough cycles it can be seen that the average period of each cycle was six years. In general, the period of the actual demand cycle of color TV sets after the year 1979 tended to be longer, the period extended from four years in the first cycle to seven years in the fourth and fifth cycles, and the average period was about six years, which was shorter than the period of the actual demand cycle of refrigerators and washing machines.

Table 8.3 Evolution characteristics of actual demand cycles of color TV sets in China, 1978–2012

Trough year	*Peak year*	*Peak-to-peak (years)*	*Trough-to-trough (years)*	*Trough-to-peak (years)*	*Peak-to-trough (years)*
1979	1981			2	
1983	1985	4	4	2	2
1989	1991	6	6	2	4
1993	1996	5	6	3	2
2000	2003	7	7	3	4
2007	2010	7	7	3	4

Source: calculated based on the data on color TV set production provided by WIND.

Period of actual demand cycle of passenger vehicles

Based on peak-to-peak calculation, there were three complete actual demand cycles of passenger vehicles during the period from 1975 to 2011 (Table 8.4; Figure 8.6): the 1975–1985 cycle with a period of ten years, the 1985–1993 cycle with a period of eight years and the 1993–2010 cycle with a period of 17 years. The average period of all cycles was 12 years. Based on peak-to-peak calculation, the actual demand for passenger vehicles had three cycles: the 1983–1990 cycle with a period of seven years, the 1990–1998 cycle with a period of eight years and a new cycle after the year 1998; this new cycle had lasted for 14 years till 2012, but it has not been confirmed whether the year 2012 was the trough of a new round of the cycle. Taking the fact that the latest cycle has not ended into consideration, the average period of the actual demand cycle of vehicles should be more than ten years based on the trough-to-trough calculation.

Table 8.4 Evolution characteristics of actual demand cycles of passenger vehicles in China, 1978–2012

Trough year	*Peak year*	*Peak-to-peak (years)*	*Trough-to-trough (years)*	*Trough-to-peak (years)*	*Peak-to-trough (years)*
	1975				
1983	1985	10		2	8
1990	1993	8	7	3	5
1998	2010	17	8	12	5

Source: calculated based on the data on civilian passenger vehicle ownership provided by WIND.

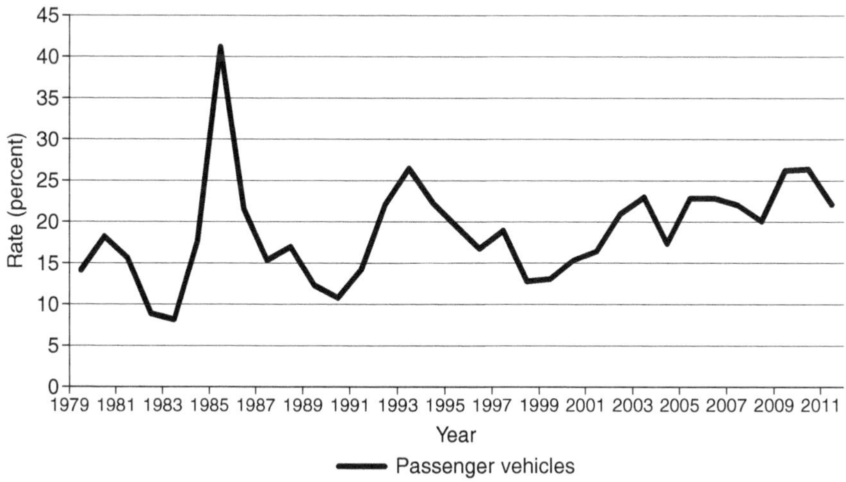

Figure 8.6 Fluctuations of growth of civilian passenger vehicle ownership in China, 1975–2011 (%).

Source: calculated based on the data on civilian passenger vehicle ownership provided by WIND.

In general, the period of the actual demand cycle of vehicles was obviously longer after the year 1975, and the average period of all cycles was 12 years, which was obviously longer than the period of the actual demand cycle of household electrical appliances.

Influence of the demand for consumer durables on urban and rural households' consumption expenditure structure in China

Among urban and rural households' six major categories of non-food consumption expenditures, household appliances and automobiles are two kinds of typical expenditures on consumer durables. Corresponding to the changes in the number of consumer durables owned by every 100 households, the structure of urban and rural households' expenditure on consumer durables in China also has clear periodical characteristics: Before 1991, as household electrical appliances entered urban and rural households, urban and rural households' expenditure on consumer durables was dominated by household appliances and services. After 1991, along with the rapid increase of civilian passenger vehicle ownership, the scale and proportion of urban and rural households' expenditure on automobiles increased rapidly and became the priority of urban and rural households' consumption expenditure.

Specifically, during the period from 1982 to 1991, the weights of household appliances and housing in urban households' consumption expenditure had increased significantly; the weight of household appliances and services in urban households' consumption expenditure increased from 9.22 percent in 1982 to 13.46 percent in 1988, and then gradually fell to 9.62 percent in 1991, with an average of 10.27 percent for the period from 1982 to 1991, ranking as the third largest consumption expenditure item following clothing and housing. During this period, the number of household electrical appliances owned by every 100 urban households increased significantly. In 1991, every 100 urban households had on average 66.96 color TV sets, 80.91 refrigerators and 47.47 washing machines.

After 1991, urban households' consumption expenditure on automobiles experienced a rapid expansion. Its weight increased significantly from 1.36 percent in 1991 to 14.73 percent in 2012 and overtook housing as urban households' largest consumption expenditure item since 2010. At the same time, the total civilian passenger vehicle ownership increased from 1.8525 million vehicles in 1991 to 61.2413 million vehicles in 2010, and the number of civilian passenger vehicles owned by every 100 urban households also increased from 0.34 in 1999 to 13.07 in 2010 (Figure 8.7).

Similar to the changes in urban households' consumption expenditure structure, as electrical appliances such as TV sets, refrigerators and washing machines entered rural households after 1980, rural households' consumption expenditure on household appliances and services experienced a rapid expansion. Its proportion increased significantly from 3.79 percent in 1980 to 9.47 percent in 1983,

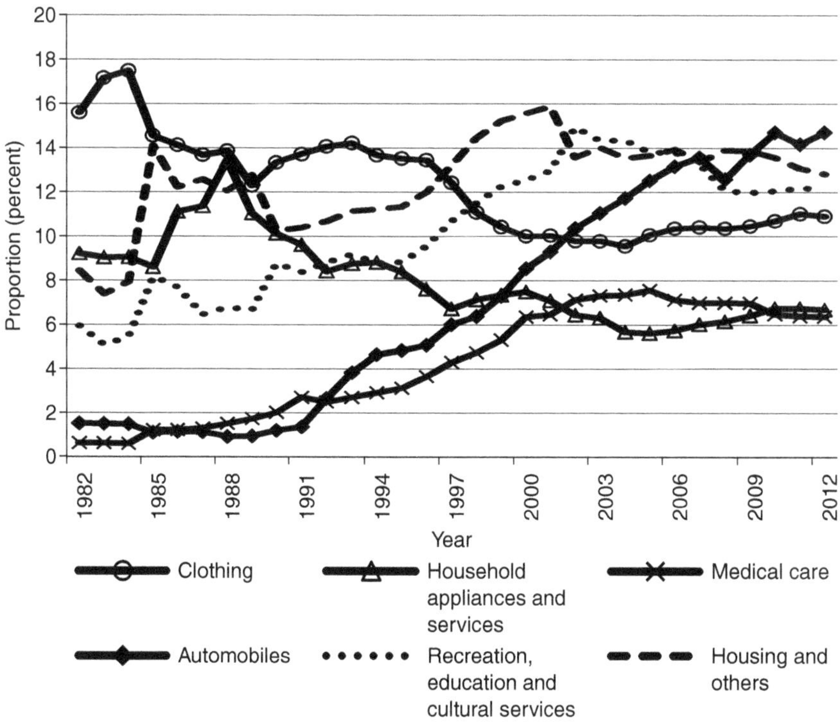

Figure 8.7 Proportion of urban households' non-food consumption expenditure in China, 1982–2012 (%).

Source: calculated according to the data on urban households' consumption expenditure provided by WIND.

and then stabilized at a high level around 8.56 percent till 1993, ranking as the third largest non-food consumption expenditure item, following housing and clothing. The weight of automobiles in rural households' consumption expenditure also increased significantly after 1990. It increased continuously from 2.24 percent in 1990 to 11.96 percent in 2006, and then gradually fell to 7.54 percent in 2012. The weight of automobiles in rural households' consumption expenditure averaged 9.58 percent from 2000 to 2012, ranking as the third largest consumption expenditure item, following housing (averaged at 18.15 percent) and cultural and educational entertainment (averaged at 11.58 percent) (Figure 8.8).

Influence of the consumer durables demand cycle on the period of the economic cycle in China

Consumer durables consumption is the demand-side foundation for economic growth and cyclical economic fluctuations during the period of industrialization,

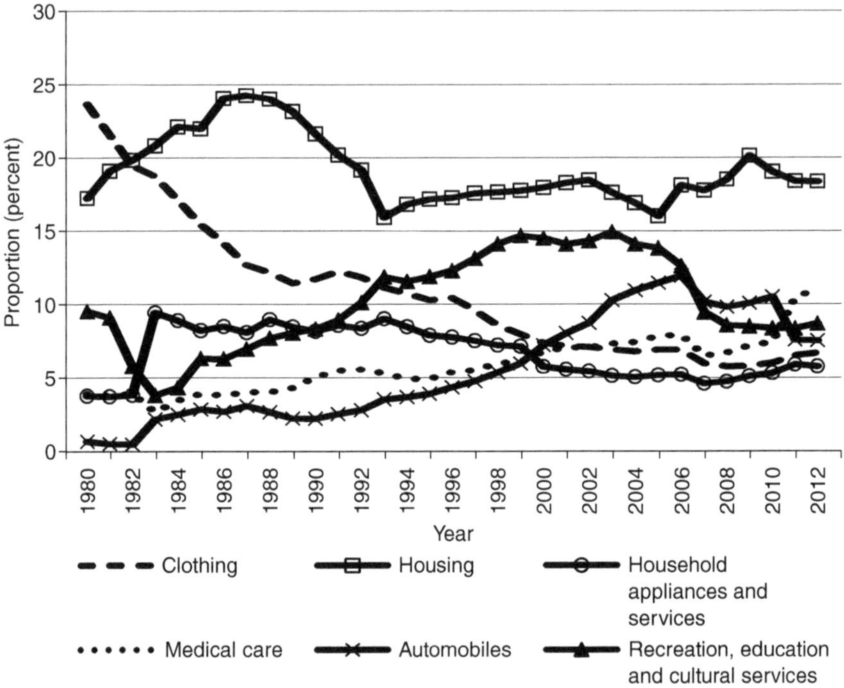

Figure 8.8 Proportion of rural households' non-food consumption expenditure in China, 1980–2012 (%).

Source: calculated according to the data on rural households' consumption expenditure provided by WIND.

and the actual demand cycle of consumer durables is also very important in determining the trend of the overall economic cycle. China's economy experienced three cycles after 1977, and the period and the rising and falling stages of each cycle have become progressively longer. One of the decisive factors for this is that the demand for consumer durables has shifted from household electrical appliances with relatively lower prices and shorter product lives to family passenger vehicles with relatively higher prices and longer product lives, thus transforming the industrial structure from focusing on light industry to heavy industrialization.

Gradual extension of the period of economic cycles in China since 1977

Based on peak-to-peak calculations, China's GDP growth experienced three complete cycles during the period from 1977 to 2012 (Table 8.5; Figure 8.9): the 1978–1984 cycle with a period of six years, the 1984–1992 cycle with a period

Table 8.5 Evolution characteristics of GDP cycles in China in 1977–2012 (years)

Time point of peak	*Time point of trough*	*Time from peak to trough*	*Time from trough to peak*
1978	1981	3	
1984	1990	6	3
1992	1999	7	2
2007	2013	6	8

Source: according to the data in the 1990–2012 *China Statistical Yearbooks*.

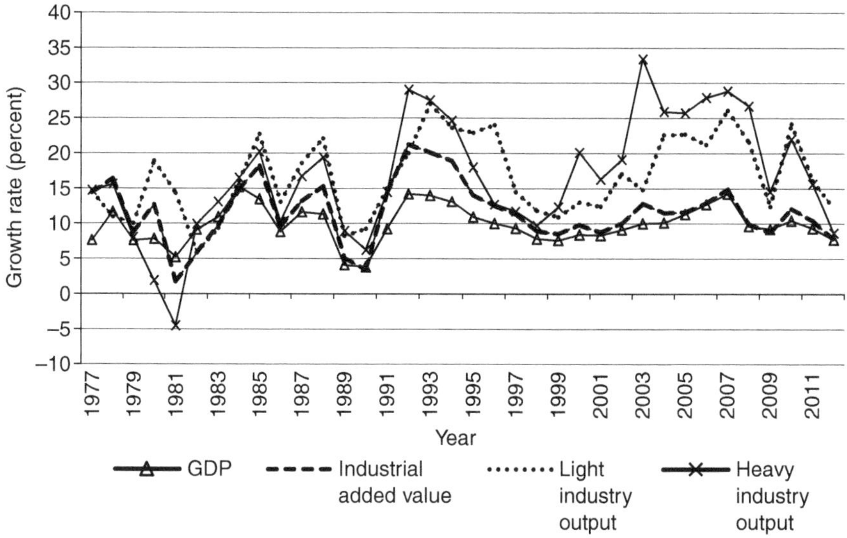

Figure 8.9 Actual growth rates of GDP, industrial added value, light industry output and heavy industry output in China, 1977–2012 (%).

Source: calculated according to the data in the 1990–1990 *China Statistical Yearbooks*.

of eight years and the 1992–2007 cycle with a period of 15 years. Based on the trough-to-trough calculation, China's GDP growth rate experienced two complete cycles: the 1981–1990 cycle with a period of nine years and the 1990–1999 cycle with a period of nine years. The third cycle, which began in 1999, has lasted for 14 years till now; the question of whether the third cycle reached its trough in 2013 has not yet been determined. From the period and the length of rising and falling stages of the three cycles, it can be seen that China's GDP cycles have had three features since 1977. First, the period of economic cycles has become gradually longer, with an extension from six years to eight years and 15 years based on peak-to-peak calculation; second, the rising stage of a cycle has become continuously longer, with a substantial extension from 2–3 years in the early stage to eight years; third, the falling stage of a cycle has also become gradually longer, with an extension from the first three-year falling stage to the second six-year falling stage and then to the third seven-year falling stage, so it is expected that the fourth falling stage beginning in 2007 will last seven years at least.

Short-cycle fluctuation of the demand for household electrical appliances was an important factor leading to the relatively shorter period of the 1978–1984 GDP cycle

During the period from 1978 to 1984, household electrical appliances such as color TV sets, washing machines and refrigerators entered urban and rural households, and production was in a state of rapid growth; among them, the production growth rates of color TV sets and household refrigerators were the highest, and they were also the priority of the urban and rural households' consumption expenditure on consumer durables. During this period, the growth rate of light industry output was significantly higher than that of heavy industry output, and the fluctuation shape of the growth rate of industrial added-value was highly consistent with that of light industry output. The fluctuations of GDP growth rate were dominated by the fluctuations of industrial added-value, which was determined by the fluctuations of the growth rate of light industry output, while the period of the cycle of light industry output was mainly determined by the period of the actual demand cycle of household electrical appliances such as color TV sets and refrigerators. The relatively shorter period of the actual demand cycle of household electrical appliances was the important factor that led to the relatively shorter period of this round of the GDP cycle.

After 1978, household electrical appliances such as color TV sets, washing machines and refrigerators began to enter urban and rural households (Table 8.6). The production and consumption of household electrical appliances became the new source of economic growth in China. In the 1978–1984 GDP cycle, the production scale of newly emerging color TV sets, refrigerators and washing machines expanded rapidly from 3,800 sets, 28,000 sets and 400 sets in 1978 to 1.3395 million sets, 547,400 sets and 5.7806 million sets in 1984, respectively, with an inter-year average growth rate as high as 165.78 percent, 64.13 percent and 393.54 percent respectively.

Table 8.6 Average growth rates of household electrical appliances and civilian passenger vehicles in China during different periods (%)

Period	*Refrigerators*	*Washing machines*	*Color TV sets*	*Civilian passenger vehicles*
1978–1984	64.13	393.54	165.78	13.74
1984–1992	31.38	2.57	33.27	18.99
1992–2007	15.82	12.25	13.13	19.31
2007–2012	13.89	10.98	8.63	23.68

From the shapes of cycles of GDP, industrial value-added, light industry output and heavy industry output, it can be seen that the GDP growth rate entered the falling stage of this cycle in 1978 and reached its trough in 1981; the period from 1981 to 1984 was the rising stage of this cycle. The falling stage of the growth rate of industrial added-value and that of heavy industry output coincided with the falling stage of GDP growth rate, but its rising stage was one year longer than the rising stage of GDP growth rate (one-year lag after the second peak). The falling stage of light industry began in 1980, its trough (1982) had a lag of one year when compared with the troughs of the growth rate of GDP, industrial added-value and heavy industry output, and its second peak overlapped with the second peak of the growth rate of heavy industry output and that of industrial added-value.

From the consumer durables demand cycle, it can be seen that the lagging trough of the growth rate of light industry output was induced by the lagging trough of the demand cycle of color TV sets; the trough of refrigerators in 1981 was consistent with the trough of the growth rate of GDP and that of industrial added-value, and the trough of the growth rate of the demand for color TV sets in 1983 had a lag of two years when compared with the troughs of the growth rates of GDP, industrial added-value and heavy industry output. The second peaks of the cycles of industrial added-value, light industry output and heavy industry output had a lag of one year when compared with the second peak of the GDP cycle, and they were jointly determined by the lagging peak of the consumer durables demand cycle. The second peak of the growth rate of the demand for household refrigerators in 1984 coincided with the second peak of the GDP growth rate; but the second peak of the growth rate of the demand for color TV sets and automobiles occurred in 1985, when the growth rate of the demand for washing machines was still at the rising stage of its cycle, thereby determining that the second peak of the growth rates of light industry output, heavy industry output and industrial added-value was in 1985, which had a lag of one year when compared with the second peak of GDP growth rate. Table 8.7 offers a comparison of the cycles.

It can be seen that the period of this round of the GDP cycle was only six years, which was obviously shorter than the period of the following cycles. One important reason for this is that the period of the demand cycle of color TV sets and refrigerators was only four years during this period, and the period of the cycle of light industry output was only five years.

Expansion of demand for household electrical appliances and accelerating demand for passenger vehicles lengthened the period of the 1984–1992 GDP cycle

The period of the second GDP cycle was eight years (1984–1992), which was obviously longer than the period of the 1978–1984 cycle. From the change of consumer durables demand structure, it can be seen that as middle-income households, which account for the largest proportion of the population, began to

Table 8.7 Comparison of the cycles of GDP, industrial added value, light industry output, heavy industry output and demand for consumer durables based on peak-to-peak calculation (years)

GDP cycle	Fluctuation range	1978–1984	1984–1992	1992–2007	2007–2012
	Period of cycle	6	8	15	5
Growth cycle of industrial added value	Fluctuation range	1978–1985	1985–1993	1993–2007	2007–2012
	Period of cycle	7	8	14	5
Growth cycle of light industry output	Fluctuation	1980–1985	1985–1993	1993–2007	2007–2012
	Period of cycle	5	8	14	5
Growth cycle of heavy industry output	Fluctuation range	1978–1985	1985–1992	1992–2007	2007–2012
	Period of cycle	7	7	15	5
Demand cycle of color TV sets	Fluctuation range	1981–1985	1985–1991	1991–1998	1998–2003
	Period of cycle	4	6	7	5
Demand cycle of refrigerators	Fluctuation range	1980–1984	1984–1988	1988–1994	1994–2003
	Period of cycle	4	4	6	9
Demand cycle of washing machines	Fluctuation range	1982–1993		1993–2004	2004–2010
	Period of cycle	11		11	6
Demand cycle of vehicles	Fluctuation range	1975–1985	1985–1993	1993–2010	
	Period of cycle	10	8	17	

Source: according to the data in the 1990–2012 *China Statistical Yearbooks*.

demand color TV sets and refrigerators, the scale of the demand for color TV sets and refrigerators expanded, thus lengthening the period of the demand cycle. In addition, the acceleration of demand for passenger vehicles with a relatively longer period led to an increase of the growth rate of heavy industry output. As a result, these two factors were the fundamental demand-side factors that determined the extension of the period of this round of the GDP cycle.

After 1984, the demand for household electrical appliances such as color TV sets and refrigerators expanded from the early-stage, high-income households to the middle-income households, which account for the largest proportion of the population, so the production scale of color TV sets and refrigerators expanded rapidly. Compared with 1984, the production of color TV sets and refrigerators increased 9.95 times and 8.87 times respectively in 1992, with a cross-year average growth rate as high as 33.27 percent and 31.38 percent respectively. As the scale of the demand for color TV sets and refrigerators expanded and extended to middle-income households, the period of the demand cycle of color TV sets and refrigerators became obviously longer; the period of the demand cycle of color TV sets extended from four years in the 1981–1985 cycle to six years in the 1985–1991 cycle, and the period of the demand cycle of refrigerators extended from four years in the 1984–1988 cycle to six years in the 1988–1994 cycle, thus the period of the cycle of light industry output extended from five years in the 1980–1985 cycle to eight years in the 1985–1993 cycle.

After 1984, the automobile industry also experienced accelerated growth. Production increased 3.37 times from 316,400 vehicles in 1984 to 1.0667 million vehicles in 1992; civilian passenger vehicle ownership increased 4.02 times from 562,800 vehicles in 1984 to 2.2616 million vehicles in 1992, with an inter-year average growth rate of 18.99 percent, which was obviously higher than the cross-year average growth rate of 13.74 percent during the period from 1978 to 1984. The increase of the growth rate of the demand for civilian passenger vehicles induced the increase of the growth rate of heavy industry output, and the average growth rate of heavy industry output increased from 8.64 percent during the period from 1978 to 1984 to 15.64 percent during the period from 1985 to 1992. Compared with the average growth rate of light industry output during the corresponding periods, the gap between them narrowed from 3.54 percent during the period from 1978 to 1984 to 0.48 percent during the period from 1985 to 1992. Pulled by the increase of the growth rate of the demand for civilian passenger vehicles, the growth of heavy industry output was accelerated; the trough of this round of the GDP cycle occurred in 1990 and coincided exactly with the troughs of the cycles of industrial added-value, light industry output and heavy industry output; but after the trough, the peak of the GDP cycle occurred in 1992 and coincided with the peak of the cycle of heavy industry output, but it was one year earlier than the peak of the cycle of industrial added-value and that of light industry output.

Expansion of the demand for household electrical appliances and the sustained and rapid increase of demand for civilian passenger vehicles greatly lengthened the period of the 1992–2007 GDP cycle

After 1992, China's GDP growth rate entered the long cycle with a falling stage of seven years and a rising stage of eight years. From the structure of the demand for consumer durables, it can be seen that due to the expansion of export and rural households' demand, the period of the cycle of the demand for household electrical appliances became longer, thus greatly extending the cycle of light industry output and playing an important role in greatly lengthening the period of the GDP cycle, but the sustained and rapid growth of demand for civilian passenger vehicles was the decisive factor of the greatly extended period of this round of the GDP cycle.

Expansion of the groups with demand for household electrical appliances lengthened the period of the cycle of light industry output

After 1992, urban households' demand for household electrical appliances gradually reached a phase of saturated demand, and the urban households' demand for household electrical appliances such as color TV sets, refrigerators and washing machines entered a period with low-speed growth, which was dominated by renewal demand and the demand for novel products. But during the period from 1992 to 2007, the actual demand cycle of color TV sets experienced two cycles with an average period of six years each; the actual demand cycle of washing machines experienced one cycle with a period of 11 years; and the period of the actual demand cycle of refrigerators extended from six years in the 1988–1994 cycle to nine years in the 1994–2003 cycle. At the same time, during the period from 1992 to 2007, after the urban households' demand for household electrical appliances reached a phase of saturated demand, the actual demand growth rate of color TV sets and that of refrigerators experienced a relatively substantial drop when compared with their growth rates during the period from 1984 to 1992, but they still maintained a relatively fast average annual growth rate of 13.13 percent and 15.82 percent respectively; the average growth rate of the actual demand for washing machines was as high as 12.25 percent, with an increase of nearly 10 percent when compared with the average growth rate during the period from 1984 to 1992 (2.57 percent). During this period, the relatively fast growth of the actual demand for household electrical appliances and the extension of the period of the demand cycle were mainly induced by the expansion of demand.

First, demand for household electrical appliances had expanded to rural households, thus lengthening the period of the actual demand cycle of household electrical appliances. After 1992, rural households' demand for household electrical appliances entered a period of scale expansion, and the rural household groups with a demand for household electrical appliances expanded from the highest-income households in 1992 (in 1992, the number of color TV sets, refrigerators and washing machines owned by every 100 rural households was 8.08 sets, 2.17 sets and 12.2 sets respectively, i.e., only the highest-income households, which accounted for 10 percent of total rural households, fulfilled their demand for household electrical appliances) to the high- and middle-income households (in 2007, the number of color TV sets, refrigerators and washing machines owned by every 100 rural households increased to 94.38 sets, 26.12 sets and 45.94 sets respectively). In addition to the growing domestic demand for household electrical appliances driven by rural households' growing demand, the widening income inequality between different groups of people with demand for household electrical appliances induced by the expansion of domestic consumer groups also lengthened the period of the actual demand cycle of household electrical appliances at the same time.

Second, the continuous expansion of export scale lengthened the period of the actual demand cycle of household electrical appliances. Taking the export of color TV sets as an example, the export scale of China's color TV sets continued to expand substantially during the period from 1995 to 2006 and increased 18.43 times from 5.73 million sets in 1995 to 105.62 million sets in 2006, with an average annual growth rate of 30.33 percent (Figures 8.10 and 8.11). The sustained and rapid growth of the export of household electrical appliances not only drove the actual growth of demand for household electrical appliances, but also lengthened the period of the actual demand cycle of household electrical appliances.

Due to the expansion of groups with demand induced by the expansion of export and rural households' demand for household electrical appliances, the

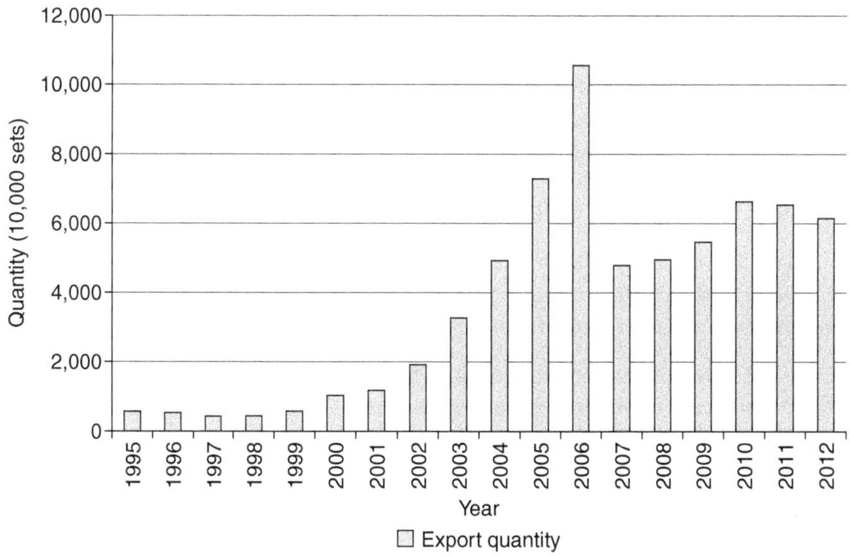

Figure 8.10 Quantity of color TV sets exported from China, 1995–2012 (10,000 sets).

Source: China Macroeconomic Database provided by WIND.

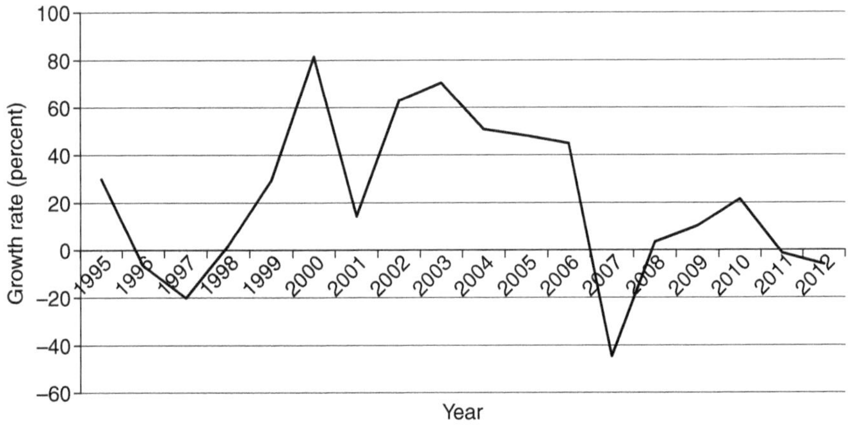

Figure 8.11 Growth rate of the quantity of color TV sets exported from China, 1995–2012 (%).

Source: China Macroeconomic Database provided by WIND.

period of the actual demand cycle of household electrical appliances and the period of the cycle of light industry output were extended. At the same time, due to the mismatch between the peaks and troughs of the actual demand cycles of color TV sets, refrigerators and washing machines during the period from 1992 to 2007 (for example, the year 1998 was the trough of the demand cycle of refrigerators and washing machines, but it was also the peak of the demand cycle of color TV sets), the falling stage and the rising stage of the growth of light industry output in this round of the cycle were extended. Especially in the rising stage from 1999 to 2007 of this cycle, the growth rate of light industry output slowed a little on three occasions, which was closely related to the mismatch between the peaks and troughs of the demand cycles of household electrical appliances and other light industrial products.

Sustained and rapid growth of the demand for civilian passenger vehicles greatly lengthened the period of the cycle of heavy industry output

After 1992, the continuous expansion of the demand for civilian passenger vehicles became an important demand-side factor in determining the fluctuation trend of the cycles of heavy industry and the whole economy.

From the trend of the growth rate of civilian passenger vehicle ownership and that of heavy industry output, it can be seen that the trend of the growth rate of heavy industry output was highly consistent with that of commercial passenger vehicle ownership during the period from 1992 to 2010, and the cycle of the household demand for passenger vehicles was a decisive factor for the cycle of heavy industrial output. After 1992, the growth rate of civilian passenger vehicles declined continuously, the growth rate of civilian passenger vehicle ownership decreased from 26.45 percent in 1993 to 12.79 percent in 1998, and the growth rate of heavy industry output decreased continuously from 27.5 percent in 1993 to 9.7 percent in 1998. After 1998, the growth rate of the demand for civilian passenger vehicles resumed the rising trend, and the growth rate of civilian passenger vehicle ownership increased to 26.4 percent in 2010; the growth rate of heavy industry output also rebounded synchronously and increased to a peak of 28.8 percent in 2008 and then dropped to 14.52 percent in 2009 before rebounding again to 22 percent in 2010.

From the influence of the period of the demand cycle of civilian passenger vehicles on the period of the cycle of heavy industry output and GDP, it can be seen that civilian passenger vehicle ownership maintained a sustained and rapid growth during the period from 1992 to 2007, with an average annual growth rate as high as 19.31 percent, which was not only higher than the average growth rate of 18.99 percent during the period from 1984 to 1992 and the average growth rate of 13.74 percent during the period from 1978 to 1984, but also significantly higher than the average growth rate of the production of color TV sets, refrigerators and washing machines during the same period, i.e., 13.13 percent, 15.82 percent and 12.25 percent respectively. The sustained and rapid growth of the demand for civilian passenger vehicles is what enabled the growth rate of heavy industry output to be higher than that of light industry output during this period. The average growth rate of heavy industry output was 20.91 percent during the period from 1992 to 2007, which was 1.94 percent higher than the average growth rate of light industry output during the same period (18.97 percent). Consequently, the influence of heavy industry on the period of the GDP cycle also increased. The period of this round of the GDP cycle was the same as the period of the cycle of heavy industry output, and the peak of the GDP cycle coincided with that of the cycle of heavy industry output, but the trough of the cycle of heavy industry output (1998) was one year earlier than that of the GDP cycle (1999).

After 2007, the declining actual demand growth rate of consumer durables and its cyclical correction were the fundamental demand-side factors for GDP growth rate to enter a mid-to-long-term correction period

After 2007, China's GDP growth rate entered a period of cyclical correction, and then the outbreak of the American financial crisis in 2008 led to the global economic recession; thus, China's exports dropped dramatically, which deepened the depth of the cyclical correction of China's economic growth rate. From the demand for consumer durables it can be seen that domestic households' demand for household electrical appliances gradually entered a phase of slower growth and saturated demand, and coupled with a substantial decline in the export growth rate of household electrical appliances, the actual demand cycle of household electrical appliances entered a period of cyclical downturn. This induced continuous decline in the growth rate of light industry output, which was one of the fundamental demand-side factors for the sustainable correction of the economic growth rate. The domestic demand for passenger vehicles still maintained a rapid growth after 2007, but the actual demand cycle of passenger vehicles also entered a period of cyclical downturn after 2010, and coupled with a substantial decline in passenger vehicle's export growth rate, the passenger vehicles' role in driving heavy industry output and GDP growth rate was significantly impaired.

Declining growth rate of the demand for household electrical appliances and its cyclical correction caused the growth rate of light industry output to decrease continuously

After 2007, urban households' demand for household electrical appliances and rural households' demand for color TV sets entered a phase of saturated demand, and coupled with the substantial decline in the export quantity and growth rate of color TV sets and other household electrical appliances (see Figure 8.10), the actual demand for household electrical appliances entered a phase of slower growth; during the period from 2007 to 2012, the average growth rate of the actual demand for color TV sets, refrigerators and washing machines was 8.63 percent, 13.89 percent and 10.98 percent respectively, with a decrease of 4.5 percent, 1.93 percent and 1.27 percent respectively when compared with the average growth rate during the period from 1992 to 2007. With the decrease of the actual demand growth rate, the actual demand for color TV sets, refrigerators and washing machines entered a period of cyclical downturn after 2007; among them, the actual demand growth rate of refrigerators entered a period of cyclical downturn in 2010, and the actual demand growth rate of color TV sets and that of washing machines entered a period of cyclical downturn in 2011. The declining growth rate of the demand for household electrical appliances and its cyclical correction caused the growth rate of light industry output to slow down from its peak of 26.1 percent in 2007 to 12.2 percent in 2012, which was one of the fundamental demand-side factors that enabled the GDP growth rate after 2007 to enter a period of mid-to-long-term correction.

Cyclical correction of the actual demand cycle of passenger vehicles and a sharp decline of vehicle export led to a sharp decline of the growth rate of heavy industry output

The expansion of family passenger vehicles from the highest-income urban households to high-income urban households occurred during the period from 2007 to 2012. The number of passenger vehicles owned by every 100 households increased from 6.06 sets in 2007 to 21.5 sets in 2012. The number of personal vehicles owned also expanded from 31.9599 million in 2007 to 74.7837 million in 2012, with an annual average growth rate of 23.68 percent. This is the most rapid period of average growth rate since 1978 (as shown in Table 8.6),

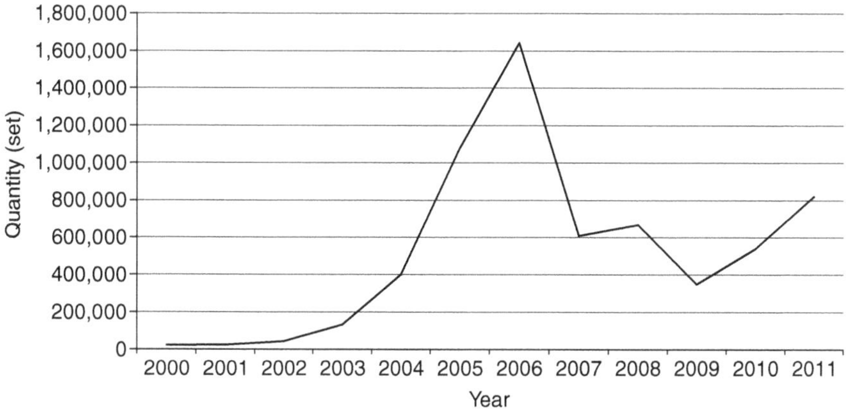

Figure 8.12 Exported quantity of motor vehicles and chassis from China during 2000–2011 (vehicle).

Source: China Macroeconomic Database provided by WIND.

which formed an important source of domestic consumption to support relatively high economic growth. But motor vehicle and chassis export dropped dramatically during this period, with the export quantity decreasing from 1.6424 million vehicles in 2006 to 350,000 vehicles in 2009 and rebounding only to 820,000 vehicles in 2011 (Figure 8.12). The dramatically decreased vehicle exports partly counteracted the pulling effect of the rapid expansion of domestic demand for passenger vehicles on economic growth; at the same time, the cycle of domestic households' actual demand for passenger vehicles reached its peak in 2010 and entered a period of cyclical downturn in 2011; therefore, its pulling effect on economic growth also declined relatively. Influenced by the cyclical correction of domestic demand for passenger vehicles and the dramatically decreased vehicle exports, the growth rate of heavy industry output fell continuously from 28.8 percent in 2007 to 8.6 percent in 2012, which was an important factor of the in-depth correction of China's GDP growth rate.

Conclusions and policy recommendations

From the income distribution cycle of urban and rural households' demand for consumer durables in China, it can be seen that urban households' demand for household electrical appliances, such as color TV sets, refrigerators and washing machines, has entered a phase of saturated demand, and rural households' demand for color TV sets has also reached a phase of saturated demand, rural households' demand for refrigerators and washing machines has passed its peak period as two-thirds of rural households had fulfilled their demand for refrigerators and washing machines in 2012. The future domestic urban and rural households' demand for household electrical appliances will be dominated by renewal demand and innovation demand, and strengthening efforts in product innovation of household electrical appliances will be the main method to stimulate domestic demand for household electrical appliances.

From the actual demand growth rate of household electrical appliances in recent years it can be seen that in the case of full domestic demand, the production of household electrical appliances has still maintained relatively rapid growth, and the speedy growth of the export of household electrical appliances is the decisive factor for this; the export quantity of color TV sets has accounted for more than 50 percent of the domestic production of color TV sets since 2007. As a result, expanding the export of household electrical appliances is the key to maintaining the sustainable growth of the household electrical appliance industry. Household electrical appliances are one of the important demand-side foundations to support the development of light industry. In 2012, the actual demand cycles of household electrical appliances such as color TV sets, refrigerators and washing machines were close to their troughs. At present, it is necessary to resume the implementation of the policy of "household electrical appliances going to the countryside" as soon as possible in order to stimulate the rebound of domestic demand for home appliances. Meanwhile, it is also necessary to encourage home appliances export so as to enable the actual demand cycle of household electrical appliances to shift to its rising stage as soon as possible and to curb the deep downturn momentum of the growth rate of light industry output.

Family passenger vehicles have not only been the key point of urban households' consumption of consumer durables in China in recent years, but also the important demand-side foundation for the sustainable and rapid growth of heavy industry output and GDP. In 2012, the highest- and high-income households, which accounted for 20 percent of total urban households, had fulfilled their demand for passenger vehicles. Therefore, in the next 5–10 years, most of the initial demand for passenger vehicles will come from middle-income urban households, which account for 60 percent of total households. From the income distribution cycle of consumer durables, it can be seen that the realization of high-income households' demand for family passenger vehicles means that the period of accelerated growth of the initial demand for passenger vehicles has finished, the growth rate of the initial demand for passenger vehicles, which is dominated by middle-income households' demand, will decline gradually, but the actual demand for passenger vehicles will continue to maintain rapid growth due to the influence of renewal demand and innovation demand.

At the same time, the gradual realization of high-proportion middle-income urban households' demand for family passenger vehicles means that the scale of the demand for passenger vehicles will be greatly expanded, the proportion of the output of passenger vehicles in heavy industry and in total economic output will increase continuously, so will its impact on the economic growth rate. Before middle-income urban households meet their demand for family passenger vehicles in 2020, the rapid growth of the actual demand for passenger vehicles, which was mainly dominated by high-income households' renewal demand and middle-income households' initial demand, will provide China's heavy industry and economy with an important demand-side support to develop rapidly. From the perspective of extending the cycle of the demand for passenger vehicles and improving passenger vehicles' contribution to economic growth, it is necessary to intensify the support for domestic vehicle models developed through indigenous innovation and encourage domestic enterprises to expand exports and conduct more product innovation.

9 The influence of household income distribution on urban household passenger vehicles and the economic cycle in China

Both urban and rural household income in China are subject to a normal distribution that has the median value of the income group with the highest household ratio as the expected value. Due to the characteristics of normally distributed household income, the demand for consumer durables in China is also subject to a normal distribution and the income inequality among households has an important impact on the production of consumer durables at the growing and maturing stages of their development. Reducing the income inequality can improve the growth rate of the demand for consumer durables at the growing and maturing stages and benefit present economic growth. However, it can impair the support of demand to the manufacturing enterprises of consumer goods at their initial stage of development, which is unfavorable to long-term economic growth. Therefore, moderate income inequality is a necessary condition to ensure sustainable and rapid economic growth. Household passenger vehicles are the most important consumer durables in the process of industrialization in heavy and chemical industries, because the production chain of household passenger vehicles involves various industries ranging from the mining industry and chemical industry to transportation infrastructure industry and to the industry that has an important influence on the transformation of industrial structure and economic growth.

By taking the development of Chinese urban household passenger vehicles as an example, this chapter analyzes and verifies the influence of household income distribution structure on consumer durables and economic growth. The analysis shows that Chinese urban household passenger vehicles were at the initial stage of development during the period from 1990 to 2005, were in the growing stage of development during the period from 2006 to 2010, and began to enter the maturing stage of development in 2011. From the demand function of household passenger vehicles at the growing stage of development, it can be seen that China's saloon production is subject to a normal distribution with an expected value of inter-year income of 91,300 yuan and variance of 10.61 for revenue. Passenger vehicle production is subject to a normal distribution with an expected value of inter-year income of 106,700 yuan and variance of 13.96 for revenue. Therefore it is expected that saloon production and passenger vehicle production will reach the maximum value in 2015 and 2016 respectively.

According to the regression analysis for various explanatory factors, the widening income inequality among urban households played an important role in promoting saloon production at the initial stage of development from 1990 to 2005, and the reducing income inequality among urban households has accelerated the expansion of the scale of saloon production at the growing stage of development since 2005. The results of industry correlation analysis show that the multiplier from automobile production to total output value of heavy chemical industries was 1.2 from 2000 to 2010.

Urban households' demand for passenger vehicles becomes an important internal driving factor after the year 2000, when China's economy entered a new stage of heavy and chemical industrialization development. This is also the foundation of domestic demand on which China's economy entered a new round of the cycle with the longest rising stage and the highest average growth rate since 2000. As Chinese urban households' initial demand for passenger vehicles has already passed the growing stage at a rapid growth rate and entered the maturing stage, urban households' initial demand for passenger vehicles has entered a stage with a declining growth rate; the initial demand for passenger vehicles will reach the maximum value around 2016. In order to maintain the important role of the automobile industry in driving the growth of heavy and chemical industries and China's economy, it is not only necessary to encourage high-income households' renewed demand for new passenger vehicles, expand exports and open up new markets for family passenger vehicles, but also to further reduce the income inequality between households and encourage lower-middle-income urban households and rural households to gradually realize their demand for household passenger vehicles.

The structural changes and different development stages of the production of Chinese urban households' passenger vehicles

The passenger vehicles industry has developed rapidly in China in recent years, and passenger vehicle production increased 3.95 times from 3.9318 million in 2005 to 15.5244 million in 2012, with an average annual growth of 21.68 percent. The saloon has become the main vehicle model of urban household passenger vehicles in China. Saloon production expanded from 42,400 vehicles in 1990 to 10.7698 million vehicles in 2010 and increased by 3.89 times during the period from 2005 to 2012, with an average annual growth rate of 21.42 percent. However, the proportion of saloons in passenger vehicle production decreased from 75.2 percent in 2007 to 69.37 percent in 2012. The MPV is mainly used as a commercial passenger vehicle and its production increased 3.13 times from 157,100 vehicles in 2005 to 491,900 vehicles in 2012, with an average annual growth rate of 17.71 percent. The MPV accounts for a relatively lower proportion of passenger vehicle production, averaging only 3.13 percent. The SUV has become the fastest-growing model in passenger vehicle production in recent years. Its production increased by 10.25 times from 194,700 vehicles in 2005 to 1.9955 million vehicles in 2012, with an average annual growth rate of 39.43

percent, and its proportion in passenger vehicle production increased from 4.95 percent in 2005 to 12.85 percent in 2012. The pick-up truck has become the second biggest model among different passenger vehicles, but its growth rate is the slowest among all kinds of passenger vehicles. Its production increased only by 2.79 times from 811,800 in 2005 to 2.2672 million in 2012, with an average annual growth rate of 15.8 percent. Its proportion of passenger vehicle production decreased from 20.65 percent in 2005 to 14.6 percent in 2012. From the structural changes of passenger vehicles, it can be seen that they have developed rapidly in China and the saloon has always been the main passenger vehicle model since 2005, while the SUV has been an emerging passenger vehicle model and will become the second most common model. Table 9.1 offers a breakdown of the figures.

Here we investigate which stage the Chinese urban household passenger vehicle industry has entered. In the previous theoretical analysis, it can be seen that the demand for consumer durables is subject to a normal distribution, and based on its three turning points and two extreme points of the growth rate we can divide the lifecycle of consumer durables into six stages. These six stages are expressed via the proportion of households that achieve their consumption demand. The initial stage has a proportion ranging from 0 to 4.18 percent. The growing stage has a proportion ranging from 4.18 percent to 15.87 percent. The maturing stage has a proportion ranging from 15.87 percent to 50 percent. The declining stage has a proportion ranging from 50 percent to 84.13 percent. The dusk stage has a proportion ranging from 84.13 percent to 95.82 percent. The terminal stage has a proportion ranging from 95.82 percent to 100 percent. Based on the changes in the quantity of passenger vehicles owned by every 100 urban households, it can be seen that in 2001 every 100 urban households had only 0.6 motor vehicles, which means only 0.6 percent of households had a car (Figure 9.1). According to the division of the stages mentioned above for the production lifecycle of consumer durables, family passenger vehicles in China were still at the early initial stage of development in 2001. The quantity of vehicles owned by every 100 urban households increased to 4.32 vehicles in 2006, which means about 4.32 percent of households realized their demand for passenger vehicles; this proportion of households exceeded the upper limit of the initial stage of development (4.18 percent). Therefore, the development of family passenger vehicles began to enter the growing stage of development in 2006. The quantity of vehicles owned by every 100 urban households increased to 13.07 vehicles in 2010, which means that 13.07 percent of households realized their demand for passenger vehicles, and this proportion was approaching the upper limit of the growing stage of consumer durables (15.87 percent), indicating that the growing stage of the development of household passenger vehicles in China was coming to an end. The quantity of vehicles owned by every 100 urban households increased to 18.58 vehicles in 2011, which means that 18.58 percent of households realized their demand for passenger vehicles, and this proportion of households exceeded the lower limit of the maturing stage of passenger vehicles (15.87 percent). Therefore China's household passenger vehicle production entered the maturing stage in 2011.

Table 9.1 The development of passenger vehicles in China in 2005–2012

Year	*Production (10,000 vehicles)*					*Structure (%)*			
	Passenger vehicles	*Saloon*	*MPV*	*SUV*	*Crossover*	*Saloon*	*MPV*	*SUV*	*Crossover*
2005	393.18	276.82	15.71	19.47	81.18	70.41	4.00	4.95	20.65
2006	519.71	384.48	19.41	22.75	93.08	73.98	3.73	4.38	17.91
2007	638.00	479.75	22.45	35.94	99.86	75.20	3.52	5.63	15.65
2008	672.87	502.91	19.17	44.71	106.07	74.74	2.85	6.64	15.76
2009	1,036.42	745.53	25.10	65.61	200.18	71.93	2.42	6.33	19.31
2010	1,388.67	957.49	45.02	133.00	253.16	68.95	3.24	9.58	18.23
2011	1,451.27	1,014.29	50.57	162.46	223.94	69.89	3.48	11.19	15.43
2012	1,552.44	1,076.98	49.19	199.55	226.72	69.37	3.17	12.85	14.60

Source: China Macroeconomic Database provided by WIND.

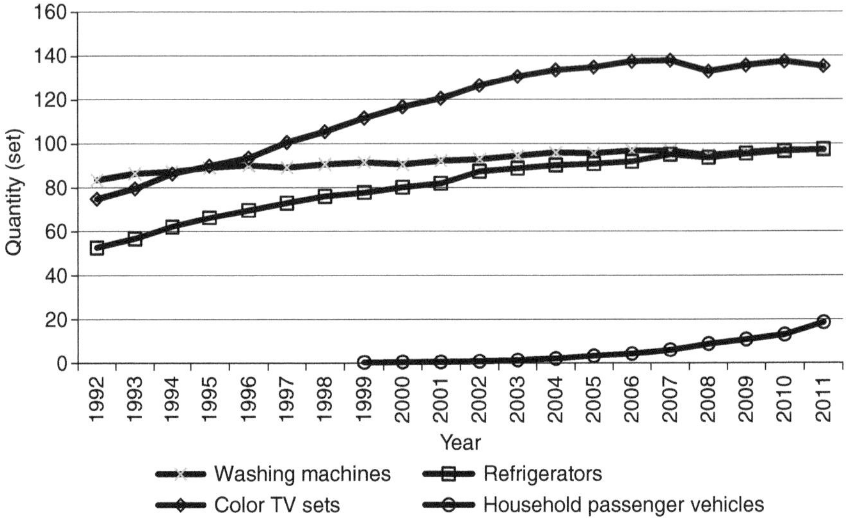

Figure 9.1 Quantity of consumer durables owned by every 100 urban households, 1992–2011 (set/vehicle).

Source: China Macroeconomic Database provided by WIND.

Evolution of income inequality among Chinese urban households

The average income level of urban households has improved continually in China since 1990, while income inequality continued to expand during the period from 1990 to 2005, but started to reduce after 2005. This change in the income inequality corresponds exactly to the initial and growing stages of the development of family passenger vehicles mentioned in the last paragraph.

According to the per capita disposable income of urban households and the average household population across all income groups, we can calculate and obtain the disposable income of urban households across all income groups based on their income levels during the period from 1990 to 2011. By taking the national average disposable income of urban households as the expected value and by weighting the proportion of households of each income group, we can calculate and obtain the variance of the disposable income of urban households during the period from 1990 to 2011. As shown in Table 9.2, along with the improvement of the average household income level, the variance of the disposable income of urban households increased from 0.0141 in 1990 to 12.4425 in 2011. As the income variance depends on two factors, namely the average household income level and income inequality, the expansion of income variance does not mean the enlargement of the income inequality among households. Thus, we take the ratio of the standard deviation of household disposable income

Table 9.2 Average disposable income of urban households in China in 1990–2011 (10,000 yuan)

Year	*National average*	*Lowest*	*Low*	*Lower-middle*	*Middle*	*Above-average*	*High*	*Highest*
1990	0.5330	0.3517	0.4179	0.4699	0.5197	0.5797	0.6506	0.7679
1991	0.5876	0.4016	0.4661	0.5166	0.5683	0.6420	0.7078	0.8456
1992	0.6848	0.4395	0.5227	0.5877	0.6643	0.7479	0.8550	1.0256
1993	0.8550	0.5154	0.6221	0.7064	0.8122	0.9435	1.1061	1.3834
1994	1.1488	0.6453	0.7991	0.9225	1.0836	1.2890	1.5072	1.9214
1995	1.3834	0.7060	0.8745	1.0217	1.1946	1.4078	1.6459	2.1031
1996	1.5484	0.7697	0.9717	1.1279	1.3270	1.5734	1.8323	2.3697
1997	1.6461	0.8749	1.1088	1.3247	1.5614	1.8559	2.1934	2.7883
1998	1.7143	0.8693	1.1297	1.3513	1.6330	1.9239	2.2845	3.0146
1999	1.8382	0.9136	1.1839	1.4313	1.7473	2.0853	2.4774	3.2264
2000	1.9656	0.9445	1.2354	1.5165	1.8519	2.2237	2.7076	3.5407
2001	2.1265	0.9838	1.3035	1.6076	1.9799	2.4248	2.9361	3.9903
2002	2.3417	0.8261	1.2188	1.5782	2.0237	2.5810	3.2728	5.0909
2003	2.5501	0.8807	1.3022	1.6831	2.2055	2.8021	3.6220	5.8524
2004	2.8076	0.9618	1.4350	1.8675	2.4418	3.1385	4.1020	6.7250
2005	3.1059	1.0470	1.5731	2.0803	2.7111	3.5163	4.6104	7.5961
2006	3.4690	1.1812	1.7730	2.3342	2.9988	3.9197	5.1295	8.3754
2007	4.0117	1.3893	2.0815	2.7147	3.4682	4.4897	5.8474	9.4904
2008	4.5922	1.5829	2.3710	3.1198	4.0414	5.2756	6.8775	10.9471
2009	4.9635	1.7283	2.6363	3.4180	4.3736	5.6959	7.4089	11.7533
2010	5.5035	1.9569	2.9713	3.8360	4.8572	6.2620	8.1025	12.9093
2011	6.2594	2.2691	3.4150	4.3640	5.5117	7.0541	9.1439	14.8870

Source: calculated according to the per capita disposable income of urban households and the average household population across all income groups provided by the National Bureau of Statistics.

to the national average household disposable income as an indicator to demonstrate the income inequality among households. We can see that the income inequality among urban households expanded continually during the period from 1990 to 2005, and the ratio of the standard deviation of income to average household disposable income increased from 0.2228 in 1990 to 0.5947 in 2005 (Table 9.3). The income inequality among urban households fell after 2005, and the ratio of the standard deviation of income to average household disposable income dropped to 0.5587 in 2010 and rebounded to 0.5635 in 2011. In 2005, income inequality among urban households experienced a shift from expansion to contraction, and 2005 was also the turning point at which Chinese urban household passenger vehicle production moved from the initial stage to the growing stage. The following analysis will show that the time point at which the income inequality among urban households converted from expansion to contraction has an important influence on different stages of the development lifecycle of Chinese urban household passenger vehicles.

The demand function of China's passenger vehicle production and its future development trend

Based on the normally distributed density function of the demand for consumer durables, we run a regression of the logarithm of saloon production on the average urban household income and the ratio of income variance to squared income inequality. The results show that at different stages of development, China's saloon production has been subject to a normal distribution that takes the average urban household income and the ratio of annual income variance to income inequality as explanatory variables. However, at different stages of development there exist bigger differences in the expected value of inter-year income and the income variance. The variance and expected value of inter-year income were relatively smaller (37,200 yuan and 69,800 yuan respectively) at the initial development stage of family passenger vehicles during the period from 1990 to 2004, which means that the distribution curve of saloon production was very steep, with a very high extremum (21.6074 million vehicles) and therefore has relatively shorter growing and maturing stages. Based on this, it can be estimated that the maximum value would appear in 2012. But along with the improvement of income level, the inter-year income variance and the expected value of income rose to 106,100 yuan and 91,300 yuan at the growing stage of the development of family passenger vehicles during the period from 2005 to 2011, and the increase of income variance caused the distribution curve of saloon production to flatten out. Thus the maximum value of future saloon production will reduce to 16.1317 million vehicles; the time at which saloon production will reach maximum value will be delayed to 2015. At the same time, according to the results of the normal estimation of the demand function of passenger vehicle production during the period from 2005 to 2011, passenger vehicle production was normally distributed, with an inter-year income variance of 13.96 and an expected value of 106,700 yuan. Based on the 12 percent annual

Table 9.3 The variance of average disposable income of Chinese urban households and the income inequality in 1990–2011

Year	*Income variance*	*Lowest*	*Low*	*Lower-middle*	*Middle*	*Above-average*	*High*	*Highest*	*Income inequality*
1990	0.0142	0.0033	0.0026	0.0008	0.0000	0.0004	0.0014	0.0055	0.2228
1991	0.0162	0.0035	0.0030	0.0010	0.0001	0.0006	0.0014	0.0067	0.2165
1992	0.0285	0.0060	0.0053	0.0019	0.0001	0.0008	0.0029	0.0116	0.2467
1993	0.0630	0.0115	0.0108	0.0044	0.0004	0.0016	0.0063	0.0279	0.2935
1994	0.1347	0.0254	0.0245	0.0102	0.0008	0.0039	0.0128	0.0597	0.3226
1995	0.1898	0.0459	0.0518	0.0262	0.0071	0.0001	0.0069	0.0518	0.3149
1996	0.2480	0.0606	0.0665	0.0354	0.0098	0.0001	0.0081	0.0674	0.3216
1997	0.3085	0.0595	0.0577	0.0207	0.0014	0.0088	0.0300	0.1304	0.3374
1998	0.3778	0.0714	0.0684	0.0264	0.0013	0.0088	0.0325	0.1691	0.3585
1999	0.4516	0.0855	0.0856	0.0331	0.0016	0.0122	0.0409	0.1927	0.3656
2000	0.5703	0.1043	0.1067	0.0403	0.0026	0.0133	0.0551	0.2481	0.3842
2001	0.7549	0.1306	0.1355	0.0538	0.0043	0.0178	0.0656	0.3474	0.4086
2002	1.4726	0.2297	0.2522	0.1166	0.0202	0.0115	0.0867	0.7558	0.5182
2003	1.9824	0.2787	0.3115	0.1504	0.0238	0.0127	0.1149	1.0905	0.5521
2004	2.6451	0.3407	0.3768	0.1768	0.0268	0.0219	0.1675	1.5345	0.5793
2005	3.4116	0.4239	0.4699	0.2104	0.0312	0.0337	0.2263	2.0162	0.5947
2006	4.1241	0.5234	0.5753	0.2576	0.0442	0.0406	0.2757	2.4073	0.5854
2007	5.2127	0.6877	0.7451	0.3364	0.0591	0.0457	0.3370	3.0017	0.5691
2008	7.0407	0.9056	0.9868	0.4336	0.0607	0.0934	0.5223	4.0384	0.5778
2009	7.9925	1.0466	1.0831	0.4777	0.0696	0.1073	0.5980	4.6102	0.5696
2010	9.4548	1.2578	1.2824	0.5561	0.0836	0.1148	0.6755	5.4846	0.5587
2011	12.4425	1.5922	1.6181	0.7185	0.1118	0.1263	0.8320	7.4435	0.5635

Source: calculation based on the data in Table 9.2.

Note
The income inequality is the ratio of the standard deviation of income and the national average disposable income of urban households.

average growth rate of urban household income during the period from 2005 to 2011, it is expected that the maturing stage of the demand for passenger vehicles in China will last until 2016, which means passenger vehicle production will reach the maximum value of 31.1489 million vehicles in 2016.

The factors affecting development of household passenger vehicles and its demand function

Past theoretical analysis shows that under the condition of normally distributed inter-year household income, the demand for consumer durables is normally distributed, and its demand function shall be $Q(x)=\frac{1}{\sigma\sqrt{2\pi}}e^{-\frac{(x-u)^2}{2\sigma^2}}$, of which x is the income–price ratio, and u and σ are the expected value and standard deviation of the income–price ratio respectively. Since there is no saloon price data since 1990, we cannot conduct a rigorous normality analysis of the demand function of household passenger vehicles, and we can only estimate the influence of average disposable income of urban households and the changes in income inequality on saloon production without considering the influence of saloon price on the demand for saloons. According to the function of the demand for consumer durables, if we take the inter-year average household income as an explanatory variable and take the expected value and variance of the inter-year average income distribution as constants, we can see that there exists a non-linear relationship between average household income and the demand for consumer durables. After logging the demand function, there still exists an exponential relationship between the logarithm of demand and household income, and it can be expressed as

$$\log Q(x)=\log\left(\frac{1}{\sigma\sqrt{2\pi}}\right)-\frac{u^2}{2\sigma^2}-\frac{1}{2\sigma^2}X^2+\frac{u}{\sigma^2}X \qquad (1)$$

In Equation 1, the squared average household income X^2 can be converted to the ratio of inter-year income variance to squared income inequality, thus the mathematical expression of the logarithm of the demand for consumer durables can be converted into

$$\log Q(x)=\frac{u}{\sigma^2}x-\frac{1}{2\sigma^2}\frac{\rho^2}{\theta^2}+\log\left(\frac{1}{\sigma\sqrt{2\pi}}\right)-\frac{u^2}{2\sigma^2} \qquad (2)$$

where ρ^2 and θ represent inter-year income variance and income inequality respectively. Equation 2 shows that there exists a linear relationship between the average income level and the logarithm of the demand for consumer durables, and the higher the income level is, the greater the logarithm of the demand for consumer durables will be. It also shows that there exists an exponential relationship between the income variance, the income inequality and the logarithm of the demand for consumer durables, and if the income variance is greater and the income inequality is smaller, then the logarithm of the demand for consumer durables will be smaller.

The factors affecting China's saloon production and its demand function

In Equation 2 of the demand function of consumer durables, the demand depends on three variables, namely the per capita income level, the variance of income in each year and the income inequality, but there are also another two constant parameters, the expected value of inter-year income u and the income variance σ^2. In a fixed period of time, the expected value of inter-year income and the income variance are given, but from a dynamic perspective, along with the widening of the interval, the increase of income level and the change of income inequality would increase the expected value of inter-year income and the income variance. The function of the inter-year demand for consumer durables is still normally distributed, but the shape of the distribution curve and the length of development stages can vary along with the change of inter-year income variance. Therefore, even for the same kind of consumer durables there exists a certain degree of difference in their demand function at different stages of development. Take saloon production as an example: The demand function during the period from 1990 to 2011 differs significantly from the demand functions in another two periods from 1990 to 2004 and from 2004 to 2011.

Based on Equation 2 of the demand function of consumer durables, we conduct a regression analysis of the logarithm of saloon production during the period from 1990 to 2011, and the results are as follows.

During the period from 1990 to 2011, the average urban household income and the ratio of income variance to the squared income inequality were significantly correlated with the logarithm of saloon production. Every 10,000 yuan increase of average household income could cause the logarithm of saloon production to increase by 1.7352, and every 0.1 percent expansion of the ratio of income variance to income inequality could cause the logarithm of saloon production to fall by 0.1351. Regression Equation 1 is completely consistent with Equation 2, thus indicating that China's saloon production was normally distributed during the period from 1990 to 2011. According to Equation 2 and the regression Equation 1, we can see that the income variance of saloon production function is approximately 4.2 $\left(\frac{1}{2\sigma^2} = 0.119,\ \sigma^2 = 4.2016\right)$, and the expected value is approximately 6.67 $\left(\frac{u}{\sigma^2} = 1.5879,\ u = 6.6717\right)$. Thus, the demand function of China's saloon production is the normal distribution density function with an expected value of 6.67 and an income variance of 4.2. The function can be expressed as $Q(x) = A \times \frac{1}{2.05\sqrt{2\pi}} e^{-\frac{(x-6.67)^2}{3.4}}$, of which A is a constant factor and the mean value is 4,768.52 during the period from 1990 to 2011.

The regression Equation 1 of saloon production (JCCL) on average urban household income (JTSR), the income variance (SRFC) and income inequality (SRCJ) from 1990 to 2011 is as follows:

$$\log(\text{JCCL}) = 1.5879 \times \text{JTSR} - 0.119 \times \text{SRFC/SRCJ}^2 + 1.676 + [\text{AR}(1) = 0.4146]$$
$$(8.03) \qquad (-4.5) \qquad (5.45) \qquad (2.53)$$

R^2=0.987732; adjusted R^2=0.985567; DW=1.44. AR(1) is the first-order autoregressive residual component.

At different time intervals, it can be seen that at the initial stage of the development of family passenger vehicles during the period from 1990 to 2005, the average urban household income and the ratio of income variance to squared income inequality were also in a highly significant correlation with the logarithm of saloon production. The influence of the average household income and the ratio of income variance to income inequality on the logarithm of saloon production are 1.8758 and –0.1343 respectively. The regression Equation 2 is also completely consistent with Equation 2, which indicates that China's saloon production was also normally distributed during the period from 1990 to 2005, but the variance and expected value of inter-year income differ significantly from the expected value and variance of the demand function during the period of 1990 to 2011. According to Equation 2 and regression Equation 2, it can be calculated that the income variance of the demand function of saloon production is 3.72 $\left(\frac{1}{2\sigma^2} = 0.1343,\ \sigma^2 = 3.7217\right)$, the expected value is approximately 6.98 $\left(\frac{u}{\sigma^2} = 1.8758,\ u = 6.9813\right)$, and the demand function of saloon production during this period is $Q(x) = A \times \frac{1}{1.93\sqrt{2\pi}} e^{-\frac{(x-6.98)^2}{7.44}}$.

The regression Equation 2 of the saloon production (JCCL) on average urban household income (JTSR), the income variance (SRFC) and income inequality (SRCJ) from 1990 to 2004 is:

$$\log(\text{JCCL}) = 1.8758 \times \text{JTSR} - 0.1343 \times \text{SRFC/SRCJ}^2 + 1.1302$$
$$(4.35) \qquad (-1.1) \qquad (3.33)$$

R^2=0.94506; adjusted R^2=0.936608; DW=0.91. The validity of the equation is verified with a Q test.

At the growing stage of the development of household passenger vehicles during the period from 2005 to 2011, the average urban household income and the ratio of income variance to squared income inequality are also significantly correlated with the logarithm of saloon production, and the influence of the average household income and the ratio of income variance to income inequality on the logarithm of saloon production is 0.8608 and –0.0417. Regression Equation 3 is also completely consistent with Equation 2, thus indicating that saloon production was also normally distributed during this period. However, compared to the initial stage of development, the inter-year income variance increases obviously and the expected value declines during this period. According to Equation 2 and regression Equation 3, it can be calculated that the income variance of the demand function of saloon production is 10.61 $\left(\frac{1}{2\sigma^2} = 0.0471,\ \sigma^2 = 10.6117\right)$, the expected value is approximately 9.13 $\left(\frac{u}{\sigma^2} = 0.8608,\ u = 9.1347\right)$ and the demand function of saloon production during this period is $Q(x) = A \times \frac{1}{3.26\sqrt{2\pi}} e^{-\frac{(x-9.13)^2}{21.22}}$.

The regression Equation 3 of the saloon production (JCCL) on the income variance (SRFC) and income inequality (SRCJ) and average urban household income (JTSR) from 2005 to 2011 is:

$$\log(\text{JCCL}) = \underset{(1.94)}{0.8608} \times \text{JTSR} - \underset{(-0.99)}{0.0471} \times \text{SRFC/SRCJ}^2 + \underset{(3.46)}{3.4503} \qquad (3)$$

R^2=0.957008; adjusted R^2=0.935512; DW=2.45.

By comparing the saloon demand functions in three intervals during the periods from 1990 to 2011, from 1990 to 2005 and from 2005 to 2011, it can be seen that the expected value and variance of the demand functions in these three intervals differ significantly from the expected value and variance of the demand function in the whole interval. The inter-year income variance at the initial stage of development (1990–2005) is lower than the inter-year income variance in the whole interval, but the expected value of inter-year income is slightly higher than the expected value of income in the whole interval. Along with the increase of income level, the inter-year income variance and the expected value at the growing stage of development (2005–2011) are significantly greater than the inter-year income variances and the expected values at the initial stage of development and in the whole interval. From the above analysis, it can be seen that the income inequality among Chinese urban households expanded continually at the initial stage and tended to reduce at the growing stage, and the increase of inter-year income variance and expected value at the growing stage was mainly caused by the improvement of average household income level. However, the increase of income variance and expected value at the growing stage have important influence on the extreme value of saloon production and the length of its development stages, and the increase of income variance extends the length of the growing and maturing stages of the demand for saloons and reduces the maximum value of demand. In the whole interval, it can be seen that the average disposable income of Chinese urban households was 62,600 yuan in

2011, which was approaching the expected value 66,700 yuan of the demand function of China's saloon production during the period from 1990 to 2011. This indicates that the scale of the initial demand dominated by urban households for saloons would reach its maximum value in 2012 (10.55 million vehicles). In the subintervals, it can be seen that the expected value of the demand function of China's saloon production during the period from 1990 to 2005 was 69,800 yuan. According to the 12 percent annual growth rate of average urban household income during the period from 2005 to 2011, it can be estimated that the average urban household income reached the expected value of the demand function of saloon production in 2012, which means that saloon production reached the maximum value of 21.6074 million vehicles in 2012. After the increase of income variance at the growing stage, the expected value of average urban household income rose to 91,300 yuan, and the maximum value of saloon production fell to 16.1317 million vehicles. According to the 12 percent annual growth rate of average urban household income during the period from 2005 to 2011, it can be estimated that the point at which saloon production would reach its maximum value would be delayed to 2015.

The influence factors affecting the production of China's passenger vehicle and its demand function

The saloon is the basic passenger vehicle type in China, but along with the rapid development of other passenger vehicle types such as SUVs, the proportion of saloons in passenger vehicle production began to decline continuously from 2008; therefore, the development trend of saloon production cannot fully demonstrate the development trend of passenger vehicles. Thus, we took the data of passenger vehicle production during the period from 2005 to 2011 as samples and carried out a regression analysis according to Equation 2, and the results are as follows. During the period from 2005 to 2011, the average urban household income, income variance and income inequality were highly and significantly correlated with passenger vehicle production. Every increase of 10,000 yuan in average household income could cause the logarithm of passenger vehicle production to increase by 0.7645; every 1 percent drop in the ratio of income variance to income inequality could cause the logarithm of passenger vehicle production to increase by 0.0358.

According to Equation 2 and regression Equation 4, we can calculate that the variance of normally distributed demand function of passenger vehicles is 13.9637 $\left(\frac{1}{2\sigma^2}=0.0358,\ \sigma^2=13.9637\right)$ and the expected value is 10.6753 $\left(\frac{u}{\sigma^2}=0.7645,\ u=10.6753\right)$, which indicates that China's passenger vehicle production is subject to a normal distribution with an expected value of 10.67 and a variance of 13.96, and its expression shall be $Q(x)=\mathrm{A}\times\frac{1}{3.74\sqrt{2\pi}}e^{-\frac{(x-10.67)^2}{27.98}}$, of which A is a constant factor.

In 2011, the average disposable income of Chinese urban households was 62,600 yuan, which had a greater disparity than the expected value of 106,700 yuan of the demand function of passenger vehicle production. This means that when the demand for family passenger vehicles entered the maturing stage in 2011, the deceleration in growth of the demand for household passenger vehicles would continue for a period of time, and China's passenger vehicle production would continue to expand for the next few years. According to the 12 percent annual growth rate of average urban household income during the period from 2005 to 2011, it can be estimated that the average income of Chinese urban households could reach the expected value of the demand function of passenger vehicles (106,700 yuan) in 2016, i.e., China's passenger vehicle production will reach its maximum value around 2016. According to the demand function of passenger vehicles, it can be estimated that the extreme value of passenger vehicle production will be about 31.1489 million vehicles.

The regression analysis Equation 4 of passenger vehicles production (CYC) on the income variance (SRFC) and income inequality (SRCJ) and average urban household income (JTSR) from 1990 to 2011 is:

$$\log(\text{CYC}) = 0.7645 \times \text{JTSR} - 0.0358 \times \text{SRFC/SRCJ}^2 + 3.9633 \qquad (4)$$
$$(1.51) \qquad (-0.66) \qquad (3.49)$$

R^2=0.946884; adjusted R^2=0.920326; DW=2.33.

The influence of average urban household income level and income inequality on passenger vehicle production

According to the regression analysis equations of saloon production and passenger vehicle production, we can only determine the contribution of the average urban household income to saloon production and passenger vehicle production; it is difficult to distinguish the specific influence of income variance, especially income inequality, on passenger vehicle production. In order to analyze the influence of average urban household income and income inequality on the demand for family passenger vehicles in a more intuitive manner, we run regressions of the logarithm of saloon production and passenger vehicle production on the explanatory variables of average urban household income and income inequality. The results show that in the total interval from 1990 to 2011, the improvement of household income level and the enlargement of income inequality could stimulate the increase of the logarithm of saloon production. In the sub-intervals, when the family passenger vehicles were at the initial stage of development before 2005, the improvement of average urban household income level and the enlargement of income inequality could stimulate the increase of the logarithm of saloon production. However, during the period from 2005 to 2011, when the family passenger vehicles were at the growing stage of development and income inequality was reduced, the reduction of income inequality stimulated the increase of the logarithmic values of saloon production and passenger vehicle production.

The influence of average household income and income inequality on saloon production from 1990 to 2011

In the whole interval from 1990 to 2011, average urban household income and income inequality are highly and significantly correlated with the logarithm of saloon production. The increase of every 10,000 yuan in average household income could cause the logarithm of saloon production to increase by 0.5164, and every 0.1 percent expansion of household income inequality could cause the logarithm of saloon production to increase by 0.524. Overall, the improvement of average household income level and the expansion of income inequality could stimulate the growth of saloon production.

The regression Equation 5 of the saloon production (JCCL) on the income variance (SRFC), income inequality (SRCJ) and average urban household income (JTSR) from 1990 to 2011 is:

$$\log(\text{JCCL}) = \underset{(5.91)}{0.5164} \times \text{JTSR} + \underset{(4.67)}{5.2396} \times \text{SRCJ} + \underset{(2.93)}{0.9806} + \underset{(5.72)}{[\text{MA}(1) = 0.6957]} \quad (5)$$

$R^2=0.98162$; adjusted $R^2=0.978557$; DW=2.23. MA(1) is the first-order auto-regressive residual component.

The influence of average household income and income inequality on the saloon production at the initial development stage (1990–2005)

At the initial stage of the development of household passenger vehicles, the expansion of household income inequality could stimulate the growth of saloon production. The results of regression analysis show that during the period from 1990 to 2005, the logarithm of saloon production was highly and significantly correlated with average urban household income and income inequality. The increase of every 10,000 yuan average household income could cause the logarithm of saloon production to increase by 0.6364, and every 0.1 percent expansion of household income inequality could cause the logarithm of saloon production to increase by 0.3656. According to the regression coefficient of average household income and income inequality on the logarithm of saloon production during this period, the average household income and the income inequality were improved by 25,730 yuan and 0.3719 respectively, and this led to the increase of the logarithm of saloon production by 1.6373 and 1.3596 respectively. This accounted for 39.19 percent and 32.54 percent of the increase of the logarithm of saloon production (4.1784) during the same period. This means that among the 2.7253 million saloons production during this period, 1.0679 million and 886,700 of them could be explained by the improvement of urban household income level and the expansion of income inequality respectively.

The regression Equation 6 of the saloon production on average urban household income as well as income inequality from 1990 to 2005 is:

$$\log(\text{JCCL}) = 0.6364 \times \text{JTSR} + 3.656 \times \text{SRCJ} + 1.4914 + [\text{AR}(1) = 0.3698]$$
$$(2.69) \qquad (2.67) \qquad (6.32) \qquad (2.85) \qquad (6)$$

$R^2 = 0.986208$; adjusted $R^2 = 0.982447$; DW = 2.47.

The changes of the influence of average household income and income inequality on saloon production at early and late initial stages of development

At the initial stage of the development of passenger vehicles, although the average urban household income and the income inequality increased continually, the average annual increases of average household income and income inequality at the late initial stage of development were much greater than those at the early initial stage of development, and their influence on saloon production also clearly increased. At the early initial stage from 1990 to 2001, the contributions of average income and income inequality to the logarithm of saloon production were obviously lower, and were only 0.5071 and 0.1864 respectively, which was only equivalent to 80 percent and 51 percent of the average contribution at the entire initial stage of development. According to the coefficients of average household income and income inequality on the logarithm of saloon production, the average household income and the income inequality were improved by 15,935 yuan and 0.1858 respectively, and this caused the logarithm of saloon production to increase by 0.8081 and 0.3463 respectively, which accounted for 28.77 percent and 12.83 percent of the increase of the logarithm of saloon production (2.8087) during the same period, respectively. Among the 661,100 saloon produced in the early initial stage of development, 190,600 and 81,500 vehicles could be explained by the improvement of urban household income level and the expansion of income inequality; the remaining 41 percent of the increased saloon production was induced by other factors.

Due to the significantly increasing income inequality from 2001 to 2006 or, say, at the late initial stage of development, the influence of average household income and income inequality on the logarithm of saloon production increased significantly; their coefficient is 0.7233 and 0.4114 respectively, which was equivalent to 143 percent and 221 percent of the contribution at the early initial stage of development. According to the contribution of average household income and income inequality to the logarithm of saloon production, average household income and income inequality were increased by 13,426 yuan and 0.1768 respectively, thus causing the logarithm of saloon production to increase by 0.971 and 0.7274, accounting for 56.96 percent and 42.67 percent of the increase of the logarithm of saloon production (1.7048) during the same period, and accounting for 99.36 percent in total. This means that the increase in saloon production scale was almost entirely caused by the improvement of average household income and the expansion of income inequality. After converting into the increase of saloon production scale, it can be seen that among the increased saloon production of 3.166 million vehicles at the late initial stage of development, 1.8033 million and 1.3509 million vehicles were directly caused by the improvement of urban household income level and the expansion of income inequality respectively. Compared to the early initial stage of development, the enlargement of income inequality among urban households was an important factor in the great expansion of saloon production at the late initial stage of the development of family passenger vehicles.

The regression analysis Equation 7 for the saloon production and average urban household income, as well as income inequality, from 1990 to 2001 is:

$$\log(\text{JCCL}) = \underset{(1.45)}{0.5071} \times \text{JTSR} + \underset{(0.57)}{1.864} \times \text{SRCJ} + \underset{(1.86)}{2.3853} + [\text{AR}(1) = \underset{(2.85)}{0.5658}] \quad (7)$$

$R^2 = 0.978959$; adjusted $R^2 = 0.969942$; DW = 2.28.

The regression analysis Equation 8 for the saloon production and average urban household income, as well as income inequality, from 2001 to 2006 is:

$$\log(\text{JCCL}) = \underset{(3.15)}{0.7233} \times \text{JTSR} + \underset{(2.52)}{4.114} \times \text{SRCJ} + \underset{(1.96)}{1.0175} \quad (8)$$

$R^2 = 0.967318$; adjusted $R^2 = 0.94553$; DW = 2.94.

The influence of average household income and income inequality on saloon production at the growing stage of development (2005–2011)

At the growing stage of the development of family passenger vehicles during the period from 2006 to 2011, the average urban household income increased continually, but the income inequality fell in the same manner. As shown in the previous analysis, at the growing and maturing stages of the development of consumer durables, the reduction of income inequality can shorten the length of growing and maturing stages and boost the demand for consumer durables and the demand growth rate. The results of the regression analysis show that during the period from 2005 to 2011, the average household income was significantly and positively correlated with the logarithm of saloon production, and its contribution was 0.289. The income inequality among households was negatively correlated with the logarithm of saloon production, and its contribution was –13.7076, which means every 1 percent decrease in income inequality could cause the logarithm of saloon production to increase by 0.1371.

By comparing the contribution of average household income and that of income inequality, it can be seen that the contribution of the reduced income inequality to the logarithm of saloon production was much greater than the contribution of the average household income during the period from 2005 to 2011. But the average annual increase of average household income during this period is much greater than that at the initial stage of development, while the average annual reduction of income inequality is much smaller than the average annual increase of income inequality at the initial stage of development. Therefore, according to the influence of average household income and income inequality on the logarithm of saloon production, the increase of the logarithm of saloon production induced by the improvement of average household income is much greater than that induced by the reduction of income inequality. Specifically, the average urban household income was increased by 31,350 yuan and the income inequality was reduced by 0.0311 during the period from 2005 to 2011, thus the logarithm of saloon production was improved by 0.9113 and 0.427 respectively. These changes of urban household income and income inequality account for 68.59 percent and 32.14 percent, respectively, of the increase of the logarithm of saloon production (1.3286) during the same period and in combination account for 100.73 percent. Among the total saloon production, production of 5.2693 million and 2.4689 million vehicles were directly caused by the improvement of average household income and the reduction of income inequality respectively, which means that all the increase of saloon production during this period was induced by the improvement of average household income and the reduction of income inequality. The improvement of average household income was the major factor, and the reduction of income inequality made a very high marginal contribution; but due to the limited reduction of income inequality, its influence on increasing saloon production was still lower than the influence from the improvement of average income level.

The regression Equation 9 of saloon production on average urban household income, as well as income inequality, from 2005 to 2011 is:

$$\log(\mathrm{JCCL}) = 0.289 \times \mathrm{JTSR} - 13.7076 \times \mathrm{SRCJ} + 12.8968$$
$$(4.47) \qquad (-2.39) \qquad (3.63) \qquad (9)$$

$R^2=0.977949$; adjusted $R^2=0.966924$; DW=2.41.

Table 9.4 offers a summary.

The influence of average household income and income inequality on passenger vehicle production in 2005–2011

The results of the regression analysis show that from 2005 to 2011, the average household income has a significantly positive correlation with the logarithm of passenger vehicle production, and its coefficvient is 0.3039. The income inequality among households has a negative correlation with the logarithm of passenger vehicle production, and its coefficient is –13.0815, which means every 1 percent reduction in income inequality could cause the logarithm of passenger vehicle production to increase by 0.131. Specifically, during the period from 2005 to 2011, the average urban household income is improved by 31,350 yuan and the income inequality is reduced by 0.0311, thus the logarithm of passenger vehicle production is improved by 0.9583 and 0.4081 respectively, accounting for 73.38 percent and 31.25 percent of the increase of the logarithm of passenger vehicle production (1.3059) during the same period, and in combination accounting for 104.63 percent.

Table 9.4 Contribution of average urban household income and income inequality to saloon production in 1990–2011

Interval	*Change of average income*	*Change of income inequality*	*Change of the logarithm of saloon production*	*Contribution of average income changes*	*Contribution of income inequality changes*	*Proportion of the contribution of average income changes*	*Proportion of the contribution of income inequality changes*
1990–2001	1.5935	0.1858	2.8087	0.8081	0.3463	28.77	12.33
2001–2006	1.3462	0.1768	1.7048	0.9710	0.7274	56.96	42.67
1990–2005	2.5730	0.3719	4.1784	1.6373	1.3596	39.19	32.54
2005–2011	3.1535	–0.0311	1.3286	0.9113	0.4270	68.59	32.14

Source: calculated according to the data in Table 9.1 and Table 9.2 and the contribution of each factor to the logarithm of saloon production.

Among the total saloon production, production of 8.5066 million and 3.6171 million vehicles were directly caused by the improvement of average household income and the reduction of income inequality respectively. In short, during the period from 2005 to 2011, the improvement of average urban household income level and the reduction of income inequality were the important factors in the rapid expansion of passenger vehicle production scale.

The regression analysis Equation 10 of the saloon production (CYC) on average urban household income (JTSR) as well as income inequality (SRCJ) from 1990 to 2005 is:

$$\log(\text{CYC}) = 0.3039*\text{JTSR} - 13.0815*\text{SRCJ} + 12.7903$$
$$(3.84) \qquad (-1.86) \qquad (2.94) \qquad (10)$$

$R^2 = 0.968444$; adjusted $R^2 = 0.952666$; DW = 1.96.

The influence of Chinese urban households' passenger vehicles on the automobile industry and economic growth

Boosted by urban households' demand for passenger vehicles, the saloon replaced trucks and coaches to become the dominant sector in the automobile industry after 2001. China's automobile industry then entered a period of rapid expansion due to the rapid growth of saloon production, and the whole economy also entered a new stage of heavy and chemical industrialization that enabled China's economy to enter a new cycle with the longest rising stage and the highest average growth rate since the Reform and Opening Up Policy. As seen from the results of the regression analysis, automobile production increased synchronously with the total output value of the automobile industry. Every 1 percent increase in the total output value of automobile production caused the total output value of heavy industry to increase by 1.21 percent, and the multiplier coefficient from automobile production to heavy industry output value was approximately 1.2. Therefore the rapid development of urban household passenger vehicles has been an important driving force to maintain sustained and high-speed economic growth since China's economy entered the new stage of heavy and chemical industrialization in 2000.

Rapid expansion of the output of the automobile industry caused by urban households' consumption of passenger vehicles

The output of China's automobile industry has expanded continuously since 1990; in particular, saloon production has experienced a sustained and rapid growth. The whole development process can be divided into two different stages either side of 2001, when large amounts of passenger vehicles were consumed by urban households.

Before 2001, the development of China's automobile industry was relatively slow; automobile production grew only from 708,800 to 2.3415 million during the period from 1991 to 2001 and increased by 3.3 times, among which trucks, passenger vehicles and saloons increased by 1.78 times, 4.75 times and 8.68 times respectively (Figure 9.2). During this period, saloon production increased quickly, and the percentage of saloon production in the whole of production increased continually from 11.44 percent in 1991 to 30.05 percent in 2001. However, trucks, as the dominant sector in the automobile industry at that time, increased slowly, and caused the development of the whole automobile industry to be relatively slow.

After 2001, as more and more households purchased passenger vehicles, saloon production increased substantially and the proportion of saloon production among the whole automobile industry began to exceed the proportion of truck and coach production since 2002 (Figure 9.3). The saloon has replaced trucks and coaches to become the dominant sector in the automobile industry, and the output scale of the whole automobile industry expanded rapidly due to the speedy expansion of saloon production. Automobile production increased to 18.2647 million vehicles in 2010, an increase of 7.8 times compared to 2001. The production of trucks, coaches and saloons increased by 4.88 times, 5.71 times and 13.61 times respectively, and the proportion of saloons in the whole of automobile production increased to 52.43 percent by 2010.

Along with the rapid expansion of the output of the automobile industry, the total output value of the automobile industry also expanded rapidly from 198.58 billion yuan in 2000 to 1.89378 trillion yuan in 2010, increasing by 9.54 times. As seen from the results of the regression analysis of automobile production and the total output value of the automobile industry during the period from 2001 to

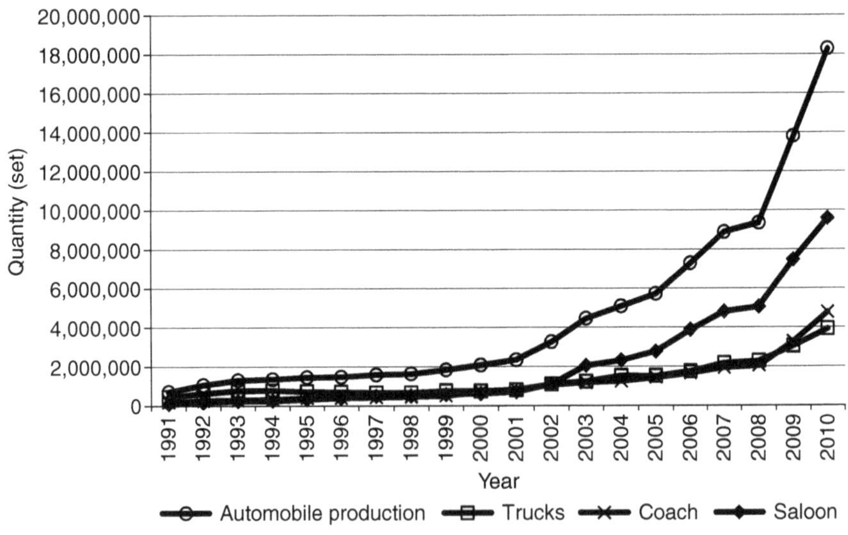

Figure 9.2 Changes in automobile production in 1991–2010 (vehicle).

Source: China Macroeconomic Database provided by WIND.

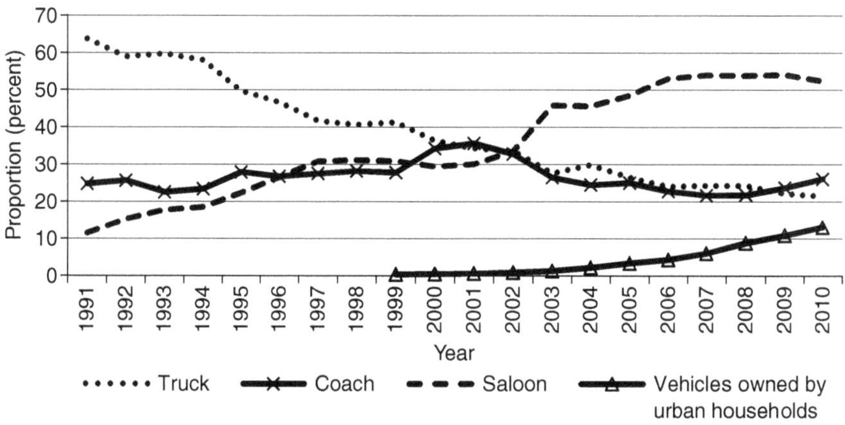

Figure 9.3 Quantity of vehicles owned by every 100 households and the structural change of the automobile industry, 1991–2010 (%).

Source: calculation according to the data provided by the China Macroeconomic Database of WIND.

2010, every 1 percent increase in automobile production caused the total output value of the automobile industry to increase by 0.9926 percent, i.e., the total output value of the automobile industry increased almost synchronously with automobile production. Automobile production experienced the fastest growth during the period from 2001 to 2010, so it was the biggest contributor to the total output value of the automobile industry during that period.

The correlation between the saloon production (JCCL) and the total output value of the automobile industry (QCCZ) during the period from 2001 to 2010 is:

$$\log(\text{QCCZ}) = 0.9926 \times \log(\text{QCCL}) + 2.4163 + [\text{MA}(1) = 0.7955]$$
$$(21.35) \qquad\qquad (8.02) \qquad\qquad (3.22) \qquad\qquad (11)$$

$R^2 = 0.993989$; adjusted $R^2 = 0.992487$; DW = 2.67.

The sustained expansion of the automobile industry that led to a new accelerating growth stage of heavy and chemical industrialization of China's economy

After the development of new light industry induced by the rapid expansion of the home appliance industry during the period from 1990 to 1997, China's economy gradually entered a new stage of heavy and chemical industrialization, beginning in 1998 (Figures 9.4 and 9.5). The proportion of the total output value of heavy industry in the total industrial output value continued to increase from 58.03 percent in 1998 to 71.85 percent in 2011, and the growth rate and fluctuation of

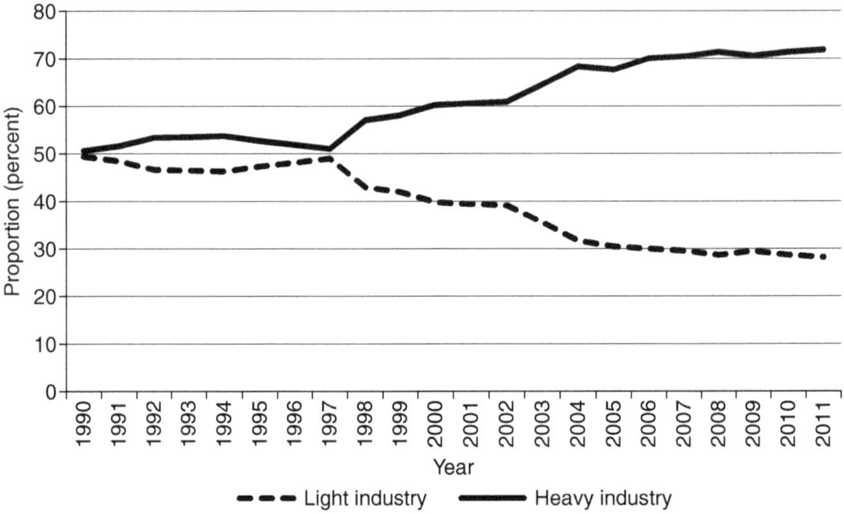

Figure 9.4 Structural changes of China's total industrial output value, 1990–2011 (%).

Source: China Macroeconomic Database provided by WIND.

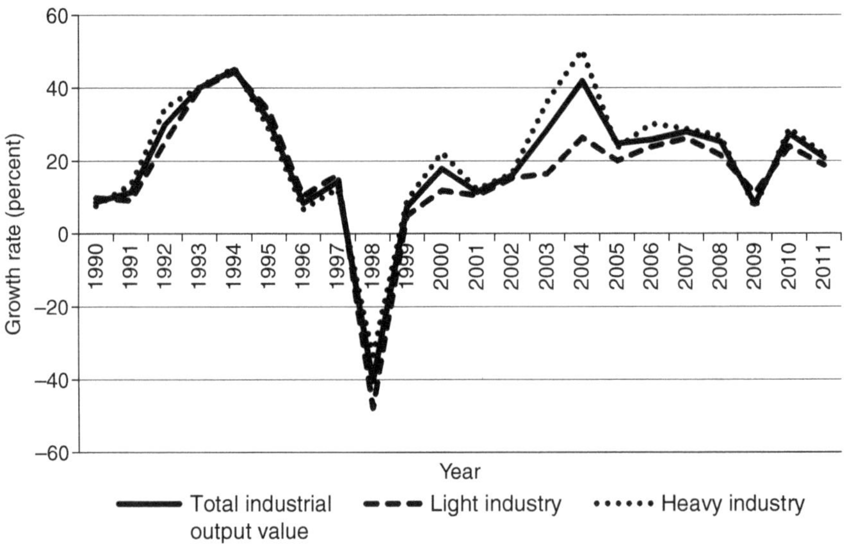

Figure 9.5 Changes of the nominal growth rate of China's total industrial output value in 1990–2011 (%).

Source: China Macroeconomic Database provided by WIND.

total industrial output value mainly depended on the growth rate and trend of the total output value of heavy industry during this period. At the same time, the share of secondary lines' added-value and the industry's added-value in GDP remained at a high level of around 46.5 percent and 40.6 percent respectively. The rise of the share of the tertiary industry's added-value in GDP was related to the rapid development of the manufacturing-related service industry that served the secondary industry. For example, the share of the added-value of the wholesale trade and financial sectors in GDP increased from 8.22 percent and 4.18 percent in 2000 to 9.18 percent and 5.66 percent in 2011 respectively. The heavy and chemical industry was the major industrial element that determined China's GDP growth rate and the driver of its fluctuations after 2000. That is to say, the reason that China's GDP growth rate increased from 8.4 percent in 2000 to 14.2 percent in 2007, and then slowed to 9.3 percent in 2011, with large fluctuations in the GDP growth rate, is mainly the large fluctuations in the growth rate of the added-value in the heavy and chemical industry. This is also the basic characteristic of economic growth fluctuations at the stage of heavy and chemical industrialization in a country's economy. The average annual growth rate of China's GDP was 10.37 percent during this period, which is the longest rising economic growth period of eight consecutive years, from 2000 to 2007, and which has the highest average economic growth rate since the Reform and Opening Up Policy.

Domestic consumption and export are the basic demands that determine economic growth. China's economy has entered a new stage of heavy and chemical industrialization since 2000, which is jointly determined by the expansion of the scale of trade and the structural upgrading of domestic consumption. From the perspective of domestic consumer demand, the influence of the structural upgrading of consumption on heavy and chemical industry is shown in two ways. The first is the rapid expansion of the automobile industry and its related industries, caused by increasing household demand. The other aspect is the rapid expansion of the real estate industry and its related industries, caused by the improvement of urban households' housing conditions.

The production chain of the automobile industry is relatively longer than that of the real estate industry, so the former has a greater influence on the development of heavy and chemical industry. From the results of the regression analysis of the total output value of the automobile industry and that of heavy industry during the period from 2000 to 2010, it can be seen that there exists a highly significant correlation between them, and the goodness-of-fit (correlation of determination) is as high as 0.97557, while the elasticity coefficient of the total output value of the automobile industry to that of heavy industry is 1.2066, i.e., every 1 percent increase in the growth rate of the total output value of the automobile industry causes the growth rate of the total output value of heavy industry to increase by 1.2066 percent. This coefficient can be regarded as the multiplier from the growth rate of the automobile industry's output to the growth rate of heavy industry's output. At the same time, according to the results of a regression analysis of automobile production and the total output value of the automobile industry, every 1 percent increase in automobile production can cause the total output value of the automobile industry to increase by 0.9926 percent. The multiplier of the growth rate of automobile production and that of the growth rate of heavy industry's total output value is approximately 1.1976 during the period from 2000 to 2010. That means that every 1 percent increase in automobile production can cause the total output value of heavy industry to increase by 1.1976 percent. Based on this, it can be concluded that since China's economy entered a new stage of heavy and chemical industrialization in 2000, the rapid development of passenger vehicles in urban households has become an important driving force for sustained and high-speed economic growth.

At the same time, China's economic growth has entered a mid-to-long-term adjustment period after the second half of 2007. In addition to the decreased export growth rate caused by the US financial crisis, the falling growth rate of automobile production caused by the falling growth rate of saloon production is also an important factor. During the period from 2001 to 2007, the average growth rates of China's saloon production and automobile production were as high as 34.31 percent and 23.15 percent respectively. However, during the period from 2008 to 2011, the average growth rates of saloon production and automobile production fell to 21.48 percent and 20 percent, and compared to the average annual growth rate in the period from 2001 to 2007 they fell by 12.83 percent and 3.15 percent respectively. According to the multiplier effect of automobile production on the total output value of heavy industry, it can be calculated that during the period from 2008 to 2011, the average annual growth rate of the total output value of heavy and chemical industry decreased by 3.78 percent due to the falling growth rate of automobile production.

The correlation between the total output value of the automobile industry (QCCZ) and the total output value of heavy industry (ZGYCZ) during the period from 2000 to 2010 is:

$$\log(\text{ZGYCZ}) = 1.2066 \times \log(\text{QCCL}) + 1.4396 + [\text{MA}(1) = 0.9999]$$
$$(9.72) \qquad\qquad (1.3) \qquad\qquad (9.06) \qquad\qquad (12)$$

$R^2 = 0.975572$; adjusted $R^2 = 0.969465$; DW $= 1.99$.

Conclusions and policy recommendations

Since 2000, the household passenger vehicle industry has been the foundation of China's domestic demand and has enabled China's economy to enter a new stage of heavy and chemical industrialization and to maintain its rapid growth. As seen in the different stages of the development of household passenger vehicle industry in China, this saloon-dominated industry sector for urban households has already experienced the growing stage of rapid development and has entered the maturing stage with a declining growth rate. As the middle-income urban households gradually realize their demand for saloons, the scale of the initial demand for household passenger vehicles that was dominated by saloons will reach its maximum value during the period from 2015 to 2016. Urban households' initial demand for family passenger vehicles is an important demand foundation to support rapid economic growth at the stage of heavy and chemical industrialization. In addition, the multiplier effect between automobile production and the total output value of heavy industry is as high as 1.2. Therefore, the falling growth rate of this initial demand would inevitably cause the economic growth rate to decline.

In order to maintain the automobile industry's role in driving the heavy and chemical industry and in sustaining economic growth, it is necessary to encourage automobile-manufacturing enterprises to put more effort into product innovation, to stimulate high-income households' demand to renewing their vehicles, to open up new markets for household passenger vehicles, to encourage lower-middle-income urban households and rural households to gradually realize their demand for passenger vehicles, to expand vehicle exports and to open up foreign markets. As there is a relatively large income inequality among urban and rural households in China, reducing the income inequality is an effective measure to stimulate domestic demand for passenger vehicles and to speed up the development of the automobile industry at the present stage.

10 The characteristics of and factors affecting the evolution of China's economic cycle and its dynamic equilibrium

The characteristics of the evolution of China's economic cycle and its dynamic equilibrium

The cyclical fluctuation of the economic growth rate is normal in an economy, and at any stage of the cyclical fluctuation there always exists a dynamic equilibrium of growth (see Chapter 7). After separating the cycles of China's quarterly cumulative GDP growth rate by using BP filtering (full sample asymmetric [Christiano-Fitzgerald]) and HP (Hodrick-Prescott) filtering during the period from the first quarter of 1992 to the fourth quarter of 2014, we can categorize the fluctuation of GDP growth rate by short-term fluctuation, mid-term fluctuation, mid-to-long-term fluctuation, long-term fluctuation and dynamic equilibrium. Based on the features of fluctuation, it can be seen that the GDP growth rate always fluctuates around the residual value, where GDP growth rate is stripped by short-term fluctuation;

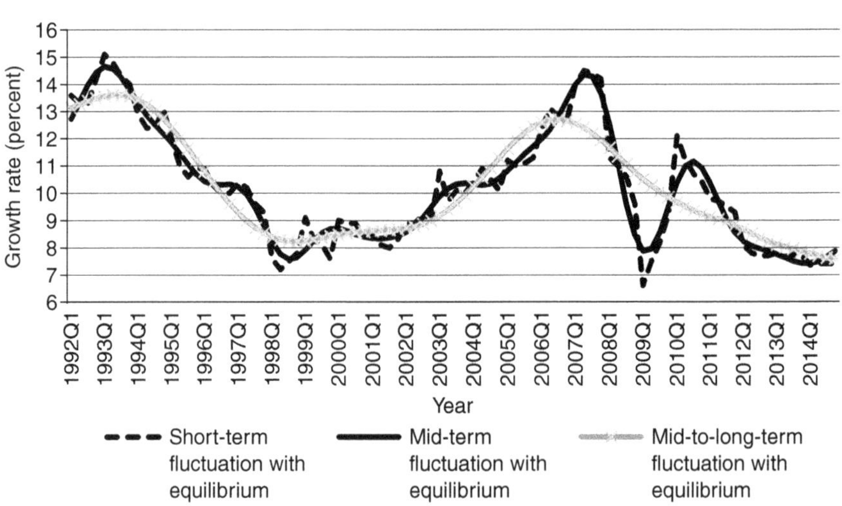

Figure 10.1 The short-term, mid-term and mid-to-long-term fluctuations with equilibrium of GDP growth rate from the first quarter of 1992 to the fourth quarter of 2014 (%).

Source: the data filtering is based on the data on GDP growth rate provided by WIND.

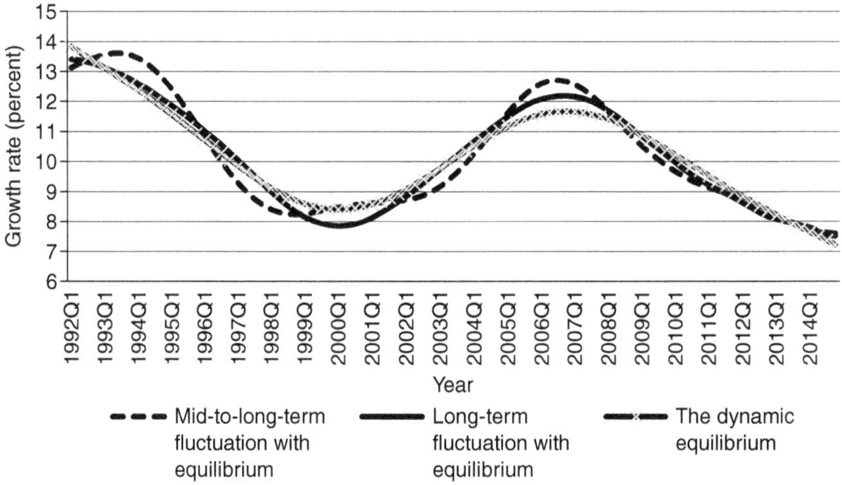

Figure 10.2 Mid-to-long-term, long-term fluctuations with equilibrium and the dynamic equilibrium of GDP growth rate from the first quarter of 1992 to the fourth quarter of 2014 (%).

Source: the data filtering is based on the data on GDP growth rate provided by WIND.

hereinafter we call the residual value the mid-term fluctuation with equilibrium. Similarly, the mid-term fluctuation with equilibrium always fluctuates around the mid-to-long-term fluctuation with equilibrium, the mid-to-long-term fluctuation with equilibrium fluctuates around the long-term fluctuation with equilibrium, and the long-term equilibrium with equilibrium fluctuates around the dynamic equilibrium. All these mean that the short-term fluctuation with equilibrium always fluctuates around the longer-term fluctuation with equilibrium and takes the longer-term fluctuation with equilibrium as its dynamic equilibrium (as shown in Figures 10.1 and 10.2). After removing all sorts of fluctuations' equilibrium, it can be seen that China's GDP growth rate has a variety of cyclical fluctuations with different characteristics. Short-term and mid-term fluctuations have relatively larger amplitudes and are mainly influenced by external factors, mid-to-long-term fluctuations have a declining amplitude and tend to converge, long-term fluctuations have increasing cyclical peak and trough values, and the dynamic equilibrium of GDP growth rate shows a trend of cyclical decline.

Short-term fluctuation has an indistinct regular pattern and is significantly influenced by external factors and shocks

During the period from the first quarter of 1992 to the fourth quarter of 2014, there were a total of 16 cycles, of which the average wavelength was 5.4 quarters. These cycles have three major characteristics as follows (Table 10.1 and Figure 10.3).

Table 10.1 Short-term fluctuations of GDP growth rate from the first quarter of 1992 to the fourth quarter of 2014

Cycle	*Time point of peak*	*Peak value (%)*	*Time point of trough*	*Trough value (%)*	*Peak-to-trough decrease (%)*	*Trough-to-peak rise (%)*	*Peak-to-peak (quarter)*	*Trough-to-trough (quarter)*
	1992Q1	0.87	1992Q3	–0.67	1.54			
1	1993Q1	0.44	1994Q2	–0.47	0.91	1.11	4	3
2	1994Q4	0.92	1995Q2	–0.46	1.38	1.39	7	4
3	1996Q1	0.47	1998Q1	–0.62	1.09	0.93	5	6
4	1997Q4	0.47	1998Q1	–0.62	1.09	0.79	7	5
5	1999Q1	1.18	1999Q4	–1.09	2.27	1.80	5	7
6	2000Q3	0.40	2001Q3	–0.37	0.77	1.50	6	7
7	2002Q1	0.32	2002Q4	–0.41	0.73	0.69	6	5
8	2003Q1	0.92	2003Q2	–0.48	1.39	1.33	4	2
9	2004Q2	0.60	2004Q4	–0.44	1.05	1.08	5	6
10	2005Q1	0.37	2005Q4	–0.42	0.79	0.82	3	4
11	2006Q2	0.75	2006Q4	–0.72	1.47	1.17	5	4
12	2007Q4	0.53	2008Q1	–1.24	1.77	1.25	6	5
13	2008Q4	1.14	2009Q1	–1.28	2.42	2.38	4	4
14	2010Q1	1.72	2011Q1	–0.56	2.28	3.00	5	8
15	2011Q4	0.74	2012Q3	–0.26	1.00	1.30	7	6
16	2013Q4	0.27	2014Q4	–0.47	0.74	0.53	8	5
Average		0.71		–0.61	1.32	1.32	5.4	5.1

Source: the data filtering is based on the data on GDP growth rate provided by the National Bureau of Statistics.

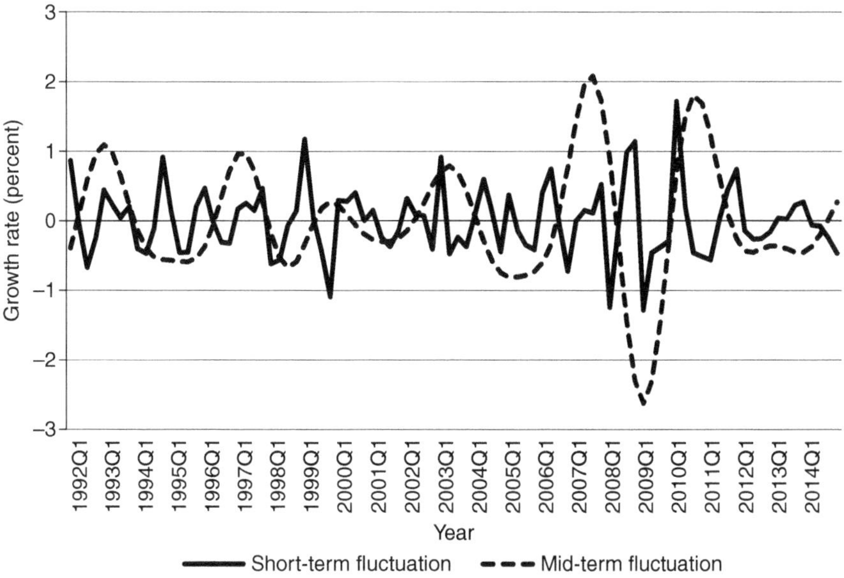

Figure 10.3 Short-term fluctuations and mid-term fluctuations of GDP growth rate after removing equilibrium from the first quarter of 1992 to the fourth quarter of 2014 (%).

Source: the data filtering is based on the data on GDP growth rate provided by WIND.

Relatively larger amplitude of short-term fluctuations

The average amplitude of 16 cycles is as high as 1.32 percent. Both the decreased amplitude from the peak to the trough (periodical decrease) and the largest increased amplitude from the trough to the peak (periodical increase) occurred between the fourth quarter of 2008 and the first quarter of 2010. The cyclical decreased amplitude and the cyclical increased amplitude were 2.28 percent and 3 percent respectively. The minimum amplitude occurred during the period from the third quarter of 2000 to the first quarter of 2001, and its cyclical decreased amplitude and cyclical increased amplitude were 0.73 percent and 0.69 percent respectively.

Relatively large changes of the short-term fluctuation's wavelength

Calculated by the interval of peak-to-peak and trough-to-trough, the average wavelength of short-term fluctuations of 16 cycles is 5.4 quarters and 5.1 quarters respectively. But there are bigger differences in the wavelength of different cycles. In the cycle with the shortest wavelength, the wavelength is only three quarters (from the second quarter of 2004 to the first quarter of 2005), and in the cycle with the longest wavelength, the wavelength is as high as eight quarters (from the fourth quarter of 2011 to the fourth quarter of 2013).

Short-term fluctuation is significantly influenced by external shocks

The largest amplitude of short-term fluctuation occurred during the US financial crisis from the first quarter of 2008 to the first quarter of 2010, and the fluctuations ranged from –1.28 percent in the first quarter of 2009 to 1.72 percent in the first quarter of 2010, with an amplitude as high as 3 percent. At the same time, after the Asian financial crisis in 1997, the short-term fluctuation also had a large amplitude as high as 2.27 percent, with a decline from 1.18 percent in the first quarter of 1999 to –1.09 percent in the fourth quarter of 1999. In addition, the amplitude of other cycles with short-term fluctuations was at around 1.5 percent.

The recent peak of short-term fluctuations occurred in the fourth quarter of 2013, with a peak value of 0.27 percent, and the short-term amplitude fell to –0.47 percent in the fourth quarter of 2014.

Mid-term fluctuation has a very large amplitude and relatively strong regularity, but is still significantly influenced by external factors and shocks

During the period from the first quarter of 1992 to the fourth quarter of 2014, there were a total of five mid-term cycles: the 1993Q1–1997Q1 cycle, the 1997Q1–1999Q4 cycle, the 1999Q4–2003Q2 cycle, the 2003Q2–2007Q3 cycle and the 2007Q3–2010Q3 cycle. The main characteristics of these fluctuations are as follows (Table 10.2).

The amplitude of mid-term fluctuation is very large

The average percentage of the decreased amplitude of the five cycles is 2.08 percent and the average percentage of the increased amplitude is 2.18 percent. This amplitude is significantly higher than that of the short-term fluctuation. The largest amplitude occurred during US financial crisis period from the third quarter of 2007 to the third quarter of 2010, with its periodical decreased amplitude and periodical rising amplitude being 4.7 percent and 4.43 percent respectively. The smallest amplitude occurred during the Asian financial crisis period from the second quarter of 1997 to the fourth quarter of 1999, with its cyclical decreased amplitude and cyclical increased amplitude being only 0.58 percent and 0.95 percent respectively.

The wavelength of mid-term fluctuation tends to become longer, and its falling stage is longer than its rising stage

Calculated by the interval of the peak-to-peak and trough-to-trough, the average wavelength of five cycles is 13.4 quarters and 14.4 quarters. The peak-to-peak length of five cycles tends to become shorter, with a reduction from 17 quarters in the first cycle to 12 quarters in the fifth cycle; the trough-to-trough length of five cycles tends to become longer, with an increase from 12 quarters in the first

Table 10.2 Mid-term fluctuations of GDP growth rate from the first quarter of 1992 to the fourth quarter of 2014

Cycle	*Time point of peak*	*Peak value (%)*	*Time point of trough*	*Trough value (%)*	*Peak-to-trough decrease (%)*	*Trough-to-peak rise (%)*	*Peak-to-peak (quarter)*	*Trough-to-trough (quarter)*
	1993Q1	1.09	1995Q3	–0.59	1.68			
1	1997Q2	0.97	1998Q3	–0.67	1.64	1.56	17	12
2	1999Q4	0.276	2001Q2	–0.303	0.58	0.95	10	11
3	2003Q2	0.79	2005Q1	–0.81	1.60	1.10	14	15
4	2007Q3	2.08	2009Q1	–2.62	4.70	2.89	13	16
5	2010Q3	1.81	2013Q3	–0.45	2.26	4.43	12	18
Average		1.17		–0.91	2.08	2.18	13.4	14.4

Source: the data filtering is based on the data on GDP growth rate provided by WIND.

cycle to 18 quarters in the fifth cycle. From the rising stage and the falling stage of each cycle, it can be seen that the falling stage of the first cycle is ten quarters, which is longer than its rising stage (seven quarters); the rising stage and the falling stage of the second cycle are five quarters; the falling stage of the third cycle is six quarters, and its rising stage is eight quarters; the falling stage of the fourth cycle is seven quarters, and its rising stage is six quarters; the falling stage of the fifth cycle is six quarters, and its rising stage is six quarters; the falling stage of the new cycle after the third quarter of 2010 is eight quarters. In general, the wavelength of the mid-term fluctuations of GDP growth rate tends to become longer, and the falling stage of a cycle is longer that the rising stage.

Mid-term fluctuation is significantly influenced by external shocks

During the Asian financial crisis, the mid-term fluctuations of GDP growth rate had the minimum amplitude, thus indicating that the Chinese government took proper measures to cope with the Asian financial crisis around that period. China's economy managed the negative impact of external shocks without any sharp decline in economic growth rate or any steep rebound in the later economic growth that might be caused by expansionary stimulus. During the US financial crisis, the amplitude of the mid-term fluctuations of China's GDP growth rate was very large, and the important reason for that is that when the shock of the US financial crisis hit China's economy, China overreacted and the policy responses were too late. In addition, there was an internal reason: the fluctuation of the economic growth rate is expected to be quite large at the stage of heavy and chemical industrialization.

The recent trough of the mid-term fluctuations of GDP growth rate occurred in the third quarter of 2013. After that, the mid-term fluctuations of GDP growth rate entered a cyclical rising stage, with the amplitude range increased to 0.27 percent in the fourth quarter of 2014.

Mid-to-long-term fluctuation tends to converge

During the period from the first quarter of 1992 to the fourth quarter of 2014, there were a total of two complete cycles in the mid-to-long-term fluctuations of GDP growth rate. According to the peak-to-peak calculation, they are the 1994Q1–2000Q2 cycle with a wavelength of 25 quarters and the 2000Q2–2006Q2 cycle with a wavelength of 24 quarters. According to the trough-to-trough calculation, they are the 1997Q2–2003Q2 cycle with a wavelength of 24 quarters and the 2003Q2–2009Q2 with a wavelength of 24 quarters respectively, namely, the wavelength of the mid-to-long-term fluctuations of GDP growth rate is approximately 24 quarters (Table 10.3; Figure 10.4).

The important feature of the mid-to-long-term fluctuations of GDP growth rate is that its amplitude decreased continually and the fluctuation tended to converge. Since the first quarter of 1992, the peak value of the mid-to-long-term fluctuations of GDP growth rate decreased continually and gradually from 0.85 percent in the first quarter of 1994 to 0.66 percent in the second quarter of 2000, and then to 0.54

Table 10.3 Mid-to-long-term fluctuations of GDP growth rate from the first quarter of 1992 to the fourth quarter of 2014

Cycle	*Time point of peak*	*Peak value (%)*	*Time point of trough*	*Trough value (%)*	*Peak-to-trough decrease (%)*	*Trough-to-peak rise (%)*	*Peak-to-peak (quarter)*	*Trough-to-trough (quarter)*
	1994Q1	0.85	1997Q2	–0.79	1.64			
1	2000Q2	0.66	2003Q2	–0.60	1.26	1.45	25	24
2	2006Q2	0.54	2009Q2	–0.36	0.90	1.14	24	24
3	2014Q4	0.09				0.44		
Average		0.53		–0.58	1.27	1.01	24.50	24

Source: the data filtering is based on the data on GDP growth rate provided by WIND.

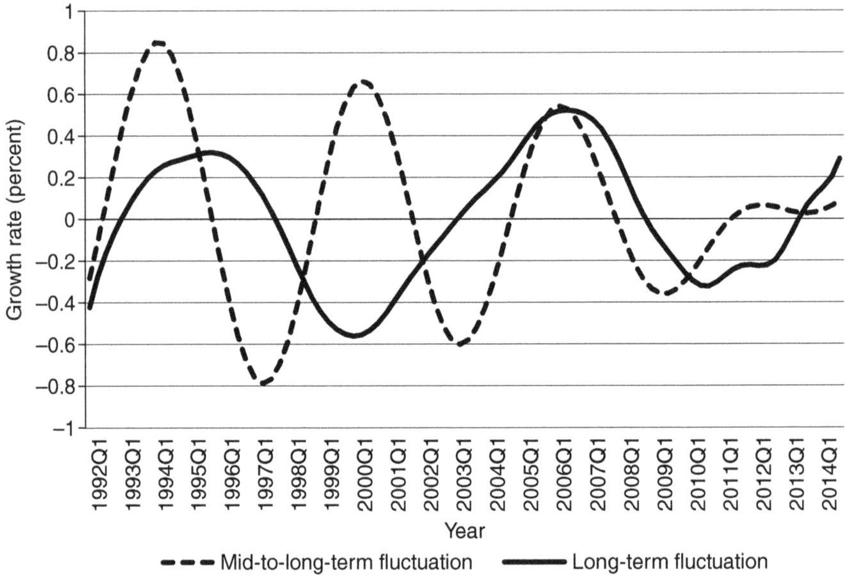

Figure 10.4 Mid-to-long-term fluctuations and long-term fluctuations of GDP growth rate from the first quarter of 1992 to the fourth quarter of 2014 (%).

Source: the data filtering is based on the data on GDP growth rate provided by WIND.

percent in the second quarter of 2006. At the same time, the trough value of mid-to-long-term fluctuations increased continually and gradually from –0.79 percent in the second quarter of 1997 to –0.6 percent in the second quarter of 2003 and then to –0.36 in the second quarter of 2009. With the combined influence of the declining peak value and the rising trough value, the amplitude of the mid-to-long-term fluctuations of GDP growth rate decreased continually; the cyclical decreasing amplitude fell gradually from 1.64 percent in the 1994Q1–1997Q2 period to 1.26 percent in the 2000Q2–2003Q2 period and then to 0.9 percent in the 2006Q2–2009Q2 period. The cyclical rising amplitude also increased gradually from 1.45 percent in the 1997Q2–2000Q2 period to 1.16 percent in the 2003Q2–2006Q2 period and then to 0.42 percent in the 2009Q2–2012Q2 period.

The recent trough of the mid-to-long-term fluctuations of GDP growth rate occurred in the second quarter of 2009. After that, the mid-to-long-term fluctuation of GDP growth rate entered a cyclical rising stage. The fluctuating value increased to 0.08 percent in the fourth quarter of 2014.

Cyclical rising trend of the long-term fluctuation

Since the first quarter of 1992, there has been only one complete cycle in the long-term fluctuation of GDP growth rate. This is to say, according to the peak-to-peak calculation it is the 1995Q4–2006Q3 cycle with a wavelength of 43 quarters, and according to the trough-to-trough calculation it is the 2000Q1–2010Q4 cycle with a wavelength of 43 quarters (Table 10.4). The long-term fluctuations of GDP growth rate have two important features. First, the cyclical peak value and the cyclical trough value tend to be greater; second, the fluctuations show a cyclical rising trend. The peak value of cyclical fluctuations increased from 0.32 percent in the fourth quarter of 1995 to 0.52 percent in the third quarter of 2006, and the trough value of cyclical fluctuations increased from –0.56 in the first quarter of 2000 to –0.32 percent in the fourth quarter of 2010. At the same time, the cyclical decreasing amplitude of long-term fluctuations tends to be smaller, falling from 0.88 percent in the 1995Q4–2000Q1 period to 0.84 percent in the 2006Q3–2010Q4 period. The cyclical rising amplitude tends to be greater, increasing from 0.74 percent in the 1992Q1–1995Q4 period to 1.08 percent in the 2000Q1–2006Q3 period.

The long-term fluctuations reached a new trough in the fourth quarter of 2010. The long-term fluctuating value turned positive in the third quarter of 2013, thus indicating entry into a new round of expansion. The fluctuating value increased to 0.29 percent in the fourth quarter of 2014.

The dynamic equilibrium of GDP growth rate shows a trend of cyclical decline

After removing all sorts of cyclical fluctuations, the dynamic equilibrium of GDP growth rate still shows a state of cyclical fluctuation. The equilibrium value fell from 13.83 percent in the first quarter of 1992 to 8.4 percent in the first quarter of 2000, and then rebounded to 11.66 percent in the fourth quarter of 2006 (Figure 10.5). After that, it entered a falling trend again and slowed to 7.22 percent in the fourth quarter of 2014. Based on the linear trend of long-term equilibrium value, it can be seen that the cyclical fluctuations of dynamic equilibrium showed a declining trend, and its linear trend value decreased from 11.55 percent in the first quarter of 1992 to 9 percent in the fourth quarter of 2014.

Factors affecting cyclical fluctuations and the dynamic equilibrium of China's economic growth rate

The evolution trend of cyclical fluctuations and the dynamic equilibrium of the economic growth rate are the major reflection of the status of an economy. Various factors affecting the economy ultimately affect the cyclical fluctuations of the economic growth rate. Taking actual investment growth rate, actual household consumption[1] growth rate, export growth rate, import growth rate and actual growth rate of the funds occupied by industrial enterprises' finished products (hereinafter referred to industrial inventory) as explanatory variables of the GDP growth rate, we carried out regression analysis to decompose the factors affecting the GDP growth rate. The results show that since the first quarter of 1992, the cyclical fluctuations of actual household consumption growth rate have become the most important factor of demand that determines the cyclical fluctuations of China's GDP growth rate. The cyclical fluctuations in export growth rate have had a greater

Table 10.4 Long-term fluctuations of GDP growth rate from the first quarter of 1992 to the fourth quarter of 2014

Cycle	*Time point of peak*	*Peak value (%)*	*Time point of trough*	*Trough value (%)*	*Peak-to-trough decrease (%)*	*Trough-to-peak rise (%)*	*Peak-to-peak (quarter)*	*Trough-to-trough (quarter)*
			1992Q1	–0.42	0.42			
1	1995Q4	0.32	2000Q1	–0.56	0.88	0.74		32
2	2006Q3	0.52	2010Q4	–0.32	0.84	1.08	43	43
3	2014Q4	0.29				0.61	32	
Average		0.38		–0.44	0.72	0.81	37.50	37.50

Source: the data filtering is based on the data on GDP growth rate provided by WIND.

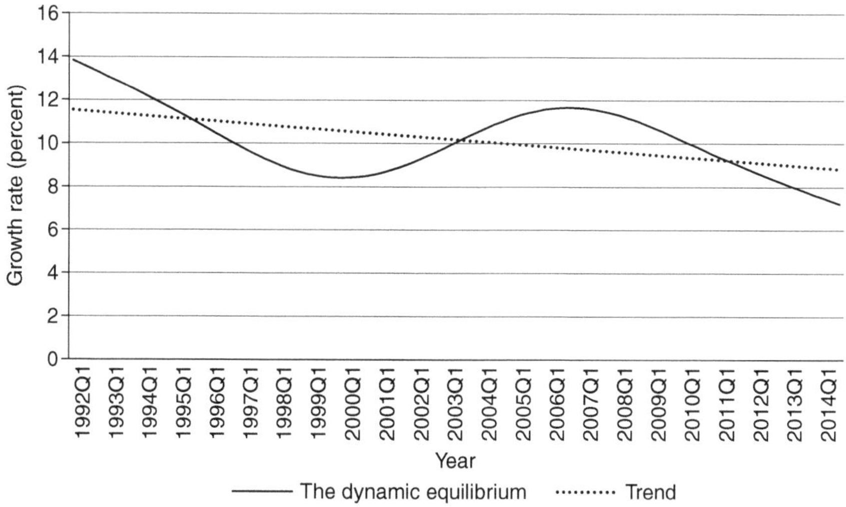

Figure 10.5 Dynamic equilibrium of GDP growth rate and its inherent trend from the first quarter of 1992 to the fourth quarter of 2014 (%).

Source: the data filtering is based on the data on GDP growth rate provided by WIND.

influence on the cyclical fluctuations of GDP growth rate than those of actual investment growth rate, and the cyclical fluctuations of import growth rate and actual industrial inventory growth rate have had an important effect of inhibiting the amplitude of the cyclical fluctuations of the GDP growth rate. The trend of the cyclical fluctuation of the GDP growth rate's dynamic equilibrium demonstrates the special characteristics of China's economy in its evolving phase from light industrialization to heavy and chemical industrialization and then to the late stage of industrialization. Such features are jointly determined by the cyclical fluctuation trends of the dynamic equilibrium of the actual growth rates of consumption, export and investment. The upgrading and transformation of household consumption structure and export structure are the foundation that determines the cyclical trend of the GDP growth rate's dynamic equilibrium

Factors affecting short-term fluctuations of GDP growth rate

The short-term fluctuations of different demand growth rates are the fundamental factors that affect short-term fluctuations of economic growth rate. The influence of other factors such as policy adjustment and external shocks on economic growth also have effects through the short-term fluctuations of demand growth rates. However, some factors that are difficult to quantify can also affect short-term fluctuations and cause them to have weak regularity. Taking the short-term fluctuations of the actual growth rates of investment (TZAGW), household consumption (XFZAGW), export (CKZW), import (JKZW), government expenditure (FISEAGW) and industry inventory (INDHARGW) as explanatory variables for the short-term fluctuations of GDP growth rate (GDPAGW), we carried out a regression analysis to decompose the factors affecting the short-term fluctuations of GDP growth rate. The results of the regression analysis show that the goodness-of-fit of equation (R^2) is 0.71, and the adjusted goodness-of-fit is only 0.67, which means all demand factors (explanatory variables) can only explain 70 percent of the short-term fluctuations of the GDP growth rate, while the other 30 percent of short-term fluctuations is difficult to explain using the actual growth rates of short-term fluctuations of various demand factors (Table 10.5).

Based on the elasticity effect of various demand factors on the short-term fluctuations of the GDP growth rate, it can be seen that the short-term fluctuations of the actual household consumption growth rate have the greatest influence on the short-term fluctuations of the GDP growth rate. The elasticity effect here means the change of the range of the dependent value caused by every 1 percent change of certain explanatory variables. It can be seen that every 1 percent increase of the short-term fluctuating value of the consumption growth rate can cause the short-term fluctuating value of the GDP growth rate to increase by 0.1857 percent, which indicates that the elasticity effect of the short-term fluctuations of the actual household consumption growth rate on the short-term fluctuations of the GDP growth rate is 0.1857 percent. The elasticity effect of the short-term fluctuations of the actual growth rates of investment, export and import are approximately the same, namely 0.0363 percent, 0.0365 percent and 0.0358 percent respectively, while the short-term fluctuations of the actual industrial inventory growth rate have a very low elasticity effect to the short-term fluctuations of the GDP growth rate (only 0.0059 percent).

From the actual effects of various demand factors on the short-term fluctuations of GDP growth rate, it can be seen that the declining growth rates of investment, consumption, import and export jointly caused the increasing decline in the short-term fluctuating value of the GDP growth rate in 2014, especially that the substantially decreased export and import growth rates were the important factors that

Table 10.5 Short-term fluctuating values of GDP growth rate and actual demand growth rates from the first quarter of 2013 to the fourth quarter of 2014 (%)

Period	*GDP*	*Investment*	*Household consumption*	*Export*	*Import*	*Industrial inventory*
2013Q1	0.044	1.474	–0.579	4.515	–1.568	2.392
2013Q2	0.023	0.962	–0.255	–1.148	–0.644	–0.005
2013Q3	0.225	1.098	0.046	0.642	3.696	–0.536
2013Q4	0.274	–2.890	–0.305	4.637	6.413	–3.209
2014Q1	–0.062	–0.227	0.884	–4.241	1.312	1.480
2014Q2	–0.077	0.396	–0.263	–0.218	–0.484	1.369
2014Q3	–0.254	–0.713	–1.156	1.123	–3.888	0.878
2014Q4	–0.469	–0.888	0.949	–2.167	–8.316	–0.227

Source: the data filtering is based on the data on GDP growth rate and demand growth rate provided by WIND.

caused the continuously increasing decline in GDP growth rate in the second half of 2014 (Table 10.6).

From the simulation conducted by utilizing the regression equation to decompose the influence from various factors, it can be seen that because of the relatively low goodness-of-fit, the deviation between simulated value and actual value during the period from 2003 to 2010 is relatively larger and the deviation after 2010 tends to be smaller, and thus various demand factors can explain relatively more of the short-term fluctuation of the GDP growth rate (Figure 10.6).

Table 10.6 Actual influences of short-term fluctuations of actual growth rates of various demand factors to short-term fluctuation of GDP growth rate (%)

Period	*GDP*	*Investment*	*Household consumption*	*Export*	*Import*	*Industrial inventory*
2013Q1	0.044	0.054	–0.108	0.165	–0.056	0.014
2013Q2	0.023	0.035	–0.047	–0.042	–0.023	0.000
2013Q3	0.225	0.040	0.009	0.023	0.132	–0.003
2013Q4	0.274	–0.105	–0.057	0.169	0.229	–0.019
2014Q1	–0.062	–0.008	0.164	–0.155	0.047	0.009
2014Q2	–0.077	0.014	–0.049	–0.008	–0.017	0.008
2014Q3	–0.254	–0.026	–0.215	0.041	–0.139	0.005
2014Q4	–0.469	–0.032	0.176	–0.079	–0.298	–0.001

Source: calculated according to the data in Table 10.5 and the effect of each factor.

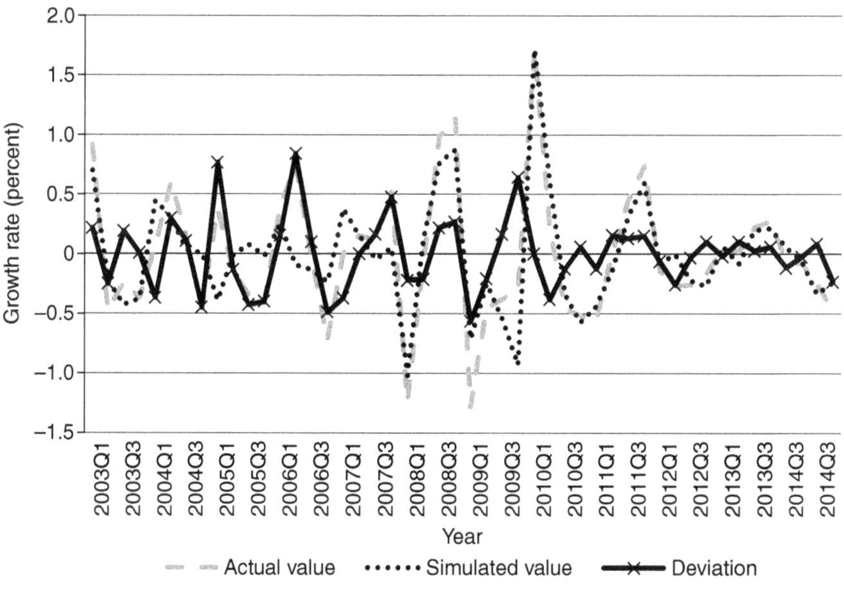

Figure 10.6 Simulated value and deviation of short-term fluctuations of GDP growth rate from the first quarter of 2013 to the fourth quarter of 2014 (%).

However, the deviation between simulated value and actual value in the fourth quarter of 2014 expands again to –0.23 percent, which is equivalent to 49.6 percent of actual short-term fluctuating value. The actual contribution value of various demand factors to the short-term fluctuations of GDP growth rate is only –0.234, which is equivalent to 50 percent of the short-term fluctuating value of the GDP growth rate (–0.469 percent), thus indicating that some other factors have a greater influence on the short-term fluctuations of GDP growth rate beyond only demand factors.

The factors affecting the short-term fluctuations of the GDP growth rate can be decomposed as the following equation:

$$\mathrm{GDPAGW} = 0.0363 \times \mathrm{TZAGW} + 0.1857 \times \mathrm{XFZAGW} + 0.0365 \times \mathrm{CKZW} + 0.0358 \times \mathrm{JKZW} + 0.0059 \times \mathrm{INDHARGW} - 0.0027$$

$R^2 = 0.709573$; adjusted $R^2 = 0.674998$; $\mathrm{DW}^2 = 2$.

Factors affecting the mid-term fluctuations of GDP growth rate

The mid-term fluctuation of the GDP growth rate has the largest amplitude among four kinds of cyclical fluctuations, and its regularity is relatively stronger, but it is still significantly affected by external shocks. The influence of two regional and global financial crises since 1992 and the influence of domestic policy responses on China's economic growth rate are mainly reflected in mid-term fluctuations. From the demand factors that directly affect the mid-term fluctuations of GDP growth rate, it can be seen that the mid-term fluctuations of actual growth rates of investment (TZAGWS), consumption (XFZAGWS), export (CKZWS), import (JKZWS) and industrial inventory (INDHARGWS) show wide-ranging fluctuations. Since the mid-term fluctuations of GDP growth rate have relatively stronger regularity, we can also regard the mid-term fluctuating value of first-order-lag GDP growth rate as an explanatory variable, while taking demand factors as explanatory variables. That is, by incorporating the lagged variable into the construction of a difference equation, the inherent cyclical fluctuation characteristics of variables can be shown. The results of regression analysis show that the influence factor decomposition equation of mid-term fluctuations has a very high goodness-of-fit, thus indicating that the mid-term fluctuations with the actual growth rate of various demand factors and the inherent cyclical fluctuations of the GDP growth rate's mid-term fluctuation can well explain the mid-term fluctuation of the GDP growth rate (Table 10.7).

From the elasticity effects of various factors on the mid-term fluctuating value, it can be seen that in addition to the inherent cyclical fluctuation factors of the mid-term fluctuations (first-order-lag mid-term fluctuating value), the mid-term fluctuations of actual household consumption growth rate are the most important factor that affects the mid-term fluctuations of the GDP growth rate, with its contribution being 0.3158 percent. Other important factors are the mid-term fluctuations of export and investment growth rates, with an elasticity effect

Table 10.7 Mid-term fluctuating values of the GDP growth rate and actual growth rate of each demand factor from the first quarter of 2013 to the fourth quarter of 2014 (%)

Period	*GDP*	*GDP (T−1)*	*Investment*	*Household consumption*	*Export*	*Import (T−1)*	*Industrial inventory*
2013Q1	−0.362	−0.360	3.031	−1.275	2.067	0.311	0.060
2013Q2	−0.405	−0.362	2.252	−1.523	1.615	2.170	−1.914
2013Q3	−0.451	−0.405	1.474	−1.267	−0.819	1.094	−3.162
2013Q4	−0.451	−0.451	0.597	−0.674	−3.655	−1.637	−3.539
2014Q1	−0.369	−0.451	−0.437	0.002	−5.234	−4.074	−3.142
2014Q2	−0.199	−0.369	−1.521	0.530	−4.603	−4.652	−2.255
2014Q3	0.032	−0.199	−2.395	0.789	−1.904	−2.904	−1.235
2014Q4	0.274	0.032	−2.768	0.788	1.787	0.445	−0.380

Source: the data filtering is based on the data on GDP growth rate and demand growth rate provided by WIND.

of 0.0547 percent and 0.0518 percent respectively. The mid-term fluctuations of actual growth rates of import and industrial inventory have negative elasticity effects on the mid-term fluctuation of GDP growth rate, namely −0.0044 percent and −0.0569 percent respectively.

From the trend of mid-term fluctuations of each demand factor and the actual influence on the mid-term fluctuations of the GDP growth rate during the period from the first quarter of 2013 to the fourth quarter of 2014, it can be seen that the fluctuation range of the mid-term fluctuating value of each demand factor was higher than the mid-term fluctuation range of the GDP growth rate. The trend of the mid-term fluctuations of household consumption growth rate was basically consistent with that of the GDP growth rate, thus household consumption had the largest actual influence on the mid-term fluctuations of economic growth rate and became the most important demand factor that determined the trend of the mid-term fluctuations of the GDP growth rate.

The mid-term fluctuations of export growth rate lagged one quarter behind the mid-term fluctuations of the GDP growth rate and became the second largest demand factor that determined the trend of the mid-term fluctuations of the GDP growth rate. The mid-term fluctuations of actual investment growth rate lagged greatly behind the mid-term fluctuations of the GDP growth rate, thus restraining the amplitude of the mid-term fluctuations of the GDP growth rate. The mid-term fluctuations of import growth rate lagged two quarters behind the mid-term fluctuations of the GDP growth rate, and the trend of the mid-term fluctuations of actual industrial inventory growth rate was basically consistent with that of the GDP growth rate, but these two major demand factors had negative elasticity effects on the mid-term fluctuations of the GDP growth rate, thus restraining the amplitude of the mid-term fluctuations of the GDP growth rate. In general, the gradual recovery of the mid-term fluctuating value of the GDP growth rate after the third quarter of 2013 was mainly driven by the recovery of the mid-term fluctuating values of household consumption and export growth rates. The continuous decline in the mid-term fluctuating value of investment growth rate and the recovery of the mid-term fluctuating values of import growth rate and actual industrial inventory growth rate had important effects of inhibiting the recovery of the mid-term fluctuating value of the GDP growth rate, which is the major reason why the recovery of the mid-term fluctuating value of the GDP growth rate was significantly lower than the recovery of the mid-term fluctuating values of household consumption and export growth rates (as shown in Table 10.8).

The factors affecting the mid-term fluctuations of the GDP growth rate can be decomposed as the following equation:

$$\text{GDPAGWS} = 0.7376 \times \text{GDPAGWS}(-1) + 0.0518 \times \text{TZAGWS} + 0.3158 \times \text{XFZAGWS} + 0.0547 \times \text{CKZWS} - 0.0044 \times \text{JKZWS}(-1) - 0.0569 \times \text{INDHARGWS} + 0.0248 + [\text{AR}(1) = 0.7277, \text{MA}(2) = 0.9177]$$

$R^2 = 0.999669$; adjusted $R^2 = 0.9996$; DW = 0.4. AR(1) and MA(1) are first-order autoregressive and moving average residual components respectively.

The mid-term fluctuations of actual investment growth rate are inconsistent with the trend of the mid-term fluctuations of GDP growth rate, and therefore it has an effect of inhibiting the amplitude of the mid-term fluctuations of GDP growth rate (Figure 10.7). The underlying reasons for this are as follows. First, investment is highly affected by policy adjustments because China's policy control on its economy is mainly on the regulation of investment. Second, with the increasing degree of marketization, enterprises' judgments on future economic trends directly affect their investment decision-making, thus the mid-term fluctuations of actual investment growth rate have always been ahead of the mid-term fluctuations of GDP growth rate since 2000. For example, the actual investment growth rate reached the peak value of its mid-term fluctuations in the third quarter of 2006, while the GDP growth rate reached the peak value of its mid-term fluctuations in the third quarter of 2007.

After the actual investment growth rate reached the peak value of its mid-term fluctuations in the third quarter of 2009, the GDP growth rate reached the peak value in the third quarter of 2010. The main reason that the economic growth rate can reach a peak value of fluctuation soon after the launch of investment is the subsequent cyclical rise of consumption and export. However, after the new mid-term fluctuation peak of investment in the third quarter of 2012, there was no new mid-term fluctuation peak of economic growth rate in 2013. An important reason for this is that the household consumption growth rate entered a recession of mid-term fluctuation in 2013, thus causing a sharp drop in its fluctuating value.

Although the export growth rate entered the rising stage of mid-term fluctuation, the increase in the mid-term fluctuating value of export was relatively smaller due to a weak recovery in the international economy, severe trade protection and other factors. Therefore it failed to make up for the negative influence of declining domestic household consumption growth rate on the GDP growth rate. In 2014, domestic household consumption entered the rising stage of the mid-term fluctuation again, but the increase was small. Moreover, the sharp decline in the

Table 10.8 Actual influences of the mid-term fluctuating value of actual growth rate of each demand factor on mid-term fluctuating value of GDP growth rate from the first quarter of 2013 to the fourth quarter of 2014 (%)

Period	*GDP*	*GDP (T–1)*	*Investment*	*Household consumption*	*Export*	*Import (T–1)*	*Industrial inventory*
2013Q1	–0.362	–0.266	0.157	–0.403	0.113	–0.001	–0.003
2013Q2	–0.405	–0.267	0.117	–0.481	0.088	–0.009	0.109
2013Q3	–0.451	–0.298	0.076	–0.400	–0.045	–0.005	0.180
2013Q4	–0.451	–0.333	0.031	–0.213	–0.200	0.007	0.201
2014Q1	–0.369	–0.333	–0.023	0.001	–0.287	0.018	0.179
2014Q2	–0.199	–0.272	–0.079	0.167	–0.252	0.020	0.128
2014Q3	0.032	–0.147	–0.124	0.249	–0.104	0.013	0.070
2014Q4	0.274	0.024	–0.143	0.249	0.098	–0.002	0.022

Source: calculation based on the data in Table 10.7 and the elasticity effect of various factors.

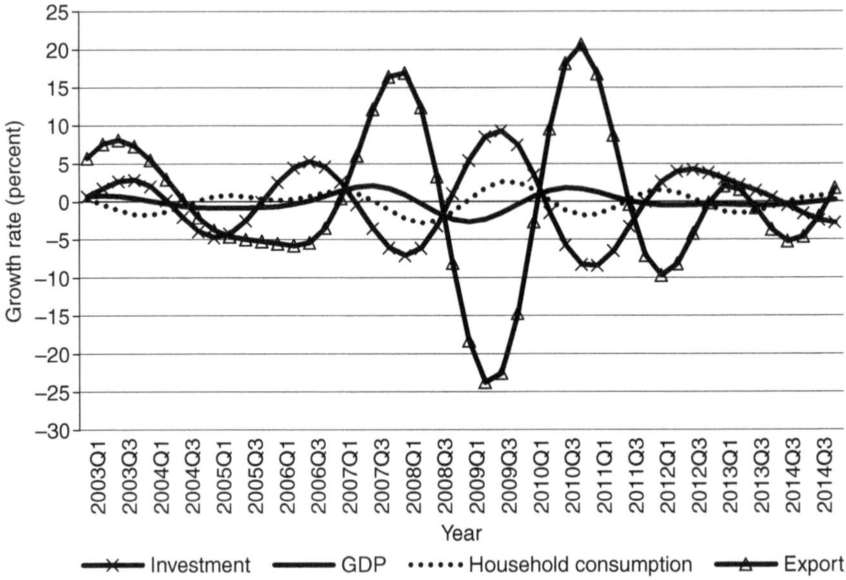

Figure 10.7 Mid-term fluctuations of GDP growth rate and actual investment growth rate from the first quarter of 2000 to the fourth quarter of 2014 (%).

Source: the data filtering is based on the data on GDP and investment provided by WIND.

Note

The right axis is for the mid-term fluctuation of GDP growth rate, the left axis is for mid-term fluctuation of the other three demand growth rates.

mid-term fluctuating values of actual growth rates of export and investment caused the mid-term fluctuating value of GDP growth rate to rebound slowly, which became an important reason for the decline in GDP growth rate.

Factors affecting mid-to-long-term fluctuations of the GDP growth rate

Since the first quarter of 2003, mid-to-long-term fluctuations of the GDP growth rate tended to converge, which is mainly because the mid-to-long-term fluctuations of the actual growth rates of investment and household consumption tended to converge. Taking the mid-to-long-term fluctuations of actual growth rates of investment (TZAGWM), household consumption (XFZAGWM), export (CKZWM), import (JKZWM) and industrial inventory (INDHARGWM) as explanatory variables for the mid-to-long-term fluctuation of the GDP growth rate (GDPAGWM), we carried out a regression analysis. The results of the regression analysis show that the goodness-of-fit of the influence factor decomposition equation is very high, and the demand factors explain the cause of the mid-to-long-term fluctuations of the GDP growth rate (Figure 10.9).

Table 10.9 Mid-to-long-term fluctuating values of actual growth rate of GDP and each demand factor from the first quarter of 2013 to the fourth quarter of 2014 (%)

Period	*GDP*	*Investment*	*First-order-lag investment*	*Household consumption*	*Export*	*First-order-lag export*	*Import*	*Industrial inventory*
2013Q1	0.0474	−1.9728	−1.9664	0.0954	2.1770	3.7484	−4.2720	2.2659
2013Q2	0.0372	−1.8378	−1.9728	0.0118	0.6026	2.1770	−6.0155	2.9252
2013Q3	0.0298	−1.5848	−1.8378	−0.0714	−0.8676	0.6026	−7.3106	3.4094
2013Q4	0.0276	−1.2442	−1.5848	−0.1469	−2.1404	−0.8676	−8.1005	3.7034
2014Q1	0.0320	−0.8508	−1.2442	−0.2082	−3.1430	−2.1404	−8.3651	3.8039
2014Q2	0.0438	−0.4408	−0.8508	−0.2500	−3.8275	−3.1430	−8.1209	3.7194
2014Q3	0.0626	−0.0488	−0.4408	−0.2690	−4.1732	−3.8275	−7.4181	3.4685
2014Q4	0.0872	0.2949	−0.0488	−0.2639	−4.1864	−4.1732	−6.3348	3.0788

Source: the data filtering is based on the data on actual growth rates provided by WIND.

According to the elasticity effect of each demand factor on the mid-to-long-term fluctuations of the GDP growth rate, it can be seen that the mid-to-long-term fluctuations of actual household consumption growth rate is the most important demand factor that affects the mid-to-long-term fluctuations of GDP growth rate, and its elasticity effect is 0.9452 percent. The mid-to-long-term fluctuations of the export growth rate is another important factor, the elasticity effect of the mid-to-long-term fluctuations of current export is 0.6938 percent, and the elasticity effect of the mid-to-long-term fluctuations of the first-order-lag export is –0.5799 percent, so the comprehensive elasticity effect of the mid-to-long-term fluctuations of export is 0.1139 percent. The elasticity effect of the mid-to-long-term fluctuations of actual growth rate of current investment to the mid-to-long-term fluctuations of GDP growth rate is 0.266 percent, but the elasticity effect of the mid-to-long-term fluctuations of the actual growth rate of first-order-lag investment is –0.3421 percent, so the comprehensive elasticity effect of the mid-to-long-term fluctuations of the actual growth rate of investment on the mid-to-long-term fluctuations of GDP growth rate is–0.076 percent. The mid-to-long-term fluctuations of actual growth rates of import and industrial inventory have negative elasticity effects on the mid-to-long-term fluctuation of the GDP growth rate, namely –0.1461 percent and –0.0629 percent respectively.

According to the actual influence of each demand factor on the mid-to-long-term fluctuations of the GDP growth rate, it can be seen that the modest recovery in the mid-to-long-term fluctuating value of GDP growth rate after the first quarter of 2013 was mainly driven by the mid-to-long-term fluctuations of actual investment growth rate in its cyclical rising stage. Moreover, the decline in the mid-to-long-term fluctuations of the import growth rate was greater than the decline in that of the export growth rate, so this also played an important role in supporting the recovery of the mid-to-long-term fluctuations of the GDP growth rate. The declining mid-to-long-term fluctuating value of the actual household consumption growth rate and the increasing mid-to-long-term fluctuating value of the actual industrial inventory growth rate had important effects of inhibiting the recovery of the mid-to-long-term fluctuating value of the GDP growth rate (as shown in Table 10.10).

The factors affecting the mid-to-long-term fluctuations of GDP growth rate can be decomposed as the following equation:

$$\begin{aligned}&\text{GDPAGWM}=0.266\times\text{TZAGWM}-0.3421\times\text{TZAGWM}\\&(-1)+0.9452\times\text{XFZAGWM}+0.6938\times\text{CKZWM}-0.5799\times\text{CKZWM}\\&(-1)-0.1461\times\text{JKZWM}-0.0629\times\text{INDHARGWM}-0.0106\end{aligned}$$

$R^2=0.999927$; adjusted $R^2=0.999914$; DW=0.46.

From the fluctuation range and trend, it can be seen that the amplitude of the mid-to-long-term fluctuations of the GDP growth rate tended to converge after the first quarter of 2003, and the important reason for this is that the mid-to-long-term fluctuations of actual growth rates of household consumption and investment tended to converge after the first quarter of 2003.

Table 10.10 Actual influences of the mid-to-long-term fluctuations of each demand factor on mid-to-long-term fluctuations of GDP growth rate (%)

Period	*GDP*	*Investment*	*Household consumption*	*Export*	*Import*	*Industrial inventory*
2013Q1	0.0474	0.1480	0.0902	–0.6632	0.6242	–0.1426
2013Q2	0.0372	0.1861	0.0112	–0.8443	0.8790	–0.1841
2013Q3	0.0298	0.2072	–0.0675	–0.9514	1.0682	–0.2146
2013Q4	0.0276	0.2112	–0.1389	–0.9819	1.1837	–0.2331
2014Q1	0.0320	0.1993	–0.1967	–0.9394	1.2223	–0.2394
2014Q2	0.0438	0.1738	–0.2363	–0.8329	1.1867	–0.2341
2014Q3	0.0626	0.1378	–0.2543	–0.6758	1.0839	–0.2183
2014Q4	0.0872	0.0951	–0.2494	–0.4846	0.9257	–0.1938

Source: calculation based on the data in Table 10.9 and the elasticity effects of various factors.

In addition, during the period from the first quarter of 2003 to the fourth quarter of 2011, the amplitude and trend of the mid-to-long-term fluctuations of the GDP growth rate were basically consistent with those of the actual household consumption growth rate (Figure 10.8). However, since then the amplitude has been significantly smaller than the amplitude of the mid-to-long-term fluctuations of the actual

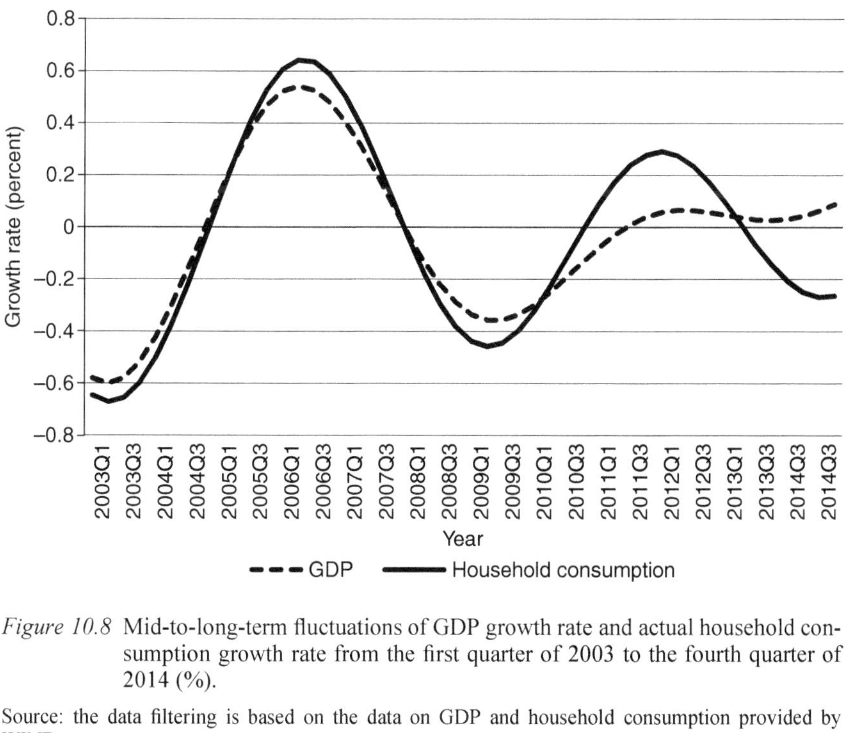

Figure 10.8 Mid-to-long-term fluctuations of GDP growth rate and actual household consumption growth rate from the first quarter of 2003 to the fourth quarter of 2014 (%).

Source: the data filtering is based on the data on GDP and household consumption provided by WIND.

household consumption growth rate, and when the mid-to-long-term fluctuations of the actual household consumption growth rate entered a cyclical declining stage in the second quarter of 2013, the mid-to-long-term fluctuations of the GDP growth rate rebounded again, thus the trend of mid-to-long-term fluctuations of the GDP growth rate deviated from the trend of mid-to-long-term fluctuations of the actual household consumption growth rate. There are three reasons for this. First, the range of the decline in the mid-to-long-term fluctuations of the actual household consumption growth rate was relatively smaller, so it had a limited effect on pulling up the decreasing trend of mid-to-long-term fluctuating value of the GDP growth rate. Second, the mid-to-long-term fluctuations of the actual household consumption growth rate entered a cyclical recovery after the first quarter of 2013, so the reduced range of the decline in the mid-to-long-term fluctuating value of the actual household consumption growth rate had a gradually decreasing influence on contracting the mid-to-long-term fluctuating value of the GDP growth rate. Third, and the most important factor, is that the range of the decline in the mid-to-long-term fluctuations of the import growth rate was larger than the decline in that of the export growth rate, so the increased net exports caused the mid-to-long-term fluctuating value of the GDP growth rate to increase rather than decrease.

The factors affecting long-term fluctuations of the GDP growth rate

The long-term fluctuations of the GDP growth rate have a very significant regularity. In order to show the inherent regularity of the long-term fluctuations of the GDP growth rate and the influence of demand factors, we took the long-term fluctuating values of the first-order-lag GDP growth rate and the long-term fluctuating values of the actual growth rates of investment (TZAGWL), household consumption (XFZAGWL), export (CKZWL), import (JKZWL) and industrial inventory (INDHARGWL) as explanatory variables and carried out the regression analysis to decompose the factors affecting the long-term fluctuations of the GDP growth rate (GDPAGWL). The results of regression analysis show that these factors can well explain the trend of the long-term fluctuations of GDP growth rate (Figure 10.9; Table 10.11).

According to various factors' elasticity effects on the long-term fluctuations of the GDP growth rate, it can be found that the long-term fluctuations of the first-order-lag GDP growth rate have a relatively higher elasticity of 0.7531 percent, which shows that the long-term fluctuations of the GDP growth rate have very strong inherent regularity. Among various demand factors, industrial inventory (the funds occupied by industrial enterprises' finished products) has the highest elasticity effect of 0.0525 percent, which shows that the inventory change has a relatively greater influence on the long-term fluctuations of the GDP growth rate. Moreover, the export has an elasticity effect of 0.0438 percent, which is significantly higher than the elasticity effects of household consumption and investment (0.0365 percent and 0.0229 percent respectively), showing that the influence of the long-term fluctuations of export growth rate on the long-term fluctuations of GDP growth rate is greater than that of household consumption and investment. The

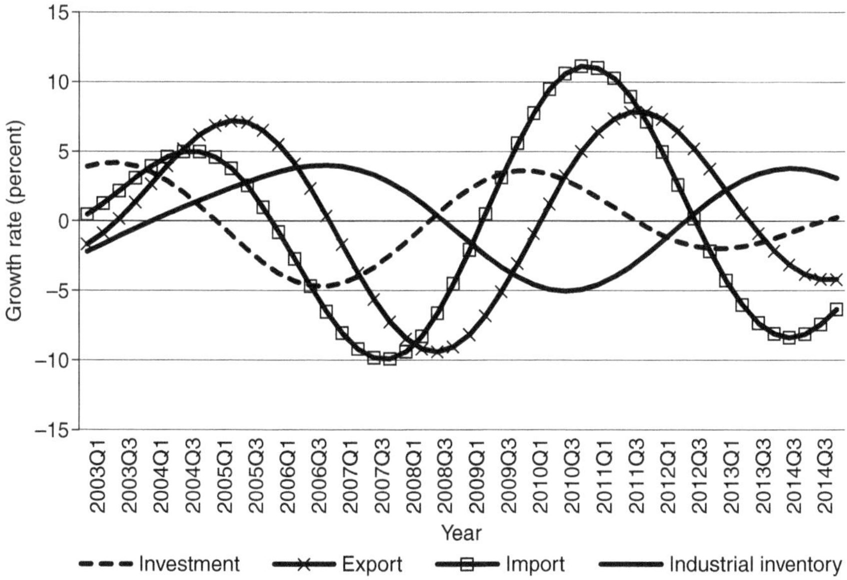

Figure 10.9 Mid-to-long-term fluctuations of actual growth rates of investment, import, export and the funds occupied by industrial enterprises' finished products from the first quarter of 2003 to the fourth quarter of 2014 (%).

Source: the data filtering is based on the data provided by WIND.

effects of the long-term fluctuating values of current and first-order-lag import growth rates on the long-term fluctuating value of the GDP growth rate are 0.0324 percent and –0.0422 percent respectively. Comprehensively, it can be seen that the elasticity effect of the long-term fluctuations of the import growth rate on the long-term fluctuations of the GDP growth rate is –0.0098 percent.

According to the actual influences of various factors obtained through the calculations based on these factors' elasticity effects and their long-term fluctuating values since the first quarter of 2013, it can be found that in addition to the factor of GDP growth rate long-term fluctuations' inherent rising cycle (the rising actual influence of the first-order-lag long-term fluctuating values), the sustained recovery of the long-term fluctuating value of export growth rate had the largest actual influence on the long-term fluctuations of GDP growth rate, which was also the main demand factor that resulted in the rising long-term fluctuating value of GDP growth rate after the first quarter of 2013 (Table 10.12; Figure 10.10). The sustained recovery of the long-term fluctuating values of household consumption's actual growth rates and industrial inventory also played an important role in promoting the recovery of the long-term fluctuating value of the GDP growth rate. Due to the decline in the long-term fluctuating value of actual investment growth rate, the actual influence of investment factors on the

Table 10.11 Long-term fluctuating values of GDP growth rate and actual growth rates of various influencing factors from the first quarter of 2013 to the fourth quarter of 2014 (%)

Period	*GDP*	*First-order-lag GDP*	*Investment*	*Household consumption*	*Export*	*Import*	*First-order-lag import*	*Industrial inventory*
2013Q1	–0.147	–0.198	0.310	–0.148	–0.135	–0.505	–0.245	–0.108
2013Q2	–0.075	–0.147	0.934	–0.119	–0.185	–0.369	–0.505	–0.125
2013Q3	0.002	–0.075	1.231	–0.092	–0.182	0.138	–0.369	–0.093
2013Q4	0.068	0.002	1.124	–0.084	–0.015	0.767	0.138	0.027
2014Q1	0.115	0.068	0.725	–0.086	0.378	1.164	0.767	0.242
2014Q2	0.152	0.115	0.276	–0.072	0.977	1.069	1.164	0.525
2014Q3	0.201	0.152	0.025	–0.009	1.698	0.480	1.069	0.826
2014Q4	0.290	0.201	0.095	0.122	2.448	–0.307	0.480	1.097

Source: the data filtering is based on the data provided by WIND.

Table 10.12 Actual influences of long-term fluctuations of actual growth rates of various influence factors on long-term fluctuating values of GDP growth rate from the first quarter of 2013 to the fourth quarter of 2014 (%)

Period	*GDP*	*First-order-lag GDP*	*Investment*	*Household consumption*	*Export*	*Import*	*Industrial inventory*
2013Q1	–0.147	–0.149	0.007	–0.005	–0.006	–0.006	–0.006
2013Q2	–0.075	–0.111	0.021	–0.004	–0.008	0.009	–0.007
2013Q3	0.002	–0.075	0.028	–0.003	–0.008	0.020	–0.005
2013Q4	0.068	0.001	0.026	–0.003	–0.001	0.019	0.001
2014Q1	0.115	0.051	0.017	–0.003	0.017	0.005	0.013
2014Q2	0.152	0.087	0.006	–0.003	0.043	–0.015	0.028
2014Q3	0.201	0.115	0.001	0.000	0.074	–0.030	0.043
2014Q4	0.290	0.151	0.002	0.004	0.107	–0.030	0.058

Source: calculated based on the elasticity effects of various factors and the data in Table 10.11.

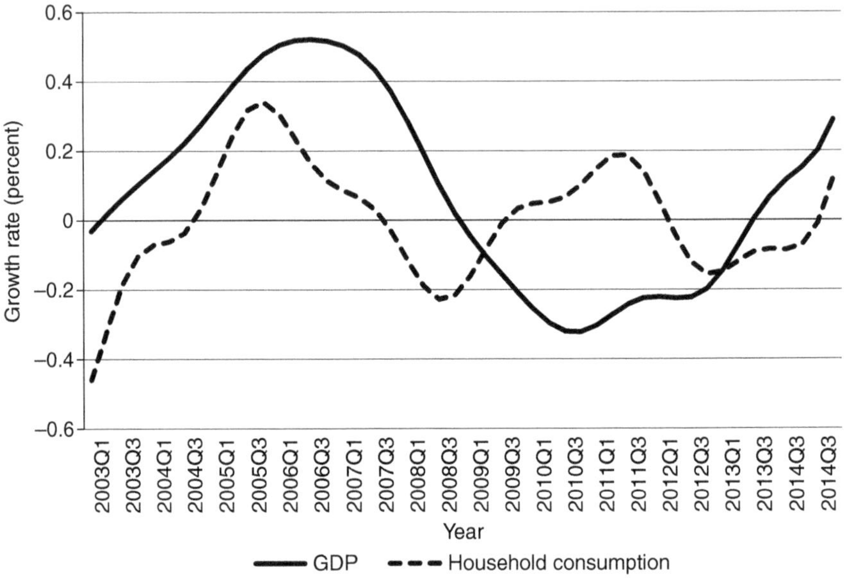

Figure 10.10 Long-term fluctuations of actual growth rates of GDP and household consumption from the first quarter of 2003 to the fourth quarter of 2014 (%).

Source: the data filtering is based on the data provided by WIND.

long-term fluctuating value of GDP growth rate decreased continually. The increase of the long-term fluctuating value of the import growth rate had an increasing effect of inhibiting the recovery of the long-term fluctuating value of the GDP growth rate.

From the overall trend of the long-term fluctuating values of various demand factors and the long-term fluctuating value of the GDP growth rate, it can be found that from the first quarter of 2003 to the fourth quarter of 2014, the wavelength of the long-term fluctuations of actual household consumption growth rate was shorter than that of the long-term fluctuations of GDP growth rate, but most of the time the trend of long-term fluctuations of the actual household consumption growth rate was consistent with that of the GDP growth rate (Figure 10.11). Moreover, the trend of long-term fluctuations of the export growth rate was basically consistent with that of the GDP growth rate, and the long-term fluctuations of actual growth rates of household consumption and export were the fundamental demand factors that determined the trend of the long-term fluctuations of the GDP growth rate. Although the long-term fluctuations of the actual growth rates of investment, investment-based import and industrial inventory exceeded or lagged behind the long-term fluctuations of GDP growth rate, their overall trends were basically consistent with the trend of long-term fluctuations of the GDP growth rate, which were the important factors that determined the trend and shape of the long-term fluctuations of the GDP growth rate.

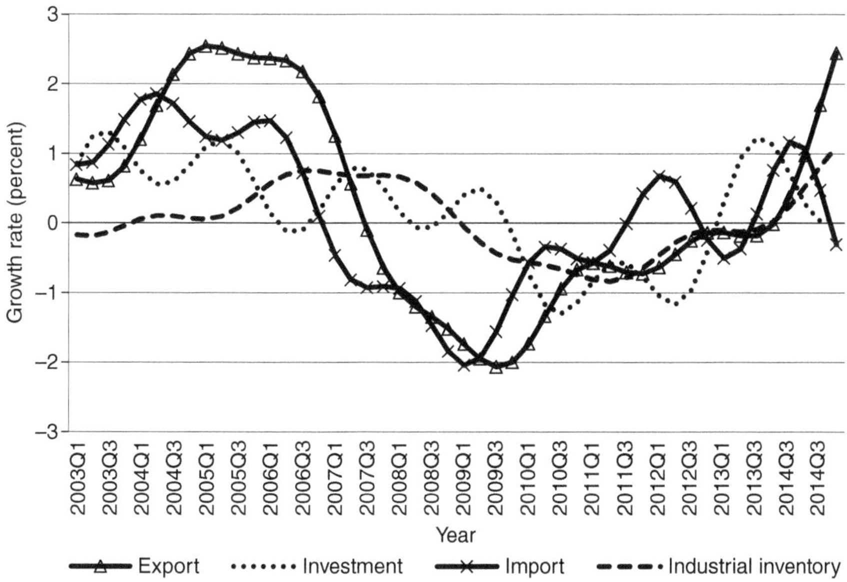

Figure 10.11 Long-term fluctuations of actual growth rates of investment, import, export and funds occupied by industrial enterprises' finished products from the first quarter of 2003 to the fourth quarter of 2014 (%).

Source: the data filtering is based on the data provided by WIND.

The factors affecting the long-term fluctuations of the GDP growth rate can be decomposed as the following equation:

$$\text{GDPAGWL} = 0.7531 \times \text{GDPAGWL}-1) + 0.0229 \times \text{TZAGWL} + 0.0365 \times \text{XFZAGWL} + 0.0438 \times \text{CKZWL} + 0.0324 \times \text{JKZWL} - 0.0422 \times \text{JKZWL}-1) + 0.0525 \times \text{INDHARGWL} + 0.01003$$

$R^2 = 0.998689$; adjusted $R^2 = 0.998459$; DW = 0.19.

Factors affecting the dynamic equilibrium of the GDP growth rate

The trend of cyclical fluctuation of the dynamic equilibrium of the GDP growth rate from the first quarter of 1992 showed the characteristics of the evolution of China's economic development in different phases. By taking the dynamic equilibrium of actual growth rates of household consumption (XFZAGTTL), investment (TZAGTTL), export (CKZTTL), import (JKZTTL) and industrial inventory (INDHARGTTL) as explanatory variables of the dynamic equilibrium of the GDP growth rate (GDPAGTTL), we carried out a regression analysis. The results of the regression analysis show that the dynamic equilibrium of five major demand factors explain the trend of the dynamic equilibrium of the GDP growth rate.

From the elasticity effect of each demand factor, it can be seen that the dynamic equilibrium of the household consumption growth rate affects the dynamic equilibrium of the GDP growth rate most, with an elasticity effect of 1.4033 percent, while the elasticity effects of the dynamic equilibrium of actual growth rates of export and investment are 0.2605 percent and 0.2152 percent respectively (Table 10.13). The dynamic equilibrium of actual growth rates of import and industrial inventory have negative elasticity effects on the dynamic equilibrium of the GDP growth rate, which means that the improvement of the import growth rate and industrial inventory growth rate can reduce the dynamic equilibrium of the GDP growth rate, and their elasticity effects are –0.3147 percent and –0.0424 percent respectively.

From the actual effects of the demand factors that improved the dynamic equilibrium of the GDP growth rate, it can be seen that during the period from the first quarter of 2013 to the fourth quarter of 2014, the dynamic equilibrium of the actual household consumption growth rate had the highest actual influence on the dynamic equilibrium of the GDP growth rate, followed by the dynamic equilibrium of the actual investment growth rate, which had the third largest actual influence after consumption and investment. Due to the continual downward trend of the dynamic equilibrium of actual growth rates of consumption, investment and export, their actual effects also decreased continuously from 13.46 percent, 4.4 percent and 2.53 percent in the first quarter of 2013 to 12.56 percent, 4.36 percent and 2.13 percent in the fourth quarter of 2014 respectively. This means that since the first quarter of 2013, the continued decline in the dynamic equilibrium of the GDP growth rate has been jointly determined by the continued decline in the dynamic equilibrium of actual growth rates of consumption, investment and export.

Based on the actual influences of the demand factors that restrained the dynamic equilibrium value of the GDP growth rate, it can be seen that due to the continued decline in the dynamic equilibrium of the import growth rate, its inhibiting effect on the dynamic equilibrium of the GDP growth rate decreased,

Table 10.13 Dynamic equilibrium of GDP growth rate and actual growth rate of each demand factor from the first quarter of 2013 to the fourth quarter of 2014 (%)

Period	*GDP*	*Investment*	*Household consumption*	*Export*	*Import*	*Industrial inventory*
2013Q1	8.217	20.460	9.591	9.719	12.780	10.010
2013Q2	8.070	20.422	9.499	9.462	12.592	10.066
2013Q3	7.925	20.388	9.407	9.223	12.409	10.131
2013Q4	7.781	20.358	9.315	8.998	12.231	10.202
2014Q1	7.640	20.328	9.223	8.783	12.055	10.279
2014Q2	7.499	20.298	9.131	8.576	11.879	10.359
2014Q3	7.358	20.269	9.039	8.373	11.704	10.441
2014Q4	7.218	20.239	8.948	8.127	11.528	10.523

Source: the data filtering is based on the data provided by WIND.

and its actual contribution evolved from –4.02 percent in the first quarter of 2013 to –3.63 percent in the fourth quarter of 2014 (Table 10.14). After the first quarter of 2013, the dynamic equilibrium of the actual industrial inventory growth rate increased continually and its inhibiting effect on the dynamic equilibrium of the GDP growth rate also increased continually, of which the actual contribution evolved from –0.43 percent in the first quarter of 2013 to –0.45 percent in the fourth quarter of 2014.

The factors affecting the dynamic equilibrium of GDP growth rate can be decomposed as the following equation:

$$\text{GDPAGTTL} = 0.2152 \times \text{TZAGTTL} + 1.4033 \times \text{XFZAGTTL} + 0.2605 \times (\text{CKZTTL} - 100) - 0.3147 \times (\text{JKZTTL} - 100) - 0.0424 \times \text{INDHARGTTL} - 7.739 + [\text{MA}(1) = 0.9546]$$

$R^2 = 0.999994$; adjusted $R^2 = 0.999999$; DW = 0.24.

As can be seen from different stages of development, the dynamic equilibrium of growth of the GDP growth rate since the first quarter of 1992 shows the transition of China's economy's in the phases from light industrialization to heavy and chemical industrialization and then to the late stage of industrialization (Figures 10.12 and 10.13):

1 From the first quarter of 1992 to the first quarter of 2000, China's economy was at the late and declining stage of light industrialization. After the first quarter of 1992, China's economy entered the middle and late stages of light industrialization, and the dynamic equilibrium of actual domestic commodity consumption growth rate (total retail sales of consumer goods) entered a stage of slight increase. The growth rate of commodity export, which was dominated by light industrial and textile products, had relatively larger fluctuations, and its dynamic equilibrium fell gradually from 21.4 percent in the

Table 10.14 Actual influences of various demand factors on dynamic equilibrium value of GDP growth rate from the first quarter of 2013 to the fourth quarter of 2014 (%)

Period	*GDP*	*Investment*	*Household consumption*	*Export*	*Import*	*Industrial inventory*	*Constant term*
2013Q1	8.217	4.403	13.459	2.532	–4.022	–0.425	–7.739
2013Q2	8.070	4.395	13.330	2.465	–3.962	–0.427	–7.739
2013Q3	7.925	4.388	13.200	2.402	–3.905	–0.430	–7.739
2013Q4	7.781	4.381	13.071	2.344	–3.849	–0.433	–7.739
2014Q1	7.640	4.375	12.942	2.288	–3.793	–0.436	–7.739
2014Q2	7.499	4.368	12.813	2.234	–3.738	–0.439	–7.739
2014Q3	7.358	4.362	12.685	2.181	–3.683	–0.443	–7.739
2014Q4	7.218	4.356	12.556	2.129	–3.628	–0.446	–7.739

Source: calculation based on the data in Table 10.13 and the elasticity effects of various factors.

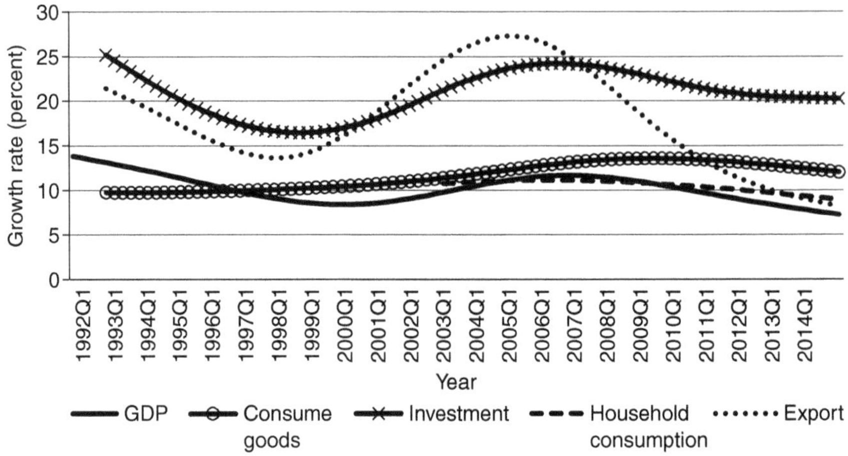

Figure 10.12 Dynamic equilibrium of actual growth rates of GDP, household consumption, consumer goods, export and investment from the first quarter of 1992 to the fourth quarter of 2014 (%).

Source: the data filtering is based on the data provided by WIND.

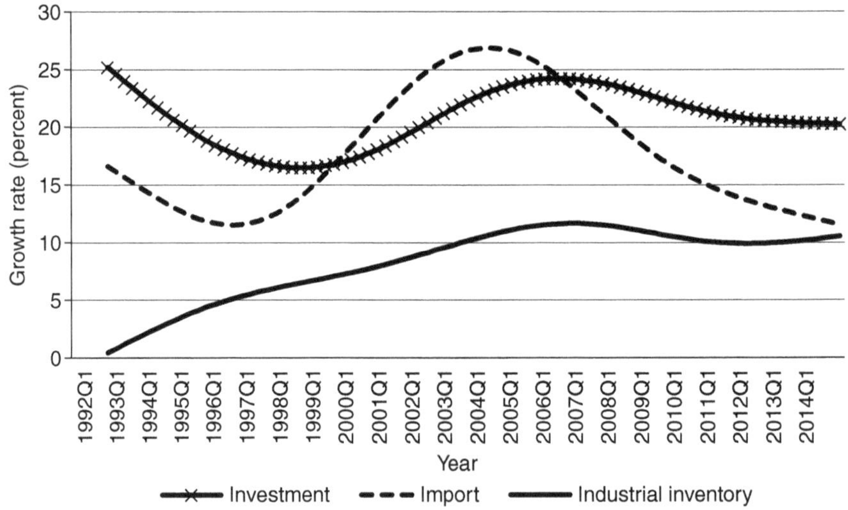

Figure 10.13 Dynamic equilibrium of actual growth rates of investment, import and industrial inventory from the first quarter of 1992 to the fourth quarter of 2014 (%).

Source: the data filtering is based on the data provided by WIND.

first quarter of 1993 to 13.64 percent in the first quarter of 1998. The dynamic equilibrium of the actual investment growth rate determined by domestic commodity consumption and export also fell from 25.2 percent in the first quarter of 1993 to 16.47 percent in the fourth quarter of 1998. As a joint result of the continued declines in the dynamic equilibrium of export's actual growth rates and investment, as well as the slow increase in the dynamic equilibrium of the commodity consumption growth rate, the dynamic equilibrium of China's GDP growth rate also fell from 13.11 percent in the first quarter of 1993 to 8.4 percent in the first quarter of 2000.

2 From the first quarter of 2000 to the fourth quarter of 2006, China's economy was at the stage of heavy and chemical industrialization with accelerating growth. After 2000, China's economy entered a new stage of heavy and chemical industrialization, and the domestic household consumption of home and electrical appliances reached a state of saturation and entered a low-speed growth state that mainly relied on renewal demand for newer and better home appliances. However, housing and automobile consumption entered a stage of rapid growth as well as commodity consumption and whole household consumption. The dynamic equilibrium of commodity consumption increased from 10.44 percent in the first quarter of 2000 to 13.57 percent in the second quarter of 2009, and the dynamic equilibrium of the actual household consumption growth rate increased from 10.75 percent in the first quarter of 2003 to 11.14 percent in the second quarter of 2006. While the dynamic equilibrium of the consumption growth rate increased continually, the dynamic equilibrium of the export growth rate also increased from 16.01 percent in the first quarter of 2000 to 25.3 percent in the first quarter of 2005 at the same time. Boosted by the rapid growth of consumption and export, the dynamic equilibrium of the investment growth rate also increased from 16.96 percent in the first quarter of 2000 to 24.24 percent in the third quarter of 2006. Boosted by the increasing dynamic equilibrium of actual growth rates of consumption, export and investment, the dynamic equilibrium of China's GDP growth rate was improved constantly after the first quarter of 2000 and reached a peak of 11.66 percent in the fourth quarter of 2006. The whole economy was also in a state of accelerated growth; the underlying demand-supported factors were that the domestic consumption shifted from light industrial consumer goods such as household electrical appliances to heavy industrial consumer goods such as housing and automobiles. Moreover, the upgrading and the transformation of the export product structure from the focus on light industrial products to heavy and chemical industrial products is another important factor (see Chapter 8).

3 After the fourth quarter of 2006, China's economy was at the late stage of heavy and chemical industrialization, with continually declining growth. Restricted by increasing export scale, relatively insufficient international market demand and some other factors, the dynamic equilibrium of China's export growth rate entered a process of continual decline after the first

quarter of 2005. Along with the decline in the household electrical appliances consumption growth rate and the declining automobile consumption growth rate, the rising range of the dynamic equilibrium of domestic commodity consumption's actual growth rate declined after the first quarter of 2006, and its dynamic equilibrium began to enter a process of decline in the fourth quarter of 2009. The dynamic equilibrium of the actual household consumption growth rate began to enter a process of decline in the third quarter of 2006. The dynamic equilibrium of the actual investment growth rate determined by consumption and export also began to enter a process of decline in the fourth quarter of 2006, and therefore the dynamic equilibrium of China's GDP growth rate also continued to decline from 11.66 percent in the fourth quarter of 2006 to 7.22 percent in the fourth quarter of 2014.

Conclusions and policy recommendations

The cyclical fluctuations of GDP growth rate show the inherent pattern of regularity of China's economic development and the influence of external shocks on economic growth. The short-term fluctuations of GDP growth rate have irregular characteristics and the effect of demand factors on short-term fluctuations is rather low, which indicates that the different influences of external shocks and policy adjustment on various demand factors cause the short-term fluctuations of each demand factor's growth rate to deviate from the relationship between various demand factors. The mid-term fluctuations show stronger regularity than short-term fluctuations. However, the mid-term fluctuations still show huge waves during the US financial crisis, indicating that policy adjustment and external shocks can have a significant influence on regular economic fluctuations.

The convergence tendency of the mid-to-long-term fluctuations, the increase of long-term fluctuations' peak and trough values and the cyclical fluctuation trends of dynamic equilibrium reveal the basic characteristics of China's economic development and transition in different phases. From the direct influence of various demand factors on the cyclical fluctuations of the economic growth rate, it can be seen that household consumption and export are the fundamental factors that determine the cyclical fluctuations of economic growth rate and its dynamic equilibrium. The elasticity effect of investment is lower than that of household consumption and export, but due to large fluctuations of investment growth rate its actual influence on the fluctuations of economic growth rate is very high.

Since policy adjustment has a significant influence on the short-term and mid-term fluctuations of demand and economic growth rates, the effective way to stabilize the cyclical fluctuations of the economic growth rate and promote steady and rapid economic growth is to enhance the forward-looking elements and accuracy of macroeconomic regulation and control policies. Especially at the moment, China's economy is at the bottom of a cycle with a relatively low economic growth rate, so the adoption of moderate stimulus policies and measures is a necessary approach to prevent a deep economic downturn and to promote steady economic growth. From the perspective of mid-term and long-term development, stabilizing and promoting the dynamic equilibrium of the economic growth rate are the fundamental measures to maintain sustained and rapid economic growth. In the case that the dynamic equilibrium of investment and consumption growth rates have very strong endogeneity, the improvement of the export growth rate should be the main choice for stabilizing the dynamic equilibrium of the economic growth rate.

Notes

1 Household consumption is obtained through the calculation based on the per capita consumption expenditure of urban and rural households and the annual population of urban and rural households. The actual household consumption growth rate refers to the actual growth rate with deduction of a consumer price factor from the nominal growth rate of household consumption.

2 From the simulation, it can be seen that the goodness-of-fit of short-term fluctuations is relatively low, but the DW statistics are approximately 2, and the goodness-of-fit of mid-term, mid-to-long-term and long-term fluctuations and dynamic equilibrium value are very high, but the DW statistics are very low.

11 The development trend of China's economic cycle in the next decade

Cyclical fluctuation is the norm in any functioning economy, and an intertemporal equilibrium of growth can exist at any stage of it (Chapter 7). From the demand-determined perspective, an economy can be considered as a semi-closed circulation system, with the cyclical fluctuation of the consumption demand as its starting point, and that of export enhancement and policy intervention as its exogenous variables. The same set of consumption and export fluctuations and the dynamic equilibrium state of growth will become the foundation for the dynamic equilibrium of investment and even the whole economic growth, which in turn will decide the consumption side of the scenario. The future trend of the above-mentioned fluctuation and equilibrium not only lies in the inherent law of fluctuation and the direct impact of demand, but more on the interaction between various internal variables of the economic circulation system.

To this end, we built an endogenous cycle model of the economic cycle, which contains 21 variables, to simulate and predict the cyclical fluctuation and dynamic equilibrium value of economic growth rate respectively. Results show that the next decade will witness a periodic deceleration in China's economic growth, with the average growth rate falling from the eye-catching 10 percent in the past to a still-fast 6.5 percent, and its fluctuation ranging from 5 percent to 8 percent.

This development trend reflects the phased characteristics of China's economy, which is in transition from heavy industrialization to late-industrialization and finally post-industrialization. For promoting steady and rapid economic growth, and for upgrading the economic structure, China should enhance the forward-looking elements and pertinence of macro-control policies, give full play to short-term regulation in stabilizing short-term and mid-term fluctuations, and promote smooth economic growth in the next decade, according to the law of cyclical fluctuation. Moreover, it is also necessary to formulate effective mid-term and long-term regulatory policies according to the basic law of economic transformation and upgrading, to focus on stabilizing exports, upgrading consumption structure and encouraging enterprise innovation, and to improve the dynamic equilibrium value of the economic growth rate and the economic structure.

Tools and premises of forecasting analysis

By using the "model of the economic cycle," we simulated and predicted the cyclical fluctuations and dynamic equilibrium value of future economic growth. The model contains 21 variables, of which endogenous variables include GDP, investment, household consumption, commodity consumption (total retail sales of consumer goods), export, import, household income, inventory of industrial enterprises (capital taken up by finished goods of industrial enterprises), deposits in financial institutions, loans from financial institutions, fiscal revenue, fiscal expenditure, fiscal expenditure on social security, fiscal expenditure on education, science, culture and health, imports from major countries (the US, Europe and Japan), as well as exports of major countries. Exogenous variables include the one-year deposit rate, the weighted average interest rate of loans from financial institutions, the deposit–reserve ratio, nominal effective exchange rate of RMB, as well as the export rebate rate. All values of endogenous variables adopted the quarterly cumulative actual growth rate or the actual balance growth rate. According to the cyclical fluctuation of economic activities, we divided our model of the economic cycle into five sub-models: the short-term fluctuation model, the mid-term fluctuation model, the mid-to-long-term fluctuation model, the long-term fluctuation model and the dynamic equilibrium model.

One premise of the model-based predictive analysis is to assume that values of exogenous policy variables remain the same as those in the fourth quarter of 2014. Specifically, during the period from the first quarter of 2015 to the fourth quarter of 2025, the one-year deposit rate, the weighted average interest rate of loans from financial institutions, the deposit–reserve ratio, the nominal effective exchange rate of RMB and the export rebate rate stay at 2.67 percent, 6.56 percent, 20 percent, 146.19 percent and 15.31 percent respectively.

The second premise is to assume that the inherent trend does not change from the first quarter of 1992 to the fourth quarter of 2014, regarding the cyclical fluctuation of the import growth rate from the US, Europe and Japan. According to extrapolated results based on the previously mentioned inherent trend, a cyclical upturn is predicted for the import growth rate from the three areas. The dynamic equilibrium value will increase from 2.11 percent in the fourth quarter of 2014 to 9.49 percent in the third quarter of 2025; it will slow down to 9.42 percent in the fourth quarter of 2025. The short-term and mid-term fluctuation of this import growth rate will show a tendency of micro-fluctuation, with the amplitude of short-term and mid-term fluctuation decreasing from 14 percent and 15.26 percent in the 2014 fluctuation cycle to 2.4 percent and 3.56 percent in the 2025 cycle. The mid-to-long-term fluctuation will maintain a trend of cyclical upturn; after reaching a minimum value of –3.18 percent in the third quarter of 2014, its fluctuating value will reach a maximum value of 1.67 percent in the first quarter of 2017, and then come to a minimum value of –1.81 percent again in the fourth quarter of 2019 and a maximum value of 3.31 percent in the fourth quarter of 2024. The long-term volatility will keep a trend of the regular cyclical fluctuation, and the second quarter of 2016 is predicted to be a new peak, with a peak value of 1.65 percent; the second quarter of 2019 will be a

–1.69 percent trough. The third quarter of 2022 will be another peak, with a peak value of 1.67 percent and the same quarter of 2025 will be a –1.57 percent trough. (See Figures 11.1–11.3.) Overall, by simulating the future trend of cyclical fluctuations and dynamic equilibrium for the import growth rate from the US, Europe and Japan, the rate will show cyclical upturn trend after the fourth quarter of 2014, increasing from –3.56 percent in 2014 to 10.11 percent in 2025.

Our third premise is an adaptive environment for domestic fiscal policy in China. This is to say, the actual growth rate of the whole fiscal expenditure, including the welfare expenditure on social security, education, science, culture and health, has to go in line with the inherent development trend of economic development and actual fiscal revenue, while also open to necessary adjustments according to the characteristics of the cyclical fluctuation of economic growth. In the model-based analysis, we regarded the cyclical fluctuation of the actual fiscal revenue growth rate as the budget constraint of the cyclical fluctuation of the actual fiscal expenditure growth rate (Figure 11.4); the lagged variable of the cyclical fluctuating value of the actual fiscal expenditure growth rate as the influence factor that reflects the inherent trend of the cyclical fluctuation of the actual fiscal expenditure growth rate; and the cyclical fluctuating value of the GDP growth rate as the influence factor that reflects the adaptive regulatory policy. Results of model-based predictions show that in an adaptive policy environment, the actual growth rate of China's fiscal expenditure will maintain a cyclical downturn trend, its dynamic

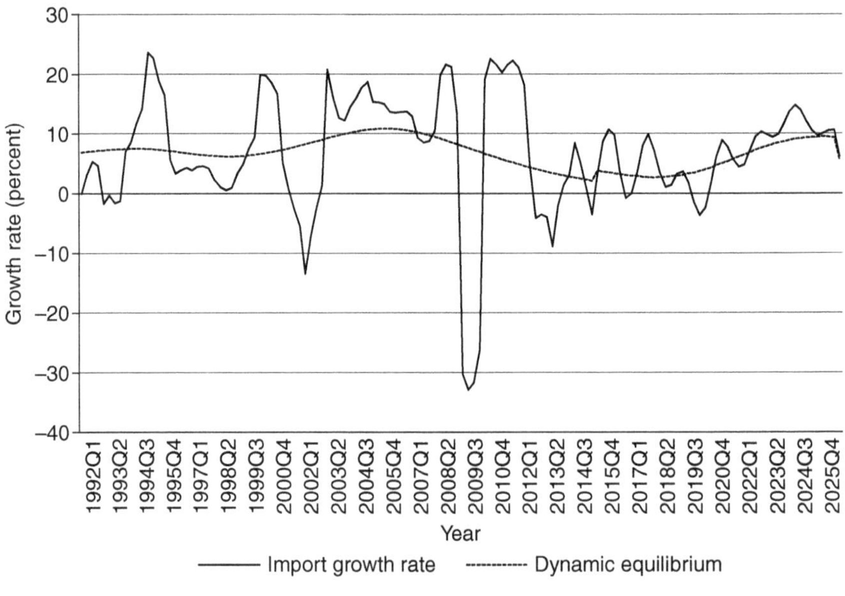

Figure 11.1 US, Europe and Japan's import growth rate and its dynamic equilibrium value from the first quarter of 2015 to the fourth quarter of 2025 (%).

Source: the data up to and including the fourth quarter of 2014 are actual values. Data after the first quarter of 2015 are obtained through extrapolation of the inherent trend regarding the cyclical fluctuation of the import growth rate from the three areas. The same applies for the following figures.

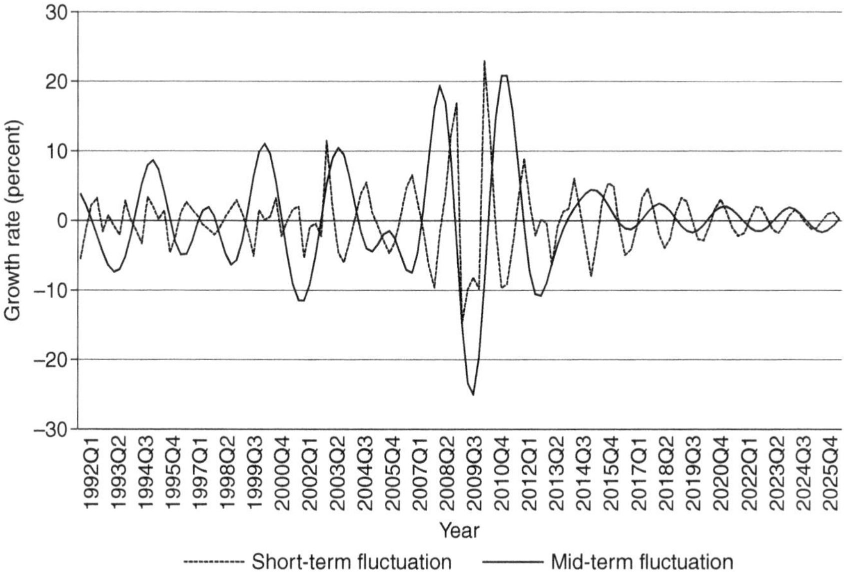

Figure 11.2 The short-term fluctuation and mid-term fluctuation of the import growth rate regarding the US, Europe and Japan from the first quarter of 2015 to the fourth quarter of 2025 (%).

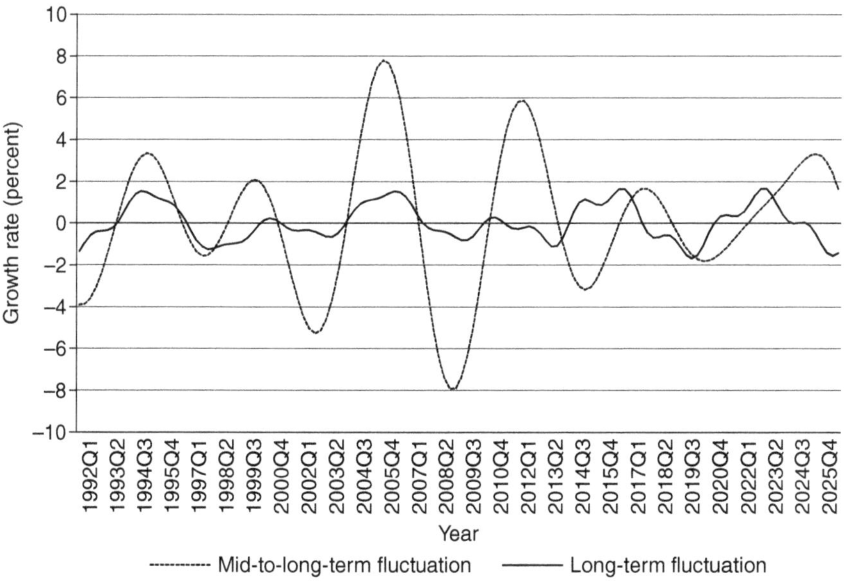

Figure 11.3 The mid-to-long-term fluctuation and the long-term fluctuation in the import growth rate regarding the US, Europe and Japan from the first quarter of 2015 to the fourth quarter of 2025 (%).

equilibrium value will fall from 14.95 percent in the fourth quarter of 2014 to 10.48 percent in the fourth quarter of 2025, and the predicted actual growth rate will drop from 7.69 percent in 2014 to 6.5 percent in 2021, and then rise to 14.69 percent in 2025. The actual growth rate of the expenditure on education, science, culture and health will also maintain a trend of cyclical downturn (Figure 11.5), and its dynamic equilibrium value and the predicted actual growth rate will decrease from 17.39 percent and 7.81 percent in 2014 respectively, to 9.03 percent and 11.01 percent in 2025. Cyclical fluctuation will be the norm for the actual growth rate of expenditure on social security, and its dynamic equilibrium value after falling from 13.4 percent in the fourth quarter of 2014 to 8.51 percent in the third quarter of 2018, will gradually increase to 16.64 percent in the fourth quarter of 2025 (Figure 11.6). The forecasted actual growth rate will fall from 9.52 percent in the fourth quarter of 2014 to 0.95 percent in the first quarter of 2020; after that, it will gradually rebound to 22.03 percent in the third quarter of 2024, and be corrected to 13.37 percent again in the fourth quarter of 2025.

Future trend of the dynamic equilibrium value of China's economic growth rate

The dynamic equilibrium value of economic growth is the foundation of future economic trends. Under the three previously mentioned premises, our forecast carried out using the dynamic equilibrium sub-models of the economic cycle

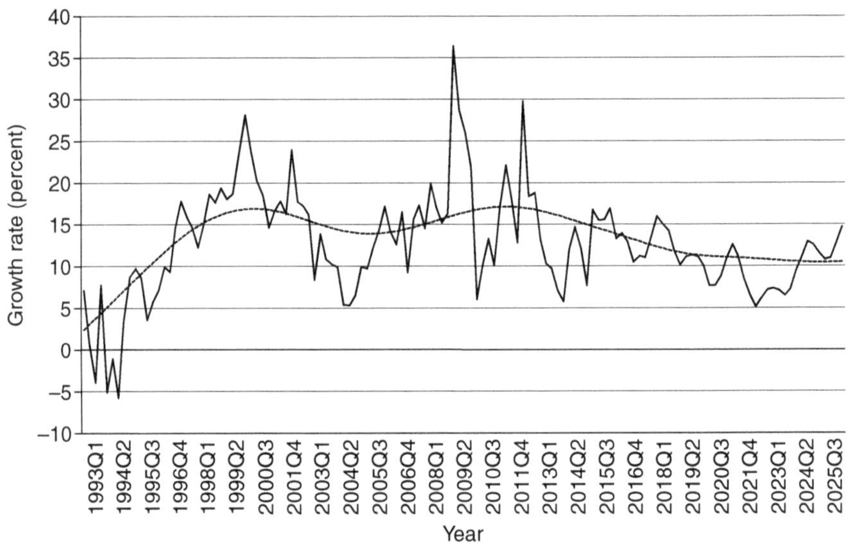

Figure 11.4 The development trend of actual fiscal expenditure growth rate and its dynamic equilibrium value from the first quarter of 2015 to the fourth quarter of 2025 (%).

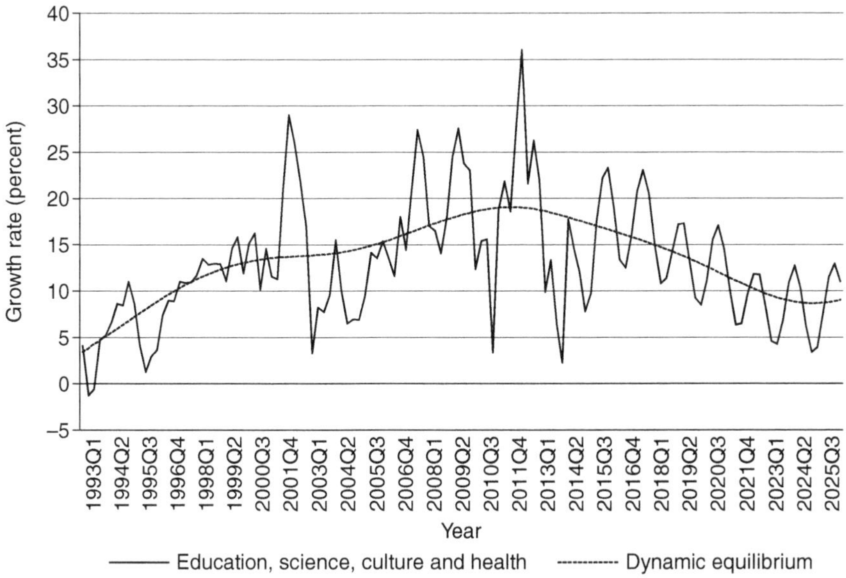

Figure 11.5 Development trends of the actual growth rate of expenditure on education, science, culture and health, and its dynamic equilibrium value from the first quarter of 2015 to the fourth quarter of 2025 (%).

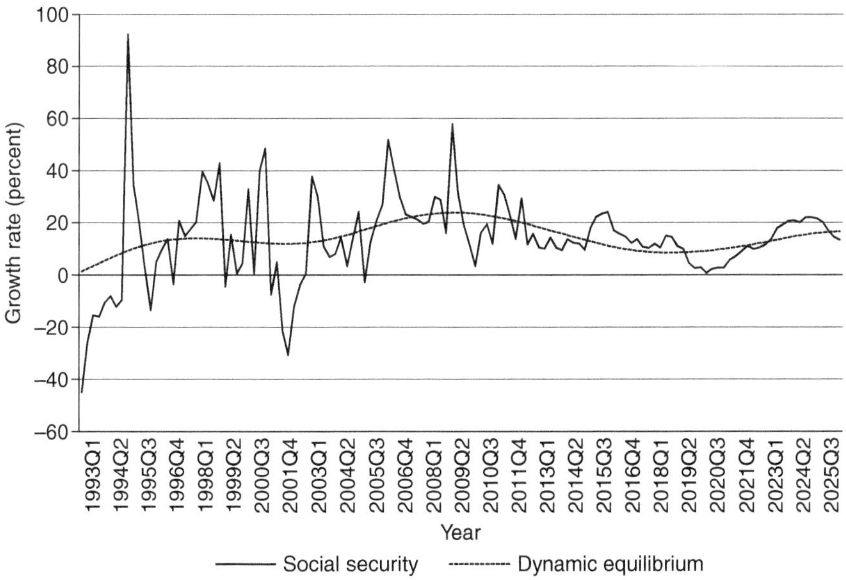

Figure 11.6 Development trend of the cyclical fluctuation and dynamic equilibrium value of the actual growth rate of expenditure on social security from the first quarter of 2015 to the fourth quarter of 2025 (%).

generates several conclusions. After the fourth quarter of 2014, the dynamic equilibrium value of China's economic growth will steadily drop with cyclical fluctuation. The dynamic equilibrium values of the actual growth rates of household income and household consumption will maintain a trend of cyclical downturn. The dynamic equilibrium value of export growth rate will rise first and then fall, with an overall relatively rapid growth rate of 7.6 percent or so, and the dynamic equilibrium values of the actual growth rates of investment and import will maintain a trend of cyclical fluctuations.

The dynamic equilibrium value of GDP growth rate will steadily drop with cyclical fluctuation

The result of our model shows that the dynamic equilibrium value of GDP growth will maintain a trend of cyclical downturn after the fourth quarter of 2014 (Figure 11.7). Specifically, the declining trend since the fourth quarter of 2006 continued until the end of 2014, when the GDP growth rate hit 7.22 percent. The trend will continue until touching the trough of 6.31 percent in the fourth quarter of 2017, and an upward trend will resume until a peak of 6.7 percent in the fourth quarter of 2020. Then, the value will fall to 6.34 percent in the fourth quarter of 2023, and increase to 6.53 percent by the end of 2025. In general, the dynamic equilibrium value of the GDP growth rate will steadily drop with cyclical fluctuations, and the average growth rate will be 6.53 percent during the period from the first quarter of 2015 to the fourth quarter of 2025. This development trend will be jointly determined by the cyclical fluctuation of

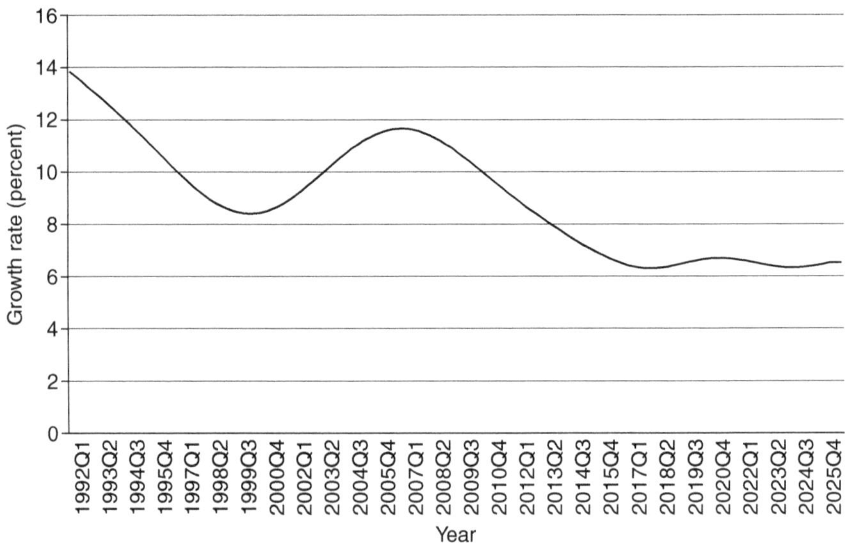

Figure 11.7 Development trend of dynamic equilibrium value of GDP growth rate from the first quarter of 2015 to the fourth quarter of 2025 (%).

the dynamic equilibrium values of actual growth rates of investment, consumption, import, export and industrial inventory.

The dynamic equilibrium value of the growth rate of actual consumer demand exhibits a trend of cyclical downturn

The dynamic equilibrium value of actual household consumption growth rate is the most important factor that determines the trend of the dynamic equilibrium value of the GDP growth rate. From our prediction, it can be seen that the dynamic equilibrium value of the actual household consumption growth rate in China will show a trend of cyclical downturn (Figure 11.8). The declining trend since the third quarter of 2006 lasts, and the value falls from 8.95 percent in the fourth quarter of 2014 to a minimum value of 8.51 percent in the third quarter of 2016. Afterwards, a trend of cyclical upturn occurs, reaching a maximum value of 9.44 percent in the first quarter of 2020, correcting to a minimum value of 8.36 percent again in the fourth quarter of 2023, and rebounding to 8.78 percent in the fourth quarter of 2025. Considering the minimum value in the fourth quarter of 2023 is lower than that in the third quarter of 2016, we predict a cyclical recession of the trend of the dynamic equilibrium value of the actual household consumption growth rate. However, the average growth rate will remain at a relatively high level, and the dynamic equilibrium value of the actual household consumption growth rate will average 8.8 percent during the period from the first quarter of 2015 to the fourth quarter of 2025.

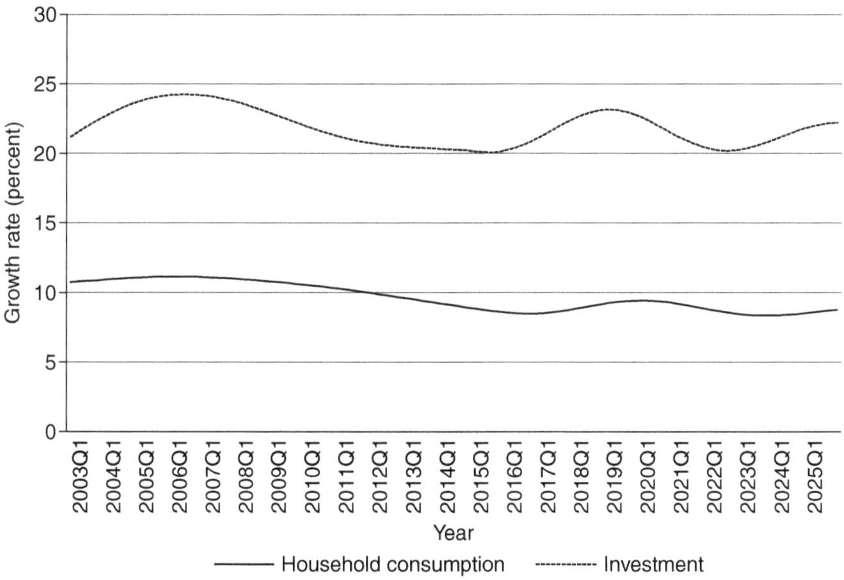

Figure 11.8 Development trends of dynamic equilibrium values of actual growth rates of household consumption and household income from the first quarter of 2015 to the fourth quarter of 2025 (%).

The cyclical declining trend of the dynamic equilibrium value of the household consumption actual growth rate is directly decided by the same trend of the actual growth rate of household income. The simulation outcome shows that the dynamic equilibrium value of the actual growth rate of household income drops from 5.96 percent in the first quarter of 2015 to 5.73 percent in the fourth quarter of 2025. Troughs appear in the first quarter of 2017 and first quarter of 2025 respectively with values of 5.76 percent and 5.39 percent, while a peak emerges in the first quarter of 2020 with a value of 5.95 percent.

The cyclical decline of the dynamic equilibrium value of the actual household consumption growth rate is closely related to the evolution of the household consumption structure. As we analyzed in Chapter 8, China's urban and rural household consumption of electrical appliances has entered a state of full demand after 2000. Urban household automobile consumption has also shifted from rapid growth between 2000 and 2012, to relatively fast growth after 2012. Household commodity consumption will enter a stage of comparatively fast growth based primarily on product upgrading (Figure 11.9). According to our prediction, the dynamic equilibrium value of the actual growth rate of China's household commodity consumption (total retail sales of social consumer goods) will steadily decrease in a cyclical downturn. The cyclical downturn since the second quarter of 2009 will continue until the fourth quarter of 2014, with a value of 12.02 percent and further decline to 10.55 percent in the second quarter of 2025. According to the experience from the US and other developed countries, once the household commodity consumption is fulfilled and changes to relatively rapid growth, the consumption of services will become the dominant driving force of household

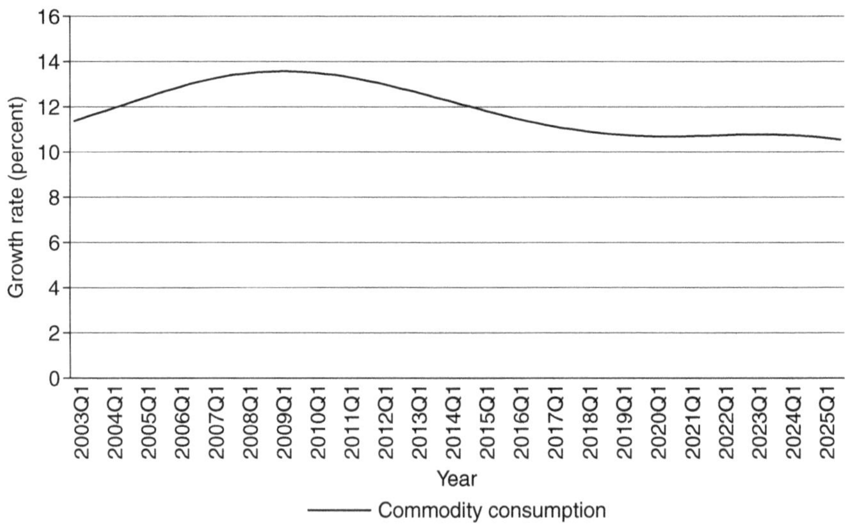

Figure 11.9 Trend of the dynamic equilibrium value of the actual growth rate of households' commodity consumption from the first quarter of 2015 to the fourth quarter of 2025 (%).

consumption growth. We don't have the statistics on urban and rural household consumption of services in China, so it is difficult to analyze it. However, judging from the cyclical downturn of the dynamic equilibrium value of actual household consumption growth rate, and the steady decrease of the dynamic equilibrium value of actual commodity consumption, we think service consumption will gradually become the driving factor of China's household consumption.

The dynamic equilibrium value of the export growth rate will fall then rise, and the dynamic equilibrium value of the import growth rate will show a trend of cyclical fluctuation

When we treat consumer demand as an endogenous variable, the dynamic equilibrium value of the export growth rate, regarded as an external demand, will become the key factor determining the trend of the dynamic equilibrium of economic growth. Based on the following two assumptions, specifically: the import growth rate from the US, Europe and Japan follows its inherent trend, and the nominal effective exchange rate of RMB and the export rebate rate remain unchanged, the dynamic equilibrium value of China's export growth rate will fall first and rise later, after the fourth quarter of 2014. After falling from 8.17 percent in the fourth quarter of 2014 to 6.97 percent in the third quarter of 2019, it will resume the rising trend and rebound to 8.56 percent in the fourth quarter of 2025, with an average value of 7.56 percent from the first quarter of 2015 to the fourth quarter of 2025 (Figure 11.10).

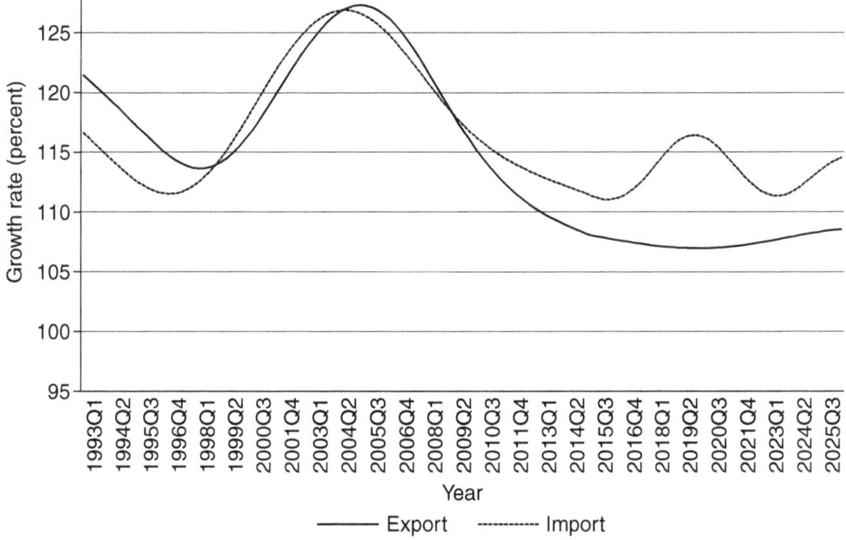

Figure 11.10 The trend of dynamic equilibrium values of import and export growth rates from the first quarter of 2015 to the fourth quarter of 2025 (%).

In the next decade, the dynamic equilibrium value of China's export growth rate will remain at a relatively faster growth rate of ~7.6 percent, which is consistent with the development experience of Germany and Japan. According to analysis of exports regarding various countries since the end of World War II, a country's commodity export will fall after its proportion reaches a certain scale in global commodity exports. Its export growth rate also gradually regresses to the average global level. For example, Japan's commodity export began to decline after its global share hit 9.86 percent in 1986. Germany's commodity export also started to shrink after it reached 12.21 percent in 1990. The average annual export growth rate in Japan and Germany also fell from 17.6 percent and 17.15 percent respectively during the period from 1950 to 1990, to 5.17 percent and 6.12 percent during the period from 1991 to 2013, while the average global export growth rate was 10.86 percent and 8.17 percent respectively in the two periods. In 2013, the proportion of China's exports in global commodity exports reached 11.74 percent, so its future export growth rate will gradually regress to the average global export growth rate.

The dynamic equilibrium value of the import growth rate depends on the dynamic equilibrium values of actual growth rates of domestic investment, consumption and inventory investment. Since more than 90 percent of the imported products are means of production, the dynamic equilibrium value of the actual investment growth is the decisive factor of the dynamic equilibrium value of the import growth rate. Our model shows the persistence of the cyclical fluctuation in the dynamic equilibrium values of the import growth rate after the fourth quarter of 2014. The declining trend started since the second quarter of 2004, persisted to 11.53 percent in the fourth quarter of 2014, and further reached a trough value of 11.06 percent in the third quarter of 2015. It will resume a trend of cyclical upturn and reach a peak value of 16.43 percent in the third quarter of 2019. After that, it will fall to a trough value of 11.35 percent in the first quarter of 2023. In the fourth quarter of 2025, it will rebound to 14.35 percent. From the first quarter of 2015 to the fourth quarter of 2025, the average value will be 13.31 percent, which is far lower than the average growth rate of 17.73 percent during the period from the first quarter of 1993 to the fourth quarter of 2014. In the next decade, the trend of cyclical fluctuation of the dynamic equilibrium value of export growth rate will basically synchronize with that of the actual investment growth rate.

Cyclical fluctuation will be observed in the dynamic equilibrium value of actual investment growth rate

Our prediction shows that after a seven-year cyclical correction starting from the third quarter of 2006, the dynamic equilibrium value of China's investment growth rate will reach a minimum value of 20.07 percent in the third quarter of 2015, and then resume a trend of cyclical upturn and reach a maximum value of 23.14 percent in the first quarter of 2019 (Figures 11.11 and 11.12). Afterwards, it will be corrected to 20.2 percent in the third quarter of 2022. In the fourth

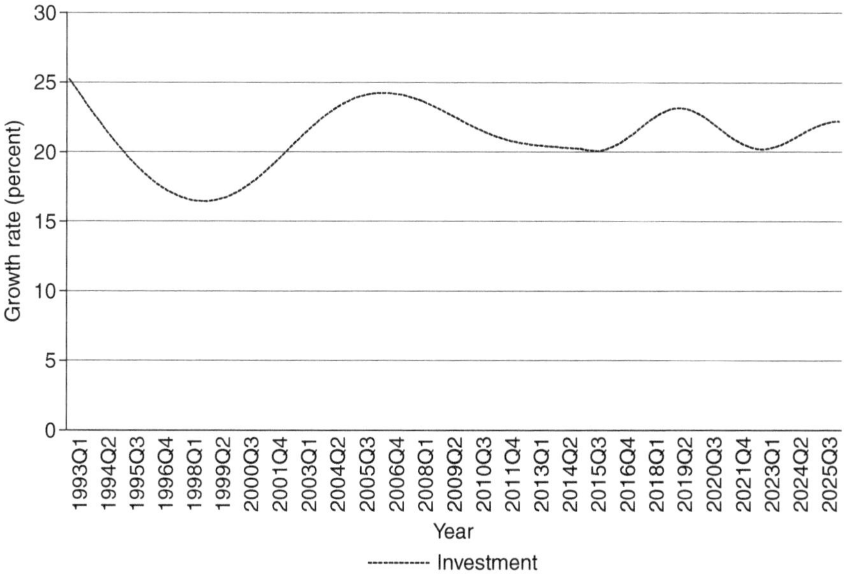

Figure 11.11 Trend of dynamic equilibrium value of actual investment growth rate from the first quarter of 2015 to the fourth quarter of 2025 (%).

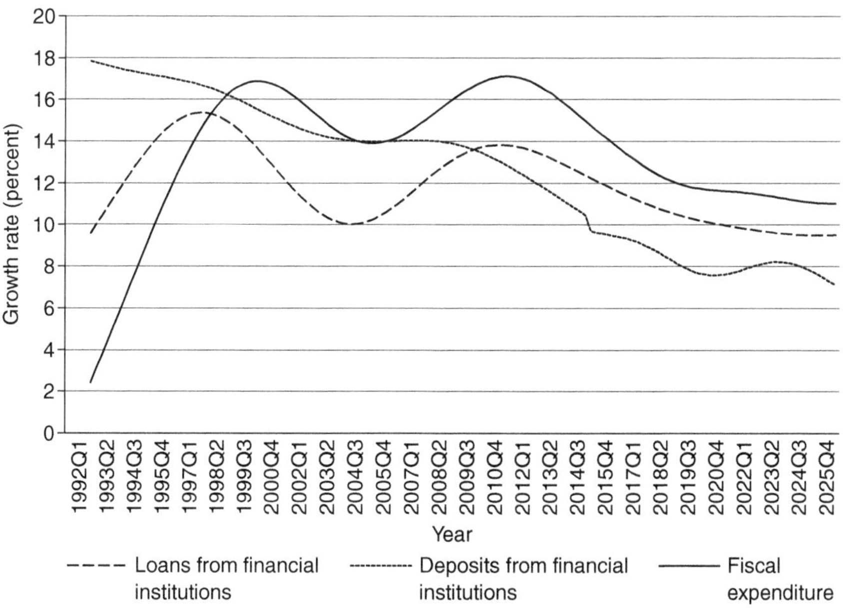

Figure 11.12 Trends of the dynamic equilibrium value of the actual growth rate of loans, fiscal expenditure and industrial inventory from the first quarter of 2015 to the fourth quarter of 2025 (%).

quarter of 2025, it will rebound to 22.21 percent. This is to say, the dynamic equilibrium value of the actual investment growth rate will show a trend of cyclical fluctuation after the fourth quarter of 2014.

By analyzing the influencing factors, it can be seen that the dynamic equilibrium value of the actual investment growth rate depends on the dynamic equilibrium values of domestic consumption and export growth rates. But the dynamic equilibrium values of actual growth rates of loans from financial institutions and fiscal expenditure are capital constraints on the dynamic equilibrium value of the actual investment growth rate in the short term. The rise of the dynamic equilibrium value of the actual inventory investment growth rate will also restrain the dynamic equilibrium value of the actual investment growth rate. We predict that the dynamic equilibrium values of actual growth rates of loans from financial institutions and fiscal expenditure will decline continuously after the fourth quarter of 2014, i.e., they will fall from 12.36 percent and 14.95 percent in the fourth quarter of 2014 to 10.34 percent and 12.07 percent in the fourth quarter of 2025 respectively. The dynamic equilibrium value of export growth rate will decline first and then rise. So the trend of the cyclical fluctuation of the dynamic equilibrium value of actual investment growth rate will be determined mainly by the cyclical fluctuation of the dynamic equilibrium values of actual growth rates of household consumption, and industrial enterprises' inventories in the next ten years.

Trend of the short-term fluctuation of China's economic growth rate

The pattern of the short-term fluctuation of China's economic growth rate is difficult to observe, because it is greatly influenced by regulatory policies and external impacts. In the short-term fluctuation model, the goodness-of-fit of the influence factor decomposition equation regarding main variables including GDP, household consumption, commodity consumption, household income, investment demand, export, import, loan, deposit and inventory, are respectively 0.71, 0.87, 0.57, 0.74, 0.67, 0.77, 0.9, 0.8, 0.85 and 0.55 in sequence. The goodness-of-fit averages at only 0.74, i.e., only about 74 percent of the short-term fluctuations of economic growth rate can be explained by the demand factors, with the remaining 26 percent determined by other factors. The trend of short-term fluctuations predicted by the short-term fluctuation model can only reflect the inherent law of the short-term fluctuations of the economic growth rate, but cannot reflect the influence of other irregular factors. According to the results of simulation, micro-fluctuation is more common for the short-term fluctuations of the GDP growth rate after the fourth quarter of 2014 – so is the short-term fluctuations of actual growth rates of import, export and industrial inventory. But after a temporary narrowing, the amplitude of the short-term fluctuation of actual growth rates of household consumption and investment will begin to enlarge again, from the first quarter of 2017.

Short-term fluctuation of the GDP growth rate tends to be microscale

Our prediction shows that in the short term, the first quarter of 2015 will witness the trough of the short-term fluctuation of the GDP growth rate, when the fluctuating value reduces to –0.5 percent. The value will rise to 0.33 percent in the second quarter of 2015 and fall to a trough value of –0.56 percent again in the second quarter of 2016. The overall trend emphasizes micro-fluctuation of the GDP growth rate during the period from the first quarter of 2015 to the fourth quarter of 2025, with the amplitude ranges gradually decreasing from 0.89 percent in the 2015–2016 fluctuation cycle to 0.53 percent in the 2024–2025 cycle (Figure 11.13). The influencing factors further show that the micro-fluctuation of the short-term fluctuation of GDP growth is mainly determined by the same trend as export growth.

Short-term fluctuation of the actual household consumption growth rate shows regular cyclical fluctuations

The short-term fluctuation of the actual household consumption growth rate is the most important demand factor that affects the short-term trend of the GDP growth rate. Our prediction shows that after the fourth quarter of 2014, the short-term fluctuation of the actual household consumption growth rate demonstrates regular cyclical fluctuation, with the amplitude of each fluctuation cycle ranging between 2.1 percent and 2.5 percent.

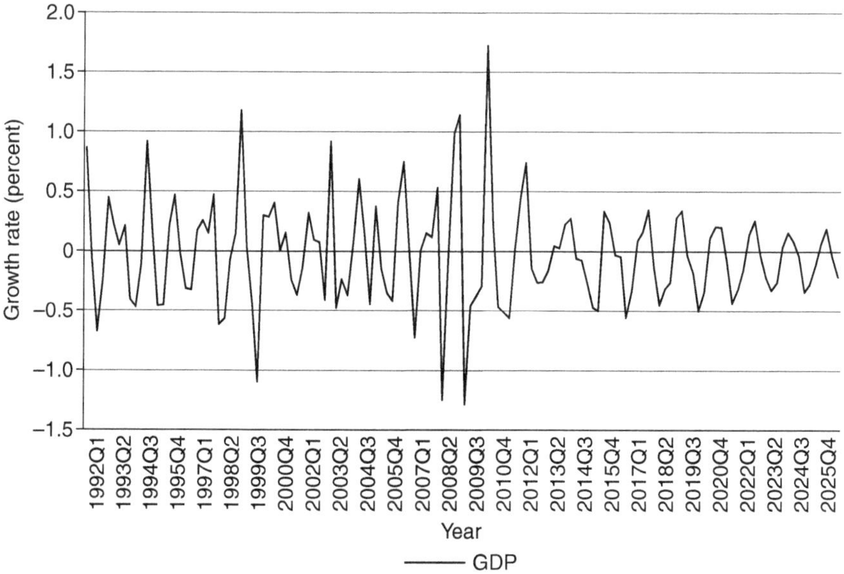

Figure 11.13 Short-term fluctuation of GDP growth rate from the first quarter of 2015 to the fourth quarter of 2025 (%).

Different from the short-term fluctuation of the actual household consumption growth rate, the short-term fluctuation of the actual growth rate regarding households' commodity consumption shows fluctuation at a minor scale after the fourth quarter of 2014 (Figure 11.14). The amplitude of its cyclical fluctuation falls gradually from 1.85 percent during the period from 2015 to 2016, to 0.63 percent in the 2024–2025 cycle. This amplitude is significantly smaller than that of the short-term fluctuation of the household consumption growth rate.

The influencing factors tell us that the short-term fluctuation of income growth rate is the key factor that determines the short-term fluctuation of household consumption and commodity consumption growth rates. By observing the fluctuation trends, both the sample interval from the first quarter of 2003 to the fourth quarter of 2014, and the predicted interval from the first quarter of 2015 to 2025, show synchronized development between the short-term fluctuation of household income growth rate, and the household consumption growth rate. Their amplitudes are basically the same, i.e., the short-term fluctuation of the household consumption growth rate is basically determined by the short-term fluctuation of the household income growth rate. This result indicates that the improvement of household income growth rate in the short term can effectively stimulate the growth of household consumption, so increasing household income can be an effective short-term regulatory policy to stimulate economic growth.

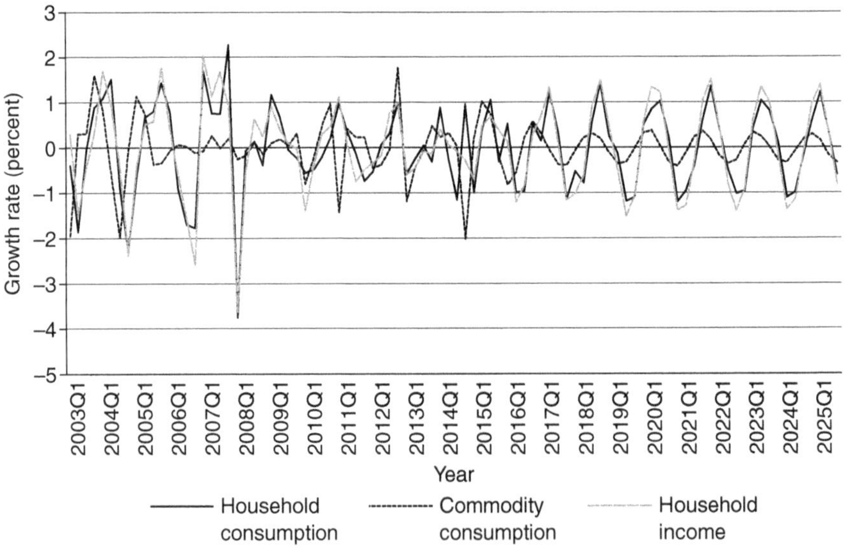

Figure 11.14 Short-term fluctuation of the actual growth rates of household consumption, commodity consumption and household income from the first quarter of 2015 to the fourth quarter of 2025 (%).

Short-term fluctuation of import and export growth rate tends to be microscale

After the fourth quarter of 2014, the short-term fluctuation of China's import and export growth rate tends to become microscale. The amplitude of the short-term fluctuation of export growth rate declines gradually from 7.88 percent in the fluctuation cycle from 2016 to 2017, to 3.85 percent from 2024 to 2025. The amplitude of the short-term fluctuation of import growth rate declines from 13.37 percent from 2015 to 2017, to 7.17 percent from 2024 to 2025 (Figure 11.15).

By observing the influencing factors, we find the short-term fluctuation of China's export growth rate is micro, because of the same pattern of short-term fluctuation regarding imports from the US, Europe and Japan (Figure 11.16). In the sample interval of our simulation analysis, the short-term fluctuation of China's export growth rate synchronizes with the import from the US, Europe and Japan, and displays the same amplitude. According to the extrapolation based on the innate tendency of the short-term fluctuation of imports from the US, Europe and Japan, the short-term fluctuation of such import growth rate fluctuates only at a microscale after the fourth quarter of 2014 (as shown in Figure 11.15), thus determining the short-term micro-fluctuation of China's export growth.

The short-term fluctuation of import growth rate depends on the trend of the short-term fluctuation of the actual growth rate of investment, consumption and industrial enterprises' inventory. Among them, the short-term fluctuation of

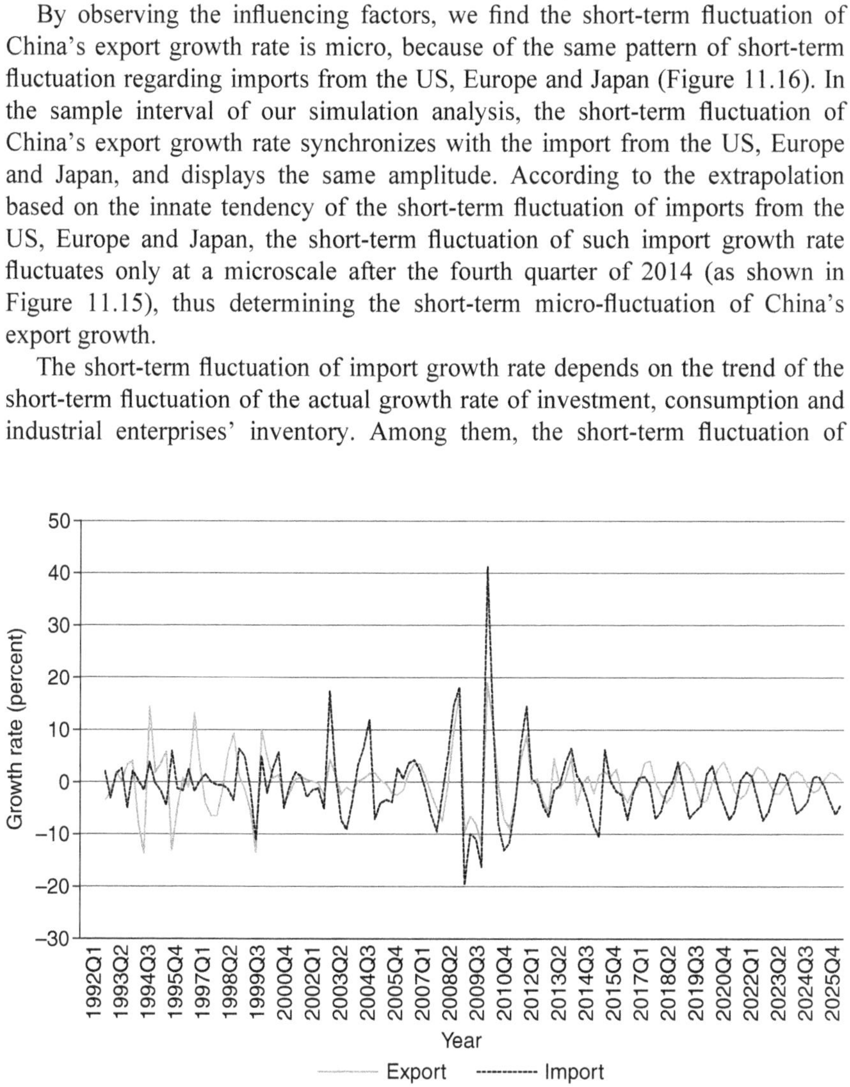

Figure 11.15 The short-term fluctuation of import and export growth rates from the first quarter of 2015 to the fourth quarter of 2025 (%).

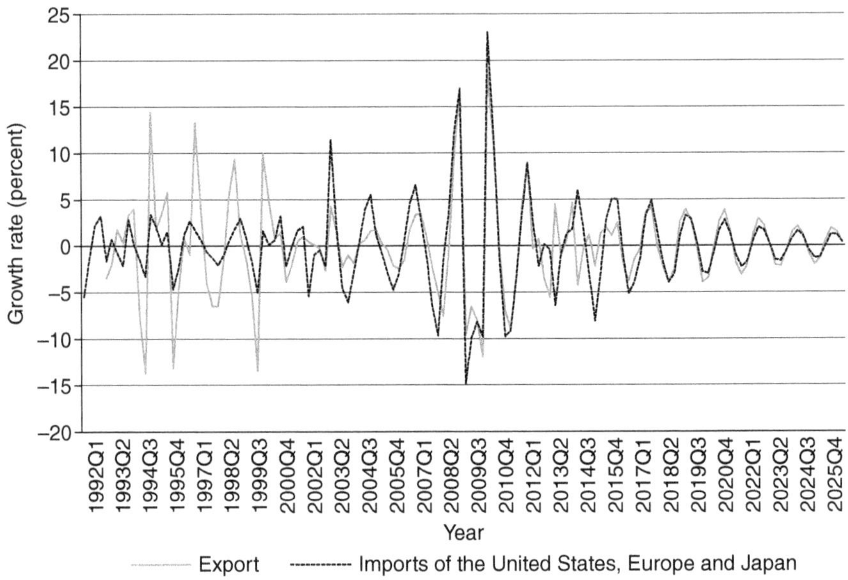

Figure 11.16 The short-term fluctuations of China's export growth rate and the import growth rate from the US, Europe and Japan, from the first quarter of 2015 to the fourth quarter of 2025 (%).

investment growth rate is a dominating factor. The short-term fluctuation of import growth rate is microscale. After 2014, this tendency will also be determined by the short-term fluctuation of the investment growth rate, which also exhibits micro-fluctuation.

Amplitude of the short-term fluctuation of the actual investment growth rate enlarges after a temporary narrowing

During the period from 1992 to 2014, the amplitude of the short-term fluctuation of the actual investment growth rate was very large (Figure 11.17), and thus had an important effect of enlarging the amplitude of the short-term fluctuation of the economic growth rate. After the fourth quarter of 2014, the short-term fluctuation of China's actual investment growth rate magnifies again after a short-term narrowing. The amplitude of the short-term fluctuation of investment growth rate narrows to 1.7 percent from the first quarter of 2015 to the fourth quarter of 2016, but will enlarge again afterwards, and ranges between 3.66 percent and 4.35 percent from the first quarter of 2017 to the fourth quarter of 2025.

Analysis of factors that affect the short-term fluctuation of the investment growth rate, including household consumption, export, industrial inventory, loans from financial institutions and fiscal expenditure (Figure 11.18), tell us that the short-term fluctuation of both export and the industrial inventory growth rate

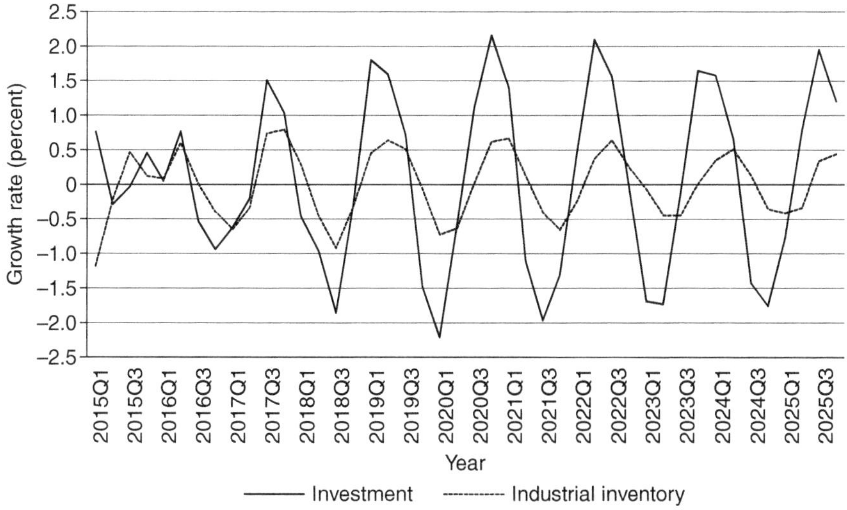

Figure 11.17 Short-term fluctuation of the actual growth rates of investment and industrial inventory from the first quarter of 2015 to the fourth quarter of 2025 (%).

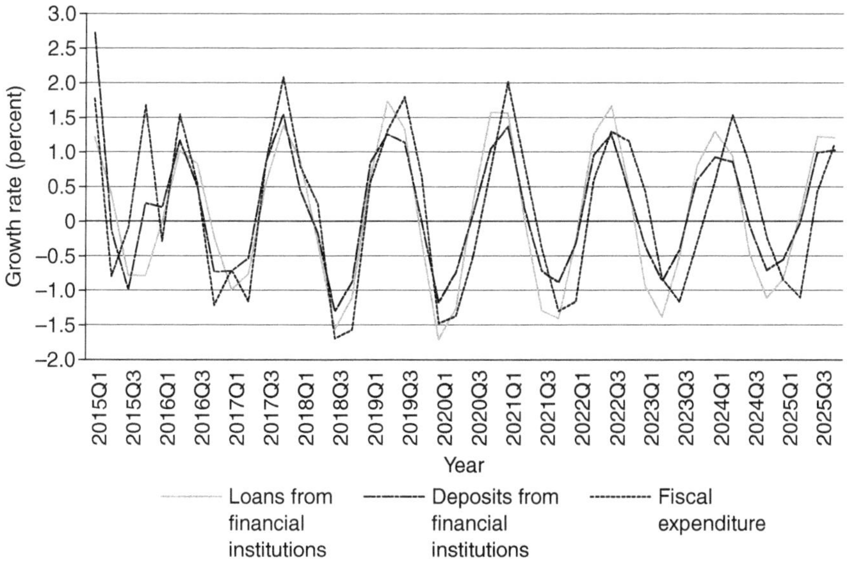

Figure 11.18 Short-term fluctuation of actual growth rate of loan, deposit and fiscal expenditure in China from the first quarter of 2015 to the fourth quarter of 2025 (%).

are micro, and the amplitude of the short-term fluctuation regarding the actual growth rates of loans and fiscal expenditure also keeps narrowing. Only the amplitude of the short-term fluctuation of actual household consumption growth rate enlarges again after a short-term narrowing. Among factors affecting the short-term fluctuation of the investment growth rate, the short-term fluctuation of the household consumption growth rate will have the highest elastic contribution. Therefore, the amplitude of the short-term fluctuation of the investment growth rate amplifies after the fourth quarter of 2016, and the increasing amplitude of the short-term fluctuation of the household consumption growth rate is the decisive factor.

Future trend of the mid-term fluctuation of China's economic growth rate

The mid-term fluctuation of the economic growth rate vibrates widely and is the important factor that affects the actual economic growth rate. The mid-term fluctuation of the economic growth rate exhibits obvious patterns, but it is still significantly influenced by policy adjustment and external shocks. According to our prediction based on the mid-term fluctuation model, it can be seen that even without any significant external impacts, the mid-term fluctuation of China's economic growth rate still shows wide fluctuations after the fourth quarter of 2014. The amplitude of the mid-term fluctuation of the actual growth rate of GDP, household consumption and investment all experience rises followed by declines, while fluctuation of the mid-term export growth rate remains in a narrow range.

Amplitude of the mid-term fluctuation of the GDP growth rate increases then decreases

After the fourth quarter of 2014, under the impact of the widely fluctuating mid-term actual growth rates of household consumption and investment, the mid-term fluctuation of the GDP growth rate will also show a wide-ranging fluctuation (Figure 11.19). There will be three mid-term fluctuation cycles in total during the period from the first quarter of 2015 to the fourth quarter of 2025. The first quarter of 2015 stands out as the peak of the mid-term fluctuation, with a value of 0.31 percent. Then the GDP growth rate will reach the trough in the third quarter of 2017 with a minimum value of –0.77 percent. In the fourth quarter of 2018 and the second quarter of 2020, the same value will reach a new peak and a new trough with values of 1.23 percent and –1.39 percent respectively. The fourth quarter of 2021, the first quarter of 2024 and the third quarter of 2025 will be peak, trough and peak respectively, with values fluctuating among 0.84 percent, –0.74 percent and 0.63 percent respectively. As illustrated by the amplitude of the mid-term fluctuation, the mid-term fluctuation of the GDP growth rate will widen first and then narrow. The descent of amplitude is merely 1.08 percent during the period from the first quarter of 2015 to the

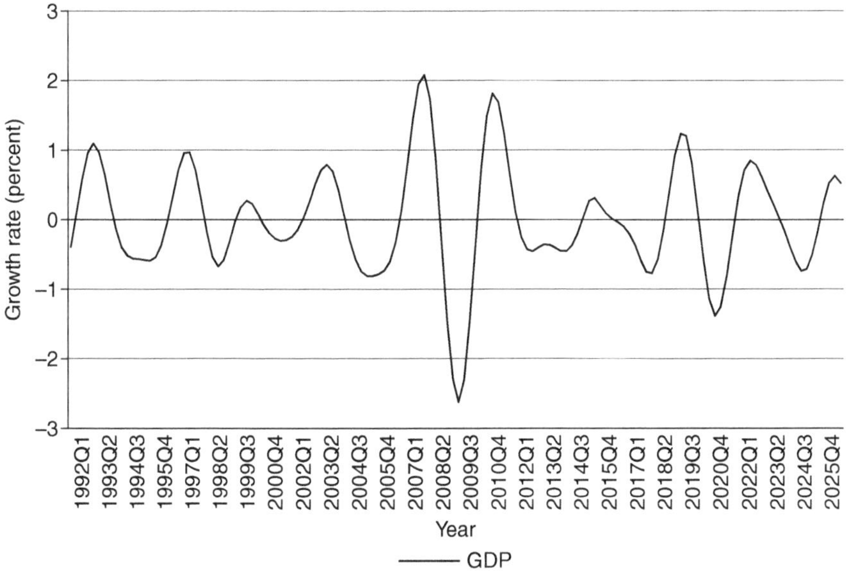

Figure 11.19 Mid-term fluctuation of China's GDP growth rate from the first quarter of 2015 to the fourth quarter of 2025 (%).

third quarter of 2017. The amplitude will increase to 2 percent during the cyclical upturn from the third quarter of 2017 to the fourth quarter of 2018. The maximum amplitude will occur during the cyclical downturn from the fourth quarter of 2018 to the second quarter of 2020, with an amplitude of 2.62 percent. After that, the fluctuation range will tend to shrink, and the amplitude during the cyclical upturn from the first quarter of 2024 to the third quarter of 2025 will only be 1.37 percent.

Amplitude of the mid-term fluctuation of the actual household consumption growth rate will also rise first and fall later

The mid-term fluctuations of the actual household consumption growth rate are the decisive factor of the mid-term fluctuations of the GDP growth rate. The result of simulation shows that the mid-term fluctuation amplitude of the actual household consumption growth rate will rise first and fall later after the fourth quarter of 2014 (Figure 11.20). The amplitude will expand gradually from 2.15 percent during the cyclical downturn from the fourth quarter of 2014 to the third quarter of 2017, to 3.52 percent during the cyclical upturn from the fourth quarter of 2017 to the fourth quarter of 2018, and then to 3.99 percent during the cyclical downturn from the fourth quarter of 2018 to the fourth quarter of 2020. Afterwards, the amplitude will tend to shrink, and narrow to 2.87 percent during the cyclical upturn from the fourth quarter of 2023 to the first quarter of 2025.

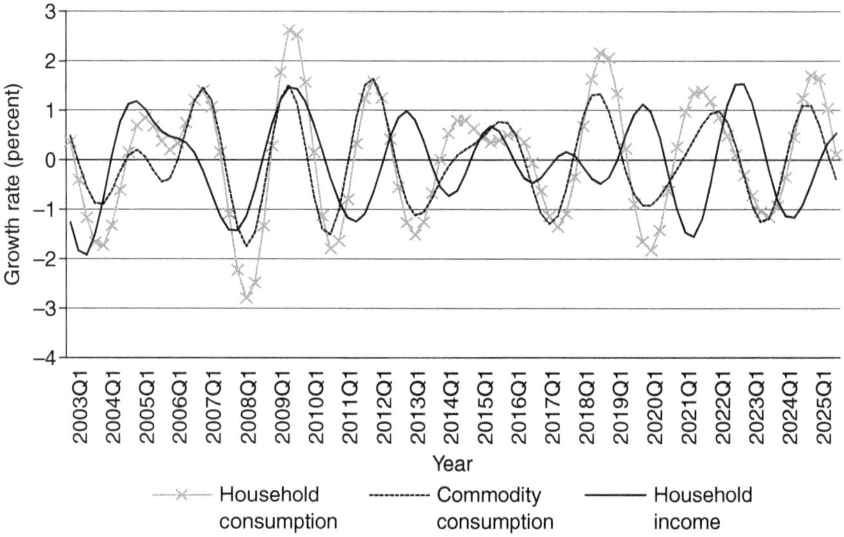

Figure 11.20 Mid-term fluctuation of the actual growth rates of household consumption, household income and commodity consumption in China, from the first quarter of 2015 to the fourth quarter of 2025 (%).

The mid-term fluctuation of actual growth rate of household commodity consumption is basically consistent with that of the household consumption growth rate; both experience a drop after an initial increase (Figure 11.21). But the peak and trough of the commodity consumption growth rate will lag behind those of the household consumption growth rate. This characteristic is a continuation of the pattern exhibited by the mid-term fluctuation of the actual commodity consumption and household consumption growth rates after the first quarter of 2010.

By looking at the influencing factors, we find the mid-term fluctuation of household consumption growth rate basically reflects the trend of household income growth rate; regardless of whether it is in the sample interval from the first quarter of 2003 to the fourth quarter of 2014, or in the predictive analysis interval from 2015 to 2025. The mid-term fluctuation trend of the actual household consumption growth rate synchronizes completely with that of the actual household income growth rate. But within the predictive interval, the mid-term fluctuation amplitude of the actual household consumption growth rate is larger than that of the actual household income growth rate. An important reason for this is that greater fluctuation of the actual growth rate regarding welfare expenditure, including fiscal expenditure on education, science, culture and health (ESCH) and on social security, can drive up the mid-term fluctuating value of household consumption. This characteristic shows that improving social security for residents, increasing household income or reducing household expenditure (increasing fiscal expenditure on ESCH) can effectively improve the household consumption growth rate.

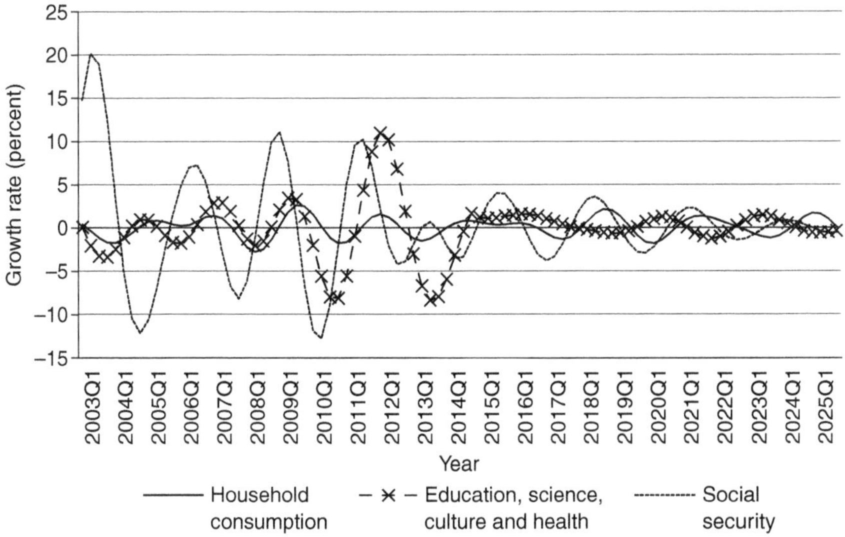

Figure 11.21 Mid-term fluctuation of the actual growth rates of household consumption; expenditure on education, science, culture and health; and expenditure on social security in China, from the first quarter of 2015 to the fourth quarter of 2025 (%).

Export and import growth rates show minor fluctuation in the mid-term

Because the mid-term fluctuation of the growth rate of imports from the US, Europe and Japan have an inherent tendency for micro-fluctuation, we can obtain through simulation that the mid-term fluctuation of China's export growth rate will also show a trend of micro-fluctuation from the first quarter of 2015 to the fourth quarter of 2025 (Figures 11.22 and 11.23). However, the amplitude of each cycle will still be very large, and the average amplitude of three fluctuation cycles from the fourth quarter of 2014 to the first quarter of 2025 will be as high as 3.5 percent. The amplitude in the cyclical downturn from the fourth quarter of 2014 to the second quarter of 2016 will be 4.47 percent, which will narrow to 3.2 percent in the cyclical downturn from the third quarter of 2023 to the first quarter of 2025.

Like the rise–fall amplitude of the mid-term fluctuation of the actual investment growth rate, the amplitude of the mid-term fluctuation of the import growth rate will also rise first and fall later after the fourth quarter of 2014. The peak value of its mid-term fluctuations will increase from 4.82 percent in the first quarter of 2015 to 9.02 percent in the fourth quarter of 2018, and then fall to 2.7 percent in the first quarter of 2023.

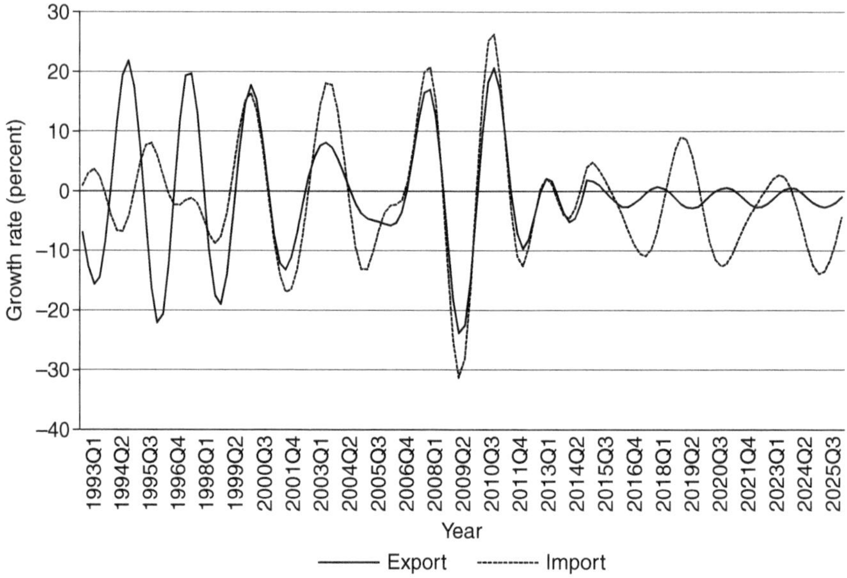

Figure 11.22 Mid-term fluctuations of China's import and export growth rates from the first quarter of 2015 to the fourth quarter of 2025 (%).

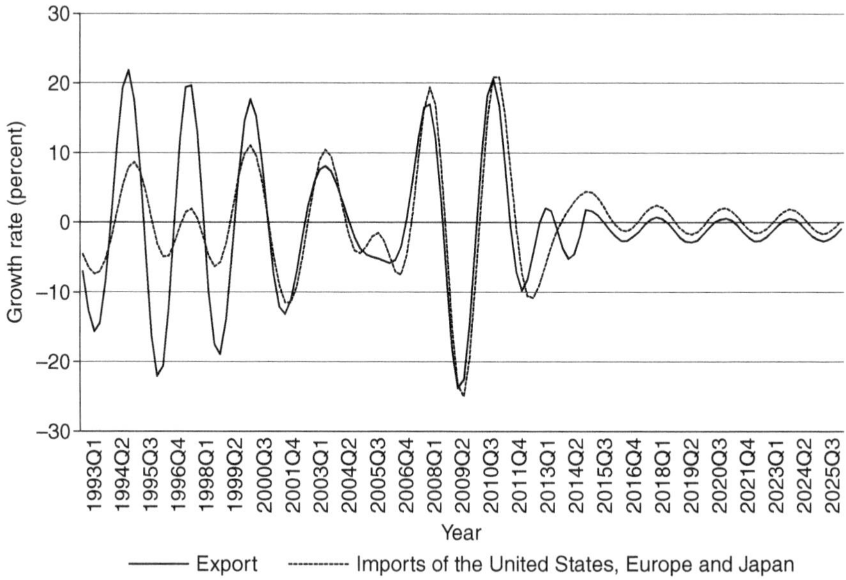

Figure 11.23 Mid-term fluctuations of the growth rates of China's export and the US's, Europe's and Japan's imports from the first quarter of 2015 to the fourth quarter of 2025 (%).

Amplitude of the mid-term fluctuation of the actual investment growth rate will rise first and fall later

The amplitude of the mid-term fluctuations of the actual investment growth rate will rise first and fall later, after the fourth quarter of 2014. The first quarter of 2015 will be the most recent trough of the mid-term fluctuation, with a trough value of –3.18 percent. The year 2018 will witness the peak, with a value of 2.28 percent; its amplitude will be 5.46 percent. The fluctuation will reach a minimum value of –5.54 percent in the second quarter of 2019, and the amplitude will be 8.72 percent. It will reach a new peak value of 4.8 percent in the fourth quarter of 2020, and the amplitude will increase to 10.34 percent. After that, the amplitude of the mid-term fluctuation will decrease continually. The amplitude will decrease to 9.52 percent in the cyclical downturn from the fourth quarter of 2020 to the third quarter of 2023, and it will further narrow to 8.3 percent in the cyclical upturn from the third quarter of 2023 to the second quarter of 2024.

Influencing factors tell us that after the fourth quarter of 2014, the mid-term fluctuation of the actual industrial inventory growth rate will fluctuate periodically (Figure 11.24). The mid-term fluctuation of the actual growth rates of fiscal expenditure and export will show a narrow range, but the mid-term fluctuation of actual growth rates of loans and household consumption will rise first and fall later. Therefore, the rise–fall trend of the mid-term fluctuation of the investment growth rate is determined by the innate trends of the mid-term fluctuation

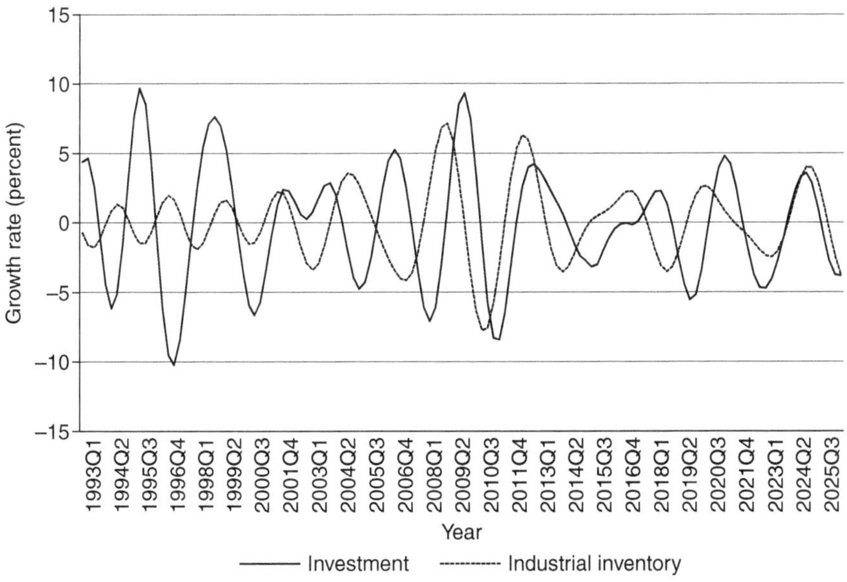

Figure 11.24 Mid-term fluctuation of the actual growth rates of investment and industrial inventory in China from the first quarter of 2015 to the fourth quarter of 2025 (%).

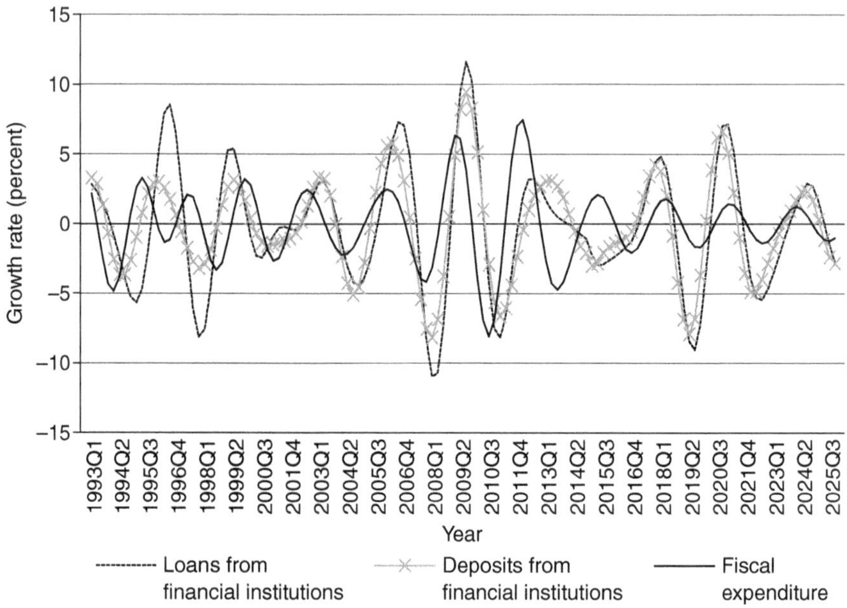

Figure 11.25 Mid-term fluctuation of the actual growth rates of loans, deposits and fiscal expenditure in China from the first quarter of 2015 to the fourth quarter of 2025 (%).

regarding both the actual growth rates of household consumption and loans from financial institutions (Figure 11.25).

Future development of the mid-to-long-term fluctuation of China's economic growth rate

The mid-to-long-term fluctuation of China's economic growth rate exhibits a regular pattern, whose important feature is its minor fluctuation. The prediction result shows that after the fourth quarter of 2014, the mid-term fluctuation of China's economic growth rate keeps fluctuating in a micro-range, and the amplitude of the mid-term fluctuation of both the GDP growth rate and the actual growth rates of demand factors such as household consumption, import, export, investment and industrial inventory all shrink gradually.

Mid-to-long-term fluctuation of the GDP growth rate maintains the micro-fluctuation trend

After the fourth quarter of 2014, the mid-to-long-term fluctuation of the actual growth rates of various demand factors tend to fluctuate on micro-levels, so the GDP growth rate repeats the trend during the period from 1992 to 2014, while

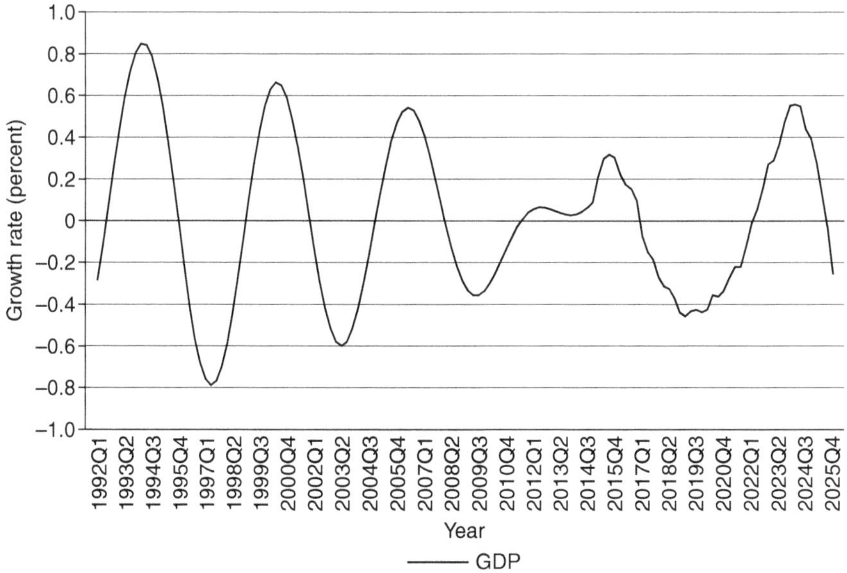

Figure 11.26 Mid-to-long-term fluctuation of China's GDP growth rate from the first quarter of 2015 to the fourth quarter of 2025 (%).

the amplitude will continue to narrow (Figure 11.26). The mid-to-long-term fluctuation of GDP growth rate will reach a peak value of 0.31 percent in the third quarter of 2015 and a new minimum value of –0.46 percent in the first quarter of 2019, and the amplitude will be 0.77 percent. After that, the mid-to-long-term fluctuation will enter the rising stage and reach a peak value of 0.56 percent in the first quarter of 2024, with an amplitude of 1.02 percent. The fluctuating value will be corrected to –0.25 percent in the fourth quarter of 2025.

Mid-to-long-term fluctuation of the actual household consumption growth rate shows regular narrow-range fluctuation

From the first quarter of 2003 to the fourth quarter of 2014, the mid-to-long-term fluctuation of the actual household consumption growth rate showed micro-fluctuation (Figure 11.27). After the fourth quarter of 2014, the amplitude of the mid-to-long-term fluctuation of the actual household consumption growth rate will enlarge. But it will maintain regular oscillation and fluctuation, and its fluctuating value will keep up with the recovery trend after the third quarter of 2014, and reach a peak value of 0.39 percent in the second quarter of 2017. Afterwards, it will enter a cyclical downturn. It will reach a minimum value of –0.41 percent in the second quarter of 2020, and the falling range will be 0.8 percent. It will reach a new maximum value of 0.27 percent in the first quarter of 2023, and the increasing range will narrow to 0.68 percent. It will again touch the

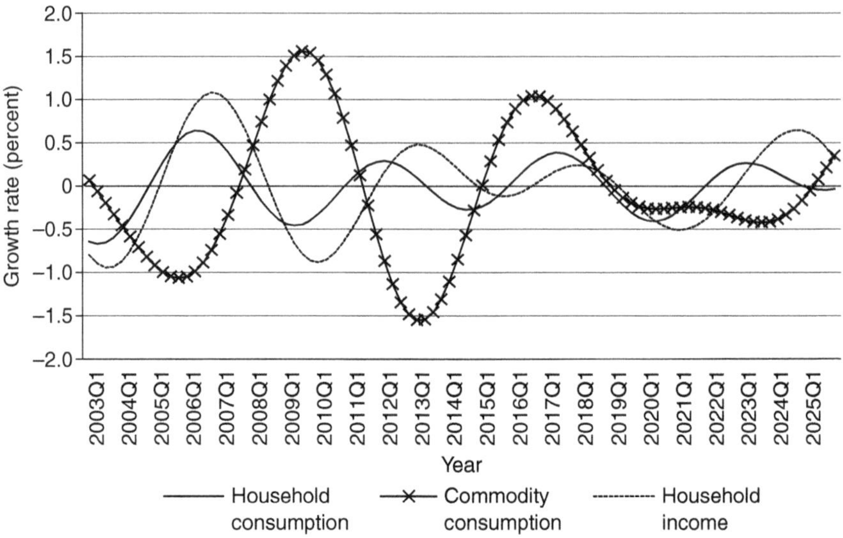

Figure 11.27 Mid-to-long-term fluctuation of the actual growth rates of household consumption, household income and commodity consumption in China from the first quarter of 2015 to the fourth quarter of 2025 (%).

trough at –0.04 percent in the third quarter of 2025, with its falling range further narrowing to 0.3 percent. This is to say, the amplitude of the mid-to-long-term fluctuation of the actual household consumption growth rate will slightly enlarge first and resume the tendency of micro-fluctuation later, thus showing a trend of regular narrow-range fluctuation.

The mid-to-long-term fluctuation of the actual growth rate of household commodity consumption will maintain the trend of micro-fluctuation from the first quarter of 2003 to the fourth quarter of 2014, with its fluctuating value repeating a cyclical upturn after the first quarter of 2013 and reaching a peak value of 1.04 percent in the third quarter of 2016. After that, it will enter a cyclical downturn and reach a trough value of –0.42 percent by the third quarter of 2023, and the falling range will narrow to 1.46 percent. The fluctuating value will rebound to 0.35 percent by the fourth quarter of 2025.

By examining the influencing factors, we discover that after the first quarter of 2015, the enlargement of the amplitude of the mid-to-long-term fluctuation of the household consumption growth rate is mainly caused by the enlargement of the amplitude of household income growth rate. The mid-to-long-term fluctuation value of the actual household income growth rate will maintain the earlier trend of micro-fluctuation during the period from the first quarter of 2015 to the fourth quarter of 2018, but the fluctuation range will inflate after that. Specifically, the fluctuating value will reach a trough value of –0.12 percent in the fourth quarter of 2015 and a peak value of 0.24 percent in the first quarter of

2018, and the amplitude will only be 0.36 percent. Next, the amplitude will expand, and the fluctuating value will fall to a trough value of –0.51 percent by the first quarter of 2021, and the amplitude will expand to 0.75 percent. The fluctuating value will reach a peak value of 0.64 percent in the third quarter of 2024, with the amplitude further expanding to 1.15 percent.

Amplitude of the mid-to-long-term fluctuation of export and import growth rates narrows significantly

From 2004 to 2014, influenced by the US financial crisis and the following policy responses, among other factors, the mid-to-long-term fluctuation of China's import and export growth rates also experienced a process of wide-ranging fluctuation, and the maximum amplitude of the fluctuation of export and import growth rates from 2008 to 2011 reached 16.5 percent and 20.96 percent respectively. The main reason for the wide-ranging oscillation of export growth rate was the wide-ranging oscillation of the mid-to-long-term fluctuations of US, European and Japanese import growth rate, while the wide-ranging oscillation of the mid-to-long-term fluctuation of import growth rate stemmed from the same pattern of the domestic investment growth rate (Figure 11.28).

After the fourth quarter of 2014, the amplitude of the mid-to-long-term fluctuation of China's export growth rate will narrow significantly, which is mainly

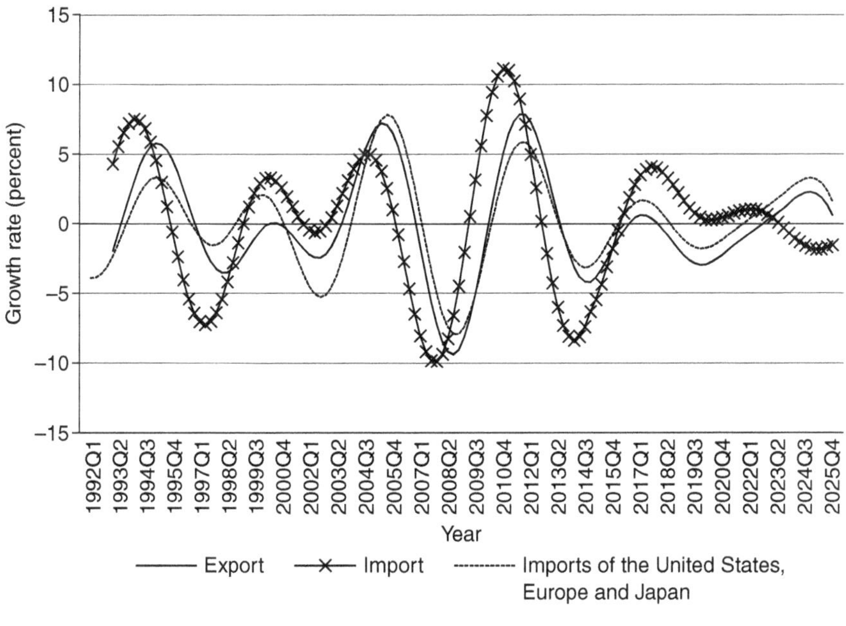

Figure 11.28 Mid-to-long-term fluctuation of China's import and export growth rates, and the growth rate of imports from the US, Europe and Japan, from the first quarter of 2015 to the fourth quarter of 2025 (%).

caused by the economic stability in the US, Europe and Japan, as well as the significant narrowing of the fluctuation amplitude of imports from these areas. The mid-to-long-term fluctuation of China's export growth rate will begin to resume a cyclical upturn in the first quarter of 2015. Its fluctuating value will increase gradually from a trough value of –4.19 percent in the fourth quarter of 2014 to a peak value of 0.62 percent in the first quarter of 2017. Afterwards, it will reach a trough value of –2.96 percent in the fourth quarter of 2019 and a peak value of 2.27 percent in the fourth quarter of 2024.

Influenced by the continuous narrowing of the fluctuation amplitude of the mid-to-long-term actual growth rates regarding investment and industrial enterprises' inventory, the amplitude of the mid-to-long-term fluctuation of China's import growth rate will also narrow accordingly after the fourth quarter of 2014. The peak value of the long-term fluctuation will rise from –5.47 percent in the first quarter of 2015 to 4.08 percent in the third quarter of 2017, followed by a cyclical downturn. After hitting a minimum value of 0.25 percent in the second quarter of 2020, it will rebound slightly to a maximum value of 1.04 percent in the first quarter in 2022. Then, it will again fall to a minimum value of –1.86 percent in the first quarter of 2025.

The mid-to-long-term fluctuation of the actual growth rates of investment and industrial inventory maintains micro-fluctuation with decreasing amplitude

The amplitude of the mid-to-long-term fluctuation of investment growth rate has been decreasing since 2000, and so does the fluctuation of the actual investment growth rate after the fourth quarter of 2014 (Figure 11.29). The value of fluctuation sustains the cyclical upturn after the first quarter of 2013, and reaches a peak of 1.05 percent in the fourth quarter of 2015. Thereafter, the trend will change to a cyclical downturn, touching a trough value of –2.25 percent in the first quarter of 2018. In the following cycle, the value again reaches a peak of 1.42 percent in the second quarter of 2021 and a trough of –1.61 percent in the third quarter of 2025 respectively. In general, the amplitude of the mid-to-long-term fluctuation of investment growth rate after the first quarter of 2015 will rock between 3 percent and 3.7 percent, which is significantly smaller than the amplitude of cyclical fluctuation during the period from 2000 to 2014.

From the demand side, in addition to the narrowing fluctuating amplitude of the household consumption and export growth rates, the micro-fluctuation of the actual growth rate of industrial enterprises' inventory is also an important factor that reduces the amplitude of the investment growth rate fluctuation in the mid-to-long term after the fourth quarter of 2014. The previous micro-fluctuation of the actual growth rate of industrial inventory continues after the fourth quarter of 2014, with the fluctuating value dropping continuously from a peak of 3.81 percent in the first quarter of 2014 to a trough of –3.2 percent in the second quarter of 2018. It will resume the cyclical upturn afterwards, reaching a peak

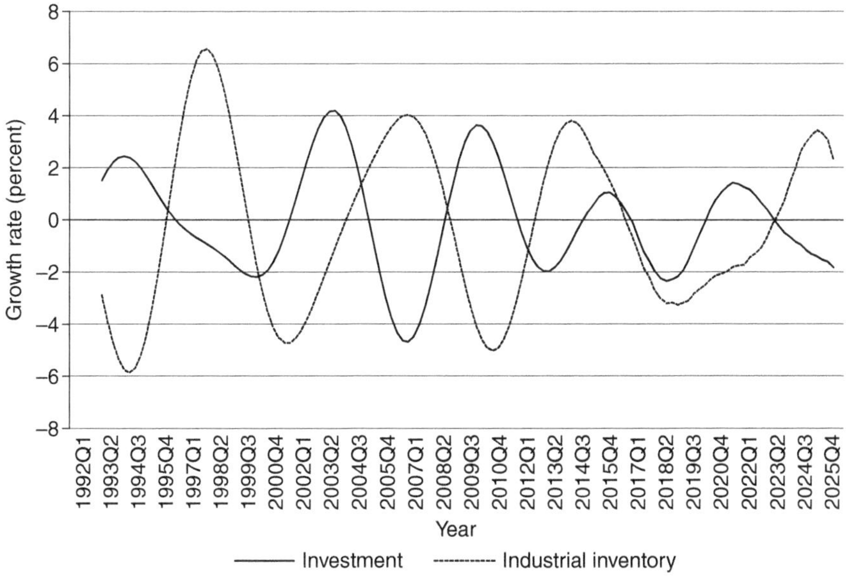

Figure 11.29 Mid-to-long-term fluctuation of the actual growth rates of investment and industrial inventory in China, from the first quarter of 2015 to the fourth quarter of 2025 (%).

value of 3.31 percent in the second quarter of 2025. Its amplitude will narrow from 7.12 percent in the cyclical downturn to 6.51 percent in the cyclical upturn.

Let's look at the sources of funds. After the fourth quarter of 2014, the previous pattern of micro-fluctuation continues for both the actual growth rates of loans from financial institutions and fiscal expenditure (Figure 11.30). They are the important factors that determine the micro-fluctuation of investment growth rate in the mid-to-long term. Among them, the mid-to-long-term fluctuation of fiscal expenditure growth rate will reach a peak value of 2.97 percent in the first quarter of 2017 and a trough value of –2.72 percent in the fourth quarter of 2021. The amplitude will narrow from 6.47 percent averaged in the cyclical upturn from the first quarter of 2012 to the fourth quarter of 2017, to a value of 5.69 percent averaged in the cyclical downturn from the first quarter of 2017 to the fourth quarter of 2021. The mid-to-long-term fluctuation of the growth rate of loans from financial institutions will reach a peak value of 1.78 percent in the second quarter of 2015 and a trough of –1.13 percent in the first quarter of 2021. The corresponding amplitude in the cyclical downturn will only be 2.91 percent. After that, the fluctuating value will reach a peak value of 1.77 percent in the second quarter of 2024, and the amplitude will be 2.9 percent.

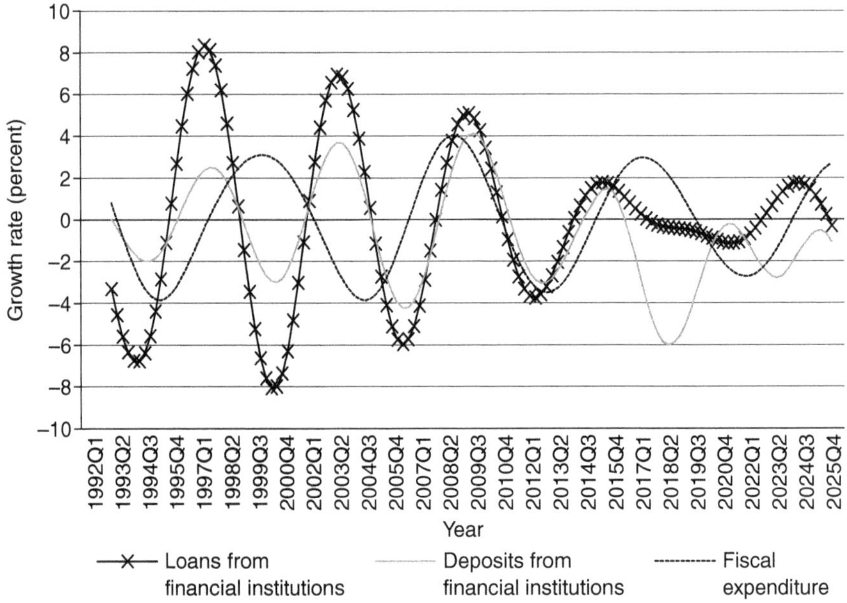

Figure 11.30 Mid-to-long-term fluctuation of the actual growth rates of loans, deposits and fiscal expenditure in China, from the first quarter of 2015 to the fourth quarter of 2025 (%).

Future development of the long-term fluctuation of China's economic growth rate

The long-term fluctuation of the economic growth rate shows strong regularity, while the impact of other factors including policy adjustment and external shocks is tiny. According to the prediction of the long-term fluctuation model, after the fourth quarter of 2014, the long-term fluctuation of China's economic growth rate will maintain a trend of cyclical upturn, while the long-term fluctuation of actual growth rates of household consumption, investment and export will express irregular cyclical fluctuations.

The long-term fluctuation of GDP growth rate will show cyclical upturn

During the period from the first quarter of 1992 to the fourth quarter of 2014, the peak and trough of the long-term fluctuation of GDP growth rate increased continually in cyclical upturns (Figure 11.31). After the fourth quarter of 2014, the long-term fluctuation of the GDP growth rate will maintain the earlier trend of cyclical upturn. After increasing from 0.29 percent in the fourth quarter of 2014 to a peak of 0.55 percent in the first quarter in 2016, the fluctuating value will

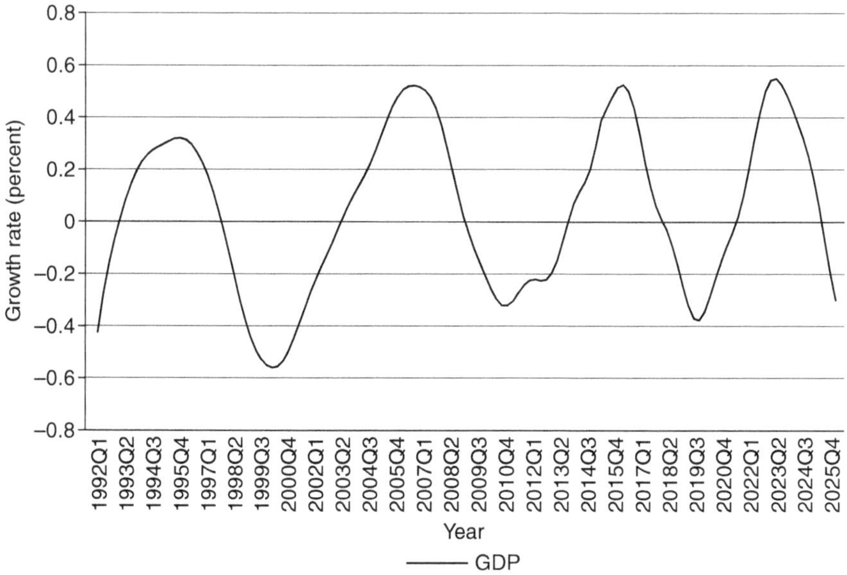

Figure 11.31 Long-term fluctuation of China's GDP growth rate from the first quarter of 2015 to the fourth quarter of 2025 (%).

enter cyclical downturn and reach a trough value of –0.34 percent in the second quarter of 2019. It will rebound to a peak value of 0.46 percent in the fourth quarter of 2022 and drop to –0.22 percent by 2025.

Long-term fluctuation of the actual household consumption growth rate will appear irregular

When separating the cycles by using BP and HP filtering techniques, because the BP filtering cannot extract the cyclical fluctuating factors with a wavelength shorter than two quarters, we have to classify the cyclical fluctuation with a wavelength shorter than two quarters, or a wavelength longer than ten years, as long-term fluctuation. Affected by the ultra-short-term fluctuation with a wavelength shorter than two quarters, the long-term fluctuation of the actual household consumption growth rate experienced irregular fluctuation during the period from the first quarter of 1992 to the fourth quarter of 2014. But in general, the long-term fluctuation of the household consumption growth rate still shows very strong regularity. Our model demonstrates that after the fourth quarter of 2014, the long-term fluctuation of the actual household consumption growth rate will exhibit irregular fluctuation. Its fluctuating value will maintain the rising trend after the fourth quarter of 2012 and reach a peak value of 0.37 percent in the third quarter of 2015. After that, it will enter a cyclical downturn and be corrected to a trough value of –0.19 percent by the third quarter of 2020. It will be corrected again to a peak value of 0.37 percent in the third quarter of 2023, and then be corrected to 0.04 percent in the fourth quarter of 2025.

The long-term fluctuation of the actual growth rates of household commodity consumption and household income will maintain the same trend as the long-term fluctuation of actual household income growth rate. The peaks and troughs of the three kinds of fluctuation coincide in timing, while in fluctuating values the long-term household income and commodity consumption growth rates are slightly lower than that of the household consumption growth rate (Figure 11.32). Considering that the long-term fluctuation of household income growth rate is the main factor that determines the trends of the long-term household consumption and commodity consumption growth rates, the synchronous fluctuation of the three shows that increasing household income and improving the long-term fluctuating value of the household income growth rate can effectively improve the growth rates of household consumption and commodity consumption.

The long-term export growth rate will show great fluctuation, and the long-term fluctuation of import growth rate will exhibit continuous decline

Because the long-term US, European and Japanese import growth rates will fluctuate widely due to their inherent nature after the fourth quarter of 2014, the long-term fluctuation of China's export growth rate will repeat the same trend (Figure 11.33). The fluctuating value will increase from 2.45 percent in the

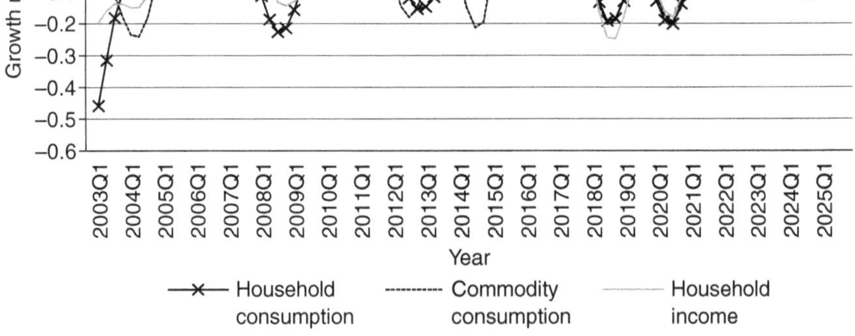

Figure 11.32 Differences between the long-term fluctuation of actual growth rates of household consumption, household income and commodity consumption in China, from the first quarter of 2015 to the fourth quarter of 2025 (%).

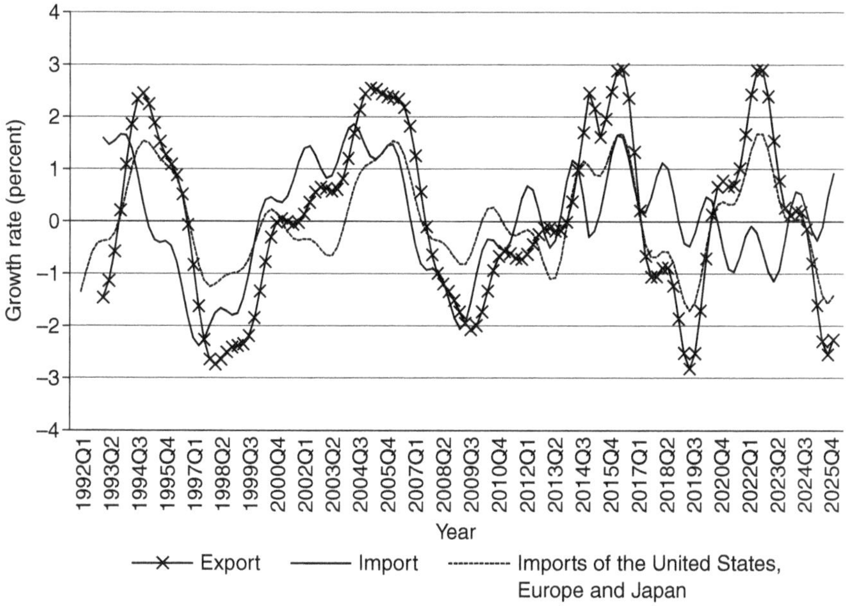

Figure 11.33 Long-term fluctuation of China's import and export growth rates, and the growth rate of imports from the US, Europe and Japan, from the first quarter of 2015 to the fourth quarter of 2025 (%).

fourth quarter of 2014 to 2.85 percent in the second quarter of 2016. Afterwards, it will enter a cyclical downturn and drop to –2.68 percent in the second quarter of 2019. It will rebound to a peak value of 2.88 percent by the second quarter of 2022 and then correct to –2.21 in the fourth quarter of 2025.

Influenced by the irregular long-term fluctuation of the actual growth rates of household consumption, investment and industrial inventory, the long-term fluctuation of import growth rate will also show a trend of irregular fluctuations after the fourth quarter of 2014. The fluctuating value will rise from –0.31 percent in the fourth quarter of 2014 to 1.6 percent in the second quarter of 2016. Afterwards, it will fall to –0.78 percent in the second quarter of 2021 and then rebound to 0.5 percent by the fourth quarter of 2025.

Amplitude of the long-term fluctuation of the actual investment growth rate will rise first and fall later

Similar to the long-term fluctuation of the household consumption growth rate, the long-term fluctuation of the actual investment growth rate was irregular due to the impact of ultra-short-term fluctuation from the first quarter of 1992 to the fourth quarter of 2014 (Figure 11.34). The amplitude of the long-term fluctuation of the actual investment growth rate will still show a trend of irregular fluctuation after

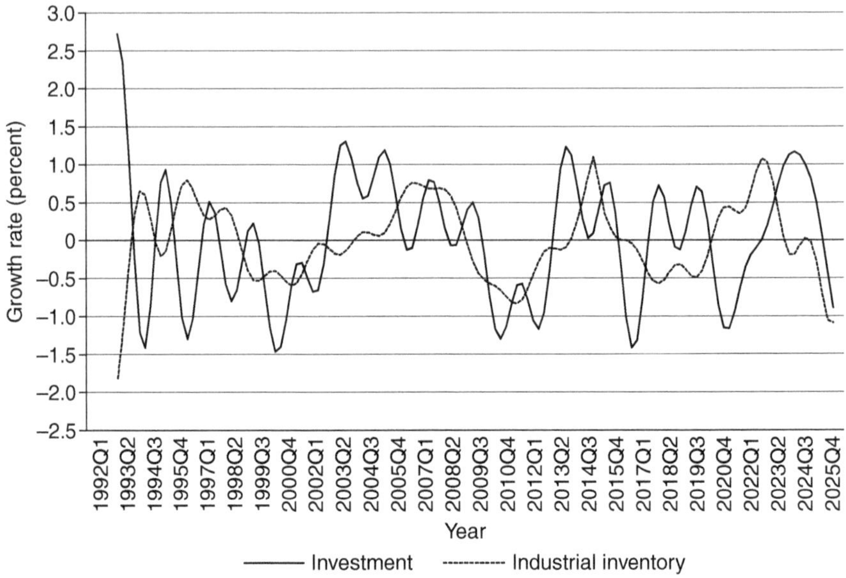

Figure 11.34 Long-term fluctuation of the actual growth rates of investment and industrial inventory in China from the first quarter of 2015 to the fourth quarter of 2025 (%).

the fourth quarter of 2014. Its fluctuating value will rebound to 0.96 percent in the third quarter of 2015, from 0.1 percent in the fourth quarter of 2014. After that, it will fall to –1.34 in the fourth quarter of 2016. By the fourth quarter of 2019, it will reach a peak of 1.14 percent. It will be corrected to a trough value of –1.26 percent in the first quarter of 2021 and rebound to a peak value of 1.63 percent in the first quarter of 2024. In the fourth quarter of 2025 it will be corrected again to –0.03 percent.

By looking at influencing factors, the long-term fluctuation of the actual industrial inventory growth rate will maintain irregular fluctuation after the fourth quarter of 2014, but its regularity is higher than the long-term fluctuation of the investment growth rate. Its fluctuating value reached a peak in the fourth quarter of 2014, and will reach a trough value of –0.62 percent in the third quarter of 2017 and rebound to a peak value of 0.84 percent in the third quarter in 2022. After that, it will correct to –0.81 percent by the fourth quarter of 2025. After the fourth quarter of 2014, the long-term fluctuation of the actual growth rates of loans and fiscal expenditure will be very irregular, which is the main factor affecting the irregular trend of the long-term fluctuation of investment growth rate (Figure 11.35).

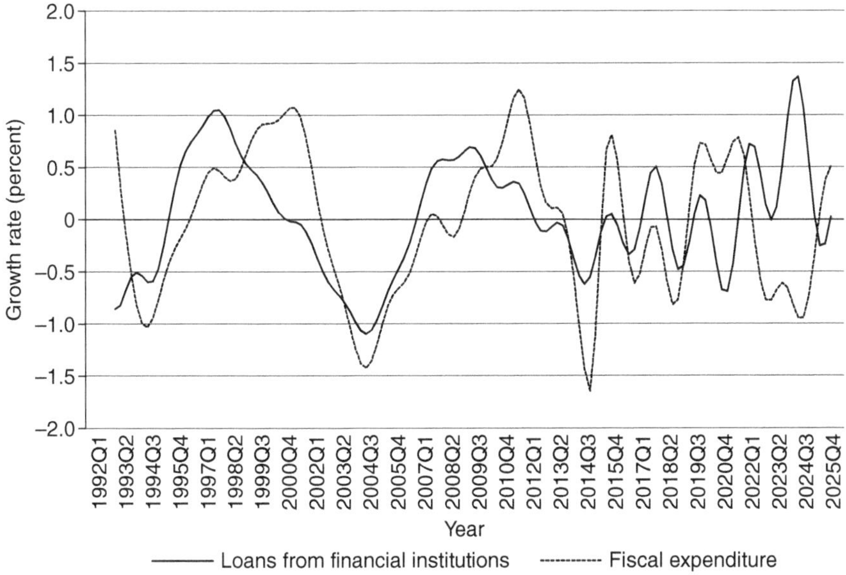

Figure 11.35 Long-term fluctuation of the actual growth rates of loans and fiscal expenditure in China from the first quarter of 2015 to the fourth quarter of 2025 (%).

Future development of China's economic growth rate

By using our model that predicts the economic growth rate's dynamic equilibrium value and four kinds of cyclical fluctuation, we obtain the predictive value of China's economic growth rate from the first quarter of 2015 to the fourth quarter of 2025. The predicted results are based on unchanged monetary policy, the adoption of adaptive fiscal policies, as well as the constant internal growth trend of the international market demand. Although this is only one of the many scenarios of China's economic development, it reveals the basic trend of China's economic development.

GDP growth rate will dip in 2017, but the overall growth rate will remain stable

After the fourth quarter of 2014, the dynamic equilibrium value of China's GDP growth rate will decrease steadily (Figure 11.36). But influenced by cyclical fluctuation, the GDP growth rate will show relatively larger fluctuation, and will fall to 5.02 percent and 4.92 percent respectively in the fourth quarter of 2017 and the fourth quarter of 2019, that the lowest rate of GDP growth might be much lower. After the fourth quarter of 2019, the dynamic equilibrium value will rebound in a limited manner, and the highest GDP growth rate will only reach 7.92 percent in the first quarter of 2021. In general, during the period from the

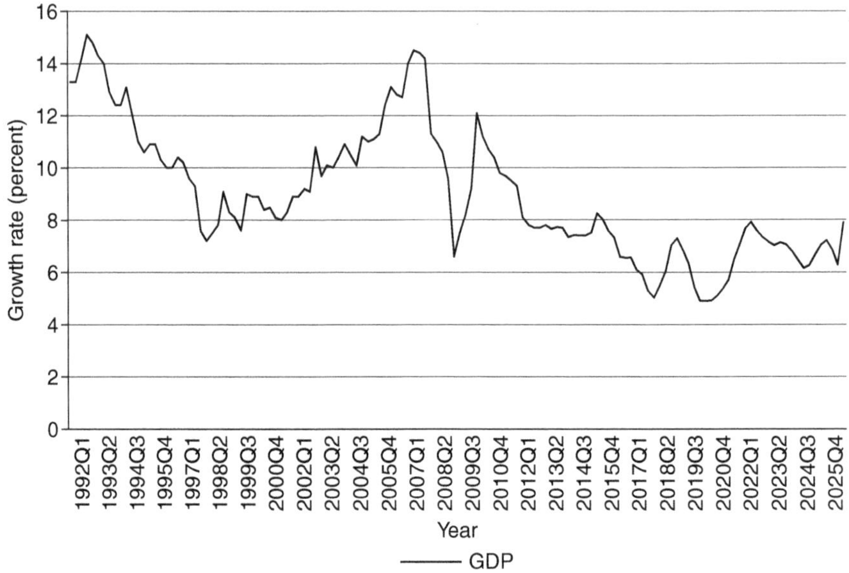

Figure 11.36 Simulated predictive value of China's GDP growth rate from the first quarter of 2015 to the fourth quarter of 2025 (%).

first quarter of 2015 to the fourth quarter of 2025, the GDP growth rate will decrease from a high-speed growth with an average growth rate of 10.21 percent from the first quarter of 1992 to the fourth quarter of 2014, to a relatively fast growth with a growth rate of 6.55 percent or so.

Growth rates of household consumption and household income will show regular cyclical fluctuation; commodity consumption growth rate will show cyclical downturn

After the fourth quarter of 2014, China's household consumption growth rate and household income growth rate will display wide-ranging cyclical fluctuation (Figure 11.37). The household consumption growth rate will fluctuate between 7 percent and 12.6 percent, the household income growth rate will fluctuate between 4 percent and 8.5 percent; their average growth rate will be 9.11 percent and 5.9 percent respectively from the first quarter of 2015 to the fourth quarter of 2025, which are significantly lower than the average growth rate of 10.35 percent and 7.16 percent respectively from the first quarter of 1992 to the fourth quarter of 2014. The growth rate of households' commodity consumption will keep the trend of cyclical downturn, with the highest growth rate of 13.86 percent in the third quarter of 2015. It will fall to 11.14 percent in the fourth quarter of 2025 in the cyclical downturn. From the first quarter of 2015 to the fourth quarter of 2025, the average growth rate will be 11.06 percent, which will

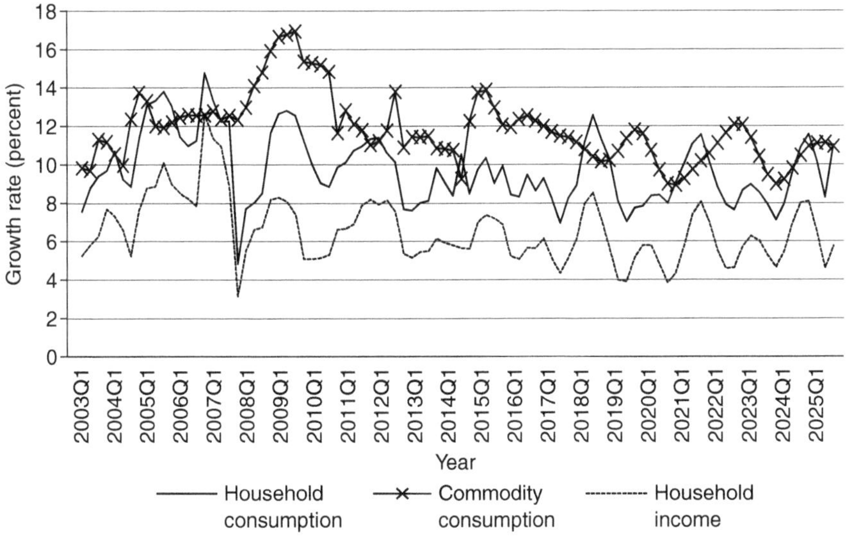

Figure 11.37 Predictive values of the actual growth rates of household consumption, household income and commodity consumption in China, from the first quarter of 2015 to the fourth quarter of 2025 (%).

fall by 0.53 percent from the average growth rate of 11.59 percent during the period from the first quarter of 1992 to the fourth quarter of 2014.

Import and export growth rates will decline and keep relatively low

Restricted by the slow growth of international market demand and the inherent downtrend of exports, China's export growth rate will maintain relatively low from the first quarter of 2015 to the fourth quarter of 2025, with a growth rate between –3.5 percent and 12.1 percent (Figure 11.38). The average growth rate will be 6.3 percent or so, which is far lower than the average growth rate of 17.83 percent during the period from 1992 to 2014.

Influenced by the declining domestic consumption and investment growth rates, as well as the relatively higher growth rate of investment in industrial inventory, the import growth rate will drop dramatically after the fourth quarter of 2014, with wide fluctuation ranging from –4.8 percent to 29.5 percent. But during the period from the first quarter of 2015 to the fourth quarter of 2025, the average growth rate will be only 7.67 percent, which is far below the average growth rate of 17.69 percent during the period from 1992 to 2014.

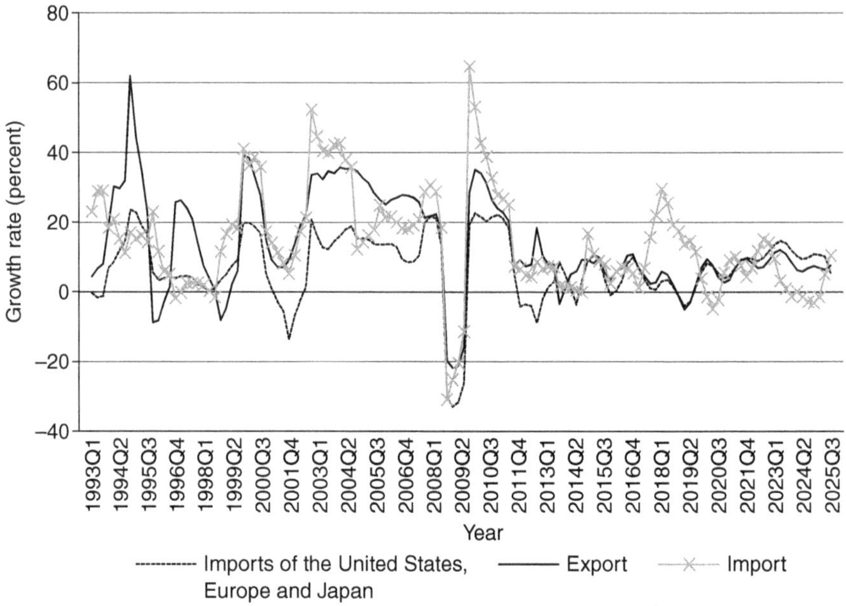

Figure 11.38 Predictive values of China's import and export growth rates, and growth rate of imports from the US, Europe and Japan, from the first quarter of 2015 to the fourth quarter of 2025 (%).

Investment and industrial inventory growth rates will show a relatively stable trend of cyclical fluctuation

After the fourth quarter of 2014, the investment and industrial inventory growth rates will expand around their dynamic equilibrium values (Figure 11.39). Among them, the investment growth rate will lay between 16.4 percent and 28.4 percent, with an average growth of 20.6 percent from the first quarter of 2015 to the fourth quarter of 2025, which will fall by 0.47 percent from the average growth rate of 21.07 percent during the period from 1992 to 2014. The industrial inventory growth rate will rest between 3.9 percent and 19 percent, with an average growth of 11.08 percent from the first quarter of 2015 to the fourth quarter of 2025, which will increase by 3.07 percent from the average growth rate of 7.99 percent during the period from 1992 to 2014.

Growth rates of deposits and loans of financial institutions will fluctuate with wide amplitudes

Influenced by the declining economic growth rate and household income growth rate with relatively great fluctuations, the deposit growth rate will also decline and show relatively greater fluctuation after the fourth quarter of 2014 (Figure 11.40).

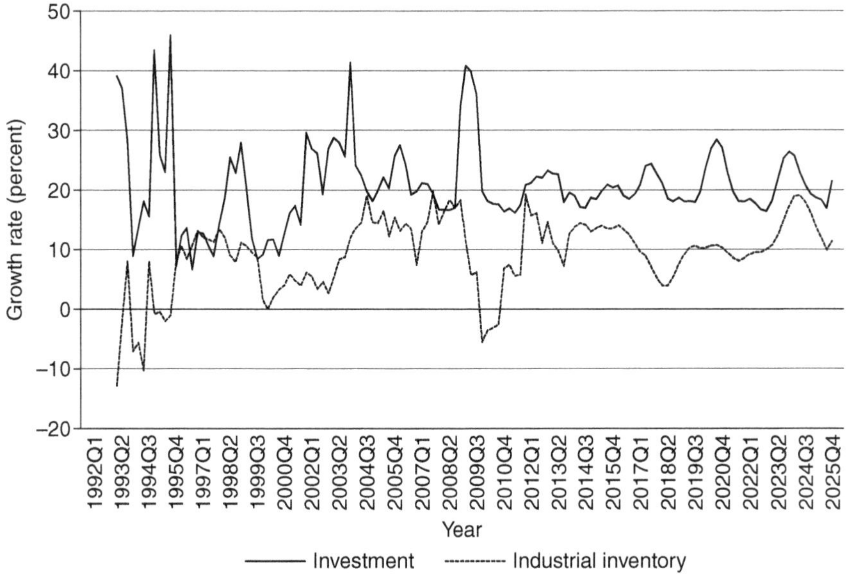

Figure 11.39 Long-term fluctuation of the actual growth rates of investment and industrial inventory in China, from the first quarter of 2015 to the fourth quarter of 2025 (%).

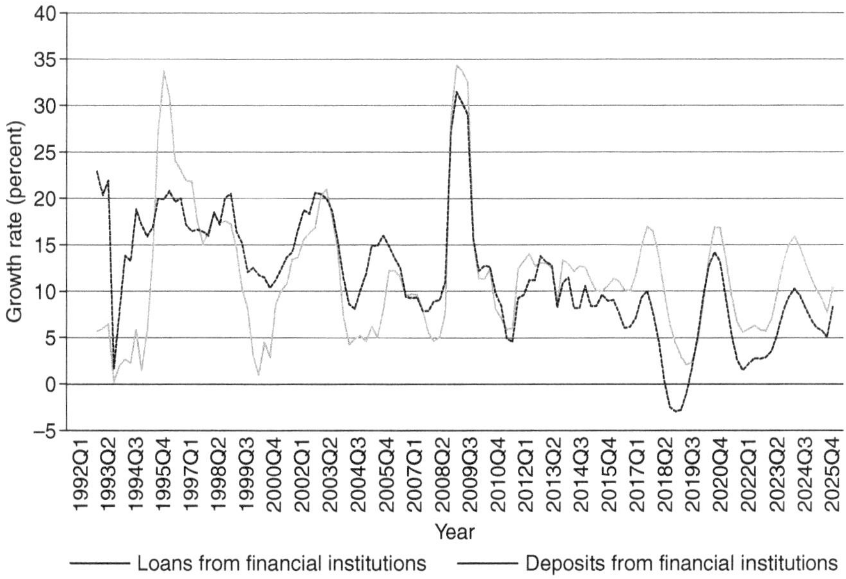

Figure 11.40 Simulated predictive values of the actual growth rates of deposits and loans of financial institutions in China, from the first quarter of 2015 to the fourth quarter of 2025 (%).

During the period from the first quarter of 2015 to the fourth quarter of 2025, the deposit growth rate will be between –3 percent to 14.2 percent, with an average growth rate of 6.11 percent, which will fall by 8.45 percent from the average growth rate of 14.56 percent during the period from the first quarter of 1992 to the fourth quarter of 2014. The lowest point will also appear during the deep correction of the economic growth rate in 2019.

Restricted by the decline in deposit growth rate, the loan growth rate will also drop substantially after the fourth quarter of 2014. From the first quarter of 2015 to the fourth quarter of 2025, the deposit growth rate will rest between 2 percent and 16.8 percent, with an average growth rate of 10.13 percent, which will fall by 2.18 percent, compared with the average growth rate of 12.31 percent from the first quarter of 1992 to the fourth quarter of 2014, and the lowest point will also appear during the deep correction of the economic growth rate in 2019.

Fiscal revenue and expenditure will maintain a relatively stable and rapid growth

In the simulation analysis, we treat fiscal expenditure as an endogenous variable of the model, so as to reflect the rigidity of fiscal expenditure and the intrinsic orientation of adaptive fiscal policy (Figure 11.41). The results of our prediction show that the fiscal expenditure growth rate will fall first and rise later, after the fourth quarter of 2014. The growth rate will experience a cyclical downturn,

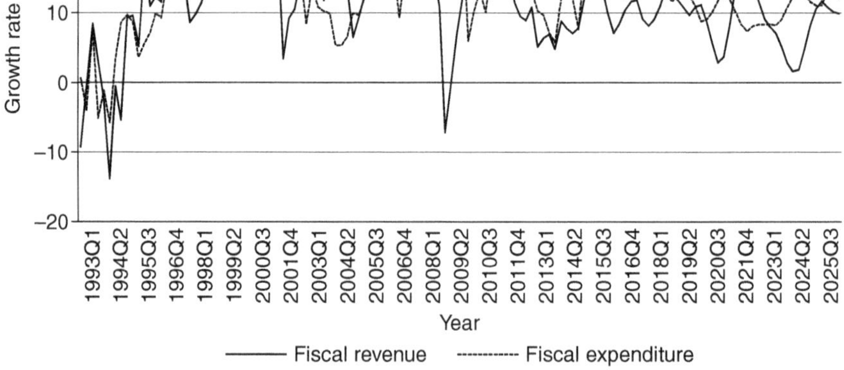

Figure 11.41 Simulated predictive values of the actual growth rate of fiscal revenue and expenditure in China, from the first quarter of 2015 to the fourth quarter of 2025 (%).

falling from 17.18 percent in the first quarter of 2015 to 7.36 percent in the first quarter of 2022. Later, it will gradually rebound to 14.3 percent in the fourth quarter of 2025, and the average growth rate is estimated to be 12.47 percent during the period from the first quarter of 2015 to the fourth quarter of 2025, falling 1.02 percent compared to the average growth rate of 13.49 percent from the first quarter of 1992 to the fourth quarter of 2014. Over the same period, the fiscal revenue growth rate will maintain cyclical fluctuation, and the growth rate will rest between 3 percent and 18 percent, with an average growth rate of 9.87 percent, falling 3.65 percent compared to the average growth rate of 13.52 percent during the period from the first quarter of 1992 to the fourth quarter of 2014.

Conclusions and policy recommendations

If analyzed from the structure of demand, China's economy is in the midst of transformation from the heavy and chemical industrialization stage to the late stage of industrialization, and expected to enter the post-industrialization stage in the next decade. According to the basic law of economic development, the next ten years will also witness China's economic growth rate gradually slowing down from the high speeds reached during the stage of heavy and chemical industrialization, to the rapid pace at the late stage of industrialization, and then to the relatively fast rate in the period of post-industrialization. The results in this chapter roughly reflect the economy's basic pattern of the above-mentioned transition in the next decade. In brief summary, viewed from the trend of the dynamic equilibrium value of the economic growth rate, China's economic growth can roughly maintain a relatively fast growth rate of ~6.5 percent for the next ten years. Taking into consideration the cyclical fluctuation of the economy, the economic growth rate will range between 5 percent and 8 percent in the upcoming decade. In light of the phased shift and cyclical fluctuation of China's economy, short-term policies should concentrate on minimizing short-term fluctuation and stabilizing economic growth, while the mid-to-long-term policies should focus on steadying exports, upgrading consumption structure, encouraging enterprise innovation and advancing the economic structure. A virtuous circle between the steady and relatively rapid economic growth and the optimization and upgrading of the economic structure is the ultimate goal.

1 *Strengthen the foresightedness and pertinence of macro-control policies, and stabilize the short-term and mid-term fluctuation of the economic growth rate.* In the next ten years, China's economic growth rate will maintain a relatively rapid growth on the whole, but the short-term and mid-term fluctuations, which are greatly influenced by policy adjustments and external shocks, will cause the economic growth rate to fluctuate greatly. In particular, when the short-term and mid-term fluctuations coincide in cyclical decline, the economic growth rate will experience a deep downturn. Considering that policy regulation can effectively influence the trend of short-term

and mid-term fluctuations, it is necessary to implement moderate stimulus regulatory policies in advance to prevent deep dips in the economic growth rate in 2017 and 2019, which may be the years when such declines coincide.

2 *Stabilize external demand and provide the support of demand for a steady and relatively fast economic growth.* Export is an important demand factor affecting the dynamic equilibrium value of domestic consumption and economic growth rates. The decline in export growth rate can have a negative impact on economic growth. In the short run, such an external demand gap can be offset by increasing investment and stimulating consumption; but from a mid-term and long-term perspective, the domestic demand cannot replace the external demand gap. This is because the decline in export growth rate will not only reduce the economic growth rate directly, but also have indirect impacts via reducing household income and consumption growth rates, and via decelerating the growth rate of growth caused by consumption and export decline. Sound export growth rate is the key to stabilizing and promoting the dynamic equilibrium value of the economic growth rate. In the next decade, if the export growth rate stays at 6.3 percent, it will become an important support for the economy to keep a relatively fast growth rate of 6.5 percent. In order to expand exports, it is necessary to stabilize the nominal effective exchange rate of RMB and the export rebate policy in the short term, thus consolidating and improving the price competitiveness of export products. In the medium and long term, it is necessary to draw support from enterprises' technology progress and the national strategy of "One Belt and One Road." In this way, we can encourage enterprises to go global, consolidate and expand their existing share of export products worldwide, upgrade export product structure and expand the international market for export products at the same time.

3 *Deepen the reform of the income distribution system, and fully explore the consumption potential of domestic consumer durables.* The relationship between consumption and economic growth is mutually restrictive. But when the income growth rate is fixed, the optimization and adjustment of the income distribution structure can also promote the growth of consumption (Li Jianwei, 2015b). Considering the excessive income gap between households in China at present, the reform to change the income distribution system and narrow the income gap can both effectively stimulate low-income households to expand their demand for consumer durables, and encourage middle-income households to consume high-end consumer goods earlier, such as automobiles. Such reforms are important measures to boost the growth rate of domestic consumption.

4 *Improve the environment of consumption, and promote the upgrading of the consumption structure.* When the demand for most consumer durables is saturated, product upgrading will become the main growth impetus for the demand of most consumer durables. We suggest further perfecting the new-for-old policy concerning consumer durables, especially big-ticket consumer durables, to encourage the upgrading of consumer durables. At the same

time, with the gradual saturation of the demand for consumer durables, the consumption of services will become the focus of household consumption. At present, tourism, education, medical treatment and other traditional service consumption have become hot spots of domestic consumption; the internet, information, big health and other emerging services are on the rise. It is necessary to provide emerging service industries at the initial stage of development with moderate support in terms of fund-raising through capital markets, credit and loans, taxes, land, government purchase of services, etc.. It is necessary to encourage the large-scale development of enterprises and offer supply-based support for the conversion of the consumption structure from commodity consumption to service consumption.

5 *Increase investment in science and technology, promote enterprise innovation and provide technological support for economic transformation and upgrading.* Technological progress is the eternal power of economic growth. From the upgrading of the consumption structure and export structure to the shift from a big, high-volume manufacturing country to a powerful, competitive manufacturing country, technological progress is always the foundation. In order to promote technology development, it is necessary to balance the relationship between fundamental research and applied research, and between traditional industries and emerging industries. Specifically, while enhancing the capability and level of fundamental research, it is also essential to boost the transfer of fundamental research to applied industries. While actively fostering new industries, it is also vital to support the development, transformation and upgrading of traditional industries at the same time.

12 The theoretical foundation and framework of the cyclical model on China's economic growth

Theoretical foundation regarding the cyclical model of economic growth

The operation of any economy is an inherent cyclical process in which multiple variables interrelate to and interplay with each other. According to such interaction and relevant economic theories that have resulted from it, once individual equations that explore influencing factors on each variable are determined, the general time series model uses simultaneous equations to simulate and analyze the economic aggregates and economic growth. The general time series models require the existence of stable relationships between explanatory and explained variables. However, in economic reality, such stability is usually weak due to structural changes. This is particular true in the middle and late stages of industrialization, where large-scale structural changes of the economy very often lead to substantial changes in household consumption behavior, demand structure, industrial structure, as well as the mutual interaction between economic variables. That is why models constructed around the aggregates or growth rate of economic variables usually have relatively poor stability. Meanwhile, models based upon the economic structure in the past also have problems reflecting the future structural changes and trends, leading to massive deviation in mid-to-long-term predictions. In order to eliminate the influence of structural change on the stability and predictability of the economic model, we add traditional economic theories to the foundation of cyclical theories of economic growth, to enable our cyclical model of economic growth to be reflective of the various fluctuations in real economic operation.

In Chapter 3 we proved that cyclical fluctuation is the norm of economic activities. For economic growth at any stage, the cycle of income distribution determined by the normal distribution of household income, the price adjustment cycle caused by lagging supply, the cycle of demand renewal triggered by product upgrading and the cycle of demand for innovation always coexist (Chapter 5). The actual fluctuation of the economic growth rate is formed by the simultaneous fluctuation of various economic cycles. At the same time, the cyclical fluctuation of economic growth will induce the growth of its dynamic equilibrium value (Chapter 8). For these reasons, we can decompose the economic growth rate into assorted cyclical fluctuation and dynamic equilibrium values with different wavelengths and amplitudes, analyze influential factors of various cyclical fluctuations and their dynamic equilibrium values across different economic theories, and build our own cyclical model of economic growth.

In specific model construction, according to the characteristics of the cyclical fluctuation of China's economic growth since the first quarter of 1992, we applied BP filtering and HP filtering techniques to separate the economic growth rate into five parts: short-term fluctuation (with a wavelength of 2–8 quarters); mid-term fluctuation (wavelength 8–20 quarters); mid-to-long-term fluctuation (wavelength 20–40 quarters); long-term fluctuation (wavelength above 40 quarters or below 2 quarters); and the dynamic equilibrium value. We then analyzed the factors affecting various cyclical fluctuations according to related economic theories. Finally, we synthesized individual functions of influencing factor analysis into a simultaneous function, thereby forming the short-term, the mid-term, the mid-to-long-term, and the long-term fluctuation models, as well as the dynamic equilibrium value model.

When analyzing the influencing factors, the overall train of thought is to take economic operation as a semi-closed circulation system, with GDP growth rate as its core, consumption as its starting point and export and policy intervention as its exogenous variables. That is to say, short-term economic growth depends on the growth of investment, consumption, import, export and inventory investment. But from a mid-to-long-term perspective, investment depends on the growth of consumption and export, while consumption and export are basic demands that determines the mid-to-long-term economic growth. Consumer demand relies on the inherent law of consumption growth and household income, and household income further depends on economic growth. Export mainly rests with the international market demand, while import turns on the growth of domestic investment and consumption. Policy intervention has impacts on various kinds of demand. This is the logic of treating the economic operation as a circulation system.

Taking into consideration the feature of cyclical fluctuation of economic activities, the cyclical fluctuation and dynamic equilibrium growth of the economic growth rate can also be regarded as a semi-closed circulation system, with the cyclical fluctuation of the growth rate of consumer demand as its starting point, and the cyclical fluctuation of the export growth rate and policy intervention as its exogenous variables. The cyclical fluctuation and dynamic equilibrium growth of consumption and export growth rates will also become fundamental factors of the dynamic equilibrium growth of investment and the whole economy. The cyclical fluctuation and dynamic equilibrium growth of the economic growth rate will further function as decisive factors that affect the cyclical fluctuation and dynamic equilibrium growth of the consumption growth rate.

The influencing factor analysis equation of the cyclical model of economic growth

Our model consists of 21 variables. In order to simplify the analysis, we regard fiscal expenditure and imports and exports from the US, Europe and Japan as endogenous variables by using the VAR equation. We take only five policy variables as exogenous: the one-year deposit rate (CKLL), one-year lending rate (DKLL), deposit–reserve ratio (LLZB), nominal effective exchange rate of RMB (REENL) and export rebate rate (TSRAT). All the other 16 variables are endogenous: GDP (GDPAG), investment (TZAG), household consumption (XFZAG), commodity consumption (total retail sales of social consumer goods, CONAG), export (CKZ), import (JKZ), household income (SRZAG), industrial enterprises' inventory (funds occupied by industrial enterprises' finished products, INDHARG), deposits in financial institutions (FINDAG), loans from financial institutions (FINLAG), fiscal revenue (FISIAG), fiscal expenditure (FISEAG), fiscal expenditure on social security (FISESBAG), fiscal expenditure on education, science, culture and health (FISEJYAG), imports from major countries (the US, Europe and Japan) (MAINCIMG), as well as exports to major countries (MAINCEXG). Quarterly cumulative actual growth rate or the actual balance growth rate are used for all endogenous variables. Our model has five sub-models, including the short-term fluctuation model (endogenous variable suffixed with W), the mid-term fluctuation model (endogenous variable suffixed with WS), the mid-to-long-term fluctuation model (endogenous variable suffixed with WM), the long-term fluctuation model (endogenous variable suffixed with WL) and the dynamic equilibrium value model (endogenous variable suffixed with TTL). Each model can be divided into six modules, including economic growth, consumer demand and household income, investment demand and inventory investment, deposits and loans of financial institutions, fiscal revenue and expenditure, as well as import, export and international market demand.

We construct the influencing factor analysis equation of endogenous variables based on relevant economic theories. According to the equations, the influencing factor analysis equations of the mid-term, mid-to-long-term, and long-term fluctuation, as well as the dynamic equilibrium value of each variable, all exhibit very high goodness-of-fit, thus indicating that the explanatory variables can well explain each variable. But the equations of the short-term fluctuation of all variables show relatively low goodness-of-fit. Among them, the equation of the short-term fluctuation of social security growth rate has the lowest goodness-of-fit, i.e., R^2 is only 0.48 and adjusted R^2 is only 0.41. The equation of the short-term fluctuation of import growth rate has the highest goodness-of-fit, but still R^2 is only 0.9 and adjusted R^2 is only 0.87. In general, the goodness-of-fit of each equation in the short-term fluctuation model averages 0.69, and the adjusted goodness-of-fit is 0.64. An important reason for the low goodness-of-fit of equations in the short-term fluctuation model is that policy adjustments, external shocks and other factors can cause the growth rate of each variable to show abnormal fluctuation and deviation from the inherent relationship between various variables. This kind of abnormal fluctuation is mainly reflected in short-term fluctuation, and thus results in falling correlation between various variables and explanatory variables. For example, government policies to stimulate investment can lead to a rising investment growth rate that deviates from consumer demand and export, thus weakening the explanatory power of the short-term fluctuation of consumer demand and export growth rates when applying them to explain the short-term fluctuation of the investment growth rate. At the same time, the short-term fluctuation of certain individual variables induced by external shocks will impact the short-term fluctuation of other variables. For example, the falling export growth rate caused by the US financial crisis can change investors' expectations, so its negative influence on the investment growth rate is much greater than the direct influence of the falling export growth rate on investment.

Economic growth

The fundamental factors that determine the cyclical fluctuation and dynamic equilibrium value of the economic growth rate are the cyclical fluctuation and dynamic equilibrium values of the actual growth rates of five major demands: investment, consumption, export, import and industry inventory. The inherent law of cyclical fluctuation also has an important influence on the cyclical fluctuation and dynamic equilibrium value of the economic growth rate. Therefore, in the simulation equation of GDP growth rate, apart from the demand factor, we also include the lagged variable of the cyclical fluctuating value of the economic growth rate into the analysis, treating it as an influencing factor. By constructing the higher-order difference equation of the cyclical fluctuating value of economic growth rate, we try to reflect the inherent feature of the cyclical fluctuations of economic growth. Specific results are shown in Table 12.1.

Consumer demand and household income

Household income is the foundation that determines the cyclical fluctuation of actual growth rates of household consumption and commodity consumption. The cyclical fluctuation of the actual growth rate of livelihood fiscal expenditure, such as for social security, education, science, culture and health, also influence the cyclical fluctuation of the actual household consumption growth rate. Household consumption, including commodity consumption, has its own inherent law of development. When the commodity consumption reaches a state of full demand, even if the income growth rate continues to grow, the commodity consumption will maintain slow growth; at this point, the household consumption growth mainly depends on the upgrading of commodity consumption and the growth of service consumption (Chapter 8). For this reason, in addition to adopting the cyclical fluctuation of the actual growth rates of household income and the livelihood fiscal expenditure as the explanatory variables of the actual household consumption growth rate, we also use lagged variables of the cyclical fluctuating values of the actual growth rates of household consumption and commodity consumption as explanatory variables, thus reflecting the intrinsic law of the cyclical fluctuation and dynamic equilibrium value of the consumption growth rate. Specific results are shown in Table 12.2 and Table 12.3.

Table 12.1 Simulation analysis equations of the cyclical fluctuations and dynamic equilibrium value of GDP growth rate

GDP	*Model equation*	*Goodness-of-fit R^2*	*Adjusted R^2*	*DW statistics*
Dynamic equilibrium value	GDPAGTTL = 0.2673 × TZAGTTL + 1.1729 × XFZAGTTL(−1) + 0.3311 × (CKZTTL − 100) − 0.3672 × (JKZTTL − 100) − 0.438267070238 × INDHARGTTL + 0.232 × INDHARGTTL(−1) − 5.0686 + [MA(1) = 0.9616]	0.999994	0.999993	0.19
Short-term fluctuation	GDPAGW = 0.0363 × TZAGW + 0.1857 × XFZAGW + 0.03647 × CKZW + 0.0358 × JKZW + 0.0059 × INDHARGW − 0.0026	0.709573	0.674998	2
Mid-term fluctuation	GDPAGWS = 0.7376 × GDPAGWS (−1) + 0.0518 × TZAGWS + 0.3157 × XFZAGWS + 0.0547 × CKZWS − 0.00437 × JKZWS (−1) − 0.0568 × INDHARGWS + 0.0248 + [AR(1) = 0.7277, MA(2) = 0.9177]	0.999669	0.9996	0.4
Mid-to-long-term fluctuation	GDPAGWM = 0.266 × TZAGWM −0.3421 × TZAGWM (−1) + 0.9452 × XFZAGWM + 0.6938 × CKZWM − 0.5799 × CKZWM (−1) − 0.1461 × JKZWM − 0.0629 × INDHARGWM − 0.0106	0.999927	0.999914	0.46
Long-term fluctuation	GDPAGWL = 0.7531 × GDPAGWL (−1) + 0.0229 × TZAGWL + 0.0365 × XFZAGWL + 0.0438 × CKZWL + 0.0324 × JKZWL − 0.0422 × JKZWL (−1) + 0.0525 × INDHARGWL + 0.01004	0.998689	0.998459	0.19

Table 12.2 Simulation analysis equations of the cyclical fluctuations and dynamic equilibrium value of the actual household consumption growth rate

Household consumption	*Model equation*	*Goodness-of-fit* R^2	*Adjusted* R^2	*DW statistics*
Dynamic equilibrium value	XFZAGTTL = 3.7382 × XFZAGTTL (–1) – 5.3423 × XFZAGTTL (–2) + 3.4548 × XFZAGTTL (–3) – 0.8546 × XFZAGTTL (–4) + 0.0035 × SRZAGTTL – 0.0003 × FISESBAGTTL + 0.0004 × FISESBAGTTL (–1) + 0.0137	1	1	0.68
Short-term fluctuation	XFZAGW = –0.1567 × XFZAGW (–1) – 0.0479 × XFZAGW (–2) + 0.1348 × XFZAGW (–3) – 0.3077 × XFZAGW (–4) + 0.7453 × SRZAGW – 0.0276 × FISESBAGW + 0.0165 × FISEJYAGW + 0.00025	0.86832	0.842715	2.67
Mid-term fluctuation	XFZAGWS = 1.4216 × XFZAGWS (–1) – 0.8078 × XFZAGWS (–2) + 0.2272 × SRZAGWS + 0.0095 × FISESBAGWS – 0.0242 × FISEJYAGWS + 0.0457 + [AR (1) = 0.8081]	0.998284	0.998013	0.33
Mid-to-long-term fluctuation	XFZAGWM = 3.858 × XFZAGWM (–1) – 5.7199 × XFZAGWM (–2) + 3.8556 × XFZAGWM (–3) – 0.9986 × XFZAGWM (–4) + 4.1415e–06 × SRZAGWM + 3.1067e– 05 × FISESBAGWM + 5.0099e– 05 × FISEJYAGWM + 1.2747e–06	1	1	0.52
Long-term fluctuation	XFZAGWL = 1.6555 × XFZAGWL (–1) – 0.8038 × XFZAGWL (–2) + 0.0651 × SRZAGWL + 0.0106 × FISESBAGWL – 0.0216 × FISEJYAGWL – 0.0005	0.987436	0.985865	0.28

Table 12.3 Simulation analysis equations of the cyclical fluctuation and dynamic equilibrium value of the actual growth rate of households' commodity consumption

Commodity consumption	*Model equation*	*Goodness-of-fit* R^2	*Adjusted* R^2	*DW statistics*
Dynamic equilibrium value	CONAGTTL = 4.4902 × CONAGTTL (–1) – 8.3322 × CONAGTTL (–2) + 8.0097 × CONAGTTL (–3) – 3.9909 × CONAGTTL (–4) + 0.8229 × CONAGTTL (–5) + 0.0005 × SRZAGTTL + 0.0003	1	1	0.43
Short-term fluctuation	CONAGW = –0.3893 × CONAGW (–1) – 0.559 × CONAGW (–2) – 0.485 × CONAGW (–3) – 0.2686 × CONAGW (–4) + 0.1054 × SRZAGW – 0.0093 × FISESBAGW + 0.0416 × FISEJYAGW – 0.029	0.571472	0.49648	2.49
Mid-term fluctuation	CONAGWS = 3.4102 × CONAGWS (–1) – 4.8438 × CONAGWS (–2) + 3.3249 × CONAGWS (–3) – 0.9507 × CONAGWS (–4) + 0.0084 × SRZAGWS – 0.0002 × FISESBAGWS – 0.0004 × FISEJYAGWS – 0.0002	0.999928	0.999916	0.27
Mid-to-long-term fluctuation	CONAGWM = 3.6806 × CONAGWM (–1) – 5.1727 × CONAGWM (–2) + 3.2863 × CONAGWM (–3) – 0.7971 × CONAGWM (–4) + 0.0008 × SRZAGWM + 6.8391e–05 × FISESBAGWM + 0.0002 × FISEJYAGWM – 1.5452	1	1	0.33
Long-term fluctuation	CONAGWL = 0.8514 × CONAGWL (–1) + 0.7839 × SRZAGWL – 0.7352 × SRZAGWL (–1) + 0.0191 × FISESBAGWL + 0.0088 × FISEJYAGWL – 0.0029	0.924683	0.915498	0.31

Household income depends on economic growth, and livelihood fiscal expenditure – such as social security, education, science, culture and health – can also indirectly affect household income. As a result, we regard the GDP growth rate and the actual growth rate of the expenditure on social security, education, science, culture and health as the explanatory variables of the actual household income growth rate. Specific results are shown in Table 12.4.

Investment demand and inventory investment

In the long run, the actual investment growth rate depends on the actual consumer demand and export growth rate. But in the short run, the government's fiscal expenditure and loans from financial institutions can have an important impact on the actual investment growth rate because they represent sources of funds. The government's fiscal expenditure and loans from financial institutions are the mechanism through which the fiscal and monetary policies affect investment demand. Besides, improvement of the actual inventory growth rate can also inhibit future investment. On this basis, when analyzing the influencing factors of the cyclical fluctuation and dynamic equilibrium value of the actual investment demand growth rate, we adopt the actual growth rates of household consumption, export and industrial enterprises' inventory as long-term factors affecting the investment demand, and the actual growth rates of government's fiscal expenditure and loans from financial institutions as the capital constraint factors affecting the investment demand. Meanwhile, we also take into account the lagged variable of the cyclical fluctuating value of the actual investment growth rate so as to reflect the inherent trend of the cyclical fluctuation of actual investment growth rate. Specific results are shown in Table 12.5.

Inventory investment is an essential part of expenditure-based GDP. It is also a key factor affecting investment demand and import. The cyclical fluctuation of inventory investment itself is one of the important fluctuation cycles. Due to the unavailability of statistics on the whole of society's inventory investment, we have to take funds occupied by industrial enterprises' finished products as the alternative indicator of inventory investment. We also use actual growth rates of consumption, investment, export and import as the influencing factors of inventory investment. At the same time, the inherent trend of the cyclical fluctuation of the actual growth rate of industrial enterprises' inventory has been taken into consideration decomposing the factors affecting industrial enterprises' inventory. Specific results are shown in Table 12.6.

Import, export and demand of the international market

Factors affecting exports include demand of the international market and the competitiveness of Chinese products in the international market. Because the competitiveness of exported products in the international market is influenced by many factors, including technological level, industrial scale and supporting capacity, labor costs and the quality of the labor force, exchange rate and others, it is

Table 12.4 Simulation analysis equations of the cyclical fluctuation and dynamic equilibrium value of the actual household income growth rate

Household income	*Model equation*	*Goodness-of-fit* R^2	*Adjusted* R^2	*DW statistics*
Dynamic equilibrium value	SRZAGTTL = 0.5561 × GDPAGTTL − 0.05321 × FISESBAGTTL − 0.00386 × FISEJYAGTTL + 2.7606	0.964214	0.961774	0.05
Short-term fluctuation	SRZAGW = −0.2474 × SRZAGW (−1) − 0.3633 × SRZAGW (−2) − 0.2694 × SRZAGW (−3) − 0.7236 × SRZAGW (−4) + 0.4335 × GDPAGW −0.01555 × FISESBAGW + 0.0559 × FISEJYAGW + 0.0175	0.735656	0.684225	2.13
Mid-term fluctuation	SRZAGWS = 3.2032 × SRZAGWS (−1) − 4.4993 × SRZAGWS (−2) + 3.1163 × SRZAGWS (−3) − 0.9381 × SRZAGWS (−4) + 0.0082 × GDPAGWS + 0.0024 × FISESBAGWS + 0.00186850107984 × FISEJYAGWS + 0.0008	0.999959	0.999951	0.55
Mid-to-long-term fluctuation	SRZAGWM = 1.8705 × SRZAGWM (−1) − 0.9416 × SRZAGWM (−2) + 0.0236 × GDPAGWM + 0.0017 × FISESBAGWM + 0.0013	0.999967	0.999964	0.05
Long-term fluctuation	SRZAGWL = 3.3085 × SRZAGWL (−1) − 4.6739 × SRZAGWL (−2) + 3.2967 × SRZAGWL (−3) − 0.9812 × SRZAGWL (−4) + 0.0046 × GDPAGWL + 0.0007 × FISESBAGWL 0.0003	0.999791	0.999757	0.22

Table 12.5 Simulation analysis equations of the cyclical fluctuation and dynamic equilibrium value of the actual investment growth rate

Investment demand	*Model equation*	*Goodness-of-fit* R^2	*Adjusted* R^2	*DW statistics*
Dynamic equilibrium value	TZAGTTL = 13.5364 × XFZAGTTL – 12.6697 × XFZAGTTL (–1) – 1.5861 × CKZTTL + 1.6336 × CKZTTL (–1) – 8.55727 × FISEAGTTL + 7.3344 × FISEAGTTL (–1) + 12.2026 × FINLAGTTL – 11.4197 × FINLAGTTL (–1) – 1.4237 × INDHARGTTL + 31.6408	1	1	1.11
Short-term fluctuation	TZAGW = 0.7376 × CONAGW (–1) + 0.0239 × CKZW (–1) + 0.1223 × FISEAGW + 0.6542 × FINLAGW + 0.5494 × LLDK – 0.6531 × LLDK (–1) + 0.6431 + [MA (2) = –0.2109]	0.466299	0.394455	2.49
Mid-term fluctuation	TZAGWS = –1.2564 × XFZAGWS – 0.2744 × CKZWS + 0.0891 × CKZWS (–1) – 0.9821 × FISEAGWS + 1.0137 × FISEAGWS (–1) + 0.7554 × FINLAGWS + 0.8584 × INDHARGWS – 0.7647 × INDHARGWS (–1) + 0.2281 × LLDK – 0.1029 × LLDK (–1) – 0.8817	0.99728	0.996544	0.7
Mid-to-long-term fluctuation	TZAGWM = 0.1211 × TZAGWM (–1) + 2.2124 × CONAGWM + 0.1545 × CONAGWM (–1) + 1.0237 × CKZWM – 1.0754 × CKZWM (–1) – 3.1179 × FISEAGWM + 2.3981 × FISEAGWM (–1) + 0.815 × FINLAGWM – 0.7601 × FINLAGWM (–1) + 7.1549e–06 × LLDK + 1.8935e–06 × LLDK (–1) + 0.4861 × INDHARGWM – 5.845	1	1	0.36
Long-term fluctuation	TZAGWL = 3.3356 × TZAGWL (–1) – 4.6205 × TZAGWL (–2) + 3.1682 × TZAGWL (–3) – 0.9046 × TZAGWL (–4) – 0.0001	0.999605	0.999585	0.38

Table 12.6 Simulation analysis equations of the cyclical fluctuation and dynamic equilibrium value of the actual inventory investment growth rate

Inventory investment	*Model equation*	*Goodness-of-fit* R^2	*Adjusted* R^2	*DW statistics*
Dynamic equilibrium value	INDHARGTTL = 0.7714 × TZAGTTL – 0.7486 × CONAGTTL + 0.2417 × CKZTTL – 0.4302 × JKZTTL + 25.7438	0.999685	0.999655	0.12
Short-term fluctuation	INDHARGW = –0.5513 × INDHARGW (–1) – 0.5547 × INDHARGW (–2) – 0.4828 × INDHARGW (–3) – 0.1682 × INDHARGW (–4) + 0.0394 × TZAGW – 0.2236 × XFZAGW – 0.0603 × XFZAGW (–1) – 0.1402 × CKZW – 0.0106 × JKZW + 0.0125	0.548769	0.43901	2.31
Mid-term fluctuation	INDHARGWS = 3.407 × INDHARGWS (–1) – 4.8083 × INDHARGWS (–2) + 3.2668 × INDHARGWS (–3) – 0.9238 × INDHARGWS (–4) + 0.0012 × TZAGWS + 0.0085 × CONAGWS + 0.0025 × CKZWS – 0.0007 × JKZWS + 0.0002	0.999962	0.999958	0.33
Mid-to-long-term fluctuation	INDHARGWM = –0.5638 × TZAGWM – 1.3145 × CONAGWM + 0.7406 × CKZWM + 1.8336 × JKZWM – 2.5131 × JKZWM (–1) – 0.1256	0.983887	0.982498	0.08
Long-term fluctuation	INDHARGWL = –0.6081 × TZAGWL + 0.8186 × TZAGWL (–1) – 2.0271 × CONAGWL + 0.1628 × CONAGWL (–1) – 0.4783 × CKZWL + 0.6781 × CKZWL (–1) – 1.0001 × JKZWL + 0.726 × JKZWL (–1) + 0.05557 + [MA (1) = 0.979]	0.963948	0.959032	0.31

difficult to carry out a comprehensive analysis with insufficient quarterly data. As a result, we only take into account the influence of demand of the international market when analyzing the factors affecting exports. Moreover, we use the nominal effective exchange rate of RMB and the export rebate rate as the policy factors affecting exports, and also include the lagged variable of the export growth rate to reflect the inherent trend of the cyclical fluctuation of China's export growth rate at the same time. Specific results are shown in Table 12.7.

China's imports are dominated by means of production, but the percentage of consumer goods are increasing in recent years. Therefore, we regard investment, consumption and industrial enterprises' inventories as the main demand factors affecting imports, and take the nominal effective exchange rate of RMB as a policy factor. At the same time, we add the lagged variable of import growth rate to reflect the inherent trend of the cyclical fluctuation of import growth rate. Specific results are shown in Table 12.8.

Demand of the international market is the decisive factor for China's exports. We chose the imports from three big economies (the US, Europe and Japan) as the alternative indicator of international demand. In order to simplify the analysis, we only analyze the inherent trend of the cyclical fluctuations of the import growth rate from the three economies from the first quarter of 1992 to the fourth quarter of 2014. The results are shown in Table 12.9.

Deposits and loans of financial institutions

The loans from financial institutions are one of the main sources of funds for investment, and the growth rate of loans is affected by various factors such as deposits and monetary policy. In the model-based analysis, we only take into account the impact from deposits in financial institutions, deposit–reserve ratio and lending rate. At the same time, we include the lagged variable of the actual growth rate of loans from financial institutions as a factor that reflects the inherent trend of the cyclical fluctuation of the actual loan growth rate. This is how to decompose factors affecting the cyclical fluctuation of the actual growth rate of loans from financial institutions. The results are shown in Table 12.10.

The deposits in financial institutions are the main sources of funds for the loans from financial institutions, and the main body of deposits in financial institutions is composed of household saving deposits. Key factors affecting household saving deposits are household income and household consumption, while the interest rate of deposit can also have some impact. On this basis, we regard the actual growth rates of household income and household consumption, as well as the deposit interest rate, as principal factors that affect the cyclical fluctuation of the actual growth rate of deposits in financial institutions. At the same time, we take into account the inherent trend of the cyclical fluctuation of the actual growth rate of deposits in financial institutions, and decompose the factors affecting the cyclical fluctuation and dynamic equilibrium value of the actual growth rate of deposits in financial institutions. The results are shown in Table 12.11.

Table 12.7 Simulation analysis equations of the cyclical fluctuation and dynamic equilibrium value of China's export growth rate

Export	*Model equation*	*Goodness-of-fit* R^2	*Adjusted* R^2	*DW statistics*
Dynamic equilibrium value	CKZTTL = 0.9076 × CKZTTL (–1) + 0.0336 × MAINCIMGTTL + 9.7566 + [MA (1) = 0.9367]	0.999992	0.99999	0.36
Short-term fluctuation	CKZW = –0.0935 × CKZW (–1) – 0.3217 × CKZW (–2) – 0.141 × CKZW (–3) – 0.5669 × CKZW (–4) + 0.3946 × MAINCIMGW –0.0999 × REENL + 0.0896 × REENL (–1) – 0.3382 × TSRAT + 0.2821 × TSRAT (–1) + 2.4786	0.769949	0.741586	2.30
Mid-term fluctuation	CKZWS = 0.8899 × MAINCIMGWS + 0.0043 × REENL + 0.0428 × REENL (–1) – 0.0577 × TSRAT – 7.3177 + [AR(1) = 0.8338]	0.9516	0.947447	0.38
Mid-to-long-term fluctuation	CKZWM = 1.0268 × MAINCIMGWM + 0.0302 × REENL + 0.0033 × REENL (–1) + 0.0012 × TSRAT – 6.0039 + [MA(1) = 1.6334, MA(2) = 0.9998]	0.986946	0.985929	0.19
Long-term fluctuation	CKZWL = 1.6854 × MAINCIMGWL – 0.0013 × REENL – 0.0039 × REENL (1) + 0.8755 + [MA (1) = 0.9773]	0.929183	0.92577	0.18

Table 12.8 Simulation analysis equations of the cyclical fluctuation and dynamic equilibrium value of China's import growth rate

Import	*Model equation*	*Goodness-of-fit* R^2	*Adjusted* R^2	*DW statistics*
Dynamic equilibrium value	JKZTTL = 0.9767 × JKZTTL (–1) + 0.5886 × TZAGTTL – 0.6934 × TZAGTTL (–1) + 4.728 × XFZAGTTL – 4.7181 × XFZAGTTL (–1) – 1.1895e^{-05} × REENL – 0.0747 × INDHARGTTL + 5.6992	1	1	0.55
Short-term fluctuation	JKZW = –2.778 × TZAGW + 1.1657 × TZAGW (–1) + 2.9268 × CONAGW (–1) – 0.4424 × REENL + 0.5123 × REENL (–1) – 1.0431 × INDHARGW – 0.7634 × INDHARGW (–1) – 12.3568 + [MA (2) = –0.921]	0.897351	0.866937	1.76
Mid-term fluctuation	JKZWS = 0.8977 × JKZWS (–1) + 0.2377 × TZAGWS (–1) + 0.3417 × XFZAGWS – 0.0017 × REENL + 0.0132 × REENL (–1) – 1.1619 × INDHARGWS – 2.0306 + [AR(2) = 0.2531, MA (1) = 0.9652]	0.96671	0.959512	0.46
Mid-to-long-term fluctuation	JKZWM = 0.9094 × JKZWM (–1) + 0.2324 × TZAGWM + 0.9354 × CONAGWM – 0.0063 × REENL + 1.0661	0.9836	0.9828	0.07
Long-term fluctuation	JKZWL = 0.9205 × JKZWL (–1) + 0.025 × TZAGWL – 1.5427 × CONAGWL + 1.2714 × CONAGWL (–1) – 0.0017 × REENL + 0.0027 × REENL (–1) – 0.2281	0.945835	0.941772	0.29

Table 12.9 Simulation analysis equations of the cyclical fluctuation and dynamic equilibrium value of the growth rate of imports from the US, Europe and Japan

Import	*Model equation*	*Goodness-of-fit* R^2	*Adjusted* R^2	*DW statistics*
Dynamic equilibrium value	MAINCIMGTTL = 0.7325 × MAINCEXGTTL + 2.3726	0.677209	0.673623	0.01
Short-term fluctuation	MAINCIMGW = –0.0354 × MAINCIMGW (–1) – 0.3964 × MAINCIMGW (–2) – 0.2355 × MAINCIMGW (–3) – 0.6842 × MAINCIMGW (–4) – 0.0365	0.647173	0.629962	2.31
Mid-term fluctuation	MAINCIMGWS = 2.5697 × MAINCIMGWS (–1) – 2.4645 × MAINCIMGWS (–2) + 0.8595 × MAINCIMGWS (–3) + 0.0021	0.997496	0.997408	0.31
Mid-to-long-term fluctuation	MAINCIMGWM = 5.8543 × MAINCIMGWM (–1) – 14.4617 × MAINCIMGWM (–2) + 19.2868 × MAINCIMGWM (–3) – 14.6445 × MAINCIMGWM (–4) + 6.0032 × MAINCIMGWM (–5) – 1.0384 × MAINCIMGWM (–6) + 4.4849e^{-07}	1	1	0.05
Long-term fluctuation	MAINCIMGWL = 3.367 × MAINCIMGWL (–1) – 4.7523 × MAINCIMGWL (–2) + 3.3368 × MAINCIMGWL (–3) – 0.9819 × MAINCIMGWL (–4) + 0.0007	0.999649	0.999632	0.18

Table 12.10 Simulation analysis equations of the cyclical fluctuations and dynamic equilibrium value of the actual growth rate of loans from financial institutions

Loan	*Model equation*	*Goodness-of-fit* R^2	*Adjusted* R^2	*DW statistics*
Dynamic equilibrium value	FINLAGTTL = 3.7711 × FINLAGTTL (–1) – 5.3504 × FINLAGTTL (–2) + 3.3834 × FINLAGTTL (–3) – 0.8044 × FINLAGTTL (–4) + 0.0002 × FINLAGTTL + 6.0242e^{-05} × LLZB – 0.0001 × LLDK + 0.0007	1	1	0.53
Short-term fluctuation	FINLAGW = 0.4017 × FINLAGW (–1) – 0.3465 × FINLAGW (–2) – 0.3274 × FINLAGW (–3) + 0.4151 × FINLAGW – 0.0529 × LLZB + 0.05466 × LLZB (–1) + 0.0056 × LLDK – 0.0464341935909 + [MA(1) = –0.9999]	0.801783	0.780918	1.89
Mid-term fluctuation	FINLAGWS = 0.5163 × FINLAGWS (–1) + 0.6871 × FINLAGWS – 0.0257 × LLZB + 0.0328 × LLZB (–1) + 0.0109 × LLDK – 0.1805 + [MA(1) = 0.983]	0.971334	0.969184	0.38
Mid-to-long-term fluctuation	FINLAGWM = 3.8105 × FINLAGWM (–1) – 5.5723 × FINLAGWM (–2) + 3.7007 × FINLAGWM (–3) – 0.94302 × FINLAGWM (–4) + 9.91571e– 05 × FINLAGWM + 3.4383e^{-05} × LLZB – 6.1007e^{-05} × LLZB (–1) + 0.0001 × LLDK – 0.0006	1	1	0.06
Long-term fluctuation	FINLAGWL = 3.4878 × FINLAGWL (–1) – 4.9804 × FINLAGWL (–2) + 3.4739 × FINLAGWL (–3) – 0.9901 × FINLAGWL (–4) – 0.0266 × FINLAGWL + 0.0128 × FINLAGWL (–1) – 0.0005 × LLZB + 0.0006 × LLZB (–1) + 0.0009 × LLDK – 0.0002 × LLDK (–1) – 0.0053	0.99994	0.999932	0.14

Table 12.11 Simulation analysis equations of the cyclical fluctuations and dynamic equilibrium value of the actual growth rate of deposits in financial institutions

Deposit	*Model equation*	*Goodness-of-fit* R^2	*Adjusted* R^2	*DW statistics*
Dynamic equilibrium value	FINDAGTTL = 0.8881 × FINDAGTTL (–1) – 1.6711 × SRZAGTTL + 2.1834 × SRZAGTTL (–1) – 0.2033 × XFZAGTTL – 0.0044 × LLCK + 0.0074 × LLCK (–1) – 0.0034 × LLZB – 0.2472	0.999962	0.999955	0.19
Short-term fluctuation	FINDAGW = 0.4605 × FINDAGW (–1) – 0.3851 × FINDAGW (–2) + 0.0324 × FINDAGW (–3) – 0.1638 × FINDAGW (–4) – 2.3135 × GAPAGW + 0.2102 × GAPAGW (–1) + 0.2745 × XFZAGW + 0.4333 × XFZAGW (–1) + 0.0026 × LLCK – 0.00266 × LLZB + 0.0291 + [MA(1) = –0.9598]	0.854948	0.80936	2.24
Mid-term fluctuation	FINDAGWS = 5.9935 × GAPAGWS – 9.3794 × GAPAGWS (–1) – 1.56 × XFZAGWS + 0.5606 × XFZAGWS (–1) + 0.3332 × LLCK + 0.3043 × LLCK (–1) – 0.0273 × LLZB – 1.6473 + [MA(1) = 1.8112, MA(2) = 0.9041]	0.986302	0.98297	0.43
Mid-to-long-term fluctuation	FINDAGWM = 0.8099 × FINDAGWM (–1) + 1.2103 × GAPAGWM – 2.7495 × XFZAGWM + 0.6202 × LLCK – 0.03216 × LLZB – 1.3387	0.979478	0.977035	0.18
Long-term fluctuation	FINDAGWL = 3.1647 × FINDAGWL (–1) – 4.2849 × FINDAGWL (–2) + 2.8762 × FINDAGWL (–3) – 0.8123 × FINDAGWL (–4) – 0.1681 × GAPAGWL + 0.1666 × GAPAGWL (–1) + 0.0005 × LLCK – 0.0008 × LLCK (–1) – 0.0007 × LLZB + 0.0011 × LLZB (–1) – 0.0023	0.999836	0.999814	0.36

Fiscal revenue and fiscal expenditure

Fiscal revenue and expenditure are the basic tools of fiscal policy. Both have a certain extent of endogeneity. Among them, the fiscal revenue depends on economic growth, while the fiscal expenditure has a relatively stronger rigidity. In the model-based analysis, we first treat fiscal revenue as a result of economic growth, i.e., the cyclical fluctuation and dynamic equilibrium value of the actual fiscal revenue growth rate depends on those of the GDP growth rate. Then, we take the inherent trend of the cyclical fluctuation of the actual fiscal expenditure growth rate as one of the choices of fiscal policy, and consider the cyclical fluctuation of the actual growth rate of the fiscal expenditure on social security, education, science, culture and health as the result of the inherent trend of the cyclical fluctuation of the actual fiscal revenue growth rate and the actual fiscal expenditure growth rate. Meanwhile, we integrate the cyclical fluctuating value of GDP growth rate into the equations of the cyclical fluctuations of the actual fiscal expenditure growth rate as an explanatory variable, thus reflecting the influence of adaptive regulatory policy on the cyclical fluctuation of fiscal expenditure growth rate. Specific results are shown in Tables 12.12, 12.13, 12.14 and 12.15.

Operation of model simulation

By synthesizing the influencing factor analysis equations of various variable factors into a simultaneous equation, we build the short-term, mid-term, mid-to-long-term and long-term fluctuation models, and the dynamic equilibrium value model. In order to test the stability and the simulative results of these models, we use the model to test various variables within the sample interval from the first quarter of 2010 to the fourth quarter of 2014. The results show that the model-based simulative values are highly consistent with the actual values, except for the short-term fluctuation model, which generates a value that deviates widely from the actual number. Overall, the cyclical model of economic growth can effectively simulate the development of the cyclical fluctuation and dynamic equilibrium values of various endogenous variables within the sample interval. We also apply this model to analyze and forecast China's economic growth – for instance, Chapter 11 of this book summarizes by using this cyclical growth model.

Table 12.12 Simulation analysis equations of the cyclical fluctuations and dynamic equilibrium value of the actual fiscal revenue growth rate

Fiscal revenue	*Model equation*	*Goodness-of-fit* R^2	*Adjusted* R^2	*DW statistics*
Dynamic equilibrium value	FISIAGTTL = 1.2597 × GDPAGTTL + 1.7059 + [MA(1) = 1.1892, MA(2) = 0.8769]	0.996797	0.996317	0.25
Short-term fluctuation	FISIAGW = –0.1851 × FISIAGW (–1) – 0.2347 × FISIAGW (–2) – 0.4433 × FISIAGW (–3) – 0.3808 × FISIAGW (–4) + 2.4534 × GDPAGW – 0.0227	0.556081	0.527624	2.21
Mid-term fluctuation	FISIAGWS = 1.595 × FISIAGWS (–1) – 0.8839 × FISIAGWS (–2) + 0.4985 × GDPAGWS + 0.01454 + [MA(1) = 0.9997]	0.996101	0.995908	0.39
Mid-to-long-term fluctuation	FISIAGWM = 3.9091 × FISIAGWM (–1) – 5.8334 × FISIAGWM (–2) + 3.9352 × FISIAGWM (–3) – 1.0131 × FISIAGWM (–4) – 0.0092 × GDPAGWM + 0.0086 × GDPAGWM (–1) – 6.0034	1	1	0.22
Long-term fluctuation	FISIAGWL = 3.2599 × FISIAGWL (–1) – 4.5333 × FISIAGWL (–2) + 3.155 × FISIAGWL (–3) – 0.9355 × FISIAGWL (–4) + 0.09707 × GDPAGWL – 0.1257 × GDPAGWL (–1) + 0.0023	0.999606	0.999576	0.55

Table 12.13 Simulation analysis equations of the cyclical fluctuations and dynamic equilibrium value of the actual fiscal expenditure growth rate

Fiscal expenditure	*Model equation*	*Goodness-of-fit* R^2	*Adjusted* R^2	*DW statistics*
Dynamic equilibrium value	FISEAGTTL = 0.9216 × FISEAGTTL (–1) + 0.1265 × FISIAGTTL – 0.3904 + [MA(1) = 0.949]	0.999717	0.999674	0.27
Short-term fluctuation	FISEAGW = –0.2395 × FISEAGW (–1) – 0.2752 × FISEAGW (–2) – 0.1625 × FISEAGW (–3) – 0.3038 × FISEAGW (–4) – 0.1281 × FISIAGW + 0.0089 × FISIAGW (–1) – 2.3337 × GDPAGW – 0.537 × GDPAGW (–1) + 0.0008	0.494193	0.41485	2.05
Mid-term fluctuation	FISEAGWS = 1.6984 × FISEAGWS (–1) – 0.9781 × FISEAGWS (–2) + 0.0021 × FISIAGWS – 0.0166	0.992492	0.992218	0.34
Mid-to-long-term fluctuation	FISEAGWM = 3.8486 × FISEAGWM (–1) – 5.656 × FISEAGWM (–2) + 3.7596 × FISEAGWM (–3) – 0.9546 × FISEAGWM (–4) + 0.0001 × FISIAGWM + 3.0146	1	1	0.1
Long-term fluctuation	FISEAGWL = 1.8568 × FISEAGWL (–1) – 0.8613 × FISEAGWL (–2) – 0.0751 × FISIAGWL (–1) + 0.0015	0.993884	0.99366	0.48

Table 12.14 Simulation analysis equations of the cyclical fluctuations and dynamic equilibrium value of the actual growth rate of fiscal expenditure on social security

Social security	*Model equation*	*Goodness-of-fit* R^2	*Adjusted* R^2	*DW statistics*
Dynamic equilibrium value	FISESBAGTTL = 1.9862 × FISESBAGTTL (−1) − 0.9963 × FISESBAGTTL (−2) − 0.1287 × FISIAGTTL + 0.133 × FISIAGTTL (−1) + 0.0879	0.999998	0.999998	0.07
Short-term fluctuation	FISESBAGW = −0.4958 × FISESBAGW (−1) − 0.5472 × FISESBAGW (−2) − 0.2842 × FISESBAGW (−3) − 0.5257 × FISESBAGW (−4) + 0.4159 × FISIAGW + 0.3743 × FISIAGW (−1) − 2.9914 × GDPAGW + 0.1027	0.483648	0.419104	2.25
Mid-term fluctuation	FISESBAGWS = 1.6628 × FISESBAGWS (−1) − 0.9601 × FISESBAGWS (−2) + 0.0122 × FISIAGWS + 0.0139	0.991563	0.991255	0.39
Mid-and-long-term fluctuation	FISESBAGWM = 3.8843 × FISESBAGWM (−1) − 5.7757 × FISESBAGWM (−2) + 3.8901 × FISESBAGWM (−3) − 1.0018 × FISESBAGWM (−4) + 0.0054 × FISIAGWM − 0.0044 × FISIAGWM (−1) + 0.0035 × GDPAGWM + $6.3708e^{-05}$	1	1	0.06
Long-term fluctuation	FISESBAGWL = 1.7586 × FISESBAGWL (−1) − 0.8341 × FISESBAGWL (−2) − 0.4639 × FISIAGWL + 0.4486 × FISIAGWL (−1) + 0.0203	0.977967	0.976879	0.37

Table 12.15 Simulation analysis equations of the cyclical fluctuations and dynamic equilibrium value of the actual growth rate of fiscal expenditure on education, science, culture and health

Education, science, culture and health	*Model equation*	*Goodness-of-fit* R^2	*Adjusted* R^2	*DW statistics*
Dynamic equilibrium value	FISEJYAGTTL = 3.8627 × FISEJYAGTTL (–1) – 5.6337 × FISEJYAGTTL (–2) + 3.6787 × FISEJYAGTTL (–3) – 0.9097 × FISEJYAGTTL (–4) – 0.0028 × FISIAGTTL + 0.0028 × FISEJYAGTTL (–1) + 0.003	1	1	0.37
Short-term fluctuation	FISEJYAGW = –0.0053 × FISEJYAGW (–1) – 0.5408 × FISEJYAGW (–2) – 0.1075 × FISEJYAGW (–3) – 0.7381 × FISEJYAGW (–4) + 0.0058 × FISIAGW – 0.0085 × FISIAGW (–1) + 1.4491 × GDPAGW (–1) – 0.1237	0.545639	0.488843	2.51
Mid-term fluctuation	FISEJYAGWS = 0.8649 × FISEJYAGWS (–1) – 0.2269 × FISIAGWS + 0.2352 × FISIAGWS (–1) + 0.0061	0.763496	0.754948	0.32
Mid-to-long-term fluctuation	FISEJYAGWM = 3.8502 × FISEJYAGWM (–1) – 5.6728 × FISEJYAGWM (–2) + 3.7875 × FISEJYAGWM (–3) – 0.9679 × FISEJYAGWM (–4) – 0.0015 × FISIAGWM + 0.0017 × FISIAGWM (–1) – 0.0046 × GDPAGWM + 0.0037 × GDPAGWM (–1) + 5.5303e–06	1	1	0.07
Long-term fluctuation	FISEJYAGWL = 0.9399 × FISEJYAGWL (–1) + 0.7401 × FISIAGWL – 0.5054 × FISIAGWL (–1) – 1.4256 × GDPAGWL + 1.5811 × GDPAGWL (–1) – 0.0215	0.962449	0.960131	0.25

Bibliography

Arias, A., G.D. Hansen and L.E. Ohanian, "Why have business cycle fluctuations become less volatile?" *Economic theory* 32 (1) (2007): 43–58.

Barro, Robert J. and Xavier Salai-Martin, *Economic Growth and Convergence Across the United States*. Cambridge, MA: National Bureau of Economic Research, 1990.

Cao Yongfu, "Review on the research of business cycle stabilization in the United States." *Economic Research Journal*, 7 (2007): 152.

Chiang, A.C., *Fundamental Methods of Mathematical Economics*. Beijing: The Commercial Press, 1999.

Friedman, M., *The Counter-Revolution in Monetary Theory*. London: Institute of Economic Affairs, 1970.

Frisch, R., "Propagation problems and impulse problems in dynamic economics." In *Economic Essays in Honor of Gustav Cassel*. London: Allen and Unwin, 1933.

Gali, J., *Monetary Policy, Inflation and the Business Cycle: An Introduction to the New Keynesian Framework*. Beijing: China Renmin University Press, 2013.

Hall, Robert E., "The relation between price and marginal cost in US industry," *Journal of Political Economy* 96 (1) (1988): 921–947.

Hayek, F.A., *Geld the orieund Konjunktur the orie*. Leipzig: Hölder-Pichler-Tempskyag, 1929.

Jevons, W.S. (1875). "Influence of the Sun-spot period on the price of corn." A paper read at the meeting of the British Association, Bristol, 1875.

Jiang Zhongyi, *Basic Methods of Mathematical Economics*. Beijing: The Commercial Press, 1999.

Keynes, J.M., *The General Theory of Employment, Interest and Money*. Beijing: The Commercial Press, 1999.

Klein, L.R., *Economic Fluctuations in the United States, 1921–1941*. Chichester: Wiley, 1950.

Leduc, S. and K. Sill, "Monetary policy, oil shocks, and TFP: Accounting for the decline in U.S. volatility," International Finance Discussion Papers 873, Board of Governors of the Federal Reserve System, 2003.

Li Jianwei, "Correlation between consumer durables demand growth cycle and economic growth: 1978–2012." *Reform*, 7 (2013a).

Li Jianwei, "Endogenous mechanism of normally distributed household income and consumer demand growth cycle from a global perspective." *Development Research*, 8 (2013b).

Li Jianwei, "Influence of old income distribution on consumer durables and economic growth cycle." *Economic Review*, 6 (2013c).

Li Jianwei, "Normal estimation of urban and rural household income distribution in China." *Development Research*, 5 (2013d).

Li Jianwei, "Endogenous mechanism of household income distribution and economic growth cycle." *Economic Research Journal*, 1 (2015a).

Li Jianwei, "The development trend and dynamic equilibrium growth process of China's economic growth cycle." *Economic Review*, 10 (2015b).

Moore, H.L., *Economic Cycles: Their Law and Cause*, New York: A.M. Kelley, 1914.

Niemira, M.P. and P.A. Klein, *Forecasting Financial and Economic Cycles.* Beijing: China Statistics Press, 1998.

Phelps E.S. and J.B. Taylor, "Stabilizing powers of monetary policy under rational expectations." *The Journal of Political Economy*, 85. (1) (1977): 163.

Pigou, A., *Industrial Fluctuations*, trans. Gao Yaoqi. Beijing: The Commercial Press, 1999 [1928].

Samuelson, P.A., "Interactions between the multiplier analysis and the principle of acceleration." *The Review of Economics and Statistics*, 21 (2) (1939): 75–78.

Schumpeter, J.A., *Business Cycles.* Vol. 1. New York: McGraw-Hill, 1939.

Sismondi, S., *New Principles of Political Economy: The Discussion of the Connection Between a Society's Wealth and Its Demographics.* Trans. He Qin. Beijing: The Commercial Press, 1997 [1964].

Smets, F., and R. Wouters, "An estimated stochastic dynamic general equilibrium model of the Euro area." *Journal of the European Economic Association*, 1 (5) (2003).

Solow, R., *Economic Growth Essays*. Beijing: Beijing Economic Collage Press, 1989 [1969].

Tinbergen, J., *Statistical Testing of Business-Cycle Theories: I. A Method and Its Application to Investment Activity.* Vol. 1. Geneva: League of Nations, 1939.

Wang Shaoping and Hu Jin, "Periodic decomposition of China's GDP trend and lasting effect of random shocks." *Economic Research Journal*, 4 (2009): 65.

Yang Liyan and Wang Xinli, "Advances in research on real business cycle theory." *Economic Perspectives*, 2 (2004): 32–35.

Zhai Zhicheng, "Business cycle theory and current trend of macro-economy in China." *Economist*, 2 (2001): 14–20.

Index

For Product Safety Concerns and Information please contact our EU
representative GPSR@taylorandfrancis.com
Taylor & Francis Verlag GmbH, Kaufingerstraße 24, 80331 München, Germany

www.ingramcontent.com/pod-product-compliance
Ingram Content Group UK Ltd.
Pitfield, Milton Keynes, MK11 3LW, UK
UKHW020018200926
475702UK00014B/1953

* 9 7 8 0 3 6 7 1 7 9 7 9 3 *